British Propaganda during the First World War
1914-18

British Propaganda during the First World War, 1914-18

M L Sanders
Middlesex Polytechnic
and
Philip M Taylor
University of Leeds

First published 1982 by
THE MACMILLAN PRESS LTD
London and Basingstoke
Companies and representatives throughout the world

ISBN 0 333 29275 8 (hc)

Printed in Hong Kong

Contents

Acknowledgements

This book owes much to the support and encouragement of Professor James Joll who was responsible for introducing the authors to each other in 1978, and to Sarah Mahaffy of Macmillan who expressed considerable faith in the project from the very beginning. We are most grateful to Dr Keith Wilson, Dr Hugh Cecil, Dr Richard Taylor, Graham Ross and particularly to Nicholas Pronay for their invaluable comments and suggestions during the writing of the book.

The research could not have been undertaken without the assistance of the staffs of the Public Record Office at Kew in London; the British Library; the Imperial War Museum; Middlesex Polytechnic Library and the Brotherton Library at the University of Leeds; the House of Lords Records Office; Yale University Library and the Hoover Institute on War, Revolution and Peace in the United States; the Ministry of Foreign Affairs in Paris; Queens University Archives, Ontario. We are also grateful to Gordon Phillips of The Times Archive at New Printing House Square in London, to Miss V. A. Leeper for sending copies of her family letters from Australia, and to the late Lucy Masterman. Nor could the research have been undertaken without the generous assistance of the British Academy and the University of Leeds.

We are deeply indebted to the supervisors of our research degrees, namely Professor Kenneth Bourne and Professor David Dilks, and to all our colleagues at Middlesex Polytechnic and the University of Leeds for their constant encouragement and tolerance.

Finally, we should like to express our sincere gratitude to all those friends and relatives without whose support and companionship this book could not have been written.

Preface

This book re-examines the British government's involvement in propaganda during the First World War. It attempts to provide the first modern study of this controversial subject based upon unpublished primary source material held in Britain, France, the United States and Australia. Through an examination of the organisational developments, the methods employed and the content of the material produced, the book presents a revisionist interpretation of a story that has not been told accurately before. Great emphasis is placed upon the continuity of development, a feature which has been largely neglected by earlier studies which were either written at a time when the sources were not generally available or which were themselves frequently designed to serve a propagandist purpose. In the United States, for example, where many of the best studies were written during the inter-war years, several books testified to the success of British propaganda in helping to attract America into the war on the Allied side in 1917 in order to reinforce the arguments of those isolationist elements which advocated withdrawal from involvement with Europe. In Germany, historians attempted to show that the Imperial army had not been defeated on the field of battle in 1918 but had been forced to submit due to the collapse of morale from within which had been exploited by British propaganda, thereby providing a sense of 'historical legitimacy' for the 'stab-in-the-back' theory advocated by certain nationalist elements at work in Weimar Germany. Both these questions are re-examined in this book as case studies made on the basis of material which has only become available to historians over the past ten years or so.

It is, however, unlikely that the full story can ever be told. Most of the documents relating to Britain's wartime propaganda activities were either destroyed in 1920 or else 'lost' in the years that followed. No official history of this particular war activity was ever commissioned or written. This book therefore cannot aspire to be comprehensive or definitive. What it does attempt is a detailed re-appraisal based upon those sources that have survived and to establish an authoritative account as a means of clarifying the numerous contradictions which have appeared in earlier studies.

The book concentrates more on propaganda conducted abroad than that performed on the home front. This is to some extent dictated by the evidence, partly because of Cate Haste's recent examination of domestic propaganda in the First World War, *Keep the Home Fires Burning* (1977), but also because, in comparison with the Second World War at least, the British government devoted comparatively little attention to the home front between 1914 and 1918. Amateur propagandists were, of course, in abundance and there was also the enormous propagandist role played by the British press. But this book deals only with official British propaganda and, in so far as the domestic front is concerned, mainly with the work conducted by the Press Bureau, the Parliamentary Recruiting Committee and by the National War Aims Committee.

Of the various studies that have been made of Britain's wartime propaganda, by far the majority have concentrated upon the campaign overseas during the final year of the war. There are, however, several notable exceptions. The present standard work on British activity before 1918 remains that by J D Squires, *British Propaganda at Home and in the United States from 1914 to 1917* (1935). This work has borne well the test of time largely because Squires' research was based upon material held in the Hoover War Institute in Stanford, California, which managed to acquire various British archival sources in 1920 when the records were being sorted out prior to destruction. Yet although Squires was vaguely familiar with the early organisational developments, he was unable to piece together the precise connection which existed between the various official propaganda departments that sprang into being following the outbreak of war in 1914. Nor was he really able to assess the significance of the early British campaign in the United States in relation to the various unofficial activities of the numerous amateur propaganda bodies to which he devotes considerable attention. Lucy Masterman's biography of her husband, *C. F. G. Masterman* (1939), did help to throw some new light on the work of the leading official organisation before 1917 — the War Propaganda Bureau at Wellington House — but the most important study to follow that of Squires remains H. C. Peterson's *Propaganda for War: the Campaign against American Neutrality, 1914-17* (1939). This book attempted to

warn its readers of the potency of British propaganda during the
American period of neutrality in the last war and, by implication,
warned against a repetition in the next. Sidney Rogerson's
Propaganda in the Next War (1938) displayed little appreciation of the
work of Wellington House but was typical in its concentration on the
work performed during the final year of the First World War.

The reputation which Lord Northcliffe's Department of Enemy
Propaganda at Crewe House earned for its role in defeating the
Central Powers originated in 1918 when prominent enemy
personalities admitted that its material was producing an impact.
Yet, although effective, its significance has been exaggerated,
particularly by the appearance of the *Times History of the War* (vol.
21). Sir Campbell Stuart's *Secrets of Crewe House* (1920)
strengthened a reputation which was to be further reinforced by
Ludendorff's war memoirs and by Hitler's *Mein Kampf*. Henry
Wickham Steed described his activities in relation to propaganda
against Austria-Hungary in his memoirs, *Through Thirty Years*
(1924). However, the impression gained from these various works is
that little work was done before 1918 to undermine the will of the
enemy to continue the struggle. But, as Hitler recognised,
propaganda is a cumulative process which serves to condition the
mind over a period of time. Certainly, the work was intensified
during 1918, as George Bruntz recognised in what remains the best
study of its kind. *Allied Propaganda and the Collapse of the German
Empire in 1918* (1938), but the work of the important propaganda
branch of the War Office, MI7, before and indeed during the final
year of the war has not earned the attention its significance deserves.
Brigadier-General Cockerill attempted to redress the balance of
historical attention in his memoirs, *What Fools We Were* (1944), but
his plea went largely unheeded until Michael Balfour's attempt to
'demythologise' Crewe House in 1979, *Propaganda in War 1939-45*.
Whereas Balfour's argument is that British propaganda could not
have had the effect which many contemporaries maintained, the
present study suggests that Crewe House did produce an impact,
particularly in Austria-Hungary, but only because of the cumulative
effect of the work begun before its creation.

The work of Britain's first Ministry of Information under Lord
Beaverbrook has also received a disproportionate amount of
attention in relation to the activities of earlier bodies. Harold
Lasswell's pioneering work, *Propaganda Technique in the World War*

(1927), suffers from the same absence of perspective which is also apparent in Beaverbrook's *Men and Power, 1917-18* (1956). Even the more modern studies, including Doreen Collins' *Aspects of British Politics, 1904-19* (1965), Marjorie Ogilvy Webb's *The Government Explains: A Study of the Information Services* (1965) and Sir Fife Clark's *The Central Office of Information* (1970) tend to treat the early work as some sort of chaotic prelude to the order brought to the conduct of British propaganda by Lord Beaverbrook. The overall impression left by these various works is that British propaganda during the years 1914-17 was ill-organised due to a series of *ad hoc* arrangements which resulted in inefficiency, wastage of material, duplication of effort and slowness to exploit propaganda opportunities. The advent of the Ministry of Information is considered to have brought about a fundamental change. The new men were essentially journalists who are alleged to have brought with them a more positive approach to news and propaganda. They were quicker to exploit sensational stories and made greater use of the British and foreign press as well as other media such as film. In short, three years of comparative failure are said to have been followed by one year of spectacular success. The present study attempts to refocus this interpretation.

Publishers' Note
We are grateful to the Controller of HMSO for permission to quote from Crown copyright letters, and to the following for permission to quote from documents: Archives du Ministère des Affaires étrangères, Paris; Archives du Service historique de l'armée, Vincennes; National Archives, Washington; Hoover Institute on War, Revolution and Peace, Stanford; Yale University Library; House of Lords Record Office; Imperial War Museum; The Times Archive; Bodleian Library, Oxford.

Abbreviations

AWP	Arthur Willert Papers
BEF	British Expeditionary Force
BL	British Library
CAB	Cabinet Office papers
CCNPO	Central Committee for National Patriotic Organisations
CID	Committee of Imperial Defence
CPI	Committee on Public Information
DORA	Defence of the Realm Act
FO	Foreign Office papers
GHQ	General Headquarters
HIWRP	Hoover Institute of War, Revolution and Peace
HO	Home Office papers
INF	Information papers
LGp	Lloyd George papers
MP	Member of Parliament
NWAC	National War Aims Committee
PB	Press Bureau
PID	Political Intelligence Department
PM	Prime Minister
PRC	Parliamentary Recruiting Committee
T	Treasury papers
TTA	The Times Archive
USA	United States of America
WO	War Office papers
WWP	William Wiseman Papers
YUL	Yale University Library

Introduction

WHATEVER else may be said or written about the way in which the British government came to employ the weapon of propaganda during the First World War, it was undeniably an impressive exercise in improvisation. Having entered the conflict with nothing that could even remotely be described as an official propaganda department, Britain finished the conflict with the most highly developed organisation of all the belligerents for influencing public opinion. If reputation was anything to go by, it was certainly the most effective. However, the process which culminated in the establishment of a full Ministry of Information in February 1918 was neither an agreeable nor a painless one for most members of the British governing class. The path was littered with innumerable obstacles such as widespread official antipathy, inter-departmental rivalry and, at times, bitter acrimony and squabbling. So many sacred cows concerning the traditional relationship between government and governed and the rules of conduct in foreign policy were slaughtered along the way that it was almost impossible to keep count of them. Even so, by the end of the war, Britain had developed the classic model on which other governments were subsequently to base their own propaganda machinery. Between 1914 and 1918, therefore, the British government was responsible for opening a Pandoran box which unleashed the weapon of propaganda upon the modern world.

Of the numerous lessons to be drawn from the experience of the First World War, one of the most significant was that public opinion could no longer be ignored as a determining factor in the formulation of government policies. The war served to increase the level of popular interest and participation in the affairs of state to such an extent that there could be no turning back to pre-1914 conditions. The calls for the abandonment of 'secret diplomacy' and for its replacement by more open government and the creation of a League of Nations as an expression of the organised opinion of mankind were a reflection of this development. During the war, sections of the community which had previously remained uninvolved in the exigencies of national survival had found themselves directly affected by events at the front line. The gap between soldier and civilian was narrowed substantially in a struggle not merely between professional armies but between whole nations locked in mortal combat. The entire resources of the state — military, economic and psychological — had to be mobilised to the full in a total fight to the finish. The introduction of conscription, the recruitment of women into the factories, the bombardment of east coast towns by the German High Seas Fleet, Zeppelin raids in the south of England and the attempt of the German submarines to starve Britain into submission were all traumatic experiences for a nation learning the rules of modern warfare. In such a struggle, morale came to be recognised as a significant military factor and propaganda began to emerge as the principal instrument of control over public opinion and an essential weapon in the national armoury.

Despite the development of wireless telegraphy and the cinematograph in the 1890s, by far the most important medium of communication in the late nineteenth and early twentieth century remained the press. Newspapers had been rescued from their early dependence upon Treasury subsidies through an increase in circulation and the availability of more advertising space as a direct consequence of industrialisation and an expanding economy. Between 1840 and 1852, the circulation of *The Times*, for example, quadrupled from 10,000 to 40,000 copies per issue.[1] The development of a global cable network greatly accelerated the speed of international news and improved the coverage afforded to world affairs in British newspapers. The extent of this cable network may have provided a strategic headache for Britain's defence planners but it did contribute towards the establishment of Reuters as the world's leading news agency with a reputation for impartiality and freedom from official control which was to be put to invaluable use by the British government during the First World War. Reuters' leading continental rivals, Havas of France and the Wolff Bureau in Berlin, did not share the advantage of such a network. Meanwhile, the broadening base of political power following the Reform Act of 1867 and improving standards of literacy following the Elementary Education Act of 1870 and further Acts in 1888, 1891 and 1902 meant that public opinion was not only becoming an increasingly important factor in British political life but also was better informed than ever before.

Nineteenth century politicians watched these developments with considerable interest. Palmerston especially, and Canning before him, was fully aware of the growing significance of public opinion in British political life.[2] Political activists such as David Urquhart demonstrated the effectiveness of what was tantamount to a propaganda campaign.[3] The press became an indispensable feature of party politics and no government could afford to ignore its potential influence upon public opinion and the electorate, a feeling intensified after the 1832 and 1867 Reform Acts. Gladstone certainly did not in his Midlothian campaign.[4] By the last quarter of the century, political observers were beginning to express fears of large scale manipulation of opinion by politicians through the press. The abolition of taxes on newspapers, advertising and paper between 1855 and 1861 had made a further expansion of the press possible and opened the way for the 'penny populars' founded by Alfred Harmsworth (later Lord Northcliffe) and Arthur Pearson in the 1890s.

Inevitably, political interest in newspapers was concentrated on the question of domestic opinion; the possibility of influencing opinion overseas was given relatively little consideration. The prevailing official attitude remained that 'opinion, like trade and industry, should under the old liberal conception be allowed to flow in its own natural channels without any artificial regulation'.[5] It was generally maintained that the conduct of foreign affairs required a high degree of freedom from public scrutiny, whether at home where it was believed that the majority of people were incapable of appreciating the subtle intricacies of complicated diplomatic manoeuvres, or abroad where premature disclosures might prejudice British interests. Indeed, such was the special position of foreign affairs that even the House of Commons 'seldom or never presumed to press for an answer when the Foreign Secretary put a finger to his lips'.[6] As a result, the Foreign Office proved to be a generally disappointing source of information for the nineteenth century journalist. It has even been claimed that 'the foreign secretary and his officials prided themselves on their detachment from the changing moods of public opinion',[7] and there were certainly numerous complaints concerning the secrecy with which diplomats conducted their business and their notorious treatment of journalists.[8] Kennedy

Jones, for example, described how the permanent officials of the nineteenth century Foreign Office constituted 'a brick wall against which many a proprietor and editor has bruised his head' and who regarded the journalist 'who strayed into Downing Street as an unmannerly intruder to be mercilessly snubbed'.[9]

Other nations displayed a more positive attitude towards public opinion beyond their own frontiers, Germany after 1871 being a particular example. Bismarck paid considerable attention to press relations and appointed a special press agent, Moritz Busch, whose task it was to influence newspapers as far as possible on behalf of the German government in order to project an image abroad of public harmony with official policies. He manipulated the press in a way that would have been anathema in Britain where his methods were observed with interest but not imitated. The Foreign Office preferred to rely upon diplomatic relations as its means of supplying information to foreign governments. In Britain, diplomacy remained 'the special business of kings, nobles and aristocratic persons'.[10] Any attempt to influence popular opinion abroad would have stood out in sharp contrast to the traditional diplomatic etiquette of self-restraint and discretion. Diplomatic negotiations and transactions were therefore conducted beneath an umbrella of secrecy, while the Foreign Office 'abstained assiduously'[11] from creating any machinery that would serve to encourage greater public participation in the exclusive realm of international politics. It looked with distaste upon the 'gutter press' which was felt to be sensationalist and thus a danger to the smooth-running of foreign affairs. In 1896, for example, the Kruger telegram roused an intense and bitter press campaign in Britain and Germany. Queen Victoria urged Lord Salisbury to do something to mitigate the violence of this campaign. This proved easier said than done. The non-party press, jealous of its independence and freedom from political control, was not amenable to official interference. There did not exist any official channels of communication; the press was not invited to the Foreign Office. Nor was it issued with communiqués or invited to explain or support British foreign policy.

Although Lord Salisbury appreciated the power of the 'fourth estate', it was his colonial secretary, Joseph Chamberlain, who urged the need to establish regular contacts with the press. In Birmingham, Chamberlain had worked closely with William Harris of *The Birmingham Daily Post* and, on his appointment to the Colonial

Office in 1895, he made that department a ready source of official information to journalists. There was, wrote one beneficiary, 'no other Government Department at that time where a journalist was so certain of obtaining accurate and authentic information from a responsible official'.[12] Chamberlain seems to have been instrumental in persuading Salisbury to use the press as a means of securing public support for the government's policy during the Fashoda crisis of 1898 when 'for the first time Fleet Street was invited to the Foreign Office'.[13] Sanderson, the permanent under-secretary, met journalists for half an hour after the Cabinet meeting which discussed the crisis. However, while the Colonial Office under Chamberlain's successor, Alfred Lyttleton, continued to develop its innovative arrangements whereby a special officer was appointed to see press correspondents, the Foreign Office chose to return to its exclusive ways.

The concern of the Foreign Office during the Fashoda crisis to give details of official policy was a reflection of its desire to obtain public support through the medium of the press which, more often than not, tended to lead rather than follow public opinion on foreign policy matters. Foreign journalists were rarely granted the same sort of treatment. But it is important to stress that, although no system of formal contact existed, there did develop an unofficial and highly selective system of informal communication with various British journalists, mainly for the benefit of the foreign embassies in London. Sanderson continued to have some dealings with the press and, on occasion, he even requested *The Times* to moderate its anti-German or anti-Russian tone in order to ease the workings of diplomacy. He saw a Reuters agent frequently not only to provide information but also to answer questions. However, 'as there was no press secretary or press bureau, all of these conversations were highly informal and Sanderson did not go out of his way to cultivate good relations with Fleet Street'.[14]

During Sir Edward Grey's period as Foreign Secretary, contact with the press was maintained through his private secretary, Sir William Tyrrell, whose task it was to keep in touch with leading journalists, to convey information to them, and to explain the course of British foreign policy. There were, in addition, various close relationships established by Foreign Office personnel with leading journalists and editors. Cecil Spring-Rice was in regular communication with Leo Maxse of *The National Review*, St Loe Strachey of the *Spectator* and Valentine Chirol, foreign editor of *The Times* until

1912.[15] Arthur Nicolson, a permanent under-secretary who was not normally in favour of publicity, did maintain contact with W. B. Harris, *The Times* correspondent in Morocco, while Sir Edward Goschen, ambassador in Berlin 1908-14, communicated regularly with Wickham Steed in Vienna where the latter served as *Times* correspondent before replacing Chirol as foreign editor. Although J. A. Spender, editor of the *Westminster Gazette*, maintained that 'it was never the habit of the Foreign Office to inspire the newspapers',[16] it would be naive to regard these contacts solely as personal friendships. It would appear that, by confiding in trusted journalists, permanent officials hoped to avoid serious misunderstandings in the press while, at the same time, contributing towards the formation of an informed public opinion although perhaps more abroad than at home. As one writer noted in 1917, 'As long as the education of the people is left in the hands of the daily press it is useless to expect from the people any intelligent control of foreign policy'.[17] Before 1914, however, few officials were prepared to accept the democratisation of British foreign policy and the informal contacts which did exist with journalists were a reflection more of the Foreign Office's regard for the press than of any desire to involve public opinion on a large scale. Even so, as Tyrrell later recalled:

It was a comparatively easy task in pre-war days to deal with the press . . . . The issues which presented themselves to the popular mind were . . . mainly confined to Anglo-German relations, and on this subject there was practical unanimity in our Press so there was little to do on our part in the matter.[18]

An increasingly discernible regard for the power of newspaper publicity was therefore not matched by any institutional means for channelling official news and views into the medium of newspapers.

Nevertheless, the need to harness the potential of the press did occupy considerable time and energy. The Service Departments had long feared the press as a source of adverse publicity and criticism. William Russell, the legendary war correspondent of *The Times*, had demonstrated the power of both during the Crimean War. Censorship was, however, a double-edged weapon. On the one hand it was essential to preserve the flow of information in and out of Britain for imperial communications while, on the other hand, preventing communication between a hostile power and its allies.

It was just as important to prevent the publication at home of information which might adversely affect the civil population[19] as it was to prevent the transmission of information from enemy agents operating from inside Britain. The former set of considerations was ultimately to give rise to censorship and eventually to propaganda in the First World War, the latter to secret intelligence work, code-breaking and counter-espionage.

Just as the Admiralty had to consider the strategic importance of the cable network and the need for some form of control, so also did the War Office come to consider the need to censor the more sensational outbursts of the press. The War Office had first raised this question at the very moment the Foreign Office was beginning to consider greater use of press publicity during the Fashoda crisis. It was a paradox which was to hinder inter-departmental co-operation during the early phase of the First World War. The question of censorship was revived at intervals in the years after 1898, usually at times of international tension.[20] The Russo-Japanese war provided further testimony to the dangers of irresponsible publicity,[21] and in December 1904 the Committee of Imperial Defence (CID) proposed a bill restricting the freedom of the press in times of national emergency.[22] Fleet Street was not at first averse to the proposal. It fully appreciated the dangers to national security of indiscriminate publicity of the type so clearly demonstrated during the so-called Anglo-German press 'war' of 1902.[23] Indeed, at a conference held in June 1906, the Newspaper Proprietors' Association was prepared to admit the need for a bill preventing 'the publication of all news with regard to naval and military matters or the movement of ships or troops at a time when the government considered it essential in the interest of the nation to put it into operation'.[24] But when a redrafted version of the bill was placed before them two years later, the prospect of actual censorship legislation served to concentrate wonderfully the collective mind of Fleet Street. Liberal traditions were too deeply entrenched within the fourth estate by that time for it simply to allow the possibility of direct official interference — at least not without a struggle. Consequently, in 1910, the CID appointed a sub-committee under the chairmanship of the Home Secretary, Winston Churchill, to devise some form of compromise solution. Negotiations with the press proceeded at a somewhat leisurely pace until the Agadir crisis of 1911 injected an element of urgency. Churchill was replaced by the Secretary of State for War, J. A. B.

Seely, and his re-constituted sub-committee felt that during this latest crisis, the press 'might well have afforded valuable information to an enemy, and a certain risk of prejudicing the issue of diplomatic negotiations toward a peaceful settlement was in fact involved'.[25] But because Fleet Street remained opposed to any form of legislation since its volte-face of 1908, Whitehall was reduced to devising a system of voluntary censorship rather than one of compulsion. The outcome was the creation of the Admiralty, War Office and Press Committee with a permanent secretary paid for by the Newspaper Proprietors' Association which was designed to supervise the resultant 'gentleman's agreement'. However, the proprietors, 'while agreeing . . . that the publication of information of a secret or confidential character relating to naval and military subjects should thus be liable for prohibition', were nevertheless quick to stipulate that the new joint standing committee:

should not be used as a medium for the dissemination of false information, or for the purpose of stifling criticisms of policy, or, except in really important cases where national interests are at stake, for the restriction of views.[26]

With these reservations designed to prevent the press from becoming a medium for official propaganda, the proprietors accepted a system of voluntary censorship, a system which remained in force until the outbreak of war in 1914. Despite the increased danger of bureaucratic interference, Fleet Street considered this solution to be more acceptable than the prospect of an official peacetime press bureau — a suggestion occasionally voiced in some government circles.[27] It is also worth noting that in the same year as the Admiralty, War Office and Press Committee came into being — 1912 — the British Board of Film Censors was formed following an initiative by a group of film producers who were prepared to establish, also at their own expense, a censorship body headed by a permanent official who was in fact appointed by the Home Secretary which was designed to protect their industry and the public interest as they perceived it.[28]

Although these new arrangements appear to have worked quite effectively,[29] a stricter measure of government control was inevitable on the outbreak of war. In 1911, partly as a response to the latest outbreak of spy-fever,[30] the government had hastily up-dated the 1889 Official Secrets Act which had broad implications for the question of censorship. However, it was the 1914 Defence of the Realm Act (DORA) which was to lay down more specific regulations concerning the flow of information. The Act made it an offence, punishable originally by military law but subsequently altered to prosecution by civil courts, to publish information 'of such a nature as is calculated to be or might be directly or indirectly useful to the enemy'.[31] This all-embracing regulation included information relating to naval and troop movements as well as to descriptions of war material. In other words, it added coercive powers to the pre-war system of voluntary censorship. The Act further made it an offence to publish news 'likely to cause disaffection' amongst the civil and military sectors of Britain and her Allies. It must be added that DORA was not designed primarily to control public opinion, although that was certainly one of its consequences. Rather, the Act was principally concerned with preventing valuable information from reaching the enemy. It was for this reason that, on the outbreak of war, the War Office assumed responsibility for the censorship of all private and commercial communications by cables and by the postal services.[32]

The determination of the British press to avoid becoming an instrument of government before the war was matched by a reluctance on the part of the Foreign Office to develop propaganda overseas. During the Boer War, when such propaganda might have helped to improve Britain's poor image in the eyes of world opinion, no organised propaganda campaign had been undertaken.[33] In November 1899, the British ambassador in Madrid informed Lord Salisbury:

Although since the outbreak of war in South Africa the press in this country has been more than ever full of false reports and scurrilous insinuations respecting Great Britain, I have not thought it worthwhile to trouble your Lordship with specimens of these effusions, which are best treated with good humoured contempt.[34]

The British ambassador in St Petersburg held similar views. In May 1903, he reported to Lord Lansdowne a conversation he had had with Count Lamsdorff:

I said that it was certainly very disagreeable to be constantly the subject of odious and unjust charges in the public press and we could sympathise with him, as during the late war in South Africa, there appeared to be no charge or suspicion too monstrous to be credited against our Government and troops by the foreign press, and the only thing to be done was to remain calm and hope that time would do justice.[35]

This attitude was typical of by far the majority of pre-war professional diplomats. They were aware of anti-British propaganda, but they did not consider it necessary to promote or advocate a counter-campaign. Such activity would have stood out in sharp contrast to their professional sense of responsibility and would have been tantamount to opening the floodgates of international propaganda.

Sir Edward Grey made the position of the Foreign Office quite clear in a statement made to the House of Commons in November 1911. He said:

Certain representatives, newspapers and press agencies receive any communications with regard to foreign affairs which are suitable for publication. Such information is, for the most part, confined to appointments and changes in His Majesty's Diplomatic Service. If enquiries are made at the Foreign Office with regard to specific facts, they are answered when it is possible to do so without prejudice to public or private interests . . . . There is no regular organisation in connexion with the Foreign Office for inspiring any press agency or newspaper in order to put forward, either officially or semi-officially, the views of His Majesty's Government with regard to foreign affairs.[36]

Such a statement concealed the extent of the network of informal contacts which existed between publicists and diplomats and it was, in any case, an attitude which had its critics. The Royal Commission on the Civil Service, which met from 29 April to 18 July 1914, cast serious doubts upon the wisdom of the Foreign Office's attitude towards the press.[37] The Commission encountered frequent complaints that the diplomatic and consular services made little effort to accommodate the publicity requirements of the press. British officials were accused of being less conscious of journalists' needs than their French or German counterparts. After the war, George Beak, the vice-consul in Zurich, commented:

Before the war representatives of Great Britain abroad—namely the Diplomatic and Consular Service—were not encouraged to take any very great interest in the Press of the countries to which they were accredited. Reports were for the most part spasmodic and dealt with only the more extraordinary articles which happened to appear.

Practically no attempt was made in any effective manner to influence the foreign press in our favour.[38]

The war of 1914-18 changed all this. The need to mobilise opinion at home and abroad, particularly in neutral countries, became an essential weapon in the national arsenal.

It is against this background that the conduct of British propaganda in the First World War must be studied. The conflict 'brought into relief the hidden and unresolved tensions which had been gathering strength since the closing years of the nineteenth century; it weakened the framework of society and made it easier for new forces to make themselves felt'.[39] The gradual transformation of the war from being effectively a war of limited aims into one of total commitment to victory, a transformation symbolised by the introduction of conscription in 1916, necessitated the mobilisation of morale and the combating of war-weariness and pacifism. Broadly speaking, the British people entered the First World War with enthusiasm and unquestioning resignation. The appearance of Germany as the aggressor, combined with an almost forgotten treaty obligation to Belgium, provided the moral justification required for the government to take the country into a struggle which was essentially remote from the interests of the majority of British people. However, as the illusion of a short war and rapid victory faded in the wake of horrifying casualties, military stalemate and increasing mobilisation of national resources, propaganda began to play a more significant role. The struggle now appeared to depend not on events in the field of battle but on the hearts and minds of the ordinary people taking part in it. By 1916, the war had become 'a test of endurance, a match of material resources of the belligerents, of their ability to transform these into immediate tools of war, shells and guns, and of the spirit of men on both sides'.[40] The advent of Lloyd George as Prime Minister in December 1916 was to provide the nation with a leader whose determination to see the war through to victory was exceeded only by his ruthlessness in securing that goal. He was, moreover, a man convinced of the power of propaganda. Unlike the vast majority of his contemporaries, Lloyd George was quick to see that morale and public opinion could play a decisive role in affecting the final result. He initiated a new spirit of determination to win this battle which was to result in the recruitment of newspapermen into the official propaganda machinery for which he had been partly responsible for inspiring in 1914. In doing so, however, he was imposing a severe strain upon the traditional relationship between government and the press and between government and the people. Yet there could be no turning back from the innovations he was primarily responsible for launching.

PART ONE

Organisation

1 The Organisation of Official British Propaganda, 1914-16

THE precise origins of the British government's involvement in war propaganda remain clouded in uncertainty. Few records survive which throw light upon seemingly mysterious beginnings of the various organisations that sprang into being following the outbreak of the First World War. If there was any pre-war planning for such work — as is often suspected — evidence of it does not appear to exist. As a result, the picture which emerges is one of rapid improvisation, confused responsibility and empirical development. British officials unfamiliar with the management of public opinion suddenly found themselves involved in work for which they had little enthusiasm and still less experience. Before 1914, the prevailing official attitude had favoured secrecy rather than publicity. Despite the efforts of several politicians to cultivate opinion through the medium of the press, the type of atmosphere in which ideas might flourish of manipulating popular opinion on a large scale, especially in foreign countries, did not exist in nineteenth-century Britain. Indeed, even on the outbreak of the First World War, the government displayed little concern for explaining the causes or justifying British involvement to the general public at home, other than the preparation of a bluebook on the subject. The growth of Anglo-German antagonism before the war, combined with the upsurge of patriotic enthusiasm which greeted the declaration of hostilities, appeared to render unnecessary a campaign to promote domestic morale, while expectations of a short war and rapid victory worked against any urgent initiative for a concerted propaganda effort abroad. It was only as the prospect of an early victory began to fade, and the demands of total warfare began to make themselves felt, that the hollowness of these illusions bacame all too apparent.

THE PARLIAMENTARY RECRUITING COMMITTEE

On the outbreak of war, the British Regular Army totalled 160,000 men — large enough, as Bismarck had once said, for the German police force to arrest. Although it was far from being the 'contemptible little army' many Germans believed it to be, this highly professional volunteer force, which had traditionally been responsible for fighting Britain's wars, was clearly not large enough to make any decisive impact upon the course of this new struggle. Accordingly, on 8 August 1914, Lord Kitchener, the newly appointed War Secretary who believed that the war would last longer than was commonly thought, launched his appeal for men to take up the sword of justice and fight for King and Country. At first, there was no shortage of volunteers. Within a month, the figures had reached 30,000 a day.[1] Recruitment stands set up by the War Office found it difficult to cope with the sheer weight of volunteers who rushed forward to sign up in response to Kitchener's outstretched index finger inviting them to enlist simply because 'Your Country Needs You'. However, the initial flood soon became a stream and then turned into a trickle as enthusiasm began to fade. Because of the enormous casualties sustained on the western front, the shortage of volunteers grew to such alarming proportions that conscription became but a matter of time. Meanwhile the early attempts to raise a volunteer force represented the first systematic propaganda campaign directed at the civilian population by the British government. Recruitment was to remain the dominant theme of domestic propaganda until the introduction of conscription in January 1916 and was to serve as the principal focal point of the individual citizen's commitment to the national war effort.[2]

The most important recruitment organisation during the first eighteen months of the war was the Parliamentary Recruiting Committee (PRC) which operated under the auspices of the War Office. The PRC was formed following an initiative by the Prime Minister who had been impressed by the efforts of a small group of enterprising Members of Parliament who had established recruiting committees in their constituencies following Kitchener's appeal. Asquith called upon the leaders of the three major political parties to consider some form of collaborative effort in support of the war. Meetings were held on 27 and 28 August, to be followed three days later by the decision:

To form a Parliamentary Recruiting Committee for the purpose of appealing to the political associations throughout the country to give general assistance to the work of recruiting, to enlist the sympathies and help of Peers, Members of Parliament and Parliamentary Candidates, to assist County Recruiting Committees in obtaining Parliamentary speakers for public meetings, to issue and circulate suitable publications in leaflet and pamphlet form in every possible way, and to work in conjunction with the recruiting agencies.[3]

In short, the PRC was to serve as a co-ordinating agency for the direction of recruitment nationally by both the government and the numerous unofficial bodies which had already sprung into existence.[4]

The PRC was an all-party organisation led jointly by the three party leaders, Asquith, Bonar Law and Henderson, serving as its presidents. The chief Liberal and Conservative whips, respectively Percy Illingworth and Lord Talbot, served as its joint chairmen. The committee comprised 30 members consisting largely of the party whips, principal party organisers and two representatives from the War Office, Sir Henry Rawlinson and Colonel Goset, who provided the essential liaison between the military authorities which helped to finance the work, and the other recruitment bodies. The General Purposes Committee served as the PRC's executive and consisted of 14 members. Three sub-departments were formed, to deal with meetings, publications and with householders' returns and information, which were able to begin their work immediately through the offices and staff provided by the three parties at their respective headquarters. Such co-operation at the centre — a foretaste of coalition[5] — was extended to the localities through the party agents and constituency organisations. Branch committees based upon similar all-party lines were formed and, initially, the central authority in London sought to defer to local demands in deciding the nature of the propaganda campaign, although the precise organisational connection between central and local committees remains unclear.

The PRC was, strictly speaking, a political body rather than an official propaganda department in the accepted sense. It differed significantly from the various other official attempts to influence opinion during the first half of the war in that it conducted its propaganda openly and directly. Indeed, its very creation was partly designed as a propagandist move to demonstrate the political unity of the country while being, at the same time, a reassurance that it was an 'independent' body which had emerged naturally from the normal processes of a pluralistic political system at war and was not another bureaucratic imposition by the government. Yet, in reality, the PRC's function was clearly defined by the fact that its work was subordinated to the peculiar requirements of the war effort as expressed through the Cabinet and War Office. When, therefore, Lord Derby was appointed Director-General of Recruitment in October 1915, the PRC automatically co-operated with such bodies as the Joint Labour Recruiting Committee, the Local Government Board, the Ministry of Munitions and the Home Office in launching what was to prove the last great voluntary recruitment drive prior to the introduction of conscription.[6]

The PRC was also useful to the government in other, less obvious ways. It diverted a measure of parliamentary attention away from the inevitable reduction in the importance of the House of Commons in the decision-making process as the war progressed. Moreover, the use of local party organisations in the recruitment campaign enabled the government to monitor fluctuations in public opinion throughout the country. Given this particular function, it was hardly surprising that other interested departments sought to exploit the PRC. During the course of the war, a considerable number of government departments established their own propaganda and press offices and, as such, they formed part of the overall propaganda effort although they did tend to function independently of each other. Nevertheless, they often combined in various collaborative efforts and most notably in the recruitment campaign. The Ministry of Munitions, for example, worked through the various local PRC committees in its efforts to recruit workers into the factories.[7] Such instances multiplied after 1916 with the expansion in the number of wartime departments. The National War Savings Committee, the Ministry of Food, the Ministry of National Service and the Ministry of Reconstruction all exploited PRC outlets and facilities.[8] However the introduction of conscription, when compulsion replaced patriotism and propaganda in recruitment, heralded the decline of the PRC as the principal domestic propaganda organisation operating inside the United Kingdom.

CENSORSHIP AND THE PRESS BUREAU

Although the government had devoted little attention to the question of propaganda before the war, it had long appreciated the role which censorship could play in the wartime control of public opinion. It was largely from this negative perspective that more positive attitudes towards the conduct of propaganda were eventually to emerge. This is well illustrated by the British government's first offensive action against the enemy following the outbreak of hostilities. Within hours of the expiry of the ultimatum to Berlin, the cable ship *Telconia* set sail with instructions to cut the German trans-Atlantic cables. The success of this mission not only left Germany subsequently dependent upon wireless telegraphy and cable communications via neutral countries for her contact with the non-European world but was also to provide the British with an incalculable advantage in the propaganda battle to come. But how was it that the Admiralty was ready to act so promptly in severing a cable just a few inches thick lying on the bottom of the sea? Such an operation clearly required detailed advance preparation. Indeed, although detailed planning appears to have begun in 1912,[9] official recognition of the need to control the flow and content of cable communications dates from at least the 1890s, and possibly much earlier.[10]

The emergence of London during the late nineteenth century as the major news capital of the world, at the hub of a vast global cable network,[11] provided British defence planners with a severe headache. Because Fleet Street was quick to exploit the new methods of rapid communication,[12] censorship came to be recognised as a hydra-headed military and strategic problem. On the one hand, it was necessary to preserve but control the flow of information in and out of Britain while, at the same time, preventing communication between an enemy power and her allies if at all possible. On the other hand, it was essential to prevent the transmission of information from enemy agents operating inside the United Kingdom. Where the press was concerned, it was just as important to prevent the publication of information which might prove useful to the enemy as it was to prevent the publication at home of 'true or false information which might exercise a prejudicial effect on the civil population'.[13] Long before the war, therefore, the role of censorship in the shaping of morale was fully recognised.

On 5 August 1914, Lord Kitchener, the newly appointed War Minister, and Winston Churchill, First Lord of the Admiralty, summoned F. E. Smith (later Lord Birkenhead) and asked him to establish an office which would supervise the business of press censorship.[14] The event was not without its irony in view of Kitchener's well-known dislike for journalists and Churchill's earlier career as a war correspondent. Why they chose Smith for the thankless task of supervising press censorship is not clear. An intimate friend of Churchill, he was a renowned speaker with an incisive mind sharpened by a legal background — qualities which might have been considered essential in what would undoubtedly prove a delicate position. Over the next few days, Smith began to establish the official Press Bureau. Public statements relating to its activities tended to emphasise its positive functions. On 7 August, Churchill informed Parliament that the bureau had been established to ensure that 'a steady stream of trustworthy information supplied both by the War Office and the Admiralty can be given to the press'.[15] Three weeks later, Asquith described the Press Bureau as 'the mouthpiece through which communications relative to the progress of naval and military operations are made public by the Admiralty, the War Office, and other public Departments concerned'.[16] Such statements were greeted with scepticism by the press. Journalists quickly learned that the bureau was more concerned with censorship than with publicity. And whereas responsible elements of the press had adhered to the system of 'voluntary censorship' before the war, they soon came to resent the manner of control exercised by the 'Suppress Bureau'. Their resentment was compounded by the arbitrary ban imposed by Kitchener on war correspondents at the front, 'without explanation, and the initial insensitive government control over all press cablegrams poisoned within weeks the co-operative spirit painstakingly built up during the pre-war years'.[17]

The Press Bureau opened for business at 40 Charing Cross Road but was moved to the Royal United Service Institution on 17 September 1914 where it remained for the rest of the war. During its first six weeks, the work was characterised by the need for improvisation. The bureau was formed with no real terms of reference nor any specific definition of duties. F. E. Smith was, in effect, simply expected to muddle through. He divided the bureau into four sections. The Cable Department examined every telegram received and transmitted by the press and censored any information which was considered to fall within the terms of the Defence of the Realm Act. The initial concern was to prevent valuable information from reaching the enemy and, on the outbreak of war, the War Office had assumed responsibility for the censorship of private and commercial communications by cable and by the postal service.[18] However, in September 1914, the War Office transferred responsibility for the censorship of press cable communications to the Press Bureau, although the Chief Censor at the War Office, whose organisation was kept entirely separate from the bureau throughout the war, remained in charge of all cable and postal censorship other than press communications. Similarly, the Chief Naval Censor at the Admiralty supervised an organisation quite separate from the Naval Room at the Press Bureau which dealt only with press cables and newspaper articles dealing with naval matters. A third branch of the bureau, known as the Issuing Department, was theoretically responsible for serving as the normal channel through which government departments released official information to the press.[19] However the initial preoccupation with censorship made this a generally disappointing source of official information to the press during the early part of the war.

The fourth, and most controversial, branch of the Press Bureau was the Military Room which handled all press material other than telegrams. As a concession to the peacetime system of voluntary censorship, editors were allowed to submit to the bureau any material which they suspected was likely to incur the wrath of the government prior to publication. They were, however, under no compulsion to submit material beforehand. This option laid the system open to criticism on the grounds of inequal treatment. As the *Daily Chronicle* complained in January 1915:

To send an article to the Press Bureau is to invite a severity of treatment which can easily be escaped by the simple process of not sending. Some of our contemporaries escape it in this way every day . . . . If the articles were sent to it, the blue pencil would act quickly enough; but if our contemporary is not patriotic enough to send them, the Press Bureau will let it say what it pleases. A policy of this sort simply puts a premium on a newspapers' not 'playing the game', and the only marvel is — a marvel more creditable to the press as a whole than the public realises — that the majority of them continue to play it.[20]

This comment does not reveal the true extent of the legislation which the government had at its disposal under the terms of DORA. Editors were liable to prosecution for publishing anything which might be deemed subsequently to be a military or naval secret. Ignorance was no defence, nor indeed was the fact that the information might have been received from an official source, including the Press Bureau. A returned article marked 'passed by the censor' was merely an expression of the bureau's view that it did not contravene DORA. The bureau issued pamphlets advising editors of the limits to which they could go but, if that advice was ignored, the bureau itself was not empowered to issue D (Defence) Notices preventing publication — assuming, of course, that its officials were somehow informed of impending publication of dangerous material beforehand. That power rested with the Home Office, under the auspices of which the Press Bureau functioned. The marvel lies not so much in the fact that the majority of newspapers continued to 'play the game', as the *Daily Chronicle* put it, but rather in the fact that the government prosecuted so few of those which did not.

In its defence, it must be said that the Press Bureau was an unprecedented experiment and, as such, was forced to operate on the basis of experience gained as the work developed. Early mistakes were inevitable and, indeed, numerous, with the result that the press came to regard the bureau as a scapegoat for its wartime grievances against the government. It was criticised especially for its apparently arbitrary and haphazard means of reaching decisions. Yet it is unlikely that the British press would ever have felt comfortable with such an institution, no matter how efficient, because of a fundamental and perhaps irreconcilable conflict of interests. Even the most patriotic newspapers conceived their basic role in terms of being able to publicise events relating to the war in order to meet their circulation demands. In the government's rather zealous efforts to prevent valuable information from reaching the enemy, this role was being thwarted. Moreover, the press remained determined to retain its traditional freedom to criticise and to interpret the news as well as to inform its readership, within, that is, the limits of wartime restrictions. Although the Press Bureau was prepared to trust to the patriotism and responsibility of individual newspapers in this matter, the fact remains that its very existence was designed to monitor the press and, if necessary, to subordinate the functions and self-conceived duties of the fourth estate to the demands of the military, naval and diplomatic conduct of war. Fleet Street claimed to be trustworthy; the military and naval authorities, unsympathetic to the demands of journalism and more concerned with the requirements of the armed services, did not agree. And, if necessary, they had legislation to enforce their point. As a result, the enormous potential of the press as an instrument of official propaganda remained largely untapped during the early part of war. In other words, if newspapers were propagandist during this period[21] — which they undoubtedly were — it was largely of their own, rather than the government's, initiative.

The stream of criticism levelled against the Press Bureau was, however, largely misdirected. Although its director was a political figure, the bureau was in fact dominated by the Service Departments. F. E. Smith was aided by his brother Harold, an MP, and he was advised by the distinguished academic, Professor Charles Oman, and by George Riddell, owner of the *News of the World* and, more significantly, chairman of the Newspaper Proprietors' Association. But the majority of the staff was comprised of military and naval officers who had been seconded to the bureau by the War Office and Admiralty. During the spring of 1914, the Admiralty had begun to organise its own censorship department in anticipation of war and, although partly amalgamated to the Press Bureau on the outbreak of hostilities, the Chief Naval Censor, Douglas Brownrigg, admitted that it was his office at the Admiralty which retained ultimate control over all censorship policy connected with naval affairs.[22] Equally, the War Office under Kitchener's direction was so set against the publication of virtually any military information that it issued an embargo on all war correspondents at the front. Kitchener confessed his narrow view of the publicity in November 1914 when he stated that 'it is not always easy to decide what information may or may not be dangerous, and whenever there is any doubt, we do not hesitate to prevent publication'.[23] This obstructive policy towards the press, based as it was upon the misguided assumption that no news is good news, was pursued vigorously by the War Office even after war correspondents were finally allowed to visit the front in May 1915.[24] Before that time, the British press was forced to accept the unsatisfactory and unimaginative accounts of the 'official eye-witness' at the front, Sir Ernest Swinton, and the somewhat uninformative official communiqués issued by the Press Bureau from 11 August 1914 onwards.

If the value of the press as a medium for official propaganda was not widely appreciated at the start of the war because of the preoccupation with censorship, this was partly due to a lack of trust on the part of the censors in the ability of the press to refrain from sensationalism. Starved of news, Fleet Street made the most of what was available. But the shortage of information too frequently led to the publication of dubious accounts. Shortly after the creation of the Press Bureau, for example, the *Daily Mail* published 'a plausible and detailed account of an entirely fictitious naval victory'.[25] Alarmist reports were as frequent as optimistic fabrications. Although the enactment of DORA on 12 August was to make the publication of false statements an offence, in the meantime the Press Bureau had constantly to appeal for moderation and restraint. Yet by not releasing news of the despatch of the British Expeditionary Force to France until three days after it had arrived, the censors were merely aggravating an already tense atmosphere. Ironically, however, it was the failure of the bureau to censor news of the retreat from Mons, where at the end of August 1914 the British army was defeated in its first encounter with the Germans, which demonstrated the vulnerability of the system to individual self-interest. F. E. Smith allowed press reports of the retreat to be published partly out of administrative incompetence[26] and also, it seems, to strengthen the argument for reinforcements.[27] The publication in *The Times* of Arthur Moore's despatch on the retreat created a public outcry. The Press Bureau appeared to have gone from one extreme to another. The government considered that publication should have been prevented in order to avoid public demoralisation whereas the press welcomed the publicity, albeit after some initial resentment at having been 'scooped' by some of their rivals.[28] The fact that on the day after news of the retreat appeared in the press recruitment reached a record 30,000 appeared to vindicate the claims of Fleet Street that it should be allowed greater access to news about the war.[29]

The Amiens despatch on the retreat from Mons was an isolated case. The Press Bureau, inspired by the Service Departments, continued its cautious policy. F. E. Smith was determined to leave a job for which he was not well suited so that he could join his regiment but, even after his resignation from the bureau three weeks later, the wave of press criticism continued to mount. The assault was led by the Northcliffe press which, although a supporter of voluntary censorship before the war, became the Asquith government's sternest critic in wartime.[30] By the end of 1914, Colonel Repington, the controversial military correspondent of *The Times*, was arguing that the censorship was being used ' as a cloak to cover all political, naval and military mistakes'.[31] The *Audacious* affair was one such example.[32] Repington himself, in his vociferous crusade to expose this and other blunders, was a constant victim of censorship.[33]

Reports from the front and elsewhere such as those written by Repington gradually came to be regarded less in terms of military security and more in terms of their impact upon domestic morale. This development, and a further illustration of the vulnerability of censorship to personal and political self-interest, was experienced by Brownrigg in his dealings with Churchill during the Dardanelles Expedition in the spring of 1915. The failure to remove the Turks from the Straits resulting in the British withdrawal from the Gallipoli peninsula was a catastrophe of the first order. According to Brownrigg, Churchill informed him that 'for this business, I am Chief Censor, not you'. Brownrigg added:

He was also a bit of a gambler, i.e. he would hold on to a bit of bad news for a time on the chance of getting a bit of good news to publish as an offset, and I must say it not infrequently paid off.[34]

Northcliffe, however, who felt that the 'English people do not mind a bit of bad news', was not alone in considering that Churchill was responsible for 'many of the initial evils of the Press Bureau'.[35] The influence of the War Office was also evident in preventing the publication of letters from soldiers at the front testifying to the grave shortage of shells, letters which would have reinforced Northcliffe's campaign against Kitchener which was to reach its peak in May 1915. In other words, the censors came to act as propagandists in their attempts to control the flow of any information that would produce the desired effect upon public opinion.

Smith was succeeded as director of the Press Bureau by Sir Stanley Buckmaster, the Solicitor-General, on 30 September 1914. Because he inherited an organisation which was still dominated by the Service Departments, Buckmaster was unable to reverse the policy of secrecy. Some improvements did, however, take place. Buckmaster was assisted by Sir Frank Swettenham, a retired colonial administrator, and by Edward Cook, a distinguished journalist who had formerly been editor of the *Pall Mall Gazette*, *Westminster Gazette*, and the *Daily News*. The Home Secretary assumed parliamentary responsibility for the bureau, and the number of employees was increased to 50, working in shifts around the clock. Buckmaster informed the House of Commons that these improvements would not signify any change in policy towards the question of press censorship. 'It has been', he said, 'and will continue to be the policy to publish everything that can be made public without danger to the State'.[36] In view of the bureau's early record, this was hardly reassuring. The continued conservatism of the Service Departments towards publicity remained the principal factor influencing the work of the Press Bureau.

Fleet Street was not alone in regarding the censorship as unsatisfactory. In the Foreign Office it soon became apparent that the real need was for positive rather than negative forms of action. On the outbreak of war, a small News Department had been created to meet the increased demand for information from allied and neutral journalists. Although representatives of the British press were theoretically supposed to visit the Press Bureau for information relating to foreign policy matters, the uninformative nature of its communiqués caused many of them to call at a more forthcoming Foreign Office. The Press Bureau was, in fact, advised by the Foreign Office on all censorship matters relating to foreign affairs and also received information from it for release to the press. But somewhere along the way, the system was breaking down and British journalists found the original source more informative than the official mouthpiece. At first, the Foreign Office regarded the British press as a hindrance to the work of diplomacy. In October 1914, Sir Edward Grey was reported to be

receiving, almost daily, accumulating evidence of the harm which is done in neutral countries by articles which have appeared in the British press. He wishes to have the attention of editors drawn to this evil, which undoubtedly undoes much of the work which he endeavours to do with a view to securing a friendly attitude on the part of the neutrals.[37]

Despite a warning issued to the press on these lines by the Press Bureau,[38] the problem remained. The leading culprit was again felt to be the Northcliffe press and *The Times* in particular. Its foreign editor, Henry Wickham Steed, described relations during the winter of 1914-15 as being tantamount to 'a state of war . . . between us and the Foreign Office'.[39] Following a series of attacks upon Sir Edward Grey's treatment of Anglo-Turkish relations in which the Foreign Secretary was accused of mismanaging the Ottoman empire both before and after Turkey had joined the Central Powers in November 1914, the Foreign Office had closed its doors to journalists from Printing House Square. Steed, like Northcliffe, vigorously defended his paper's freedom to criticise the government if it chose to do so. Both men were adamant that relations would not improve 'until the

F.O. realises that *The Times* does not intend to be used either as a mouthpiece or as a doormat'.[40] Steed also complained of Foreign Office attempts to do 'all it can to annoy us in petty ways' which was, presumably, a reference to Foreign Office influence exerted at the Press Bureau because, by December 1914, Geoffrey Dawson, the editor, was highly critical of both bodies. 'Why in the world', he wrote, 'the P[ress] B[ureau] and the Foreign Office should always be trying to score off the newspapers I cannot for the life of me imagine'.[41]

In fact, the Foreign Office was beginning to regard its association with the Press Bureau as counter-productive. In so far as a newspaper such as *The Times* was concerned, with its efficient foreign news-gathering organisation and its high reputation abroad, severing relations was likely to produce little effect upon its editorial commentaries. It was clearly more desirable to work with such a newspaper than against it. Tension between government and the press as a whole was to some extent eased in May 1915 when, following Buckmaster's appointment as Lord Chancellor in Asquith's new coalition cabinet, E. T. Cook and Frank Swettenham were appointed to serve as co-directors of the Press Bureau. Cook's promotion, coupled with a new willingness to appoint journalists as advisers in an expanded censorship machinery of 300 staff, did serve to alleviate some of the criticism levelled against the bureau that it was ignorant of the demands of journalism. Cook fully appreciated the essentially different functions of the press and the censorship in time of war. He even informed one journalist:

You should not, in kindness or for any other reason, speak too much good of our censorship. I don't suppose you are likely to do so, but it would be a terrible blow if you did. The enterprising newspaper or news agency and an official censorship are natural enemies; and if the day should ever come when the newspapers, British and Neutral, conspired to praise the Press Bureau, it would be a catastrophe for one or the other of us; it would mean either the journalists had lost their 'go' or that our censors had been neglecting their duty.[42]

With the emergence of such realistic attitudes within the bureau, it merely remained for the more blatant sources of friction to be removed.

The cause was taken up by Lord Robert Cecil, the Parliamentary Under-Secretary of State for Foreign Affairs. Cecil was an example of that rare species of Foreign Office official who believed in the value of publicity. He recognised the propaganda potential of the press in wartime and was alarmed that this potential was not being tapped because of the continuing hostility of Fleet Street towards the Press Bureau. He argued that the bureau's powers were ill-defined and pointed to a recent decision made by the Attorney-General that opinions and deductions did not fall within the scope of the word 'mischief' specified in DORA.[43] He encountered extreme resentment on the part of journalists at the way the Press Bureau dealt with them. Wickham Steed informed Cecil in August 1915:

We have suffered so much injustice from the Press Bureau and the censorship since the beginning of the war — from the famous Amiens despatch of last August, which we were requested by the head of the Press Bureau to publish, and were afterwards reviled by the Prime Minister in Parliament for having published, down to Colonel Repington's message of last spring (on the shortage of shells), which was censored once at the front and once here and was yet represented to Parliament as not having been censored at all — that we are becoming a little sensitive. I wish the Press Bureau could understand that no decent journal cares a fig for any 'scoop' at the expense of public welfare, however much it may resent the foolish secrecy often practised in the past by people who are not in touch with, or qualified to judge, the state of public opinion.[44]

Such at least, was the view of a distinguished and respected member of a 'decent' journal. Despite the periodic thundering of *The Times*, notably over the shell-shortage crisis, it continued to be regarded essentially as the house-magazine of the British ruling establishment and, abroad, as the official mouthpiece of the government. There remained the problem of how to deal with less trustworthy behaviour on the part of the various pacifist and labour journals,[45] which could not be relied upon to operate reliably within a system of voluntary censorship. Cecil's immediate aim, however, was to improve relations between the government and the press as a whole because, as a later report put it, 'in the early days of propaganda, even Westminster was found to be too far from Fleet Street'.[46]

As the war dragged on through its first Christmas and approached its second winter with no prospect of victory in sight, the conflict came to be seen less in traditional terms of a limited war fought between small professional armies but more in terms of one nation's entire resources pitted against those of the enemy. Elements in society which had hitherto remained generally uninvolved in, and untouched by, the exigencies of national survival now found themselves directly affected by events on the field of battle. With the realisation of the concept of a home 'front', opinion and morale were viewed as military assets, while propaganda began to emerge as the chief instrument of control over them. In the Foreign Office News Department it was appreciated, albeit fundamentally, that propaganda was fast becoming a specialised weapon of warfare best conducted by people well versed in the peculiar twists and turns of public opinion at large. The Foreign Office had no wish to conduct direct propaganda. As one official pointed out, 'through showing one important editor the concrete evidence of this country's achievements, you can reach hundreds of thousands of readers'.[47] It was this attempt to utilise the press as a medium of official propaganda which prompted Cecil to campaign for the abolition of censorship on all material relating to foreign affairs, which he finally succeeded in doing on 20 December 1915.[48] Instructions were issued to the press indicating that this decision did not signify any change in the provisions of DORA, merely that responsibility for seeing that they were complied with now rested with the newspapers themselves. Thereafter, considerable latitude was extended to journalists by the Foreign Office and a new period of frankness and mutual co-operation ensued. The Press Bureau, however, was not happy with the change. In March 1917, Cook and Swettenham reported that Cecil's scheme had 'proved a failure'[49] although it is difficult to see why they should have thought so in view of the radical reduction in the number of press complaints received by the Foreign Office relating to the censorship.

Although the Foreign Office continued to advise the Chief Naval Censor at the Admiralty and the Chief Cable and Postal Censors at the War Office until 1917,[50] the severance of its direct work through the Press Bureau did enable the News Department to concentrate, as Cecil wrote, 'on what ought to be, I think, our chief work, namely propaganda'.[51] In so far as Fleet Street was concerned, this remained a delicate task. In order to avoid inevitable resentment caused by official attempts to influence public opinion through the medium of newspapers, the Foreign Office therefore adopted a personal approach. It did this by facilitating the efforts of journalists to report upon the events for themselves. Ministerial conferences held for the benefit of newspaper proprietors had begun in February 1915,[52] and weekly Press Conferences were organised by the Newspaper Proprietors' Association. But there remained little opportunity for the ordinary journalist to go about his business of gathering daily news about the war and the way it was being fought. The French allowed journalists to visit their lines, prompting Northcliffe to ask: 'If the French, why not the British?'[53] The Foreign Office agreed and repeatedly requested the War Office and Admiralty to release more information. The Service Departments refused until they could no longer resist the combined pressure of the Foreign Office and the press. British journalists were allowed to join the troops at the front in May 1915[54] and the Admiralty allowed newspapermen to visit the fleet for the first time at the end of 1915.[55] Also on Foreign Office advice, senior military and naval officers began to conduct weekly lectures for the benefit of eager correspondents, the success of which was claimed to more than justify the experiment.[56]

In all these dealings, great emphasis was placed upon personal contact between official and journalist in an attempt to forge a relationship of mutual trust and confidence. By letting the journalist see what he wanted to see (at least within reason), by arranging visits to the front, munitions factories, prisoner-of-war camps and other such places of interest, and by providing him with opportunities to discuss the course of the war with leading personalities, the British government was effectively exploiting the press as a medium of official propaganda. After the war, one MP wrote that 'there was no more discreditable period in the history of journalism than the four years of the Great War'.[57] But it was not necessarily a question of conscious acceptance on the part of the press of serving as a medium for the distribution of official propaganda, certainly not in the early days of the war when the bulk of it was conducted beneath a veil of strict secrecy. There were many occasions when newspapers were quite willing to disseminate official propaganda because of a coincidence of views. Nor was the press always the conscious handmaiden of the government in the sense that official organisations could force individual newspapers to publish certain information or articles. Such requests were made on occasions but what happened to the information once it had left its official source was generally left to the discretion and sense of patriotism of the newspaper editor himself. Even so, as one newspaper proprietor, Lord Burnham, admitted in January 1917, 'the press has undertaken the publication of a vast amount of material which it has had sent to it — a large number of articles of a propagandist character in regard to the great Departments of State which were published as a matter of courtesy'.[58]

Although the press managed to retain its freedom to criticise the government, the claim that it became part of the official propaganda machinery during the war is, therefore, largely justified.[59] In the case of perhaps the most notorious atrocity story of the war, the infamous corpse-conversion factory story of 1917, it was in fact the press which urged the story upon a more sceptical official propaganda machinery. Such examples are admittedly rare. The process more usually operated in the opposite direction. It is also important to recognise that the method of securing newspaper support operated on two different levels. In the business of everyday journalism, correspondents were provided with every opportunity to devise their own propaganda. At a higher level, the services of journalists were absorbed into the official machinery where their invaluable experience in the techniques of news selection, written communication and the propagation of opinion to a wide audience was eagerly sought after by officials who lacked similar experience and training. This process began effectively with the appointment of George Riddell as an adviser to the government shortly after the outbreak of war, continued with the appointment of such figures as E. T. Cook to serve in the Press Bureau, and reached its controversial apogee in 1918 when Lord Northcliffe and Lord Beaverbrook were appointed to take charge of all government propaganda. By absorbing whenever possible the power of the press into the service of government, by making some of its members an integral part of the defence of the realm, and by the provision of honours and appointments to certain leading editors and proprietors thereby giving them a vested interest in the survival of the system, the British government was thus able to exploit the enormous potential of the press for the duration of the war.

In short, the British press became the servant of official propaganda more out of willing acquiescence than as a result of government coercion. The press, for its part, was in the main prepared to accept the increased output of official information and improved facilities as compensation for the temporary wartime restrictions imposed by censorship upon its customary freedom. Patriotism undoubtedly played an important role in this acceptance, and it is significant that the government rarely used the powers vested in it under the terms of DORA. The Director of Public Prosecutions responded infrequently to the demands of the more extreme Cabinet and Foreign Office members who wished to initiate proceedings against recalcitrant publications.[60] The most common form of action taken was to prevent the export of particular publications because of their potential value to the enemy as counter-propaganda. The earliest example of this occurred in July 1916 with the *Tribunal* and it also happened to *The Nation* on one occasion in 1917.[61] The *Labour Leader* suffered more often because of its attacks upon the government for continuing the war and because of its repeated calls for peace negotiations.[62] Although these examples do reveal that faith had its limitations, a policy of general repression was considered undesirable. As Herbert Samuel stated during his period as Home Secretary, repressive measures 'do more harm than good. They would . . . have the effect of advertising the speeches and publications which are now, for the most part, left in obscurity'.[63] However, irresponsible publicity created a dilemma for the government. In May 1917, when the press published figures relating to the serious losses of British shipping at the hands of German submarines, the Cabinet appreciated the damaging effect which such information could have upon morale at home and in allied countries,[64] but recognised the problems of issuing a heartening piece of information to offset the press reports:

If publication were permitted, it provided the enemy with propaganda which was especially valuable to him at this moment, when he is sustaining his people mainly by encouraging hopes of a successful issue to the submarine campaign; while, on the other hand, if favourable news is published, the consumption of food in this country is greatly increased, and our allies are encouraged to clamour for more coal and similar shipping assistance.[65]

Here, then, was the official justification for the policy of secrecy. Censorship was just as important to the shaping of opinion as was publicity and propaganda. That the censorship worked at all was due, as Sir Edward Cook remarked, 'to the genius of the British people for working a logically indefensible compromise'.[66]

THE NEUTRAL PRESS COMMITTEE

Although censorship remained administratively separate from the various propaganda organisations which sprang into existence following the outbreak of war, communication with the press was a factor common to both activities. A distinction had to be made between British journalists and those from allied and neutral countries. If the former could be expected generally to accept and support the British case, the latter were likely to prove more critical. It was towards influencing favourably those observers and 'to try and counteract in an unofficial and secret way German propaganda activities'[67] that, on 11 September 1914, the Neutral Press Committee was formed under the aegis of the Home Office in connection with the Press Bureau.[68] A fortnight later, the committee was placed under the able direction of G. H. Mair, the recently retired assistant editor of the *Daily Chronicle*, on the recommendation of his editor, Robert Donald. Mair's appointment was one of the earliest examples of a newspaperman being recruited to serve in the official machinery. It was felt that journalists would receive information more willingly from someone much like themselves than they would from an official known to be a government propagandist.

Mair quickly began to organise his work into four main branches: the exchange of news services between British and foreign newspapers; the promotion of the sale of British newspapers abroad (an indication of how much the British press was considered to be a mirror of British opinion); the dissemination of news articles among friendly foreign newspapers and journals; and the transmission of news abroad by cables and wireless.[69] Mair developed the wireless service on his own initiative. It began in October 1914 and was designed to serve those foreign newspapers which could not afford to send correspondents to London or subscribe to the Reuters service. Short news messages were transmitted in morse code from the transmitter at Poldhu in Cornwall. Any foreign newspaper office receiving the messages were allowed to publish the news contained in them free of charge. But with wireless telegraphy still in its infancy, certain important areas such as the Americas were beyond the technical range of regular and reliable transmissions, and greater dependence in distant areas was placed upon the cabled news messages compiled by the Neutral Press Committee in conjunction with the Press Bureau and the Foreign Office News Department. In October 1915, Mair was able to extend his activities beyond neutral countries to encompass allied countries as well.[70]

Originally, the Neutral Press Committee was made responsible to a committee that included Lord Riddell, Lord Burnham, E. T. Cook, Robert Donald, F. E. Smith and C. F. G. Masterman who was in charge of the War Propaganda Bureau at Wellington House. This committee met rarely and was unable to establish an effective working relationship with Mair. It was therefore replaced by a smaller committee consisting of Cook, Professor Oman, two officials from Wellington House (Claud Schuster and E. A. Gowers) and Hubert Montgomery, the head of the Foreign Office News Department. At first, this group met daily and later twice weekly at the Press Bureau. But it proved no more effective than its predecessor in working with Mair and was soon disbanded, leaving Mair answerable only to the Home Office until early 1916.

If British propaganda was to be conducted efficiently overseas, it was important for the propagandists to be familiar with the changing moods of foreign opinion. From February 1915 onwards, therefore, Mair began to compile regular summaries of the foreign press. Newspapers were regarded essentially as opinion-makers as well as mirrors of opinion. An essential principle of Mair's work was that foreign journalists should be allowed to write their own articles once they had been entertained and supplied with official information by his office. This was considered to be of particular importance in dealings with American correspondents. It also had the great advantage of disguise. Official propaganda known to be such is almost useless unless, of course, you are preaching to the already converted. The recipient or target will normally treat obvious official propaganda with a higher degree of scepticism and disbelief than he will material emanating from a source such as a newspaper with which he is familiar and trusts. By appealing to opinion-makers rather than directly to the opinion itself, official bodies such as the Neutral Press Committee were effectively disguising their views from the eventual audience for which they were intended while, at the same time, avoiding comparisons with the direct techniques adopted by the Germans whose propaganda was automatically regarded as suspect.

THE NEWS DEPARTMENT OF THE FOREIGN OFFICE

The Neutral Press Committee was not the only organisation created by the government to deal with propaganda abroad. At the Foreign Office, a small News Department had been created shortly after the outbreak of war to meet the increased demand for news concerning the British contribution from allied and neutral correspondents in London. It rapidly became involved in other forms of propaganda and its involvement increased once the Foreign Office was relieved of its censorship burdens in December 1915. Initially, members of the

Foreign Office were generally wary of press propaganda. One official wrote early in 1915 that 'in this country we do not readily pander to the American taste for personal journalism, but in view of the lavish way in which interviews have been granted to American press correspondents in Germany, I believe it would be to our advantage to go some way to meet them'.[71] However, once the initial preoccupation with secrecy and censorship had subsided, officials in the News Department preferred that any proposals for increased or improved publicity through the press should originate with the journalists themselves. They perceived their own role largely in terms of suppliers of official information on demand. Those journalists who lacked discretion and who managed to escape the censorship by publishing sensitive material were damned in future. However, the fear that one of their most important sources of information might suddenly dry up seems to have served as an effective deterrent. In December 1916, one official emphasised the joint nature of the collaboration when he wrote that 'the News Department and the correspondents are constantly racking their brains to think of subjects which it will be interesting to work up'.[72] Such co-operation was possible only with foreign journalists who were broadly sympathetic to the allied cause. It was more difficult to achieve with correspondents from neutral countries. Nevertheless, the attitude of journalists from that most important of neutral countries, the United States, was recorded as being 'everything that could be wished'.[73] The only consistent exceptions were the pro-German newspapers of Randolph Hearst. In October 1914, Eustace Percy, then a junior Foreign Office official, noted on one offending article which had been brought to his attention:

We can afford to ignore Mr Hearst's malice. But, as here, he is always worth watching for his wonderful power of echoing the doubt which is at the back of the mind of the semi-ignorant man in the street. He may be trusted to point out the exact spot at which our line wants strengthening![74]

However, the persistent anti-British stance adopted by the Hearst press aggravated too many sensitive nerves to warrant the continuation of such magnanimity and, following repeated warnings over its coverage of the Easter Rising in Ireland, the battle of Jutland and the German air raids,[75] the government decided to impose an official news embargo on their London-based correspondents working for the International News Service from 1916 to 1917.[76]

Because of Britain's control over the transatlantic cables, the censors were able to reduce the effect of hostile articles sent from Berlin and elsewhere by Hearst correspondents who were cultivated by the enemy. But, in general, the American journalists working in London were considered to be 'trustworthy people' even though they did have to be 'constantly nursed and humoured'.[77] Despite the enormous linguistic advantages enjoyed by British propagandists over their enemy counterparts, the entertainment of American journalists was nonetheless considered to be 'one of the most important bits of work that the News Department has to do'.[78]

One of the most significant contributions of the Foreign Office towards the conduct of British propaganda in the First World War was the provision of agents abroad in the form of diplomatic and consular representatives. The News Department was responsible for the daily transmission of news telegrams to its overseas representatives who had instructions to make use of the information for propagandist purposes in the foreign press as they thought appropriate, according to local conditions.[79] They were, in addition, supplied with special news telegrams sent, for example, on the occasion of an important speech by a cabinet minister, and also any other suitable material produced by the various propaganda organisations. In other words, the diplomatic and consular representatives abroad acted as the distribution agents of British official propaganda. Different areas required special arrangements. In Russia, the Anglo-Russian Commission was established at Petrograd in December 1915 to receive telegrams, articles and bulletins relayed by the News Department with a view to securing publication in the Russian press.[80] Elsewhere, local committees of British residents and expatriates were formed to help missions distribute the propaganda material.[81] In Madrid, John Walter of *The Times* operated 'a kind of official Press Bureau for the Foreign Office' which received any official information, pamphlets, photographs and other material for distribution to those Spanish newspapers not under German influence.[82]

Independently of George Mair's arrangements, the News Department opened a cables and wireless branch in London's Victoria Street. This section was designed to supplement the work of the Neutral Press Committee by the nightly transmission of wireless messages in morse code to allied countries. These bulletins contained news of a general character and were known as the 'midnight messages'.[83] Although they were initially intended for overseas diplomatic missions in an attempt to alleviate the pressure on an overburdened cable network, their wider publicity potential was soon realised. Early in 1915, the Marconi company was granted exclusive rights to publish any information contained in the messages that was received by its wireless stations abroad. Marconi's own newspaper, *The Wireless Press*, enjoyed a monopoly in publishing wireless messages, including enemy transmissions intercepted by its stations, a privilege which generated considerable friction with the British press.[84]

Wireless was, however, merely an auxiliary method of telegraphic propaganda conducted by the British government. Fully 95 per cent of the work was done by cables.[85] In late 1914, the government approached Reuters and an arrangement was made whereby the news agency agreed to undertake the distribution of a certain amount of official telegraphic news to neutral countries in return for a small subsidy.[86] Although the arrangement was extended in 1915, Reuters remained conscious of the dangers of being labelled propagandist, a label which might seriously impair its cherished reputation for impartiality on the return of peace. Moreover, because of the various international agreements made before the war, Reuters was unable to introduce propaganda matter into its normal service to neutral countries 'except in a deft sort of way . . . as they are affiliated with national agencies which would not distribute what was obviously pro-Ally matter'.[87] Accordingly, an arrangement was made for Reuters to transmit official cabled news abroad by a separate venture known as the Agence Service Reuter. This service was designed to supplement the normal commercial news service and, although conducted entirely by the Reuters organisation, was financed by the British government at an annual cost of £120,000.[88] The object of the service was to secure that 'a certain class of news, of propaganda value, is cabled at greater length than would be possible in the normal Reuter Service'.[89] This arrangement benefited both parties. The government secured a cloak of legitimacy for the distribution of its news while Reuters was able to ease its acute financial difficulties.[90] But it did not prevent severe criticism from Reuters' leading rivals on the continent, Havas of France and the Wolff Bureau in Berlin, both of which enjoyed government subsidies. Nevertheless, by 1917, Reuters was sending about one million words a month abroad on behalf of the British government. Working in close collaboration with the News Department, the Agence Service Reuter was able to cable an average of 8000 words a day in English and French to Europe, Morocco, Japan and Central and South America. On occasion, as much as 60,000 words was transmitted in a single day.[91]

The official news telegrams sent directly abroad by the News Department were 'more obviously propaganda in character' than even the Agence messages.[92] They were designed to supplement the Reuters service, particularly in countries 'where experience has shown that the Service does not cover all the ground'.[93] The Foreign Office telegrams totalled 150 words for short news items, and 600 words for longer messages and articles.[94] Those scheduled for wireless transmission were broadcast twice daily, the first by Marconi's Poldhu station and the second by the Admiralty's high-powered transmitter at Caernarvon which was capable of reaching the east coast of America. Caernarvon was, in many respects, the British equivalent of the German wireless propaganda station at Nauen, but on a much smaller scale. It was devoted *inter alia* 'to exposing misrepresentations in the German wireless, and to putting forward the British case where it is necessary to supplement what goes forth in the cable services'.[95]

THE WAR PROPAGANDA BUREAU AT WELLINGTON HOUSE

If the British government had not been prepared to conduct propaganda on an organised scale when war broke out and was therefore forced to improvise the necessary machinery in the form of the Press Bureau, Neutral Press Committee and the Foreign Office News Department, the Germans had not been caught by surprise. As Rennell Rodd, the British ambassador in Rome, testified, 'German preparedness for the eventuality of war was revealed by the amount of literature with which the offices and agencies in Italy were immediately inundated'.[96] The same was true elsewhere as German propaganda spread far and wide. Posters, leaflets and pamphlets poured out from Berlin in an effort to explain Germany's entry into the war and to discredit the motives of her enemies. The British government was particularly alarmed at the virulence of the German campaign in the United States and it became apparent that immediate counter-measures were urgently required. The matter was brought to the attention of the Cabinet at the end of August 1914 by Lloyd George who 'urged the importance of setting on foot an organisation to inform and influence public opinion abroad and to confute German mis-statements and sophistries'.[97] As a result, Asquith invited his close friend, Charles Masterman, Chancellor of the Duchy of Lancaster and Chairman of the National Insurance Commission, to establish an organisation for this purpose. Masterman may have been chosen simply because he was a well-known publicist and writer.[98] But his link with the National Insurance Commission does raise an irresistible speculation. The Commission had been established in connection with the 1911 National Insurance Act and its greatest champion, Lloyd George, had chosen to recruit the services of a team of lecturers, recruited mainly from outside the civil service, to tour the country explaining the benefits of the Act to employers and workers alike.[99] This was a rare example of an organised publicity campaign conducted by a government department in peacetime prior to 1914. When Lloyd George raised the question of war propaganda shortly after the outbreak of war, he might well have had this peacetime precedent in mind. The Commission would therefore have been seen as the logical choice in any government search for a basic structure to conduct propaganda by virtue of the experience of its officials in administering the peacetime campaign. This is not to suggest that the National Insurance Commission was the forerunner of the wartime propaganda bureau but merely that the coincidence is too great to resist speculation.

Masterman was given the task of placing before the peoples of neutral countries and of the Dominions the British case for entering the war and for justifying wartime policy decisions. His first concern was how to set about this. As a preliminary measure, Masterman organised two conferences, the first with prominent literary figures and the second with representatives of the British press, in an attempt to establish the principles on which his propaganda campaign would be based and the methods he should adopt. The first conference took place on 2 September 1914 and was attended by a galaxy of literary figures including J. M. Barrie, Arnold Bennett, G. K. Chesterton, Arthur Conan Doyle, John Galsworthy, Thomas Hardy, John Masefield, Gilbert Murray, G. M. Trevelyan and H. G. Wells. The second conference was held on 7 September and was attended by E. T. Cook, Robert Donald, Geoffrey Dawson, J. L. Garvin of the *Pall Mall Gazette*, Sidney Low of *The Standard*, J. A. Spender of the *Westminster Gazette* and J. St Loe Strachey of the *Spectator*.[100] At this second gathering, four resolutions were adopted unanimously:

1. That it is essential that all the unnecessary obstacles to the speedy and unfettered transmission of news should be done away with and that all matter which has appeared or has been authorised to appear in English newspapers should be put upon the telegraph wires and cables without further censorship or delay in London.

2. That every effort should be made by the Government to procure special facilities for news messages by cable from England to neutral countries, especially those where German news at present obtains precedence.

3. It is recommended that an official be appointed by the Foreign Office to receive London correspondents representing all newspapers in the Dominions and neutral countries and to give them such information as, in the opinion of the Foreign Office, is desirable.

4. That, where no other means present themselves, British Ambassadors and Ministers should be furnished with expert journalistic assistance to enable them to deal promptly with false or misleading statements made in neutral foreign countries.[101]

The Foreign Office lent its full support to these proposals and pointed out that, in regard to resolution 3, Sir William Tyrrell, private secretary to Sir Edward Grey, had already begun this practice in the newly created News Department.[102]

Masterman then set about organising his War Propaganda Bureau in the block of flats at Buckingham Gate known as Wellington House which had previously housed the National Insurance Commission. Many of the officials who had worked there before the war such as Percy Koppel, Claud Schuster and E. A. Gowers were asked to serve in the new organisation which, for the next two years, became the principal production and distribution centre of British overseas propaganda working so effectively beneath a blanket of secrecy that even Parliament was largely unaware of its existence and activities.

Masterman appointed Schuster as his chief executive officer and Gowers as his general manager. The bureau itself was organised into sub-sections on a linguistic basis: one dealt with Scandinavia, another with Holland, and others dealing collectively with Spain, Portugal and South America, and with Italy and Switzerland. The United States was the concern of 'a most important special branch' under the direction of Sir Gilbert Parker, the Canadian-born writer and MP for Gravesend. In addition to the various officials appointed to work in the various sub-sections, Masterman also chose the novelist, Anthony Hope Hawkins, as his literary adviser and A. S.

Watt as his literary agent. Edwyn Bevan, the leading classical scholar, was recruited from Oxford University to serve as Masterman's liaison officer with military and naval intelligence, although his main task was the analysis of the German press for suitable propaganda material. J. S. Willimore, formerly of the consular service, was given a similar task with regard to the French press. The distinguished historians, Arnold Toynbee,[103] Lewis Namier[104] and J. W. Headlam-Morley[105] were appointed to serve as advisers. All these men comprised the decision-making body of Wellington House known as 'the moot' which met every day.[106] By 1917, the staff had expanded to 54,[107] making the bureau the largest organisation then in being for the conduct of propaganda abroad.

A specific set of procedures was followed by each branch of the department. It had first to monitor public opinion in the particular country with which it was concerned, chiefly through an analysis of the press. It then had to translate and publish any material likely to produce a favourable impression abroad. If suitable material was not readily available from foreign newspapers, the branch would commission a pamphlet or else circulate speeches and official documents. This material would then be distributed abroad through the diplomatic and consular officials who received it from Wellington House through the Foreign Office News Department, with which an extremely close liaison was established. Wellington House also had to deal with individuals directly, sending or receiving information and, especially in the case of the United States, encouraging press correspondents and other distinguished visitors to appreciate the British point of view. Occasionally, special envoys were sent abroad in order to ascertain the state of public opinion in the various countries and to recommend the best methods of dealing with any disaffection with British policy.

From the beginning, the guiding principle of Wellington House was that propaganda should be based upon accurate information and measured argument. As one official wrote in December 1914, 'our activities have been confined to the presentation of facts and of general arguments based upon facts'.[108] German methods were to be avoided at all costs. Instead, the British government maintained a policy of strict secrecy in its propaganda, the price of which was the recurring accusation that nothing was being done. However, given that the primary targets of Wellington House were opinion-makers rather than opinion itself, great caution was required. The facts and arguments presented in Wellington House literature had to be reliable and sensible. Mass distribution was avoided. The policy of Wellington House was 'to refrain from any general distribution, while welcoming eagerly any opportunity of approaching influential persons in foreign countries'.[109] Educated observers were even more likely to detect blatant propaganda, particularly if it was seen to originate from official sources. But if it was received from a reputable public figure or distinguished scholar, it would be regarded in a somewhat different light—provided that the recipient remained unaware that the sender was working for an official propaganda organisation such as Wellington House. Hence the vital importance of secrecy. Direct personal contacts were cultivated in an attempt to persuade the target gently of the logic and just nature of the British case. This subtle approach was especially important in the United States 'where much of the work has consisted in undoing the harm which has been done by those who have rushed impulsively to lecture the United States on her duty in the war'.[110] This was a reference to the abundance of amateur propagandists who had been galvanised into action without any official prompting or encouragement upon the outbreak of the war.

The activities of the various voluntary propaganda organisations were both a help and a hindrance to the work of Wellington House. Masterman recorded that his department found itself unconsciously directing, co-ordinating and often restraining the unofficial propagandists[111] working under the direction of such bodies as the Cobden Club, the Fight for Right Movement, the Anglican clerics, the United Workers, the Atlantic Union, the Overseas Club, the Victoria League and, perhaps most important of all, the Central Committee for National Patriotic Organisations (CCNPO).[112] The most obvious value of such organisations lay in their usefulness as distribution agencies thereby providing a cover for Wellington House. They did, however, desire a more positive role, as was illustrated by the case of the CCNPO which had as its president the Prime Minister, and Lord Rosebery and A. J. Balfour as its vice-presidents. Its chairman, Henry Cust, one time editor of the *Pall Mall Gazette*, was particularly interested in propaganda and he proposed various schemes for increasing British activity in neutral countries which invariably provoked alarm within the Foreign Office. The head of the News Department, Hubert Montgomery, warned Cust in November 1914:

Sir Edward Grey is anxious that we should not appear in any way to emulate what has been described as 'the orgy of second-rate publicity' in which the Germans have indulged, and which, by their admission, has not been a success. You will have noticed . . . that the Americans appreciate our attitude of restraint in this respect and there is a good deal of evidence that the same feeling prevails in other countries.[113]

Cust, however, was not prepared to let the matter rest. He complained that his organisation was capable of producing propaganda material more effectively and quickly than the official organisations. But the personalities connected with the CCNPO would have been associated immediately with the government, something which the Foreign Office wished to avoid. Eventually, in March 1915, 10 Downing Street was forced to warn Cust that he should confine his activities to the British Empire. But Cust was a law unto himself and had to be watched closely by the Foreign Office which even vetoed lecture tours[114] and other forms of propagandist activity sponsored by him which suggested barnstorming tactics.

Masterman was concerned to concentrate rather than dissipate the activities of Wellington House as the bureau continued to expand. In February 1916, he reported that 'our propaganda work has greatly increased in volume and the kind of work we are doing has also, in part, changed with the lengthening period of the war. Fresh methods have been and are being developed in order to preserve interest and counteract forces which are doing injury to the cause of the Allies'.[115] Following Schuster's appointment as Clerk of the Crown in July 1915, Gowers had been promoted to chief executive officer, although Schuster remained in Wellington House in an advisory capacity. A new section was created to deal with Moslem countries and another for pictorial propaganda. The bureau also became more involved in propaganda in allied countries as part of the campaign to reassure Britain's fighting partners of her determination to see the war through to the end and to emphasise the contribution being made by her people and troops.

THE RATIONALISATION OF SPRING 1916

The existence of three organisations charged with the task of conducting British official propaganda overseas raised serious problems of co-ordination and duplication of effort. The Foreign Office, as the department of state primarily responsible for Britain's relations with other countries, attempted to act as a general co-ordinating centre for the work of its own News Department, the Neutral Press Committee and Wellington House while retaining ultimate control over questions of propaganda policy. But as government departments other than the Foreign Office were drawn increasingly into greater involvement with the mechanics of propaganda, the system began to suffer from inter-departmental rivalries and jealousies — factors which proved disastrous in work which required continuity and speedy action. Robert Donald subsequently observed that:

The system was started without any policy having been defined, or any clear conception arrived at about the way propaganda should be carried on. Mr Mair drifted between the Home Office, Press Bureau and the Foreign Office — which began to take an interest in the work without being altogether reconciled to it.[116]

It was this situation, combined with a realisation that the war would be a long war of attrition, which prompted General Cockerill, the Director of Special Intelligence, to urge on 29 November 1915 that the war of words should now demand 'as much attention as the economic war'.[117] His appeal for some form of rationalisation of the propaganda system provided the signal for a series of clashes between the Foreign Office on the one hand and the Service Departments on the other.

On 10 December 1915, the War Office brought to the attention of the Foreign Office 'the multiplicity of organisations concerned and the lack of one central controlling authority [which] prove[s] a serious bar to effective action'.[118] An inter-departmental conference was proposed to discuss the means by which efficiency could be improved. The War Office was thinking in terms of entrusting the work to a central executive committee under the leadership of 'a Civil Servant of position and standing'.[119] Montgomery, who had been involved in the News Department's work from the outset, admitted the need for improved co-ordination but dismissed outright the War Office's proposals. He was particularly indignant because, hitherto, the War Office had proved reluctant to depart from its initial pre-occupation with secrecy and censorship. He wrote:

I should have thought the Army Council had plenty of other (from their point of view) more important matters to consider: moreover in the one respect in which they could really have aided us in combating enemy propaganda i.e. in giving facilities for neutral and allied correspondents to visit the front and centres of military interest, and in supplying news, they have signally failed.[120]

He felt that just because the War Office had recently come to appreciate the role which propaganda could play in a long war this was no qualification for criticising the work of those who had been involved from the beginning.

At Wellington House, Claud Schuster supported Montgomery but was even more critical of the War Office proposals:

I must say that I find it sickening that the War Office and the Admiralty, after pursuing a policy of deliberate obstruction for about seventeen months, should finally complain that the policy has produced its natural results, and then propose so wholly absurd an expedient as that described in their letter.[121]

He also pointed out that Wellington House was an independent organisation, 'if that means it pursues its own course without consultation with or direction from other authorities'.[122] But the War Propaganda Bureau was ultimately under the control of the Foreign Office and Schuster informed the War Office that if the pro-German press in neutral countries was better served with the news than those newspapers which were sympathetic to the allied cause, this was not, as the Army Council maintained, due to any lack of efficiency on the part of the three main propaganda organisations but rather to the strict policy of censorship imposed by the military and naval authorities together with their reluctance to comply with continued Foreign Office requests for them to extend their press facilities.[123] There was much justification in this retort but, as Schuster pointed out, the problem did not simply derive from the existing emphasis upon press propaganda, as the War Office maintained:

In any circumstances the course of military events would have rendered it easier for the German press than for us to influence neutral opinion through the press. The early efforts to convince neutrals that we were right were completely successful, partly because the work was, in my opinion, well done, but far more, because we had a good cause. Neutral opinion is now interested, not in the cause, but in the probable results of the war, and for obvious reasons, until we have a change in the military situation, it is far more difficult to explain that we are likely to win, than to explain that we were just.[124]

In other words, no amount of propaganda, however well conducted, could alter the harsh realities of military events and the work would continue to suffer until the government issued a coherent statement of British war aims.

On 14 December 1915, the Foreign Office informed the War Office that it had already recognised the need for improved co-ordination, which was in fact true,[125] but would make the necessary changes internally. There was accordingly no need to summon an inter-departmental conference.[126] The reply was phrased in terms which sought to check any further intrusions by the Service Departments into an area which the Foreign Office now considered increasingly its own:

... the direction in which both the War Office and Admiralty can be of the greatest assistance in influencing opinion in neutral and allied countries is in affording as many facilities as possible for newspaper correspondents to visit or accompany the British forces in the field ... and in issuing Military and Naval news as frequently and as fully as military and naval considerations will permit.[127]

This allotted subsidiary role was deeply resented, especially by the War Office which had recently conceded the point about improved press facilities by allowing journalists to visit the front. The Foreign Office response also came at a time when the War Office was beginning to envisage a greater level of involvement in propaganda through the creation of a special section known as MI7 as part of the overall reorganisation of the Imperial General Staff.[128]

Meanwhile, the Foreign Office set about putting its own house in order. On 16 December, Montgomery approached the Home Secretary with the suggestion that the anomalous position of Mair's Neutral Press Committee could be rectified by transferring responsibility for it from the Home Office to the Foreign Office. An amalgamation with the News Department, he maintained, would not only ensure greater efficiency and economy but would also provide 'more security that what is done is consistent with the interests of our foreign policy'.[129] Sir John Simon did not receive the proposal enthusiastically despite his admission that 'we have never considered him [i.e. Mair] as in any sense acting under our directions, and in fact, so far as his operations are guided by any government department, it is by the Foreign Office'.[130] Instead, the Home Secretary wished to see a return to the original conception of Mair's position whereby he acted largely on his own responsibility 'and that the Government should not be bound by anything he might have done'.[131] Although he did not rule out the possibility of further discussion, the implication of Simon's reply was that in order to maintain the policy of conducting official propaganda unobtrusively, the Neutral Press Committee should remain on the Home Office (Secret Service) Vote.

Robert Cecil remained unconvinced. He informed Simon that much of Mair's work was incidental to that conducted by the News Department and, despite a close Foreign Office relationship with him, 'as things stand we cannot and have no right to give directions to him as to what exactly he should do and what we should do. The result is a certain want of unity and loss of effort'.[132] Cecil further reassured Simon that Mair was not simply a pawn in the dispute with the War Office:

Nothing is further from my thoughts than to try and filch some work from the Home Office and give it to the Foreign Office, and if it were practicable I should only be too glad to push the whole of the propaganda business on to your shoulders, but the difficulty is that, since it affects foreign countries, it either must be done by us or under our guidance.[133]

While not seeing the need for an inter-departmental conference, Cecil nonetheless agreed to attend if one were convened, but he saw no point in asking Nicolson, the Permanent Under-Secretary at the Foreign Office, to accompany him 'because he really does not know or care anything about news or propaganda'.[134] Even allowing for a considerable degree of friction which existed between Cecil and Nicolson, it must be said that the Permanent Under-Secretary was not unusual in this respect. It was officials such as Cecil, Tyrrell and Montgomery who were the exceptions within the Foreign Office in so far as their attitude towards propaganda was concerned. But even Cecil regarded propaganda as a necessary evil of war rather than as something which could play a genuinely useful role. Nevertheless, following Simon's resignation over the issue of conscription on 1 January 1916 and his replacement as Home Secretary by Sir Herbert Samuel who was more amenable to the transfer of Mair to the Foreign Office, Cecil reluctantly agreed to attend discussions designed to rectify the various organisational anomalies and administrative problems within the existing machinery.

The long-awaited inter-departmental conference took place at the

Home Office on 26 January 1916. Representatives of the War Office took the lead in suggesting reorganisation on the lines laid down by them during the previous month, stressing particularly the proposal for an advisory committee to direct matters of policy. They cited in support of their argument the example of the French Maison de la Presse which conducted propaganda from under one roof. Thereafter, the meeting degenerated into a fiercely fought contest between the War Office and Foreign Office. Although it was unanimously agreed that greater co-ordination was an essential prerequisite to further progress, it was the different means of achieving this end which sparked off the row. Cecil, however, was eventually able to convince the conference that the War Office proposal for a centralised propaganda department was not called for by pointing out that the Foreign Office was already in possession of adequate machinery and by stating that the necessary improvements could also be made internally with a minimum of effort.[135] His success was received with considerable relief in Wellington House. A few days later, Masterman wrote to Cecil:

Heartiest congratulations to you and the Foreign Office and Grey for having slaughtered your enemies last Wednesday in what I think is the most effective destruction that any Office has given to its critics during the eighteen months of the war.[136]

The Foreign Office, however, had only triumphed in one battle; it had not yet won the inter-departmental war.

Two days after the Home Office conference, Cecil submitted a scheme for improving the efficiency and co-ordination of the existing propaganda organisations. In an attempt to improve the flow of information between government departments, special 'news officers' were to be appointed whose function it would be to obtain and supply material to the News Department which would, in turn, ensure that it was passed on to the appropriate body.[137] The Foreign Office would henceforth assume complete authority for all propaganda conducted abroad, and the Neutral Press Committee would be amalgamated into the News Department as part of this process.[138] Co-ordination with the Press Bureau would also be improved to aid domestic propaganda.[139] Wellington House was to be brought more closely under Foreign Office supervision, a move which initially caused Masterman some concern lest his bureau begin to suffer a decline in significance. He informed Cecil that he did not wish to lend his 'official, wholehearted support' for the scheme 'without making some reservations so that I may be quite clear as to the future of this office':

We have, as you know, acted in close unity with the Foreign Office for more than a year . . . . So long as we can work with you and Montgomery and can also take the initiative ourselves, we are in, what I think, is the best situation for this kind of work.[140]

Masterman was afraid that outside influences might affect the Foreign Office in such a way as to undermine the work developed thus far by Wellington House . He also feared possible delays caused by the need to submit any proposals to an advisory committee as well as being suspicious that other government departments might not co-operate so freely with his staff if Wellington House functioned as an annex of the Foreign Office. But, he continued:

If . . . we may understand that our relationships continue as they have happily done up till now, that we take on any work which your department wants us to do, and that we report to you any work which we undertake, which may in the least degree affect diplomatic matters — then I am whole-heartedly on the side of your scheme.[141]

Cecil reassured Masterman that the War Propaganda Bureau would not suffer any loss of prestige or significance and that it would continue to function as a semi-autonomous body.

In February 1916, Lord Newton became nominal head of the improved organisation for propaganda.[142] It seems that he was appointed partly 'to lend the prestige of a great name to the work'[143] and partly to appease the War Office's desire for a 'responsible head' without actually appointing a War Office man. Although Newton had little personal experience of propaganda, he managed to continue the process of reorganisation in such a way as to make the News Department an appropriate and efficient nucleus for the conduct of official propaganda overseas. He was greatly aided in this task by a talented staff including Miles Lampson (in charge of film propaganda), Alfred Noyes, the patriotic poet, John Buchan, the novelist, J. D. Gregory and Stephen Gaselee, two of the Foreign Office's 'bright young men'.[144] The Chief Naval Censor, Douglas Brownrigg, was appointed to serve as the Admiralty's news officer. Lieutenant-Colonel Sir Francis Younghusband served in a similar capacity on behalf of the India Office, T. C. Macnaughton for the

Colonial Office, H. F. Carlill for the Board of Trade and William Sutherland, one of Lloyd George's private secretaries, for the Ministry of Munitions. The War Office, which was currently in the process of establishing its own propaganda section, later appointed G. T. Davies as its liaison officer with the News Department.

By the spring of 1916, the rationalisation was complete. In March, Montgomery noted:

> Subject to certain minor changes, I think the existing arrangements are quite satisfactory; if one were beginning over again, perhaps one would aim at having one organisation, equally under the control of the Foreign Office, to carry out the work done by Mr Masterman's and Mr Mair's offices, but except for the *appearance* of separate organisations I can point to no very definite objection to the present system. I am quite convinced of one thing after an experience dating from the very early days of the war; that it is essential that the general control of propaganda in Allied and neutral countries should continue to rest with the Foreign Office and that the headquarters should be at the Foreign Office itself, as they are now.[145]

Such attitudes were shortly to come under strong attack. But Montgomery had recognised a fundamental axiom of propaganda, namely that it must be conducted in conjunction with policy. Propaganda as the servant, rather than the master, of foreign policy was something which the Foreign Office sought to maintain until the end of the war.

In May 1916, it was stated that the main object of the rationalised system was to supply the public in allied and neutral countries with as much information about the war as possible in an attempt to convince foreign opinion 'of the strength of the Allies' position, the justice of their cause and the certainty of their ultimate success, and of making clear to the Allied countries the part played by the British Empire in the war and the extent of its contribution to the common cause'.[146] In order to achieve these aims, the Foreign Office had to work quietly and carefully, avoiding any recognition of its labours and taking great care to avoid criticism that it was interfering with the internal affairs of other countries. The blatant methods adopted by the Germans were felt to be counterproductive and were thus to be avoided at all costs. Instead, the Foreign Office wished, as Robert Cecil put it, 'to do good by stealth'.[147] The price of this policy was criticism that little or nothing was being done. Once it became apparent during the second half of the war that a great deal had, in fact, been done, the Foreign Office was criticised, equally unfairly, for having done it badly.

MI7 AND THE WAR OFFICE

The War Office was comparatively slow to recognise the value of propaganda in war. In its early attempts to increase the output of official information for propaganda purposes, the Foreign Office tended to regard the military authorities as the principal obstacle to further progress. This view was not without justification. The initial preoccupation of the War Office with censorship as a means of influencing public opinion was both negative and unimaginative. However, the successful partnership of propaganda and recruitment had demonstrated the value of more positive forms of action at a time when the military authorities badly needed volunteers to offset the enormous casualties sustained on the western front. Moreover, with the introduction of conscription it became even more important to explain to the new recruits why they should fight when patriotism had not proved sufficient previously to make them enlist. At the front, it also became necessary to justify why the conscripts should continue to fight once the Germans launched a psychological offensive directed against the morale of the troops in 1916. Gradually, therefore, the War Office came to see morale as an instrument of total warfare. The growing appreciation of the importance of propaganda, combined with repeated Foreign Office requests to pay greater attention to the press, was to result in February 1916 in the creation of a specific department within the War Office to deal with propaganda conducted from a military standpoint.

It had been provisionally laid down in the War Book of August 1914 that questions of press control should be dealt with by a War Office sub-section of MO5 known as MO5(h), consisting of two general staff officers. This department was made responsible merely for issuing communiqués to the press relating to military affairs. The emphasis was upon security and brevity in the old tradition and thus it proved to be a somewhat disappointing source of news for the press. The demands of censorship and the need to appoint officers to the Press Bureau required an expansion of MO5(h) which became MO7 and functioned as the War Office branch of the bureau. The duties of MO7 in the early months of the war were confined to the censorship of press articles dealing with military affairs, the transmission of General Staff decisions to the directors of the bureau and the release of information to the press, through the Press Bureau, of both War Office communiqués and D Notices. Before long, however, the War Office found that the bureau was taking 'an unduly extended sphere of action' and it was therefore decided, 'with a view to reaffirming the military control of the press, to bring the Military Press Censors under the direct authority of a section specially charged with the leakage of military information'.[148] On 20 October 1914, MO7 reverted to its original title of MO5(h) and was brought under the immediate supervision of the War Office.

It proved to be only a temporary change of title. The reorganisation of MO5 in February 1915 which resulted in the creation of the Directorate of Special Intelligence led to the creation of MO7 to deal with press publicity. It was this body which first allowed press correspondents to visit the front in May 1915, and it was chiefly through its own work generally that the War Office gradually began to take a more active interest in propaganda. In January 1916, the Imperial General Staff underwent a major re-organisation and a new Directorate of Military Intelligence was formed with Major-General MacDonagh as its director. To him was subordinated the Directorate of Special Intelligence which dealt with counter-espionage and all matters connected with censorship. MO7 thus became MI7 with Lieutenant-Colonel Warburton Davies as its head.

MI7 was originally housed at Watergate House but, in August 1916, was moved to Adelphi Court on the Strand before reaching its final destination in Adastral House on the Victoria Embankment in October 1917. Warburton Davies was succeeded by Major (later Lieutenant-Colonel) J. L. Fisher in December 1916, by which time the staff had expanded to 24. Its aim was 'to control the British press and, in regard to military affairs, to influence it, and, through the Foreign Office, the Allied and Neutral press, in a sense advantageous to the Allies'.[149] In order to achieve this aim, MI7 was divided into four sections: MI7(a) which was responsible for the censorship of all military material in the press and in films and worked in close collaboration with the Press Bureau and the War Office Cinematograph Committee; MI7(b), the largest and most important production branch, which was divided into a further six sub-sections dealing with general press propaganda, the collection and publication of technical military information, the distribution of military propaganda in the Dominions, aerial propaganda, the compilation of home, and military propaganda by cables and by wireless; MI7(c) which arranged visits to the front; and MI7(d) which compiled foreign press summaries.[150]

By the time that Lloyd George became Secretary of State for War in July 1916, therefore, the War Office was already in possession of an elaborate propaganda department. However, it was the new minister's passionate interest and enthusiasm for the work of MI7 that was to transform it into one of the leading propaganda departments established by the government during the course of the war. Yet its creation, in many ways, marked the end of what may be described as the first stage of the British government's involvement in war propaganda. Before 1916, the organisational developments had been diverse and unco-ordinated, often giving the impression of chaos and confusion. This was subsequently interpreted as meaning inefficiency. But those officials who were charged with the task of conducting propaganda during the first half of the war were forced to operate in a largely unknown environment with only limited resources and experience at their disposal. They were asked to undertake a difficult and distasteful task without any detailed instructions as to how they should proceed or the methods they should adopt. Organisations had to be constructed from scratch and developed on the basis of experience gained as the work unfolded. They were also forced to rely upon individual initiative and intuitive understanding. No doubt the homogeneity of the British ruling establishment greatly eased the appointment of trustworthy individuals who, by virtue of their sound ideas and background, could be relied upon to perform this new wartime activity, however difficult or distasteful, in a manner favoured by the government. And although their initial instincts were not unnaturally cautious and defensive, they gradually came to recognise the role which propaganda could serve in the government's attempts to win the war. That they were able to reach the position they did in a period of just over eighteen months was a remarkable achievement. Mistakes were undoubtedly made, and the various departments concerned with the work did begin to argue amongst themselves as to which line to follow and who should be responsible overall, but this must not be allowed to disguise the considerable progress that had been made since August 1914. By the time Lloyd George became Prime Minister in December 1916, nearly every government department had come to recognise the value of propaganda in war.

There were, inevitably, several areas which remained undeveloped by the early propagandists. The system was by no means perfect or complete. The home front, for example, required more concerted attention as the length of the war increased. Propaganda in enemy countries received comparatively little consideration, at least in proportion to the significance which was to be attached to it later in the war. The original conception of propaganda had been determined first by the need to counter the virulent German campaign in neutral countries, and then by the need to reassure allies that Britain was pulling her weight, rather than by any urgent need to launch a psychological offensive against the enemy. It was not until February 1918 that a specific enemy propaganda department was created, although the important work of MI7 in military zones before then has not received the recognition its real importance deserves; nor has the work of Wellington House which, although it did not at any stage fall within its terms of reference, had found itself being drawn increasingly into a consideration of propaganda against the enemy through the work of one of its officials, S. A. Guest, who attempted to smuggle pro-ally material into Germany through neutral Holland and Switzerland. The intense secrecy in which this work was conducted meant that its existence was concealed from those contemporary critics of the government who argued that little or nothing was being done to influence foreign opinion in Britain's favour.

The most severe critics tended to be newspapermen who conceived themselves to be better qualified to conduct propaganda than permanent officials who were unversed in the techniques of mass persuasion. Newspaper proprietors such as George Riddell were certainly consulted; other journalists such as George Mair and Edward Cook were even appointed to senior positions within the propaganda machinery. But, in the main, it was not until the advent of Lloyd George as Prime Minister that Fleet Street was to be given the opportunity to play a central role in the conduct of the British official campaign. Such men might well have been better suited to conduct propaganda. They may even have understood better the demands of public opinion. But instead of resolving the problems which had plagued the campaign during the first half of the war, their promotion merely served to compound the difficulties facing the government in its attempts to rationalise the organisation of propaganda.

2 The Organisation of Official British Propaganda, 1916-18

THE assumption of complete control by the Foreign Office over all matters relating to propaganda abroad in January 1916 did little to mitigate more fundamental criticism concerning its methods, content and, above all, its organisation. Despite the improvements made in all these areas following the rationalisation of early 1916, there remained considerable dissatisfaction with the system as a whole. The War Office emerged as the principal critic of the new arrangements. In its view, Cecil's reforms had made 'no serious attempt to provide what is required' and fell 'far short of the essential minimum'.[1] The War Office argued that the new arrangements were merely a continuation of the old, but on a grander scale with all the inherent deficiencies remaining. Grave doubts were expressed about the Foreign Office's 'very limited conception of the realities of the case' stemming chiefly from what was considered to be an undue emphasis upon press propaganda:

Until the idea is grasped of combating enemy propaganda not merely by news, which it is impolitic to fabricate, but also and even mainly by views, which it is quite possible to propagate, it seems hopeless to expect that any progress will be made towards designing an organisation suited to the necessities of the case.[2]

The War Office, however, went further than providing cogent criticism and appealing for new ideas and approaches. It clearly considered that its own newly created propaganda department was better suited to the changing requirements of the war. The War Office crusade for a centralised propaganda machine was taken up at first by Lloyd George, both as War Minister and as Prime Minister, and subsequently by representatives of the press who wished to control the work themselves. In fact, the existence of MI7 merely served to confuse still further the issue of official control over foreign propaganda while simultaneously compounding the already difficult problem of co-ordination.

THE FIRST DONALD REPORT AND THE DEPARTMENT OF INFORMATION

As criticism of the Foreign Office continued to mount and gain wider support during the course of 1916, so also did the pressure for increased centralisation of the propaganda machinery. The criticism was deeply resented in the Foreign Office where it was felt that the Service Departments had only themselves to blame for not helping the News Department in its difficult task by their continued reluctance to extend their co-operation and facilities to the press. At the Admiralty, Brownrigg admitted as much. He described Montgomery and Mair as 'eager bridegrooms, ever pressing and coaxing me, the elusive bride, to grant them more and yet more favours in the shape of permits to visit the Fleet'.[3] Moreover, although the process by which the early restrictive practices of the War Office under Kitchener were gradually being discarded in favour of a more enlightened approach continued with the establishment of MI7, the squabbling persisted throughout the summer. Despite the contention of the Director of Special Intelligence, General Cockerill, that the War Office supplied information 'calculated to create the impression that the power of the Allies is on the increase, and that of the Central Powers on the wane',[4] this was not always what happened in practice. In July 1916, General Charteris of the Intelligence branch of Haig's general staff in France, observed:

Both the Foreign Office and the War Office are worrying a great deal about propaganda, particularly in France, and there seems to be great confusion at home as to who is responsible . . . . The trouble about propaganda work at home appears to be that while the Foreign Office wants to publish favourable news, the War Office wants to withhold anything that tends to show that the Germans are hard hit . . . . To the outside world, there is no doubt that we have tended to discourage confidence in ourselves by always holding back that which is favourable.[5]

Charteris also commented upon 'a little war within a war between the War Office and the Foreign Office all about films'[6] and believed that the problem was caused by the fact that the various departments 'are all working separately and each is jealous of the other'.[7]

The situation was not helped by disagreements within the Foreign Office itself. Miles Lampson, for example, had become increasingly disillusioned with what he described as the 'incredible and discreditable' lack of public interest in war films.[8] He informed Montgomery:

To be quite frank, the situation is *not* in hand at present. I know you disagree with me: but my opinion remains and *will* remain the same, until some more methodical organisation is working than is now the case.[9]

Montgomery, ever the champion of the existing regime, replied:

I am afraid we will have to agree to differ about this. I don't know in what respect the situation is not in hand! It is true that there is no one stately building that one can point to and say 'That is the Maison de la Presse where all these things are done' but *results* are the main point and results are not at all unsatisfactory.[10]

Montgomery did not state the evidence on which he based these observations. It was probably no more than mere impression. However, had he been more prepared to accept that parts of the system for which he was largely responsible were deficient and to rectify the faults, it might have served to disarm the mounting pressure for reform. As it was, his inflexible stance merely served to reinforce the belief of its critics that the Foreign Office was incapable of conducting propaganda effectively.[11]

The dispute reached a dramatic climax in December 1916 when Lloyd George became Prime Minister. Indeed, at the very first meeting of the new War Cabinet, it was decided that the entire question of propaganda required urgent attention.[12] This decision provided the signal for a renewed campaign by each of the government departments principally involved in the dispute, each one striving to secure Cabinet approval for its own particular conception of the way in which propaganda should be conducted. The Admiralty considered that hitherto British propaganda had been too defensive and passive in nature and advocated increased activity in the United States under the general supervision of the naval attachés.[13] The War Office once again reiterated its scheme for a centralised machine which would unite the various propaganda departments under one independent head — the implication being that the War Office should assume responsibility for the work. It was further suggested that special officers should be appointed overseas in order to relieve the pressure of work on the diplomatic, consular and secret services, particularly as there were certain aspects of the work 'which are hardly compatible with the dignity of His Majesty's Representatives abroad, and which, therefore, they cannot carry out satisfactorily'.[14]

The Foreign Office, not surprisingly, felt obliged to submit the longest and most comprehensive account. Indeed, far from being a mere apologia for past errors, the Foreign Office presented a thorough and convincing defence of the existing regime while, at the same time, deprecating the case for a centralised propaganda authority. After suggesting that the principal obstacle facing the News Department was the 'tradition of silence only very slowly breaking down', Montgomery wrote:

A hankering after an institution on the lines of the Maison de la Presse in Paris has from time to time manifested itself in some quarters, but I am convinced, after an experience dating from the early days of the war, that the general control of propaganda in Allied and Neutral countries should continue to rest with the Foreign Office, and that the headquarters should be at the Foreign Office, as it is now. It is that Office which is concerned with most of the current questions about which the foreign, and especially the American correspondents want daily information . . . . The correspondents . . . will come much more freely to the Foreign Office, which is the natural place for them to seek information from, than they will to an Office known to be established for propaganda purposes.[15]

Moreover, he continued,

It would be quite unworkable to have our various organisations in foreign countries independent of the Embassies and Legations, which would necessarily be the case if they were placed under the control of a separate authority in London.[16]

Robert Cecil endorsed these views entirely and, in submitting the Foreign Office case to the Cabinet, made five general observations based upon his own experience of the work conducted so far. His views reveal a fundamental understanding of the role which propaganda could play in wartime and were to remain the essential principles of Foreign Office involvement in the work. In the first place, he stated that official propaganda known to be such was 'almost useless', with the exception of published documents and State papers. Secondly, he wrote, 'it is much easier to do harm than good by propaganda' and he warned that great caution was required at all times if foreign opinion was not to be alienated. Third, 'our national habit of self-deprecation is a handicap' despite the fact that 'in many countries we are suspected of arrogance and the most moderate criticism of foreign countries is, for this and other reasons, bitterly resented'. Fourth, it remained important to avoid the appearance of conducting propaganda in the United States where the most effective action was 'to do good by stealth'. Finally, Cecil wrote, 'in wartime, it is the facts that count, not words. All we can really do to help by propaganda is to let foreigners know what is actually happening. If the events are discouraging, they will be discouraged. No doubt we may also offend people by stupid observations, but we can never explain away disagreeable facts'.[17]

Neither the Foreign Office nor the Service Departments need have gone to so much trouble. Their arguments were not considered by the War Cabinet until 24 January 1917,[18] by which time they had already been pre-empted by a Cabinet decision of some three weeks earlier to accept 'in principle' the creation of a separate propaganda organisation which would assume complete responsibility for the work, both at home and abroad.[19] Lloyd George had chosen to rely upon the apparent objectivity of a man outside the Civil Service and, on 1 January 1917, had invited his good friend Robert Donald to investigate the entire question of propaganda, and to make recommendations.[20] In his capacity as editor of the Liberal *Daily Chronicle*, Donald had been consulted on many previous occasions by the official propagandists. This involvement made him well placed, at least in Lloyd George's eyes, to conduct such an investigation. Donald's report was ready a week later which would suggest a somewhat hurried examination. Donald felt that the essential aims of British propaganda should be:

1. to maintain unity of opinion amongst the Allies;
2. to 'influence and nurse' public opinion in neutral countries;
3. to assume an offensive strategy;
4. to explain problems surrounding our peace terms — so far as they have been indicated — for the purpose of informing and influencing politicians, publicists, the intelligentsia in neutral countries.[21]

The Foreign Office would not have disagreed. But although Donald accepted the need to avoid German propaganda techniques (which were felt to have reached their zenith in 1916)[22] and also to continue British activity along lines 'which will conceal more or less its official character in neutral countries', he did question the emphasis which had been placed upon literary and press propaganda, which he judged to have been too defensive. He continued:

Considering that he has to fight against the prevailing sympathy of most neutral countries, that his communications are limited, and that his case is bad, and having regard to the overwhelming appeal which the Allies can make to the sympathies and moral support of the neutrals, it is surprising that the enemy has not been driven from the field. On the contrary, he is generally on the offensive, and our propaganda departments are too much occupied in trying to overtake lies which get a day's start, and it is almost impossible to destroy altogether their influence. This is not as it should be.[23]

Donald felt that the reason for this condition 'into which publicity and propaganda work has drifted at the present time is due to the casual way in which it originated and the promiscuous way it has expanded'. The 'rationalisation' of Spring 1916 had not introduced the necessary improvements and he rightly pointed out that there was still insufficient co-ordination between the various departments. While praising the work of Wellington House and of several News Department officials, he did not consider that Lord Newton had been a wise appointment: 'He is not solely occupied with the work[24] and he does not profess to have any knowledge of publicity methods'. Moreover, he wrote:

His chief deputies had no experience of newspaper work until sometime after the war began, and are hampered by the traditional atmosphere of the Foreign Office, its attitudes towards the press and its inability to appreciate the supreme importance of quick action.[25]

Although the role of diplomatic and consular officials serving abroad in recommending lines of action to be taken was considered 'useful', Donald's report did question the competence of such representatives to supervise work for which, he argued, they had little experience or flair and who were 'not as a rule good judges' as to the effectiveness of their labours. 'Personally', he wrote, 'the less they have to do with it the better'.[26]

The defensive character of British propaganda stemmed, Donald maintained, from the lack of overall direction. He therefore advocated a more positive approach rather than concentrating solely upon counter-propaganda. The time had come for the allies to determine common themes of action and he called for prompt decisions on the matter of war aims as well as for more rapid distribution of information to the foreign press. Donald selected as an example of the serious delays which had occurred Sir Douglas Haig's despatch relating to the British position at the battle of the Somme. It had first appeared in Britain on 30 December 1916 but had still to be transmitted abroad at the time his report was written, revealing a 'lack of appreciation of the influence which such a document would have on public opinion in every country'. Again, on 19 December 1916, Lloyd George had delivered an important speech, news of which had not been transmitted to Norway until almost a week later, by which time its immediate value as propaganda had largely been lost. These and similar delays were blamed entirely upon the News Department without any apparent appreciation that such information was passed to the Foreign Office only after it had been approved by the War Office dominated Press Bureau. Donald wrote:

It is through news that public opinion in neutral countries is most easily influenced. At present our news propaganda department seems to be asleep for more than ten hours out of twenty four (it does not work at night) and it is not alert during the rest of the time.[27]

In short, Donald felt that there was 'no clear cut organisation, no system of efficient delegation, no definite line of distinction between the work of one branch and that of another'. Nor was there any effective co-ordination due to the 'absence of harmony between one branch and another and the existence of inter-departmental jealousies'. He therefore proposed the creation of a centralised organisation under the direction of an overall head.

The Donald report appeared to confirm the validity of the proposals which the War Office had been advocating for more than a year. In fact, although it contained many valid criticisms, there were also several serious misdirected observations. The hitherto defensive nature of British overseas propaganda was not due solely to incompetence or inefficiency on the part of the Foreign Office nor to a lack of overall direction. Lord Newton, certainly, was not the right man to direct the work but he was assisted by the able Montgomery who effectively served as the head of the News Department. With the influential support of Robert Cecil, now Minister of Blockade, Montgomery had been able to overcome the considerable prejudice which existed within the Foreign Office concerning the value of propaganda. But he was not able to make much headway with other government departments, particularly the War Office, which continued to be more concerned with preventing information from reaching the enemy than with propaganda in any positive sense. Even after the departure of Kitchener, the War Office had repeatedly proved reluctant to supply the Foreign Office with information which would serve a valuable propagandist purpose, preferring instead to rely upon its own newly created department, MI7, to conduct the work from a military point of view. Moreover, the work conducted by the Foreign Office in conjunction with Wellington House was necessarily defensive not simply because the Germans had entered the war with the propaganda initiative by virtue of their pre-war preparations but mainly because of the reluctance of the British government to issue a comprehensive set of war aims around which the propagandists could construct an offensive.

This, however, was not the sort of issue which Lloyd George wanted to hear from Donald at a time when the new Prime Minister was busy tackling the delicate question of war aims in response to President Woodrow Wilson's recent appeal to all the belligerents to state clearly their reasons for continuing the fight. As it was, the views of the Prime Minister's former department held the day at a time when a change in propaganda was as important for the new government as changes elsewhere in the running of the war. It was for this reason that the policy of secrecy pursued rigorously since the start of the war was now abandoned. The government had to be seen to be doing something concerning propaganda for primarily political reasons.

Although the Cabinet had already accepted the idea of a central propaganda organisation when Lloyd George received Donald's report, it did decide to appoint a new director of propaganda with instructions to submit his own recommendations before proceeding any further.[28] Donald had suggested three deputy directors: John Buchan, who had served as Newton's liaison officer with GHQ in France; T. L. Gilmour, a former journalist currently serving on the National War Savings Committee as a munitions commissioner; and Roderick Jones, the Managing Director of Reuters. But Donald had wanted someone of even greater distinction to head the new organisation. As he later informed his fellow Liberal editor, C. P. Scott of the *Manchester Guardian*, 'I did not refer to individuals or recommend anyone for the position of Director. The position was offered to a number of Members of Parliament and others but they declined'.[29] Propaganda, it seemed, remained a subject for which few British politicians entertained sympathy. They must have recognised its value in wartime, but it continued to be regarded as a somewhat distasteful, albeit necessary, evil. Eventually, after much hesitation, Lloyd George appointed John Buchan. Lord Milner had requested the Prime Minister to interview Buchan for the job and not to rely 'on ill-informed hearsay'.[30] Consequently, Buchan was appointed Director of the new Department of Information on 9 February 1917 at the not inconsiderable salary of £1000 per annum.

Once presented with this series of decisions, the Foreign Office changed its tactics in an attempt to salvage as much control as possible over the new body. At the Cabinet meeting on 24 January 1917, it was specified that the Department of Information, though independent, was to maintain 'the closest possible association with the Foreign Office with regard to the policy to be pursued'.[31] Montgomery insisted upon this as a condition of Foreign Office acceptance of the new arrangements because, he wrote:

The general policy of propaganda in allied and neutral countries must necessarily run parallel with the Foreign Office and be subject to the Foreign Secretary, and it is essential that the person who is responsible for the administration of propaganda work should be in constant touch with the Foreign Secretary and the Minister of Blockade, or with those carrying out their directions.[32]

Eric Drummond, private secretary to the new Foreign Secretary, enlisted powerful support for this view[33] and Balfour, when he submitted Montgomery's observations to the War Cabinet, insisted that they receive careful consideration 'before any fundamental severance is effected between those who are responsible for conducting foreign policy and those who are responsible for talking about it'.[34]

The outcome was almost a classic example of compromise. In theory, the Department of Information was an independent, centralised propaganda bureau directly answerable to the Prime Minister but working in close connection with the Foreign Office. In practice, however, the department functioned as an annex of the Foreign Office. In constructing his new organisation, Buchan was fully aware of his dependence upon the facilities and co-operation which would be extended to him by the Foreign Office. It is significant that the distribution of propaganda material abroad remained in the hands of diplomatic representatives or local patriotic organisations working under their supervision. The functions of the Department of Information did, however, include propaganda at home. Buchan defined them as 'propaganda, or the putting of the Allied case in neutral countries, and the explanation of the British effort in Allied countries, with the object of ensuring a wholesome state of public opinion; and, at the same time, the direction of British opinion when direction is needed'.[35] Given this latter duty, the domination of the Department of Information by a government office whose activities were primarily concerned with foreign affairs merely served to create a fresh anomaly within the propaganda system as a whole.

Buchan divided the Department of Information into four main sections. The art and literary branch was housed at Wellington House where Masterman remained in charge of the production and distribution of books, pamphlets, periodicals, photographs and art work. 'It is a vital branch', wrote Buchan, 'but less important now than at the beginning of the war'.[36] A press and cinema division was established in the Lord Chancellor's office at the House of Lords under the supervision of T. L. Gilmour. Film propaganda had been 'greatly bungled in the past'[37] but would now be given greater emphasis. This section also employed Sir Roderick Jones who was responsible for supervising the compilation and transmission of the official cable and wireless messages through Reuters, Marconi and the normal diplomatic channels. An intelligence branch was established in Victoria Street under Lord Edward Gleichen's direction to replace Mair's Neutral Press Committee. This section was designed to ensure the rapid supply of news and information from the various government departments to the propagandists. Finally, the most important section was the administrative division under Hubert Montgomery which was responsible for the direction of policy matters relating to propaganda. Significantly, this section was created from the News Department and was located at the Foreign Office where Buchan chose to establish his headquarters. Montgomery also served as Buchan's deputy. The administrative division was responsible for financial matters and for liaising with the other government departments. The preparation of military material remained the responsibility of MI7 at the War Office, although the Department of Information in theory had the final word on any propaganda conducted in military zones. In addition, there were 14 sub-departments dealing with specific geographical areas.[38] An advisory committee was also formed to provide guidance on policy matters.[39]

The Cabinet approved Buchan's scheme on 20 February 1917.[40] No comment was made on the absence of a section to deal with home propaganda. With only a minimum of fuss, therefore, continuity in personnel and facilities had been largely preserved. Buchan felt that many officials serving in the old organisation had simply been working 'in the wrong positions .... The nucleus of a very competent staff exists both at home and abroad and it will not be hard to get hold of suitable people for new developments'.[41] Far from constituting any radical departure from the previous arrangements, the Department of Information was merely a streamlined version of the earlier machinery. Nevertheless, many of Donald's recommendations had been catered for. There was now a single head of propaganda who was directly answerable to the Prime Minister. Rationalisation had taken place with central financial control, a central record office and with greater emphasis placed upon liaison facilities in order to secure more effective co-ordination not only within the Department of Information itself but also with those other departments of State which continued to deal with propaganda in one way or another. The subordination of Wellington House to central control was ensured and a clear distinction had been drawn, as Donald had sought, between news and press propaganda on the one hand and literary propaganda on the other. The geographical sub-sections were staffed by recognised experts on the particular countries with which they dealt. Moreover, the Department of Information also promised to develop the neglected area of propaganda in enemy countries.

THE NATIONAL WAR AIMS COMMITTEE

The circumstances which had precipitated a change in government at the end of 1916 had stimulated concern about the nature and organisation of British propaganda not only in allied and neutral countries but also on the home front which, not unlike that against the enemy, had received comparatively little attention. The enthusiasm stimulated by the early recruitment campaigns was visibly in decline after the introduction of conscription, while the course of the war in 1916 indicated that still greater sacrifices would be required from the civilian population. Despite heavy German losses, the Somme offensive had not been a success. The German capture of Bucharest in December combined with the devastating effects of submarine warfare on British shipping did nothing to allay popular fears that Britain would have to face yet another year of war. This situation demanded greater consideration of the state of morale at home. Accordingly, when the Cabinet discussed the establishment of the Department of Information at its meeting on 24 January 1917, it was hoped that the new director would take steps to create 'a good home organisation as a preliminary' measure towards improving domestic propaganda.[42] This hope was not reflected in the scheme laid down by Buchan who admitted in May that 'no provision was made for the work of propaganda at home, except in so far as the War Cabinet might direct certain information to be issued to the British press'.[43] This clearly went against the original intention of Robert Donald, Lloyd George and the Cabinet which, on 30 March 1917, was 'strongly of the opinion that steps ought to be taken to educate public opinion in this country in regard to the history and potentialities of the countries, such as Mesopotamia or Palestine, where victories have been or are likely to be achieved'.[44] The Department of Information was accordingly instructed to consider the creation of a special branch to supervise this work.

There was little sign of an organisational response to this request on Buchan's part. This may have been due to the influence of the Foreign Office which regarded domestic propaganda as an area of low priority. But Buchan was reluctant to respond positively without being given the necessary finance. It is surprising, therefore, to find Buchan championing the cause of home propaganda before the Cabinet in May 1917. His change of heart was probably a response to mounting criticism of the Department of Information for not devoting its energies to this neglected area. Buchan informed the Cabinet that he had grown increasingly disturbed at the state of 'public feeling' within the country, the diminishing size of newspapers as a result of the paper shortage, and the 'almost entire cessation of public speaking, one of the best means of informing the country'.[45] He was particularly concerned about the morale of the labour force and therefore proposed the arrangement of visits to the front and reoccupied zones by workers' delegations who could relate their observations to their colleagues on returning to England. Members of Parliament, 'who have, at the moment, not very much to do', could also be recruited to aid this task. The Department of Information, however, could not in Buchan's opinion be expected to supervise the campaign at home unless the Treasury was prepared to sanction the necessary expenditure.[46] Otherwise, he could not see how his department could regard domestic propaganda as its responsibility.

The Cabinet, in its meeting on 22 May 1917, accepted Buchan's suggestions but correctly sensed that the Department of Information was not the most willing or appropriate body to take on the work.[47] A fortnight later, it felt 'that the time had come to undertake an active campaign to counteract the pacifist movement, which at present has the field to itself'.[48] As a direct consequence of this decision, the National War Aims Committee (NWAC) came into being as an organisation entirely separate from the machinery established to conduct propaganda overseas. The NWAC relied heavily upon its predecessor, the Parliamentary Recruiting Committee, for its organisational model. The same all-party emphasis was evident, although there was, of course, a coalition government in power when the NWAC was formed. Lloyd George, Asquith and G. N. Barnes, who had replaced Arthur Henderson, served as its joint presidents. F. E. Guest, the government's chief whip since March 1917, served as its chairman and Lieutenant-Colonel R. A. Sanders, a Conservative whip, served as vice-chairman — again reflecting the PRC's dependence upon the party whips. Of the NWAC's secretaries, Sir John Boraston and Arthur Peters had both been secretaries of the PRC. Thomas Cox, the general secretary of the NWAC, and G. Wallace Carter, one of the four honorary secretaries, had both served in the PRC's meetings sub-department, and there were many others who had worked for the earlier body, thereby providing continuity in personnel and experience — not surprisingly since both bodies were based upon parliamentary membership.

Also in common with the PRC, the NWAC created sub-departments to carry out the detailed work and it further emulated its predecessor by establishing meetings and publicity departments. There was felt to be less need for the NWAC to create a householders' returns section although, had modern sampling techniques been available, such a department could have proved invaluable in assessing the impact of NWAC propaganda. As it was, the NWAC chose to rely upon impressionistic reports from its speakers and local representatives. The organisation of local committees based upon party branches in the constituencies was precisely the same as the PRC. By the end of 1917, the NWAC had established committees in 269 out of 468 constituencies, 85 of which were classified as performing considerable work, 148 as doing something of value, and 36 as doing nothing.[49] By 1918, the NWAC had extended its activities into 345 constituencies.[50]

The National War Aims Committee officially came into being on 4 August 1917 — the third anniversary of the war — amidst a blaze of publicity.[51] Its aims were declared to be:

To keep before our nation both the causes which have led to the world war and the vital importance to human life and liberty of continuing the struggle until the evil forces which originated this conflict are destroyed for ever.[52]

But in order to achieve this, the NWAC urged upon the government the need for a coherent declaration of war aims 'so that the subjects with which speakers may be allowed to deal on War Aims platforms shall be clearly defined and strictly limited'.[53] This proved easier said than done in view of a July decision of Cabinet to postpone the discussion of war aims 'as long as possible as, once it was known that we were discussing these questions, the effective prosecution of the war might be rendered more difficult'.[54] It was not until January 1918 that Lloyd George made easier the work of the propagandists by defining his government's war aims. Following the German-Russian armistice at Brest-Litovsk in the wake of the Bolshevik revolution, the Italian defeat at Caporetto, the publication by the Bolsheviks of the secret treaties and growing manpower problems on the western front, a restatement of war aims became imperative in order to justify the continuation of the war. On 5 January 1918, Lloyd George made the most complete British statement of war aims to, significantly, the Trade Union leaders. This was, of course, followed by President Wilson's Fourteen Points which, apart from being a major propaganda statement in its own right, provided Allied propagandists with a greater sense of direction in their work.

The NWAC was described as an independent organisation but it was, for all practical purposes, a government department. Although the Cabinet decided on 20 August 1917 that its work should fall within the province of the government whips,[55] on the following day Sir Edward Carson was appointed 'to assume general supervision over propaganda as far as action in this country is concerned'.[56]

Shortly afterwards, Carson was instructed to extend his sphere of supervision to include propaganda overseas as well. Why he was chosen is not clear. Carson was a renowned orator and publicist but he was also a poor administrator. He was, moreover, largely unfamiliar with propaganda. It seems likely that he was chosen for political reasons, namely to distract his attention from his crusade in Ireland. This his appointment ultimately failed to do. In the meantime, with both the Department of Information and the NWAC under Carson's supervision, the role of the latter as part of the official propaganda machinery was confirmed. Furthermore, when Carson appealed to the Cabinet for financial support in October 1917, it was decided that the Treasury should finance his work.[57]

It was clear from the beginning that the NWAC was designed to monopolise the conduct of official propaganda at home. In October 1917, Carson detected 'unmistakable signs of war weariness in the nation':

At the beginning of the fourth year of the war this should cause no surprise, but in order to prevent its becoming a source of serious national weakness, it is very necessary to supply a tonic. The only effective tonic is a fuller understanding than the masses of the people at present possess as to (a) the magnitude of the issues at stake; (b) the stupendous extent of the military and economic efforts now being made by the Nation, and (c) the results which these efforts have attained up to the present, and their prospects of complete ultimate success.[58]

One of the NWAC's first tasks, therefore, was to absorb the work of such bodies as the Central Committee for National Patriotic Organisations (CCNPO) which had proved a constant irritant to the official propaganda departments.[59] In July 1917, Frederick Guest had approached the CCNPO with the suggestion of amalgamation so that the merger could be announced at the Queen's Hall meeting on 4 August when the NWAC was to be launched. He wrote:

It would seem that the most advantageous course would be for the National War Aims Committee to take up the work at the point to which you have brought it, and that, in order to avoid complications in the minds of the public and reduplication of central effort, all future meetings on these patriotic lines should be held under one name only.[60]

In short, the government now wished to control what it had not controlled before, and the CCNPO was forced to agree reluctantly to the loss of its independence.[61]

Guest, however, continued to insist that the NWAC was not an official organisation and he argued against greater integration into the government's propaganda machinery. In February 1918, he wrote:

I do not see how a Government Department can undertake Home Propaganda without its activities being liable to misconstruction and frequent attack on the grounds that it is a Government Department in disguise.[62]

Here was the old problem of conducting official propaganda openly. Guest believed that the NWAC should project the appearance of being a parliamentary organisation rather than an official department in order to enhance the credibility of its work. As it was an all-party body, the NWAC was best suited to combat pacifism and, although Guest was prepared to accept the advice of the central machinery, 'the opinion of the National War Aims Committee is unanimous that there should be no connection between themselves and any Government Department'.[63] Carson was inclined to agree but considered that it was dangerous to draw a clear distinction between home and foreign propaganda.[64] There was a fear that one body would say one thing to foreign audiences and another body something quite different to domestic opinion. Carson therefore discussed with Gerald Fiennes, the editor-in-chief of the NWAC's publicity department, means by which the Department of Information could absorb his section.[65] By that time, however, the government was about to embark upon yet another stage of reorganisation.

THE SECOND DONALD REPORT AND THE MINISTRY OF INFORMATION

While the Department of Information undoubtedly benefited from the lessons of the earlier experience in its attempts to increase the efficiency and co-ordination of British overseas propaganda, the reorganisation of 1917 ultimately failed to rectify the basic deficiencies inherent in the system. Propaganda continued to be conducted from four or five different buildings scattered about Whitehall and, once the NWAC was launched in August 1917, there was little co-ordination between the conduct of home and foreign propaganda. The absence of a ministerial head to champion the cause of the Department of Information was also a serious handicap, particularly as Buchan lacked the necessary authority and prestige to deal with other government departments on an equal basis. Moreover, one of Buchan's major innovations, the appointment of an advisory committee, proved to be a constant source of criticism, although this was admittedly of the director's own making. The committee, comprising leading newspapermen and publicity experts such as Robert Donald, C. P. Scott, Lord Burnham and Lord Northcliffe (who was replaced by Lord Beaverbrook when Northcliffe took charge of the British War Mission in the United States), was initially formed to advise Buchan on matters of propaganda policy. It was, however, rarely consulted. Buchan preferred to receive advice on policy matters from the Foreign Office where his own office was housed. As a result, Donald became dissatisfied with the arrangements for which he had partly responsible and was soon complaining that 'the propaganda headquarters are still at the Foreign Office, and are more entrenched there than ever .... Mr Buchan is under the Foreign Office almost as much, I believe, as if he were an official, and I do not think this is desirable'.[66] Both Scott Burnham agreed.[67] The latter wrote:

I quite agree with you that the position of the so-called Advisory Committee of the Propaganda Department at the Foreign Office is thoroughly unsatisfactory. I do not quite see the use of our going there merely to be brought face to face with choses jugées. Either we ought to be advised and consulted beforehand, or we should get rid of any responsibility which we did not seek, and which has no real meaning. There is only one way in which we should be consulted and that is in regular committee, with the usual equality of treatment.[68]

Donald complained to both Buchan and Lloyd George and, on 6 June 1917, the Prime Minister summoned the Director of Information for interview. Buchan was told that the advisory committee 'ought to be his cabinet and that all questions of policy relating to his department should be discussed and decided there, subject . . . to the supremacy of the War Cabinet'.[69] But although Buchan was therefore obliged to consult his committee on a more regular basis, he continued to regard it as 'an idiotic business which the PM forced on me owing to his fear of the press'.[70] The director clearly paid little attention to its views and, in July, Burnham recorded that Lloyd George had stated that Buchan 'was not the right man for the job, in which opinion we all agree'.[71] In August,

Lord Northcliffe joined the mounting chorus of criticism. *The Times* proclaimed:

We were in high hopes when Mr Buchan was created 'Director of Information', a sufficiently comprehensive title. But Mr Buchan turns out to be virtually a subordinate of the Foreign Office where he works. His work, we are sure, is of the greatest national importance. The point is that he is merely that of an addition to the existing publicity departments, not that of a supreme co-ordinating centre.[72]

Buchan, however, did not trust the press representatives. He believed that they had been appointed merely because of Lloyd George's desire to show them that something was being done in the conduct of national propaganda and to win their support. Only gradually did he realise that Lloyd George was thinking in terms of handing complete control over propaganda to them.

Buchan was well aware that his arrangements left much to be desired but increasingly found his position impossible. He pointed out that the Service Departments were still somewhat negative in their attitude towards supplying information to his organisation and he complained that, although directly answerable to the Prime Minister, he did not, in practice, have direct access to him. In September 1917, Buchan asked his old mentor and patron, Lord Milner, to raise in Cabinet the proposal that his department be placed under the supervision of a minister, 'someone to whom I can have access'.[73] The Cabinet approved the suggestion and, on 10 September 1917, Carson was instructed to extend 'his sphere of supervision and act in charge of all propaganda, whether at home or abroad'.[74] Carson did not prove a success. There was little evidence of genuine commitment to the work at a time when Carson was preoccupied with Irish affairs.[75] Buchan's initial delight at the new appointment quickly turned to disappointment as he found himself unable to stem the mounting tide of press criticism of his department's activities. On 4 October, the Cabinet commented on the considerable amount of overlapping between the Department of Information and the War Office[76] and, a month later, established a Cabinet Committee on Overlapping in the Production and Distribution of Propaganda.[77] In the meantime, on 19 October, Lloyd George had again turned to Robert Donald with a request for him to re-examine the entire system for propaganda 'on behalf of myself and the Cabinet' with a view to placing it finally on a sound organisational basis.[78]

Donald's report was ready by early December. It reiterated many of the criticisms of the first: the system was still dominated by the Foreign Office; lack of unity and co-ordination remained serious bars to efficiency; methods of procedure remained slow and time-consuming; further centralisation was essential to success. Buchan was accused of not having taken reorganisation far enough earlier in the year:

After making a due allowance for the inevitable failure to obtain a satisfactory return for the efforts made and the expenditure incurred, I am of the opinion that the Department's activities are altogether inadequate and in some cases misdirected. Much time has been lost and many opportunities missed, and the necessity for rapidity of actions is not yet fully appreciated.[79]

Donald further maintained that the foreign press was 'a weapon of which the Department has not taken full advantage' and that the work in the cables and wireless branch was amateurish — although he was opposed to the idea of handing over this work completely to Reuters: 'Reuters is a private organisation, and the government should not let go from its control the only official propaganda for which it [i.e Reuters] is responsible'.[80] Equally, he complained that dealings with the British press were inadequate: 'there seems to be a disinclination to use expert journalists, as in no case which has been brought to my notice is a journalist at the head of propaganda work abroad'.[81] Such a statement was bound to arouse Foreign Office suspicions that Lloyd George and certain Fleet Street proprietors were engaged in a conspiracy to dislodge its controlling position within the Department of Information.

Donald also took the opportunity of pointing out how many of his earlier recommendations had been ignored. Little attempt had been made to utilise telephone links between Britain and France or Switzerland; Wellington House was still issuing far too much pamphlet material; co-operation with foreign newspapers had not been conducted to the best advantage. He deplored the continued reluctance of the Department of Information to employ a recording officer as a means of testing the effectiveness of its propaganda. Moreover, no attempt had been made to find accommodation in one building and, if anything, fragmentation had increased. However, Donald left the main onslaught upon Wellington House to Arthur Spurgeon, a Treasury official who conducted a separate investigation into the work of Masterman's department. Spurgeon maintained the general tone of condemnation evident in Donald's report. He cast serious doubts upon the value of its work in the United States, especially now that America had entered the war on the side of the allies. Distribution was, he claimed, haphazard and there was a 'scandalous' waste of paper in the production of pamphlets. Even the staff was queried; Spurgeon doubted the need for a staff of 300, adding the sinister observation that many of its officials were eligible for military service.[82]

The replies of Masterman and Buchan were swift, detailed and resentful. Their staffs had been subjected to severe criticism by journalists who were suspected of pedantry and devious motives. The press had the attention of the Prime Minister; Buchan and Masterman did not. In October 1917, Buchan sensed that he was 'about to have a big row with the PM on the question of journalistic interference with my department'.[83] Newspapermen considered that they were more suited to conducting propaganda on behalf of the government than were those officials employed by the Department of Information who were untrained in publicity methods. The press was suspected of capitalising upon Lloyd George's predisposition towards it and upon his mistrust of officials. Buchan and Masterman therefore took full opportunity to reply to the accusations of Donald and Spurgeon, the more so in Masterman's case because he had not before had the chance, bound as he had been to a vow of strict secrecy.

Masterman argued that Donald's investigation had been hurried and limited. He had spent only three or four hours at Wellington House, while Spurgeon had spent merely seven afternoons there. The majority of the staff had not been questioned and the report, he claimed, was remarkable for its lack of detailed evidence in support of its conclusions. Masterman continued:

Obviously, in view of the general turning of the civilised world against Germany and the continual entrance into the war against her of one country after another, in which a frantic German propaganda has apparently been counteracted or destroyed, the general result should not be condemned offhand.[84]

He went on to state that:

As a result of the double propaganda, 19 countries have declared war against Germany and 10 have broken off relationships with her. At the same time she is continually complaining of the poor results of her own propaganda contrasted with that of the British and announcing that 'malignant British lies' have turned all the world against her.[85]

Masterman concluded with a detailed refutation of the criticisms levelled against Wellington House. In particular, he denied the charge that its work had been misdirected and inefficient and pointed out that there was as much evidence to support his assertions as those of his critics.

Buchan, in his reply to Donald's report, did not deny that the system for which he was responsible was imperfect, but he did object to the hasty manner in which the investigations had been conducted. He was particularly aggrieved that Donald had shown his supposedly confidential report to a colleague on the *Daily Chronicle* which had published an article repeating the main criticisms on 28 December 1917. British newspapers, Buchan felt, were full of preposterous tales concerning the supposed inefficiency of the Department of Information, reports which he considered to be inconsistent with 'the interests of public policy'.[86] He wrote:

Must men and all journalists consider themselves to be born propagandists, and readily point out where the Department fails? We welcome such criticism, when it is not merely ignorant gossip, for propaganda is not an occult science, but a matter on which every citizen has a right to judge, and on which his judgement is often valuable. Moreover, there is no finality to it; it may be improved but it can never be perfect.[87]

In his official reply to the report, Buchan therefore denied categorically the majority of Donald's criticisms. However, in a letter to Carson on 28 December, Buchan was more readily prepared to concede several points. Propaganda, he maintained, was a highly complex task which required the continued analysis of foreign opinion if it was to cater for its fluctuations.[88] Criticism that little or nothing was being done was wholly unjustified and derived largely from the intense secrecy which had surrounded the work.[89] Moreover, he argued, experience gained during the first three years of the war had demonstrated the value of disseminating accurate news combined with an honest and open explanation of British policy,[90] a view fully endorsed by Montgomery at the Foreign Office.[91] Montgomery also refuted the charge that the Department of

Information did not appoint journalists: 'It is not true that there is any disinclination to employ journalists as such, but a journalist is not necessarily a born propagandist'. He cited the examples of John Walter in Madrid, Hubert Walter in Switzerland and Roland Kenney in Norway all of whom were journalists working for the government abroad.[92]

The protests of Masterman, Buchan and Montgomery were not designed to prevent change. Indeed, Buchan positively welcomed the idea of reorganisation. But, as he informed Northcliffe, the Department of Information could only be made to work effectively 'under a chief who had authority with the War Cabinet, and by a director who had the confidence of that chief'.[93] Buchan considered that if Carson was replaced by a more influential and enthusiastic figure, the result would be a more effective organisation. The logical implication of his argument was the creation of a Ministry of Propaganda, an idea acceptable to Buchan provided that it was based upon past experience rather than solely upon the proposals contained in the second Donald report.

By the end of 1917, however, the war situation demanded more than simply administrative reform. The mutiny of French troops following the Nivelle offensive, the Italian defeat at Caporetto in October, the failure of the British offensive towards Passchendale in November, the critical situation in Russia in the aftermath of the Bolshevik revolution, anxieties concerning an impending German offensive and the slow progress of American intervention raised serious concern for the state of morale in Italy, France and in Britain itself where the famous Landsdowne letter published in the *Daily Telegraph* on 29 November was far from being an isolated phenomenon. The Department of Information felt that 'we have come to a period of the war when war-weariness in the European countries of the Entente and the immaturity of American opinion makes the instruction of the peoples at war with Germany as to the facts of the situation take precedence over any other line of propaganda'.[94] It was felt that the hitherto defensive character of British propaganda was no longer called for and that what was now required was an adventurous and resolute propaganda campaign directed at the civilian population of the enemy nations and not just against the troops in the field. Wellington House and the Foreign Office, followed by the Department of Information, were considered to have been too cautious in their approach, too limited in their appeal, too hesitant to expand and develop their activities in accordance with the changing demands of the war, and too casual in their treatment of proposals for change. It was now felt that:

Camouflage and the indirect appeal were no longer necessary, and that those who were in charge of the nation's propaganda could now 'speak out loud and bold', developing with special energy the most direct and effective known forms of propaganda.[95]

Moreover, the existing organisations had concentrated largely upon propaganda in allied and neutral countries; comparatively little attention had been paid to the important question of propaganda against enemy countries, except where pro-British material had reached the enemy through neutral channels. Indeed, to many outside observers, it appeared that the Foreign Office had forfeited its right to supervise British overseas propaganda and the arguments which had been put forward by the War Office since 1915 now appeared to be fully vindicated.

When Carson resigned from the Cabinet on 23 January 1918, the way was left clear for the emergence of a full Ministry of Information. That same day, Frederick Guest, Lloyd George's chief whip and director of the National War Aims Committee, wrote to the Prime Minister suggesting that Lord Beaverbrook be appointed minister in charge of propaganda because 'he is bitten with it, knows it, and I want him anchored'.[96] The suggestion was too great a temptation for Lloyd George to resist. The Prime Minister had always expressed an active interest in propaganda since at least the innovative campaign of 1912 publicising details of the National Insurance Act. It was he who had first suggested to the Cabinet the idea of an official propaganda campaign in August 1914, a proposal which resulted in the establishment of Wellington House. As Secretary of State for War in 1916, he was undoubtedly introduced to the views of his permanent officials concerning the creation of a centralised propaganda apparatus, a concept only remotely realised when he became Prime Minister. His contacts with influential journalists are as well known as his mistrust of diplomats. The role of Beaverbrook and Northcliffe in helping to bring down Asquith in December 1916 would not have gone unnoticed.[97] His interest in, and flair for, newspaper publicity was eventually underlined in 1918 when he was instrumental in buying the *Daily Chronicle*. A. J. P. Taylor has written that, in contrast to the majority of his contemporaries who disliked propaganda intensely, Lloyd George 'if anything rated the influence of propaganda and the press too highly'.[98] He certainly preferred to work with newspapermen more than permanent officials at the Foreign Office where propaganda was concerned. He had listened to their criticisms prior to the establishment of the Department of Information and there was no reason for him to change his advisers once criticism of that body began to mount, particularly as it was newspapermen who were the department's most vociferous critics.

Beaverbrook appeared to be an ideal candidate to take charge of the work, at least in Lloyd George's mind. His experience of propaganda was already considerable. In February 1915, Beaverbrook had been appointed 'recording and narrative officer' with the Canadian army in Europe. Under the title 'Eye-Witness', Beaverbrook (then Max Aitken) produced lengthy articles dealing with the activities of the Canadian troops at the front. He had written *Canada in Flanders*, a lengthy pamphlet detailing the work of the Canadian First Division. After September 1915, when the War Office allowed foreign journalists to visit the front, Beaverbrook continued to compile propagandist material and, in January 1916, he became the officer in charge of the Canadian War Records Office which issued a weekly communiqué to the Canadian and British press as well as news bulletins to the troops. It also published the *Canadian War Pictorial* and *Canada in Khaki*. In addition, Beaverbrook served as chairman of the War Office Cinematograph Committee and he further helped in initiating the Canadian War Memorial Fund which enabled leading artists, photographers and film-makers to visit the front. With this experience in mind, Lloyd George had no hesitation in taking up Guest's suggestion and, on 10 February 1918, he invited Beaverbrook to become Britain's first Minister of Information, with a seat in the Cabinet as Chancellor of the Duchy of Lancaster. His appointment marked the culmination not only of Beaverbrook's propaganda experience but also of the wartime evolution of Britain's official propaganda organisation while, at the same time, marking the end of three years of Foreign Office control over the work.

The Ministry of Information officially came into being on 4 March 1918. Its task was defined simply as being 'to direct the thought of most of the world'.[99] This was, however, far from being an easy task for the staff of about 500 officials. The organisation of the Ministry was essentially very simple. There were three main sections. The first dealt with propaganda at home and abroad. This was further divided into three sub-sections dealing with domestic propaganda, foreign propaganda and propaganda in military zones. The second section dealt with publicity and was responsible for press articles, literature, films and visual work. The third section dealt with personal propaganda and hospitality working mainly through the Overseas Press Centre. Originally, Beaverbrook assumed that the Ministry would control home propaganda through an inter-departmental committee consisting of representatives from the Ministries of Food, Munitions, War Savings and National Service, with the NWAC providing the operational machinery. However, following resistance from the NWAC, which had no desire to become ostensibly connected with a government department,[100] it was decided on 5 March that the Ministry of Information 'should not take over the political work of the National War Aims Committee and that for the present it was inadvisable for the Ministry of Information to deal with Home Propaganda'.[101] The NWAC therefore remained in charge of all official propaganda conducted within the United Kingdom, while the Ministry retained a small section to keep a watchful eye on its work.

The NWAC was not the only body which preferred to remain separate from the new Ministry. Also on 5 March, it was decided that those government departments which had established their own press and propaganda sections should be allowed to continue the initiative they had begun, at least for the time being. Lord Rhondda, the Minister for Food, had been particularly determined for his press office to resist absorption into the Ministry of Information. 'No satisfactory propaganda', he wrote, 'could be carried out by anyone who was not in daily touch with the Department and centralisation would mean loss of efficiency'.[102] The situation which resulted from this decision created numerous anomalies. Moreover, when it was decided in May 1918 that the Ministry of Information 'should undertake Home Propaganda by means of cinema films and photographs, the costs to be defrayed from their own vote',[103] the problem was compounded. Although the NWAC was drawn increasingly into the Ministry of Information's ambit, the fact that domestic propaganda continued to be conducted from a variety of different sources demonstrated an irreconcilable problem faced by Beaverbrook. Although his Ministry possessed the technical facilities, expertise and Cabinet authorisation to conduct all propaganda at home and abroad, government departments were determined to retain control over their own publicity needs even though they were less equipped to perform the work as effectively.

This situation was best illustrated by the Ministry's relationship with the Foreign Office. The section established by Beaverbrook to deal with foreign propaganda was virtually the old Department of Information. It was placed under the general supervision of John Buchan and was divided into four branches: administration, headed by Montgomery; literary and artistic propaganda, headed by Masterman; press and cinema, headed by T. L. Gilmour and assisted by George Mair, Roderick Jones and by Sir William Jury (in charge of cinema production); and intelligence under Lord Edward Gleichen. The intelligence branch provided a test case upon which Beaverbrook's authority with other Whitehall departments was to founder.

In October 1917, Robert Donald had proposed the transfer of Gleichen's intelligence bureau from the Department of Information to the Foreign Office. He wrote:

All the information which the War Office and the Admiralty Intelligence branches possess is not placed at the disposal of Lord Edward Gleichen's Intelligence Bureau, which reports to Colonel Buchan, nor does the Propaganda Department get the benefit of the knowledge of experts in the service of the War Office and Admiralty intelligence branches, some of whom are students of German psychology and authorities on conditions in enemy countries. The full co-operation of the War Office Intelligence bureau is essential in carrying propaganda into enemy countries.[104]

The problem, as ever, was that the War Office seemed reluctant to co-operate with any propaganda department operating under the auspices of the Foreign Office. Indeed, the War Office regarded the intelligence bureau as superfluous; its work was duplicated elsewhere by other, more efficient, departments such as MI7. Although Buchan denied this, he did feel that the intelligence bureau could serve a more valuable purpose in the Foreign Office than it was doing in the Department of Information. Following Donald's initiative, he requested the formal transfer of Gleichen's branch in November 1917 in the hope that it would lead to a more cordial relationship with the Service Departments in so far as supplying information was concerned.[105] Because the principal function of the intelligence bureau was the compilation of political summaries relating to the internal conditions of foreign countries, the Foreign Office also supported the idea. Montgomery pointed out that because much of British overseas propaganda 'has necessarily to be done through, or under the direction of our representatives abroad and that this entails a very considerable correspondence with them which could not be conducted by any office other than the Foreign Office, without placing them in the position of serving two masters',[106] the proposed transfer would be a great improvement in the right direction. Balfour agreed and, on 5 February 1918, the Foreign Secretary sought Cabinet approval for the transfer,[107] which he obtained on 19 February.[108] In the meantime, the Foreign Office had already begun to make the necessary arrangements to house the bureau, which would be reconstituted as the Political Intelligence Department (PID) under the direction of William Tyrrell, assisted by J. W. Headlam-Morley.

When, therefore, Beaverbrook attempted to cancel this arrangement and to secure the intelligence bureau for his new Ministry, the Foreign Office resisted vigorously. Intelligence, it argued, was not solely the concern of propaganda, its principal function being to compile from diplomatic correspondence political summaries relating to the internal situation within a given foreign country chiefly for the benefit of the policy-makers. Beaverbrook's conception was determined by much narrower considerations. Because the intelligence summaries were invaluable to propaganda work, he argued that the new PID should form an integral part of the Ministry of Information.[109] Accurate intelligence was certainly vital to effective political propaganda. But Beaverbrook's mistake was to assume that it was of value only to the propagandists. Ironically, Whitehall closed ranks on him. After nearly three years of inter-departmental rivalry and squabbling, government departments were now united behind the Foreign Office in opposition to any further transference of duties for which they had been traditionally responsible.[110] Balfour wrote:

It is quite true that propaganda must be based on knowledge; but the knowledge required covers only a fraction of that involved in the day to day work of the Foreign Office, Admiralty and War Office; and the creation of a new department, which regards it as one of its functions to co-ordinate all the most confidential information which three other departments have collected for their own purposes, is not only indefensible from the point of view of organisation, but would render secrecy even more difficult to maintain than it is at present.[111]

It was also suggested that Beaverbrook's conception was based upon a fundamental misconception: 'Propaganda and Intelligence are two entirely different functions; the former depends on the latter for inspiration, but in their inherent nature and method of operation they have nothing in common. Diplomacy and Intelligence have; the one is the essence of the other'.[112]

In the face of such determined opposition, Beaverbrook decided to submit the dispute to the War Cabinet for arbitration,[113] but the matter was referred to an inter-departmental conference which convened on 5 March 1918. Beaverbrook was successful in reversing the original arrangement: the intelligence bureau would form part of the Ministry of Information and not of the Foreign Office — which was permitted to establish its own PID if it so wished.[114] On hearing this decision, however, the staff of the intelligence bureau resigned *en bloc*, each member apparently reaching his decision not to serve under Beaverbrook independently.[115] 'None of us', wrote Rex Leeper, 'were willing to work under Beaverbrook or any other newspaper "boss"'.[116] Only R. W. Seton-Watson made reservations.[117] Faced with this development, Beaverbrook was forced to submit reluctantly; better to have an intelligence bureau in the Foreign Office than none at all. Accordingly, the staff of the PID, which included such notable figures as Headlam-Morley, Lewis Namier, Arnold Toynbee, Rex and Allen Leeper, was reinstated and became a branch of the Foreign Office.[118] The PID was known as the 'ministry of all talents'. Of its nine original members, five were recruited from Balliol and four from New College, Oxford. Many of its members were contributors to the *New Europe*, an activity which the Foreign Office allowed to continue.[119] The transfer, wrote Rex Leeper, 'is what we have always wanted'[120] partly because of the hope that the Foreign Office would keep the PID staff on permanently. The Ministry of Information had to be content with establishing a small intelligence section of its own under the supervision of John Buchan.

The struggle for control over political intelligence was, quite simply, one of power. The gradual erosion of Foreign Office involvement in propaganda during 1917 and 1918 was part of Lloyd George's broader campaign to undermine the influence of the Foreign Office in the making of British foreign policy.[121] The creation of the Department of Information in February 1917 had not seriously threatened either the traditional influence of the Foreign

Office in the formulation of policy or its wartime control over propaganda largely because John Buchan had chosen to work with, rather than against, it. Beaverbrook was not to prove as co-operative. To the older-established ministries, the Ministry of Information represented a further encroachment upon their powers which had already been undermined by the War Cabinet since December 1916. Whitehall resented the incursions of an upstart Ministry, particularly one controlled by newspaper proprietors and editors, into areas of traditional responsibility. It was not prepared to tolerate an outside, and probably temporary, department interfering with jealously guarded duties upon which government policy was formulated. Beaverbrook was made directly answerable to Lloyd George, not to Parliament, the Treasury or the War Cabinet. The Ministry of Information was suspected of being a 'quango' of the Prime Minister's — a suspicion which was not entirely without substance.

Beaverbrook's appointment might have signified the end of three and a half years of Foreign Office control over British overseas propaganda, but the Foreign Office was determined to ensure that the same did not happen with regard to policy. In other words, if the Foreign Office was prepared ultimately to accept that it was not properly equipped to deal with propaganda and was, therefore, finally prepared to surrender responsibility for such work into the hands of a group of newspapermen who claimed to understand it better, it was less willing to relinquish a responsibility which predated the wartime propaganda experience and which constituted an essential aspect of its traditional role and status. It is thus hardly surprising that the Foreign Office became alarmed when Beaverbrook began to appoint special propaganda agents in order to supervise the work in neutral countries independently of the diplomatic and consular missions. Such a development, as Beaverbrook himself admitted, provided the Ministry of Information with the potential to develop into 'a second Foreign Office at home with a new set of representatives abroad'.[122] Moreover, propaganda continued to be regarded in most official circles as a necessary evil of war, a temporary and distasteful expedient made necessary only by the activities of the enemy. Whatever its future role on the return of peace, it was assumed that established diplomatic practices would continue after the war had ended. Serious consequences might therefore arise if a group of newspapermen — or the 'press gang' as they were known — were allowed direct access to confidential intelligence which would normally have been kept from them.

In the winter of 1917-18, the Foreign Office held the trump card over both Lloyd George and Beaverbrook — provided that it could retain its traditional status and duties. This was because successful propaganda is dependent for its effectiveness not only upon accurate intelligence but, even more significantly, upon a clearly defined policy. Hitherto, the absence of a coherent statement of British war aims had deprived British propaganda of any real direction. Now that Lloyd George had committed the government to the aims laid down in his speech of 5 January 1918, this serious obstacle had been at least partially removed. But if the Prime Minister wished to reduce still further the influence of the Foreign Office in the policy-making process, and if Beaverbrook wished to reduce its influence in the conduct of British overseas propaganda, the PID would first have to be wrenched from Foreign Office control. That neither man was able to loosen that grip was a reflection of the limited power of the Ministry of Information, a situation of which Beaverbrook was fully aware. Indeed, it remained a constant source of frustration to him and he felt that, without direct control over intelligence, he would be forced to admit that the idea of a propaganda ministry '"functioning on its own" was not called for, and that, in fact, all it could do was to function as a Department of the Foreign Office'.[123] As the dispute continued throughout the final summer of the war, Beaverbrook found himself engaged in 'a remorseless battle . . . without compensations'[124] which required the full-time attention of a secretary 'simply and solely for the purpose of conducting the diplomatic correspondence with the Foreign Office, as with a neighbouring and none too friendly power'.[125] In May 1918, he despaired to Balfour:

If you face the facts the Ministry of Information is not really a Department independent of the Foreign Office, but one subsidiary to it. And what is the case in fact had much better be in name too, if friction and waste of time are to be avoided.[126]

The problem, he told Northcliffe, was that 'the War Cabinet directs him to do certain things and the Foreign Office will not allow him to do them'.[127] Balfour replied: 'For my part I am quite content to leave all details of propaganda entirely in Lord Beaverbrook's hands. I only ask that my Department should be consulted and my advice followed on matters where questions of foreign policy are concerned, and that officers who undertake propaganda in foreign countries should be under the ultimate control of the Ambassador or Minister sending him'.[128]

This was a reference to a clash which had occurred in June 1918. Beaverbrook had nominated two officials for propaganda missions in Russia and Mesopotamia. When the Foreign Office refused to grant them permission to leave, Beaverbrook complained to Lloyd George:

All that we require, and urgently, is a firm definition of the relations and respective spheres of the Foreign Office and the Ministry of Information. Without some such definition, which both parties would be compelled to observe, the present game of cross-purposes and inaction will go on for ever.[129]

The Foreign Office remained suspicious of Beaverbrook's motives, despite his reassurance that 'you can have a Ministry of semi-official propaganda following the Foreign Office in policy but carrying out that policy by a different method'.[130] However, the appointment of special propaganda agents operating outside the supervision of the diplomatic and consular services was not a method approved by the Foreign Office.

Beaverbrook's frustration was not confined to his relations with the Foreign Office. He felt that the officials of the Press Bureau should be told that 'we are a Ministry charged with the duties and powers of publicity and not a Department subordinate to themselves'.[131] The branch of the Ministry dealing with propaganda in military zones also came into conflict with the War Office. Although this branch worked in close co-operation with Colonel Fisher's MI7, the War Office retained ultimate control over all propaganda dealing with military affairs and conducted much of its work on behalf of the Ministry. Friction soon arose over the War Office's practice of censoring photographs at the front before passing them on to the Ministry of Information, by which time they had often been censored again by the Press Bureau, MI7 or by both. Beaverbrook complained that because the photographs were invaluable for propaganda purposes, they should be passed directly to the Ministry by the photographers. The War Office would then be entitled to censor them from a military point of view, but judgement concerning their suitability for propaganda purposes should rest solely with the Ministry. Beaverbrook explained:

As it is, the negatives are sent by GHQ to MI7a, from thence to the Press Bureau, then to Associated Agencies to be printed; from here the prints go back to the Press Bureau, whence in many cases they are sent to the War Office and back; then back again to the Associated Agencies; and thence, finally, after grievous delay, to the Ministry of Information, by whose staff they are actually taken in the field.[132]

This was clearly a hopeless and time-consuming process, and one which was anathema to a man who had worked in the comparatively efficient Canadian organisation.

The War Office did prove amenable to minor improvements in its arrangements with the Ministry of Information. It was a different story with the Admiralty which, Beaverbrook believed, was 'the front of the resistance to any recognition of the functions of the new ministry. Whenever I make a request to Sir Eric Geddes [First Lord of the Admiralty], it is immediately and politely refused'.[133] The main bone of contention was the supply of secret naval intelligence. Beaverbrook felt that enormous use could be made of such information by the Ministry for propaganda purposes, 'if only this knowledge were placed at its disposal'.[134] The problem, once again, was the status of the Ministry of Information. From the beginning:

the sphere of the Ministry's work was not defined with sufficient clearness. No charter of rights and duties has been drawn up and the operations of the Ministry have been and continue to be interrupted with by other Departments of State over debatable spheres of work, influence and information.[135]

In all the disputes which had taken place, Beaverbrook had been the one who had been forced to give way on every occasion without any apparent support from the War Cabinet. 'The Ministry', wrote Beaverbrook, 'is treated as a subordinate department without rights, and in consequence becomes so in fact'.[136] On 24 June he therefore resorted to a move which he was to try repeatedly in an attempt to extract a decision from Lloyd George and tendered his resignation.

The Prime Minister did not respond immediately. A week later, when Beaverbrook reiterated his desire to resign, Lloyd George summoned him to a meeting with Balfour. On 9 July, as a direct consequence of this meeting, the Ministry of Information was

confirmed as an independent organisation over which the Foreign
Office had no responsibility. It was also decided that there should be
regular consultation between the two departments, that each would
supply the other with all the required information, and that the War
Cabinet would settle any further differences of opinion.[137]
Beaverbrook withdrew his resignation. The Foreign Office, however,
was less pleased with the outcome. Balfour informed Lloyd George
on 12 July:

I am very anxious to arrive at a solution of the unfortunate
difficulties which have arisen between Lord Beaverbrook and my
Department. The conditions laid down in your memorandum would,
however, I fear not only result in increased friction but might
seriously affect the constitutional position of the Secretary of State
for Foreign Affairs. We should end having two Ministers responsible
to the Cabinet for Foreign Affairs.[138]

Balfour insisted that the Foreign Office should be allowed to
determine questions of policy with regard to the conduct of
propaganda abroad, that overseas agents should remain subject to
the authority of diplomatic and consular representatives, and that
the Foreign Office should be consulted before the Ministry decided
to send any of its own agents overseas. Beaverbrook realised his
mistake in regarding the Admiralty as the main 'front of resistance'
to his work because, he wrote:

The Foreign Office is the principal trouble. After receiving my
memorandum, the Prime Minister endeavoured to effect a settlement
between Mr Balfour and myself. The attempt failed completely and
at the end Mr Balfour was advancing far stronger claims on behalf of
the Foreign Office against the Ministry than had ever been made
before the negociation [sic] commenced.[139]

On 19 July, he again complained to Lloyd George that cabled
messages intended for his Ministry were being intercepted by the
Press Bureau and passed on to the Foreign Office before reaching his
staff and he insisted that they be sent directly. Philip Kerr, the Prime
Minister's private secretary, agreed to resolve this particular issue[140]
and, four days later, Balfour accepted his scheme with the proviso
that the Foreign Office should be consulted before any policy
decisions were reached. Balfour informed Kerr:

You state that the decision was in accordance with the arrangements come to with regard to the distribution of functions between the Foreign Office and the Ministry of Information. May I remind you that no distribution of functions has yet been determined.[141]

Balfour should have said 'agreed'. He had not yet received a reply from Lloyd George concerning his counter-proposals to the memorandum of 9 July. Lord Robert Cecil, now Assistant Foreign Secretary, Minister of Blockade and perhaps Beaverbrook's most notable Foreign Office sympathiser,[142] was becoming impatient. He informed Balfour on 29 July:

The situation is becoming intolerable and unless Beaverbrook's activities are definitely confined to propaganda, properly so-called, it will be quite impossible to conduct any business. Here is one of his agents telegraphing through the D[irector of] M[ilitary] I[ntelligence] to Beaverbrook affairs which are clearly in the province of either the War Office or the Foreign Office and are in fact being dealt with by the Russia committee.[143]

Balfour, not unnaturally, agreed, adding that the activities of the Ministry of Information were extending 'a good deal beyond anything which I, at least, have been accustomed to describe as propaganda, using that word even in the widest sense'.[144]

Lloyd George again found himself in an impossible position. He had given his full backing to Beaverbrook but he could hardly ignore Balfour's views, particularly as the Foreign Secretary enjoyed the complete support of other government departments where the Ministry of Information was concerned. The Prime Minister therefore took the line of least resistance and did nothing. Balfour, however, continued to press him for a decision on the demarcation of duties.[145] He had become particularly alarmed at the Ministry's behaviour over his famous declaration on Zionism. Although the Cabinet had approved the Balfour Declaration, the Foreign Secretary wrote:

I now find that Beaverbrook has written to you on the subject asking for a clear directive on Jewish policy. He states that he has done so because Sir Charles Henry told him that he had laid certain arguments before you which had impressed you and which you were taking into consideration; and meanwhile Zionist propaganda is being suspended.[146]

An indignant Balfour therefore demanded that a decision be made immediately. Lloyd George agreed that the relationship needed clarifying, 'otherwise friction and misunderstanding are inevitable'.[147] He reassured the Foreign Secretary that he remained a supporter of the Balfour Declaration and promised to settle the entire affair on his return from holiday in Wales.[148]

On 11 September 1918, Lloyd George finally issued a definite statement on the powers of the Ministry of Information. Photographs were to be sent directly to it after they had been censored at the front; the Press Bureau was to deal with the Ministry as it did other departments; intercepted German wireless messages were to be sent to the Ministry prior to censorship, except when naval and military matters were involved.[149] Once these detailed instructions had been relayed to the relevant departments, Beaverbrook could feel reasonably confident that he had finally established a working basis for the Ministry of Information. But he personally was unable to enjoy his triumph; he fell ill and his work had to be continued by his assistant, the novelist Arnold Bennett, and by Roderick Jones who, between them, supervised the Ministry's activities until the end of the war.

THE DEPARTMENT OF ENEMY PROPAGANDA AT CREWE HOUSE

Until the final year of the war, British propaganda was directed largely at opinion in allied and neutral countries. The creation, therefore, in February 1918 of a specific department designed 'to reveal to the enemy the hopelessness of their cause and case, and the certainty of Allied victory'[150] was certainly long overdue. Before then, enemy propaganda had been conducted by S. A. Guest at Wellington House and by MI7 at the War Office. But the establishment of Crewe House did not necessarily represent a condemnation of their work. The second Donald report had not contained any criticism of the way in which British propaganda against the enemy was being conducted. In fact, the decision to establish a separate department was sudden and unforeseen. Even Beaverbrook was initially unaware that his new Ministry was not to control this aspect of British propaganda. On 13 February 1918, Lloyd George had invited Lord Northcliffe to take charge of a psychological offensive against the enemy. The invitation was accepted only on the understanding that Northcliffe was to be responsible directly to the Prime Minister, not to Beaverbrook.

It was generally assumed at the time that this was another political calculation on Lloyd George's part. It was felt that he wished to draw the teeth of Northcliffe. Relations between the two men had always been erratic and Lloyd George, who respected the power of the press perhaps far beyond its actual significance, might well have seen the administrative reforms prompted by the second Donald report as yet another opportunity to muzzle recalcitrant or unpredictable news-papermen. Northcliffe, for his part, had indeed been a constant critic of the government and although he had accepted the post as head of the British War Mission in 1917, he generally preferred to avoid official appointments for fear that they might restrict his freedom to criticise the government if he chose to do so. Accordingly, when Lloyd George offered him a ministerial appointment on his return from the United States, the offer was politely turned down. But the fresh bait of a virtually autonomous enemy propaganda department was to prove irresistible to a man who had expressed an active, if unofficial, interest in such work since the beginning of the war. And although it was generally assumed that the bait was dangled by a Prime Minister who sought to work with, rather than against, such an influential newspaper owner, it seems more likely that the offer came, as Northcliffe himself maintained, from 'those who are doing the actual fighting in the war'[151] — which presumably meant the War Office. Northcliffe had always supported the Generals — with certain notable exceptions — and he had frequently defended their cause before Lloyd George although he was disillusioned with their failure during the Cambrai offensive in December 1917. Even so, it none-theless remains difficult to explain why the military authorities should apparently be prepared to relinquish control over work in which MI7 had been becoming increasingly involved. Perhaps, as another source suggests, the contradiction can be explained if Northcliffe was proposed by Sir William Tyrrell, the head of the PID who had been involved in propaganda from the very earliest days of the war.[152] In view of the rivalry which existed between the Foreign Office and the War Office over the question of propaganda, it is not inconceivable that Northcliffe's name was proposed by one or other department as a convenient method of solving what had become an intractable inter-departmental problem. But regardless of where the idea originated, Northcliffe eagerly welcomed the proposal. He immed-iately began to establish an enemy propaganda department, first at the London headquarters of his British War Mission and later at its more famous location of Crewe House in Curzon Street in March 1918.

Northcliffe's appointment, coupled with that of Lord Beaverbrook, created an outcry in Parliament. The attack upon Lloyd
George was led by Austen Chamberlain who argued that the
appointment of newspaper proprietors to controlling positions
within the official propaganda machinery served to remove the
demarcation lines which had previously existed between Fleet Street
and Downing Street.[153] Lloyd George was accused of trying to buy
the support of the press, 'a method of propaganda repugnant to the
traditions of our public life and to the habits of our nation'.[154] The
independence of the press, particularly *The Times*, would be
significantly impaired and its credibility as a medium of official
propaganda, conscious or otherwise, would thereby be seriously
undermined. Although Lloyd George was able to ride out the storm,
which subsided with the great German offensive in March,
he was never able to dispel altogether the suspicion that he was
attempting to establish a personal power base which transcended
traditional party politics.[155]

The creation of the Enemy Propaganda Department marked the
British government's final attempt of the war to find an adequate
organisational solution to the new problem of propaganda. It did,
however, create a fresh set of anomalies within the overall apparatus.
Crewe House was instructed to concentrate its attention upon
Germany, Austria-Hungary and Bulgaria. The Ministry of
Information, although mainly responsible for propaganda in allied
and neutral countries, was given the task of conducting propaganda
against Turkey. Moreover, in May 1918, Beaverbrook invited
Northcliffe to take charge of the work in Italy — the springboard of
any campaign against Austria-Hungary — and Northcliffe accepted.[156] This was because it was decided in Crewe House that its
initial efforts should be concentrated against the Austro-Hungarian
empire, racked by internal disaffection and ripe for a concerted allied
propaganda campaign by virtue of the subject nationalities which
had been rejuvenated by President Wilson's call for national self-
determination as part of his 'Fourteen Points' speech of 8 January
1918.

Crewe House was divided into two branches dealing with
production and with distribution. The production branch was sub-
divided into sections dealing with Germany, Austria-Hungary and
Bulgaria. The Austro-Hungarian section was placed under the
direction of Henry Wickham Steed, foreign editor of *The Times* and a

recognised expert on Austrian affairs. Steed was assisted by Dr R. W. Seton-Watson, the distinguished central European scholar who had been serving in the PID. The German section was originally headed by H. G. Wells who was able to secure the assistance of Headlam-Morley also from the PID. However, in July 1918, Wells resigned following a disagreement with Northcliffe. He was replaced by Hamilton Fyfe, a distinguished and scholarly journalist from the Northcliffe stable. Distribution was placed in the experienced hands of S. A. Guest, thereby ensuring a measure of continuity with the previous arrangements. Sir Campbell Stuart, a young Canadian whom Northcliffe had encountered during his War Mission in the United States, was appointed to serve as Northcliffe's deputy with special responsibility for administration. Liaison with the War Office was provided by Peter Chalmers Mitchell, a distinguished zoologist currently serving as a captain in MI7. Liaison with the Admiralty was provided by Commander Guy Standing and with the Foreign Office by C. J. Phillips who had supervised relations between the Foreign Office and the War Mission following a career in the Board of Education. Major questions of policy were settled by an advisory committee consisting of Robert Donald, Roderick Jones, Wickham Steed, H. G. Wells, Sir Sidney Low from the Ministry of Information, the Earl of Denbigh from the Foreign Office, the various liaison officers and two MPs, Sir Charles Nicholson and James O'Grady. This committee met regularly at first but appears to have lapsed in importance after July 1918. Crewe House was made answerable to the Ministry of Information only in respect of finance.

On 24 February 1918, Northcliffe wrote to Balfour requesting details of British policy towards Austria-Hungary. The Director of Enemy Propaganda pointed out that the previous policy of working for a separate peace with 'the Emperor, the Court, the aristocracy, on the principle of not interfering with the domestic affairs of the Habsburg Monarchy and of leaving its territory almost or quite intact' had failed.[157] He therefore proposed that Crewe House be authorised to try to 'break the power of Austria-Hungary, as the weakest link in the chain of enemy states, by supporting and encouraging all anti-German and pro-Ally peoples and tendencies'.[158] This suggestion raised policy questions of major significance. Northcliffe requested a speedy decision; Balfour had no intention of being steamrollered into making firm decisions on the delicate, and as yet undecided, issue of the subject nationalities.[159]

When, on 6 June, the government decided to publish the weak Allied Versailles declaration calling for the creation of a 'united and independent Polish State with free access to the sea' but merely expressing cautious sympathy towards the Czechoslovaks and the Yugoslavs, Northcliffe protested that this was an insufficent basis for the propaganda campaign against Austria-Hungary.[160] Balfour's explanation that the problems of inter-allied unity on this issue were so considerable that it was impossible to make any further statement at this stage[161] failed to reveal the mounting resentment of the Foreign Office at what were felt to be Northcliffe's attempts to determine the course of British foreign policy.

Northcliffe accepted Wickham Steed's definition of the connection between policy and propaganda, namely 'the same connection as between news and newspapers'.[162] But, as one historian has pointed out:

Had Crewe House been as willing as Wellington House to accept dictation from the Foreign Office on matters of foreign policy there would have been fewer problems . . . [but] Northcliffe's innovation was not that he made propaganda consistent with policy, but that he tried to alter foreign policy to make it consistent with propaganda formulated by Seton-Watson and Wickham Steed.[163]

Northcliffe was therefore afforded similar treatment to that experienced by Beaverbrook, although the history of Crewe House's relations with the Foreign Office is, overall, a happier story, perhaps due in no small part to the work of C. J. Phillips as liaison officer.[164] Even so, following Northcliffe's attempt to force Balfour's hand over the question of British policy towards Germany in June 1918,[165] the Director of Enemy Propaganda was forced to despair that 'as a people we do not understand propaganda ways . . . . Propaganda is advertising and diplomacy is no more likely to understand advertising than advertising is likely to understand diplomacy'.[166] In fact, the Foreign Office had long appreciated that propaganda depended for its success upon a clearly defined policy. This fundamental axiom of propaganda had been learned during the first three years of the war when the Foreign Office had controlled the direction of British overseas propaganda. But its work had been severely handicapped by the absence of a coherent declaration of British war aims. Beaverbrook and Northcliffe were more fortunate in this respect, having both Lloyd George's speech of 5 January 1918 and Wilson's Fourteen Points which were announced a few days after. But because they were attempting to elicit further, more detailed, declarations on specific issues from the government in order to provide their propaganda with a particular focus, they were attempting to go too far, too fast. The result was that they appeared to be subordinating policy to propaganda rather than the reverse. That they were able to do this with the apparent sanction of Lloyd George merely served to reinforce the reluctance of the Foreign Office to extend its co-operation to those who had assumed responsibility for the direction of British propaganda in February 1918.

The Foreign Office considered that it had been forced to relinquish its control over propaganda for highly dubious reasons. It stood accused before the first and second Donald reports of incompetence and inefficiency, charges which it rightly denied but which had nonetheless gained the support of Lloyd George. The Donald reports, however, do not stand up to detailed investigation. They were hastily produced (the first was written in less than a week) and contain the most sweeping generalisations about the conduct of propaganda during the early phase of the war. The more closely they are examined, the more it appears that they were the product not of an impartial observer seeking to make a detached, objective investigation, but of a highly committed individual whose ideas were firmly established long before his investigations were undertaken. Donald had been a critic of the Foreign Office and other Whitehall departments ever since the beginning of the war. He was one of many newspaper editors who became obsessed with a sense of their own importance, who made it their duty to challenge the policies of the government at virtually every turn and who believed that they held some kind of divine right to control publicity. The Donald reports emphasised the need to employ journalists and journalistic methods in the official propaganda machinery when, in fact, journalists had been recruited from an early stage of the war. But Donald wanted to see journalists control the direction of the work although when that ambition was secured in February 1918, Donald's own career as Director of Propaganda in Neutral Countries was brief and undistinguished. He was appointed on 18 February 1918 and he resigned on 2 April. By August 1918, he had returned to his old habit of criticising the organisation of propaganda.

The evidence produced by Donald was scanty and easily

countered. However, Donald's views triumphed. Masterman was frustrated at being denied a real opportunity to defend the work of Wellington House to the Prime Minister. Relations between the two men had become severely strained by 1916, stemming partly from Masterman's belief that Lloyd George was responsible for his failure to secure political re-election which had forced Masterman to resign from the Cabinet in February 1915.[167] Not only did this incident poison relations between the two men but it also denied Wellington House a champion at Cabinet level. At the end of the war, Masterman served under Arnold Bennett at the Ministry of Information who wrote, 'considering that he had been a Cabinet Minister early in the war, and that I politically a nobody, was now his superior, he behaved excellently in a very trying situation'.[168] Nor did Masterman receive any recognition from the government for the work he had done, although he was decorated by the Belgian government for the work which he had undertaken on its behalf.

From the moment that Lloyd George had become Prime Minister in December 1916, he displayed an apparent determination to weaken the grip which the Foreign Office had established, more by accident than design, on the direction of British overseas propaganda since the outbreak of the war. Unlike the majority of his contemporaries, he fully appreciated the role which propaganda could play in wartime. But he did not consider that the Foreign Office or Masterman was capable of realising its true potential. Instead, he preferred to entrust the work to newspapermen well versed in the techniques of mass persuasion. This was a dangerous ambition. He laid himself open to criticism that he was attempting to muzzle the press for political reasons when all he was probably trying to do was to harness it for the national war effort. Lloyd George defended Beaverbrook's appointment to C. P. Scott:

on the ground of Buchan's ineffectiveness and the difficulty of finding competent men for the job. Beaverbrook was extremely clever and though he was described as a 'shady financier' he was not aware of any real foundation for the charge.[169]

Beaverbrook's reputation as a propagandist was, however, already established. Lloyd George's primary interest in Lord Northcliffe's appointment was to reduce the likelihood of his maintaining his press criticism of government policy. As Lloyd George again informed C. P. Scott:

Northcliffe had been quite reasonable during the seven months he had been in America (as head of a British propaganda mission). It was necessary to find occupation for his abounding energies if they were not to run into mischief.[170]

Lord Hankey's diary confirms this desire of Lloyd George to redirect press energies into the service of government when, early in 1917, he had suggested Northcliffe as head of the War Mission:

Interesting discussion at morning War Cabinet on subject of the articles on the submarine question in *The Times* and *Daily Mail* and all the Northcliffe press which supply most valuable propaganda to the enemy, who make full use of it. Ll. G. very angry about it . . . he is now trying to persuade the War Cabinet to send Northcliffe to America to coordinate the purchases, transport arrangements etc. of the various Depts. This, of course, is really a dodge to get rid of Northcliffe, of whom he is afraid . . . [171]

This type of pragmatism was a feature of Lloyd George's premiership and it becomes difficult to distinguish between his desire to utilise the energies of people such as Beaverbrook and Northcliffe in their capacity as propaganda experts and his determination to curtail their influence as newspaper owners and critics of the government. Although he reassured C. P. Scott that neither man 'would allow their propaganda work to be determined by their personal views — and would simply take the line which they thought likely to be the most useful in the particular case', Scott commented that 'as this is not very far from being probably Lloyd George's own state of mind it did not seem much use to argue the matter'.[172]

Lloyd George's apparent determination to ignore the protestations of the Foreign Office, particularly concerning the second Donald report, regardless of their rationale or justification, was interpreted as fresh evidence of his desire to undermine the traditional role of the older-established Whitehall departments in the policy-making process when, in fact, all he was probably attempting to do was to speed up the decision-making process of a coalition government at war. Yet for a man with a rare contemporary gift for self-advertisement, he made surprisingly little effort to explain or justify his position. As a result, his determination to hand over control of the nation's propaganda to people he believed were more likely to produce effects or who were more likely to prove useful to him personally — or a combination of both — was interpreted as an assault upon the constitutional position of Whitehall. This was the key to the struggle over political intelligence and to the reluctance of Whitehall to extend its co-operation to the Ministry of Information and Crewe House.

Nor did Beaverbrook and Northcliffe help matters by their apparent determination to serve as Lloyd George's instruments in this process. Not only were they newspaper proprietors but they were also made directly answerable to the Prime Minister. As Beaverbrook admitted to Lloyd George in June 1918:

. . . since our appeal lies not to the diplomatic representatives of foreign countries, but to the public opinion of those countries, our methods must be different from those of the Foreign Office. We have a diplomacy of our own — a popular diplomacy — and for this reason we must have our own special organisation.[173]

This was the attitude which caused the Foreign Office to oppose Beaverbrook and Northcliffe, not because it did not appreciate the value of their propaganda work, nor even because it refused to accept that the time had come for broadening the audience to which British propaganda would more profitably be directed. The reason, essentially, was that the Foreign Office saw the Ministry of Information and Crewe House as further attempts by Lloyd George to erode its traditional constitutional role in the making of British foreign policy.

PART TWO

Methods, Distribution and Content

3 The Methods and Distribution of British Propaganda

WHEN Beaverbrook and Northcliffe assumed control over Britain's propaganda machinery in February 1918, their appointments held out the promise of a radical change in the methods employed by the government to influence public opinion at home and abroad. They did not, however, prove to be quite the new brooms which many critics of the previous regime might have hoped. The changes that did take place were more immediately apparent in the conduct of propaganda abroad than they were in the domestic campaign and, even then, they were changes of emphasis and scale rather than any significant departure from established wartime practices. Further, the changes were determined more by a different conception of the type of audience to be influenced than by the groundless allegation that previous methods and distribution had been ineffective or inadequate. Before 1918, the Foreign Office, together with those organisations operating under its auspices, had been reluctant to attempt direct appeals to public opinion on a mass scale. In Wellington House, for example, it was believed that 'mass activity is the easiest and that which appeals most to those who wish to produce an effect, but it is in fact the most useless as regards its results upon the population intended to be affected'.[1] The primary target of Foreign Office propaganda was clearly defined. It was directed at the opinion-makers in foreign societies — journalists, publicists, politicians, government officials, teachers — 'the principle being that it is better to influence those who can influence others than attempt a direct appeal to the mass of the population'.[2]

There were several reasons why this type of target was identified from the very beginning of the war. In many respects, it was an extension of the kind of personal diplomacy familiar to most members of the British foreign policy-making élite who were generally unfamiliar with the concept of mass popular opinion. It was, moreover, not unnaturally assumed that foreign governments would resent outside interference in the thoughts and actions of their peoples. As one official stated in December 1914, 'the intrusion of a Government, or of persons notoriously inspired by Government, into the sphere of opinion invariably excites suspicion and resentment'.[3] Or, as John Buchan maintained three years later:

Camouflage of the right kind is a vital necessity. It [i.e. propaganda] can advertise its wares but it dare not advertise the vendor. Popular opinion in every country is so delicate an instrument that attempts to play upon it in the name of a foreign Government are certain to be resented, and not only lose their value, but be positively injurious to our cause.[4]

For precisely this reason, German methods were to be avoided at all costs. In Scandinavia, for example, it was felt at the end of 1914 that:

the very friendly attitude of the Norwegians towards us is largely due to the feeling of irritation induced by the constant bombardment kept up by the Germans with all kinds of printed matter. Similarly, in Sweden, which has until lately become somewhat hostile in tone, we are told that one of the main causes of the reaction towards our side is the annoyance at the persistent German missionary work.[5]

For the first three years of the war, therefore, British overseas propaganda avoided being overt or blatant. This was not simply a device to prevent clean hands from getting dirty but the product of a genuine belief in the value of disguised and indirect propaganda.

There was much less need for caution at home. The government's first domestic propaganda campaign, that conducted by the Parliamentary Recruiting Committee with the aim of raising a volunteer army, enjoyed the enormous advantage of having a clearly defined goal and a specific target area, namely young men over the age of eighteen years. Moreover, the PRC could afford to be less cautious because it operated as a parliamentary body rather than as an official propaganda organisation and, as such, was less sensitive to charges that its work was other than patriotic. Indeed, at first, the PRC, capitalising upon the wave of patriotic euphoria that greeted the outbreak of war, concerned itself with direct, immediate appeals. But as expectations of a short war receded and the flow of volunteers diminished, it became necessary for the PRC to launch a sustained campaign, punctuated by specific pleas. The result was to broaden the method of propaganda and of its target area. The appeal for volunteers became directed at the entire population so that those who could not fight would nonetheless participate in the struggle by imposing pressure upon those who were qualified to enlist.

The principal method of direct appeal adopted by the PRC was the mass rally. The sub-department formed especially for this purpose organised more than 800 meetings and issued over four million leaflets throughout the country in order to advertise the initial recruitment campaign.[6] Nominally under central control, the character of the early rallies tended to be determined by local conditions. Joint parliamentary committees were formed under the combined leadership of the three major political parties. Their knowledge of local constituencies and their experience of canvassing during election periods made such officials best suited to determine whether a meeting should take the form of a sedate lecture with lantern slides held in a village hall or of a mass rally held in a local football ground.[7] Great care, for example, had to be taken 'to avoid unduly trespassing in districts where workers were required on Government contracts'.[8] But, as the war progressed, a pattern of campaigning on a national basis was established although each local committee retained ultimate responsibility for maintaining the sustained campaign in its own area.

The specific recruiting drives were conducted in a fashion similar to election campaigns and lasted for anything from a fortnight to a month at a time. This generally involved mass meetings in the most heavily populated areas of the country, followed by local gatherings in wards, districts and parishes. Outdoor meetings often fell victim to the English weather but, during the spring of 1915, it was nonetheless decided to adopt a policy of 'aggressive open-air propaganda'.[9] This involved the organisation of impressive patriotic pageants. Military bands led processions through the streets to meetings with rousing speeches. It was then a case of striking while the iron was hot; medical officers and local magistrates stood by to receive the new recruits caught up in the heat of the moment as cheering crowds approvingly urged them forward. Every conceivable device was used to heighten the emotional experience of the occasion. Processions of illuminated tramcars or motorised military equipment were particularly popular in areas remote from the experience of war. But the main attraction of the processions was always the military band, the most famous of which, the Highland Pipe Band, was calculated to have visited some 350 towns, travelling over 9000 miles by train and a further 3500 miles on the march in the process.[10] The powerful combination of rousing music and speeches allied to the spectacle of an organised pageant with striking visual images produced an ideal atmosphere for recruitment purposes, provided that the audience was not allowed the opportunity to become bored. Yet the pitch of excitement generated by such occasions could only be maintained for relatively short periods of time. Great care was therefore taken to avoid saturation levels which might produce resistance. Moreover, there remained the need to conduct also a permanent 'information' campaign designed to keep the issue of manpower recruitment before the public in order to provide the necessary backcloth against which the shorter, more frenzied, emotive appeals could be performed.

The most popular form of constant direct appeal was the poster, already an established means of conveying information to the public by the time of the war.[11] War posters were displayed in every available place from shop windows to country gate posts, from taxi cabs to trams and railway carriages. In May 1916, the PRC's publications sub-department calculated that it had printed nearly 12.5 million copies of 164 different posters of various shapes and sizes and, in addition, 450,000 copies of 10 different types of display card.[12] The posters attempted to combine visual imagery with simple written messages although, in many cases, they were used merely to convey written statements. It proved necessary to translate some of them into Welsh and other minority languages. The posters were distributed in a variety of ways, often reproduced in newspapers and displayed in transport companies, banks, public libraries, political clubs and anywhere the public might gather in large numbers. They were also circulated throughout the Empire and frequently found their way into other parts of the world as much through private initiative as through official enterprise.

The volume of poster production remained high until the end of July 1915 when the government suddenly called a halt to their production.[13] Although this order was reversed in the following September, Lord Derby, appointed head of recruitment on 11 October 1915, believed that the poster had lost much of its initial impact as a means of recruitment propaganda. The PRC responded by producing more in the way of leaflets and pamphlets which had previously occupied a secondary position. By May 1916, more than 34 million leaflets and some 5.5 million pamphlets had been printed by its publications sub-department. Greater emphasis was also placed upon other forms of visual propaganda such as postcards and postage stamps.

The massive increase in the number of publications immediately aroused suspicions of paper wastage. Yet distribution was widespread through the PRC's householders' returns committee which sent material to every householder listed in the Parliamentary Register. The arrival by post of literature designed to promote recruitment reinforced the other forms of appeal while simultaneously playing upon individual conscience. One recipient maintained that he was unable to enlist but could make a contribution to the war effort in the form of selling eggs to the government at three shillings a dozen (15p). There was even a dwarf who volunteered to serve as regimental mascot.[14] And although the PRC was to lose its rationale with the introduction of conscription in February 1916, the flow of propaganda was maintained by various government departments which sought to keep the war and the continued need for personal sacrifice before the British public. Labour recruitment, the raising of war loans, campaigns for food economy and the need to advertise the terms of conscription all meant that the methods and organisation pioneered by the PRC continued to be employed in the service of the government. But it was only in 1917 that the National War Aims Committee was established to ensure that the public continued to believe that the sacrifices involved in the waging of a modern war were essential to national survival and ultimate victory.

The NWAC was effectively a continuation of the PRC. It did, however, operate in a very different context and directed its propaganda to a much wider audience with a view to combating pacifism. Similar methods of propaganda were employed to achieve this aim, particularly the use of public speakers who toured the country under the guidance of the local committees. Between August and October 1917, the NWAC arranged a staggering 3192 meetings.[15] Every speaker was required to submit a report to the NWAC's central executive which issued specific instructions and useful information to them as well as visual aids such as lantern slides.[16] PRC techniques were again repeated when, on the fourth anniversary of war's outbreak, a special message by the Prime Minister was distributed in sealed envelopes to managers of theatres, cinemas and concert halls with instructions for it to be read to their audiences at 9 pm. It was estimated that the message would be heard by some 2.5 million people attending 4000-5000 such places.[17] The NWAC also used posters, postcards and other forms of pictorial propaganda, albeit on a lesser scale than the PRC had done. Greater emphasis was placed upon the use of pamphlets, including material produced by Wellington House for foreign audiences.[18] The NWAC published its own series, including *Realities* and *Searchlights*, some of which were distributed abroad. When, in October 1917, W. H. Smith & Sons offered to distribute NWAC printed material through its national chain of newsagents and booksellers, the opportunity was seized upon.[19] Further distribution was achieved through the British press. In November 1917, for example, Robert Bell, the editor of the *Observer*, was asked to print an anti-pacifist article on the Independent Labour Party so that 'it may be republished in pamphlet form as coming from that paper'.[20]

The NWAC did make much greater use of film as a medium of official propaganda, benefiting from the experience of other organisations, most notably Wellington House. Five motorised cinema vans equipped with screen and projection equipment obtained from the Department of Information toured the country showing such propaganda films as *Our Navy* and *With the Royal Flying Corps in France*. Because many cinemas were still privately owned by individual entrepreneurs, official propaganda films were not always welcome as commercial propositions.[21] The cine-motor vans were designed to ensure a measure of public exhibition although locations chosen by them frequently led to problems of an unpredictable nature. On one occasion in October 1918, when a cine-motor representative operating in Lincolnshire persuaded the wife of a local village policeman to let him use the outside wall of her house for screening purposes, the resultant traffic congestion incurred the wrath of her returning husband.[22] However, the success of the experiment generally prompted the Food Commissioner's Office in Scotland to request the use of the vans[23] which, at the end of the war, were handed over to the National War Savings Committee.[24] Indeed, the methods pioneered by the NWAC during the war provided invaluable experience for the work of subsequent propagandists in, for example, the Conservative Party which began using travelling cine-motor vans in the mid 1920s.[25]

While employing the same organisational structure as the PRC, the NWAC used a wider variety of propaganda methods and a broader range of distribution channels. The 'campaign approach' to domestic propaganda survived as a primary method of maintaining popular involvement and commitment. Large public meetings, often organised in conjunction with other government departments such as the Ministry of Food, were conducted with the same sort of vigour as the early recruitment rallies had been, complete with brass bands. With wireless telegraphy and the cinematograph still in their infancy, the former depending chiefly upon messages transmitted in morse code and the latter still confined to silent images, direct verbal communication remained perhaps the most significant medium of mass propaganda on the home front throughout the war.

Because those organisations charged with domestic propaganda acted openly on behalf of the government, there was little point in them pretending to do otherwise. Such overt operation was denied those bodies initially made responsible for conducting propaganda in allied and neutral countries. The diplomatic repercussions which might result from official British interference in foreign opinion, combined with the desire to avoid imitating the counter-productive methods of German propagandists, led organisations such as Wellington House to operate beneath a cloak of intense secrecy out of necessity as much as by choice. Even so, Wellington House was able to develop an elaborate network of world-wide distribution channels involving a wide variety of propaganda techniques.

The principal method of propaganda employed by Wellington House during the first half of the war was the pamphlet. Of the two conferences convened by Masterman in September 1914 to discuss the initiation of the propaganda campaign abroad, the first had consisted of well-known writers who were invited not solely for consultation purposes but also as potential pamphleteers. It was Masterman's intention that official pamphlets would be of the highest literary quality, academic in tone and scholarly in content, rather than simple propagandist diatribes. Such an approach derived largely from the nature of the audience to be reached. Prominent foreigners in positions of influence would, it was assumed, prove more receptive to the views of respected British authors such as John Buchan (*The Battle of the Somme*, 1916), Sir Arthur Conan Doyle (*To Arms*, 1914) and Sir Gilbert Parker (*Is England Apathetic?* 1915) than they would to those of official propagandists known to be working for the British government. Every attempt was made therefore to disguise the official nature of the pamphlets: they appeared to be written by private individuals of international repute; they were printed by private publishing houses bearing no overt indication of their origin; and they were distributed through private channels such as steamship companies which patriotically bore the costs themselves. Moreover, conscious that the brash German methods sought to impose an opinion, Masterman expected Wellington House pamphlets to be of a highly factual nature with the British case only very subtly argued. The reader was to be allowed to make up his own mind on the issues under discussion. He could thereby feel secure in the view that he had reached his own conclusions on the basis of evidence presented objectively to him by a fellow intellectual rather than having swallowed official propaganda thrust upon him by an agent of a foreign government. In order to further ease this process, a small charge was usually made for the pamphlets; people do not like to think they would buy propaganda.

Masterman's faith in this form of propaganda was reflected in the first report on the work conducted by Wellington House. The report, which was issued to the Cabinet in June 1915, revealed that some two and a half million copies of books, pamphlets and other forms of literary propaganda had been circulated in seventeen different languages since the previous September.[26] By the time of the second report in February 1916, the figure had risen to seven million copies.[27] In 1914, 45 publications had been issued, 132 in 1915, 202 in 1916 and 469 in 1917.[28] Wastage of paper was avoided by not using fly-sheets.[29] Other forms of written propaganda consisted of official publications such as the Bryce Report on German atrocities in Belgium, official white papers, ministerial speeches, messages from the King and various documentary publications relating to the origins of the war produced by most of the belligerent governments.

Simply to produce this material, however, was not enough. It was equally important to ensure that efficient distribution took place both on a large scale and on a wide front so that it could be read in as many places as possible. Methods of distribution varied considerably. In order to reach the more remote parts of the globe, use was made of the steamship companies and their agencies which dealt with leading businessmen in each target country. For example, Wellington House was able to disseminate material in the hinterlands of South America through the agents of the Royal Mail Steam Packet Company and the Pacific Steam Navigation Company. Both North and South America were supplied with material through the Cunard and White Star Shipping Lines. Pamphlets were sent to India and Australia through the Peninsular and Oriental Line, to Canada through the Canadian Pacific, and to South America by the Union Castle Line. Europe was supplied in the same way. Although pamphlets were shipped in bulk to their initial destinations, it was essential to avoid bombardment on arrival. They were therefore distributed in small numbers by foreign agents to voluntary patriotic organisations and Anglophile societies, Overseas Clubs and patriotic leagues. In China, distribution took place through the Religious Tract Society and in the Balkans through insurance companies. Voluntary organisations in England also helped to distribute pamphlets through their own private mailing lists in accordance with the general principle adopted by Wellington House that most material should be sent out on a person-to-person basis. This would avoid the flooding methods adopted by German propagandists and enhance the cultivation of personal contacts. The German propaganda network was also infiltrated. The War Office Postal Censorship department intercepted German literature, replaced it with pro-British material and sent it on its way.[30]

The assistance of the Foreign Office also proved invaluable. Diplomatic and consular representatives serving overseas frequently acted as distribution agents by ensuring that Wellington House pamphlets were placed in libraries, station waiting rooms, barber shops and doctors' surgeries where they might be picked up and read by an individual with a little extra time to spare. Every effort was made to co-ordinate the work of the various distribution agencies in order to avoid duplication. By utilising the distribution networks of voluntary organisations and the shipping companies, Wellington House was able to maintain strict secrecy for its operations. Because there was no indication that the material had originated from official sources or that it was written by people connected with the British government, this type of disguised official campaign could be described as 'black' propaganda, although this epithet did not enter common usage until many years later.

Wellington House worked in close conjunction with the publishing houses. Masterman received several requests from foreign libraries and booksellers to increase the supply of British books, not necessarily as a form of direct political propaganda but to serve a broad cultural purpose. Text books in the sciences and mathematics and works of English literature could demonstrate the richness of British civilisation and thus provide a cultural backdrop against which other forms of propaganda could profitably flourish. The French and German governments had long since recognised the value of 'cultural propaganda'. During the 1880s, they had established, respectively, the Alliance Française and the Verein für das Deutschtum im Ausland for the dissemination abroad of their national cultural achievements to serve commercial and political ends.[31] But it was not until 1917 that this particular type of activity was seriously considered by the British government. In August of that year, the Department of Information appointed a committee under the chairmanship of Sir Henry Newbolt to investigate the circulation of British books and periodicals abroad. Newbolt was President of the Royal Society of Literature, a man of letters and a devout patriot. His committee discovered that existing distribution methods were wholly inadequate to meet the demands abroad for British literature. The committee noted that:

this inadequacy has seriously affected the foreign appreciation of British thought, ideals and efficiency; and that the results of this lack of appreciation have operated in many directions to the detriment alike of British policy and of British trade.[32]

This situation was partly due to the refusal of the Post Office in 1911 to accept subscriptions from foreign readers for British newspapers and periodicals, a decision which had resulted in the establishment of British distribution houses not in London but in Liège and Cologne. Thus, 'even before the beginning of the war, the whole machinery was in the hands of the enemy'.[33] The Newbolt committee also argued that British bookselling methods were old-fashioned and lagged behind those of the Germans in so far as advance sales techniques such as 'sale-or-return' facilities and permanent display rooms were concerned. Nor was there a British book trade clearing house comparable to the German organisation in Leipzig.

Wellington House was fully aware of these deficiencies but had not been able to find an adequate solution. Ernest Gowers had approached the managing director of Williams and Norgate with a scheme which would have provided for a more efficient system of book distribution, but Williams had wanted more than the £1000 subsidy offered by the Treasury.[34] Again, in May 1916, when the British ambassador in Rome had proposed the establishment of a central book distribution depot in Milan to disseminate literature throughout Italy, the Treasury proved reluctant to finance the venture entirely.[35] Yet Wellington House retained its faith in pamphlets and books, a reflection of its commitment to intellectual propaganda. This approach was, however, based more upon assumptions concerning its impact rather than the product of scientific public opinion analysis. Indeed, there appears to have been very little consideration of the actual effectiveness of the pamphlets, how widely they were being read or which sections of the population they were ultimately reaching. Masterman accepted from the outset that 'it is in the nature of the case that we cannot be rewarded to any great extent by realising definite and overt results'.[36] No effective means of measuring the impact of propaganda was developed by Wellington House during the war. Instead, judgements concerning the efficiency of literary propaganda were based on individual perceptions and observations. Masterman was therefore careful to avoid making dogmatic claims and he generally preferred to defer to the judgement of agents serving 'on the spot'. In July and August 1915, for example, he accepted the advice of George Buchanan, the British ambassador in Petrograd, that British propaganda in Russia would more profitably benefit from the insertion of articles in the press than from the distribution of pamphlets, which the ambassador considered expensive and unpopular,[37] although a year later certain officials and journalists argued the contrary.[38]

At first, Wellington House had been reluctant to use the press as an instrument of propaganda abroad, not only because the Foreign Office News Department and the Neutral Press Committee were devoting their attention to this particular area, but also because it was considered to be a more open form of propaganda. It would undermine the policy of secrecy which was fundamental to the work of Wellington House, a policy deliberately conceived as an alternative to the explicit German methods. As Masterman argued in May 1915:

German attempts to influence Italian opinion only caused the greatest irritation, and the invitation extended to a number of Italian journalists to visit the German General Headquarters only called forth the bitterest sarcasm from the more dignified members of the Italian press.[39]

Wellington House did, in fact, place several articles in the foreign press during the early stage of the war. G. K. Chesterton's 'Letters to an Old Garibaldian' were published in the leading Italian newspaper *Il Secolo* but, in 1915, it was decided 'practically to abandon the attempt to work in this way, and to fall back upon the use of pamphlets'.[40] This proved to be only a temporary decision for it was soon realised that discreet and cautious methods could be employed by the propagandists in their dealings with many foreign journalists in London, particularly with those sympathetic to the allied cause. Masterman accepted Buchanan's advice in Russia and in China that of Sir James Jordan, the British ambassador in Peking, who advocated greater use of the local press because, as one of his officials minuted, 'every Chinaman from the highest to the beggar in rags reads the press'.[41] If Masterman was prepared to accept such advice from officials serving in countries of high illiteracy, he was even more prepared to exploit the press as a medium of British official propaganda in more advanced countries. Gradually, therefore, Wellington House fell in line with the Foreign Office on this matter while retaining its faith in pamphlets.

Journalists were not the only foreigners to receive special attention from British propagandists as part of this approach—broadly described as personal propaganda. Various public figures from the United States and Europe, including D'Annunzio, Primo da Rivera and representatives of the Russian Duma, were invited to Britain before being taken to the western front. In Britain, a typical programme included 'visits to the Clyde, munitions works, WAAC's or something similar, Chester (the type both of oldtime beauty and of liquor control), interviews with Cabinet ministers, and finally a visit to the Fleet or the Army in France'.[42] The visit of the Russian deputies in May 1916 was no exception.[43] Such exercises provided an ideal opportunity for personal propaganda amongst precisely the sort of people Wellington House wished to impress. But they could go drastically wrong. In April 1916, for example, a special guided tour was arranged for two Spanish journalists whose behaviour suggested that they were not prepared to take the whole business seriously. The visitors were reported to be 'dirty and ill-mannered', often choosing to urinate 'in any place that suited them'. One of them donned a gas-mask and conducted himself in a frivolous manner throughout the tour while the other appeared to be more interested in collecting souvenirs, even at one point delaying the entire party while he insisted upon carving his name in the bark of the nearest available tree.[44] But, in the main, the official visits were conducted in a dignified and well-ordered manner. The Cabinet considered that they even provided 'the very best education for propagandists in this country'.[45] Their success was considered to be such that, in 1917, the Department of Information decided to finance four châteaux for the benefit of foreign journalists and other visitors who wished to report on conditions at the front for themselves. This initiative was continued by the Ministry of Information's Overseas Press Centre during 1918. In organising and conducting visits, the Ministry 'aimed to convince the visitors that the Allies were going to win, to bring home to them the scope of the British effort in terms of men, money and productions, to impress on them the potentialities of the Anglo-Saxon race, and, in the case of visitors coming from the Dominions, to inculcate respect for the Crown and to show that the monarchy unites the Empire as no new-fashioned expedient could'.[46] Even the thorny problem of Ireland was tackled. A party of Australian editors was sent to Dublin by the Ministry. 'Most of these gentlemen were Home Rulers with tolerant feelings towards Sinn Fein'.[47] In Dublin, they met various political leaders, including Sinn Feiners, who:

when asked to state their aims, explained that they did not want Home Rule; they wanted a separate State, with an Army and Navy of its own, allied to Germany. Whereupon the Australian editors' tolerant attitude towards Sinn Fein came to a conclusive end.[48]

Before 1917, however, American correspondents were singled out for the most preferential treatment. Indeed, the gradual improvement in facilities for journalists working in Britain as the war unfolded was primarily motivated through a consideration of British propaganda in the United States. Their extension to correspondents from allied countries during the winter of 1915-16 was a reflection of the growing need to advertise the British point of view beyond merely neutral countries.

If one method of ensuring publicity for the British case was the cultivation of relations with foreign journalists in London, another was the establishment of press bureaux in countries where British news was in short supply. The Germans has already demonstrated the effectiveness of such bodies, most notably in Sweden where they virtually monopolised the supply of information favourable to the Central Powers through the Björnson Bureau and the Svenska Telegram Bureau. In 1915, the Allies began to challenge this monopoly. A naturalised American, S. Björkmann, was appointed British press representative in Sweden and he, together with the

British ambassador in Stockholm, Esmé Howard, met with the French ambassador to discuss the establishment of a British press bureau. It was agreed to make Björkmann a Reuters correspondent in order to disguise his connection with the British government and to transfer the existing Reuters contract with the Svenska Bureau to a newly created agency, the Stockholm Telgrambyra Bureau.[49] A similar proposal made by the British ambassador in Switzerland, Grant Duff, following discussions with his French and Italian opposite numbers, resulted in the foundation of a bureau in Basle under the direction of the Swiss journalist, Berlinger.[50] A second bureau was established in Zurich in September 1917 to supply news to the German-speaking population of Switzerland and, in the following month, a third was opened in Geneva to deal with the French-speaking area.[51]

Mounting criticism in allied countries that Britain was not pulling her weight sufficiently in the combined war effort soon led to the repetition of these experiments in France, Russia and Italy. In France, the task was greatly eased once the French government had rationalised its own propaganda organisation in October 1915 following an initiative by Aristide Briand, the newly appointed French Premier.[52] A Maison de la Presse was established with Phillipe Berthelot as its head. Informal contacts with British propagandists were established almost immediately. Then, in April 1916, Gerald Gould, the head of the French section at Wellington House, and Colonel H. A. L. Fisher visited Paris 'to arrange for co-operation, both as regards propaganda in France itself and also as regards propaganda in other countries'.[53] Arrangements were made for the exchange of address lists and propaganda material, including pamphlets and photographs, and for co-operation in placing articles in the British and French press. The British were thus able to draw upon the greater experience of the French government in dealing with the press due to the existence of a Bureau de la Presse at the Quai d'Orsay for nearly twenty years before the war.

Captain Millet, the head of the Section Anglaise in the Maison de la Presse, was made responsible for the placing of British articles in French newspapers, including Parisian dailies and provincial publications. In July 1916, he reported that:

Le Foreign Office paraît décidé à me laisser l'entière direction de la Propagande Anglaise en France. Il va mettre incessamment à ma disposition un nouveau collaborateur anglais, dont les émoluments seront à sa charge et qui m'aidera pour toute cette partie de mon service.[54]

The new English assistant, Miss Stedman, travelled to Paris at the end of August to take up her post as liaison officer between Wellington House and the Maison de la Presse, a post she was to hold until June 1917 when further reorganisation of the French propaganda apparatus rendered her position untenable.[55] In the meantime, however, the Foreign Office saw no need to establish its own press bureau in Paris, a proposal frequently voiced in official circles. It agreed with the British ambassador, Lord Bertie, that because the French changed their governments so frequently, major policy decisions might easily be reversed from one administration to the next.[56] Besides, the French press was prone to corruption and bribery; it was a relatively easy task to insert pro-British articles in the majority of newspapers. So long as the Maison de la Presse was prepared to conduct this work on behalf of the British, there was little point in establishing a press office on Parisian soil. But in June 1917, following the loss of Miss Stedman in the wake of reorganisation of both the British and the French propaganda organisations, it was finally decided to appoint a press committee in Paris comprising leading British journalists in France: Adam of *The Times*; Jerrold of *The Daily Telegraph*; and Kerr Bruce of Reuters. This body not only advised the newly created Department of Information on the requirements of British propaganda in France at a time when mistrust of Britain was increasing, but also attempted to place sympathetic articles in the French press through personal contacts with leading journalists and editors. It later served as an advisory committee to a new French propaganda bureau established in Paris during October 1917.[57]

If the British were slow to establish a press office in Paris, they were less hesitant with that other important allied partner, Russia. Early in 1916 a British press bureau was established in Moscow under the joint supervision of Robert Bruce Lockhart and Michael Lykiadopolous. Instead of issuing general press communiqués, however, a policy was adopted whereby each newspaper received its own special news bulletin, even in towns which enjoyed more than one journal. These bulletins were approximately 180-200 words in length; longer articles were rare because of the paper shortage.[58] A similar development took place in Italy in July 1917. The agent in charge of the new propaganda office in Rome, Thorold, regarded press work as his priority concern. These were typical examples of the Foreign Office's general policy of establishing local press bureaux wherever possible in allied and neutral countries. The United States was almost the only exception to this general rule.

Even in countries where press bureaux did exist, the Foreign Office remained sensitive to the charge that it was attempting to manipulate the foreign press, a sensitivity acquired chiefly through its dealings with the American press since the start of the war. In 1916, therefore, when it decided to increase its press propaganda, the Foreign Office generally avoided direct control over foreign newspapers or the provision of direct subsidies. A proposal to launch a British newspaper in Switzerland was rejected on the grounds that it would be too obvious a method of British propaganda.[59] A direct link between a foreign newspaper and the British government would merely cast doubts upon the credibility of the views expressed in that newspaper, thereby defeating the object of the entire exercise. Accordingly, when unofficial French sources indicated in July 1916 that it might be possible for the British government to obtain control of *Le Petit Journal* and possibly even *Le Temps*, the Foreign Office rejected the idea out of hand.[60] From Italy, ambassador Rodd also expressed doubts concerning the wisdom of direct official British propaganda in the press. Although it was difficult enough to place British articles in Italian newspapers, he argued, this was caused more by the lack of available space than to any residual ill-will on the part of Italian editors. Nevertheless, he did consider that it would be possible to place pro-British articles written by respected Italians which would anyway prove more effective than obvious press propaganda emanating from offical British sources.[61]

On several occasions, however, the Foreign Office did depart from its general practice of avoiding direct control over foreign newspapers. In April 1916, a new Japanese magazine was proposed to provide coverage of topical issues with English translations facing the pages written in Japanese.[62] Sir Cunningham Greene, the British ambassador in Tokyo, was opposed to the idea of a direct British subsidy by the government for the project but suggested that some other means should be found to finance it in the name of Anglo-Japanese and inter-allied relations. The Foreign Office approached S. V. Sale, a businessman with substantial Far Eastern interests, with the suggestion that he might provide the necessary funds in return for certain tax concessions. The Inland Revenue not unnaturally disapproved of such preferential treatment and proposed instead that this particular project might be financed out of Secret Service funds. Eventually, following lengthy and complex negotiations, the Anglo-Japanese review *Shin Toyo* ('The New East') was founded in February 1917 financed jointly by the Foreign Office and by Mr Sale.[63] The venture did not prove to be a success. The editor, Robertson Scott, was highly unpopular with both the British community in Japan and the local propaganda committee in Tokyo which were critical of the quality of the translations. Despite the efforts of a specially appointed committee in London to salvage the operation, *Shin Toyo* was declared bankrupt in July 1918 following the refusal of the Foreign Office and Mr Sale to provide it with any further funds.

Elsewhere, the distribution of British propaganda to foreign newspapers was determined by the particular circumstances prevailing in the country concerned. In South America, for example, the Foreign Office confined itself to the payment of subsidies in its efforts to promote and maintain pro-British sympathy. The amounts involved were generally quite small and hidden, usually not more than £20 a month as payment for advertising space.[64] In Greece, however, the payments were more substantial. Allied support for Venizelos in his struggle against the King suffered a major blow at the end of 1916 when the Greek Prime Minister was removed from office during the Salonika landings. Sir Francis Elliot, the British ambassador in Athens, proposed that a pro-allied Greek newspaper currently in financial difficulties should be given British support, and the Foreign Office agreed to provide a monthly subsidy of £500. In March 1917, Elliot further proposed that the Venizelist press be supplied with paper free of charge. Subsidies were also supplied to a number of friendly Greek newspapers, including *Patris*, *Estia*, *Ethnos*, *Ethniki*, *Astir* and *Nea Hellas*. The method of payment varied and was deliberately irregular 'to facilitate suspension of payments at any time and to prevent any paper acquiring a feeling of permanent dependence' upon British support.[65] Direct payment by members of the British legation was avoided, the funds appearing to come from a (non-existent) group of patriotic Greek exiles living in Britain. Provincial newspapers were paid only for advertising space and all Venizelist papers without correspondents in Athens were supplied free of charge with daily information by telegram from the capital, a service which cost the British embassy the sizeable sum of £650 per month.

Local conditions also dictated the nature of British press propaganda in Holland where a severe penal code empowered the Dutch authorities to impose heavy penalties for any act which might endanger the country's neutrality. In 1917, the editor of the *Telegraaf* was imprisoned for three months for having stated 'that the war had to be made by "the scoundrels of the Centre of Europe"'.[66] Mindful of these laws, the Foreign Office was careful to avoid anything which might be construed as official British propaganda. Indeed, all that the Foreign Office was able to do in Holland was to ensure that the Dutch press was supplied with a steady stream of reliable British news. Even so, news constituted an essential ingredient of the British propaganda campaign. It was carefully selected and presented in such a way as to imply a pre-determined line. Moreover, in an attempt to disguise the official nature of the information, news was supplied to the Dutch press chiefly through Reuters which provided the British government with an effective 'cover' in the distribution of official news designed, through a process of careful selection and omission, to serve a propagandist purpose. Some twenty-seven Dutch newspapers, national and provincial, were supplied by Reuters, an exercise which helped to offset the considerable influence wielded by the state-subsidised German news agency, the Wolff Bureau, in the Netherlands. At the end of 1917, the *Daily News* correspondent in Holland, George Steward, purchased the entire issue shares of the NVAW Segvoers Lutgeuers Maatschappij which held the concession for running newspaper kiosks in The Hague and Scheveningen. Steward had managed to pip the Germans to the post in this deal involving 17 kiosks, with a further nine under consideration, which could be used as distribution centres for pro-British newspapers and other propaganda material.[67]

The Reuters services were supplemented by the transmission of Foreign Office telegrams by cables and wireless to overseas representatives for distribution to the local press. During the first eighteen months of the war, the Neutral Press Committee was also involved in this type of work. George Mair's organisation was further responsible for arranging news exchanges between various leading European and British newspapers. Arrangements were made for *The Times* to exchange news with the *Novoye Vremya* of Petrograd; *The Morning Post* transmitted news bulletins to Rumania and Greece and also exchanged an abridged version of these with the

National Tidende of Copenhagen; *The Daily Telegraph* had a similar arrangement with another Danish newspaper, *Vortland*; *The Daily Chronicle* frequently exchanged news with the *Corriere d'Italia*.[68] Such arrangements provide yet another example of the British government's determination to ensure that a steady stream of pro-British news was supplied to foreign countries, news which did not ostensibly originate from official British sources but which was in fact often supplied to Fleet Street by Whitehall departments and which was subject to wartime censorship regulations. Untrustworthy newspapers were not encouraged to arrange similar news exchanges; indeed, they were frequently prevented from leaving the country. In this way, the British press became a part of the British government's propaganda campaign overseas in a manner no less significant, if less obvious, than on the home front.

The principle of disguise was maintained by Mair in his wireless news service. A special arrangement was made with the Marconi company to transmit news messages on behalf of the government from its station at Poldhu. In Spain and the Canary Islands, Marconi arranged for its agents to receive, translate and distribute the wireless messages to the local press on a regular basis. The efficacy of wireless propaganda was, however, severely limited by technological restrictions. In Bucharest, for example, reception was unreliable due to meteorological and technical factors[69] and in Greece and Norway government regulations concerning foreign wireless transmission prevented their effective distribution. Because it was still only possible to transmit messages mainly in morse code over relatively short distances, subject always to weather and official restrictions, news transmitted by wireless played a minor role in Britain's wartime propaganda campaign in comparison to other forms of telegraphic distribution, particularly cables. To ensure effective distribution of the cabled messages, special agencies were established abroad such as the English Telegraphy Agency in Bucharest and others at Amsterdam, Basle, Bilbao, Cairo and Valencia. The wireless messages were intended for newspapers which could not afford to subscribe to the normal commercial Reuters service or those which did not enjoy access to other sources of British news. They were, nonetheless, indicative of the readiness of British propagandists to employ every available means of disseminating favourable news relating to Britain's role in the war.

A further indication of this imaginative approach was in the production of illustrated magazines modelled on the lines of the *Illustrated London News* which did, in fact, provide Wellington House with its printing facilities to produce the pictorial propaganda. If the pamphlets were directed towards an intellectual audience, the illustrated magazines were designed for popular consumption. By February 1916, Wellington House was producing four such publications: *America Latina*, at first produced monthly and, from 1916, fortnightly and distributed by diplomatic and consular officials serving in South America and Spain; *O Espelho*, produced fortnightly in Portuguese, 15,000 copies of which were sent to Brazil; *Hesperia*, published weekly in Greek and sent to more than 15,000 addresses; and *Al Hakikat*, published fortnightly with translations in Arabic, Persian and Hindustani.[70] By September 1916, further editions had been launched. A new venture, *War Pictorial*, was published monthly with commentaries in English, French, Dutch, Spanish, Portuguese, Italian, Russian, Greek, Danish, Swedish and German. *Al Hakikat* introduced translations in Turkish. A new magazine, *Cheng Pao*, was launched for fortnightly distribution in China and a Japanese edition, *Senji Gaho*, was in preparation.[71] The *Warta Yang Tulus* was published in Malay, *Satya Vani* in Bengali, Hindi, Gujerati and Tamil, and *Jangi Akhbar* in Hindi and Urdu for the united provinces of India, and in Gurumkhi for the Sikhs.

The quality of these magazines varied considerably and was often the subject of considerable debate. *America Latina*, for example, was criticised for the poor quality of its translations by Professor Fitzmaurice Kelly of Liverpool University, although the Reader in Spanish at Oxford, Senõr de Arteaga, rushed to their defence.[72] In August 1916, the debate was even raised to the level of parliamentary discussion when the magazine was used as a springboard for criticism concerning the cost of British propaganda.[73] *Al Hakikat* was also attacked for the poor quality of its translated captions. In the Turkish editions, Lord Kitchener had been described as a private soldier; the Aga Khan, instead of being referred to as a sincere friend of Britain, was said to have been married to her; the firing of a torpedo had been described as the 'divorce of a shell'.[74] But despite such errors, the quality and the quantity of the illustrated magazines increased steadily as the war went on. In September 1916, 50,000 copies of *Cheng Pao* were being distributed in China; by November 1917, the figure had risen to 108,000. Every fortnight, 75,000 copies of *Al Hakikat* were distributed throughout the Arab world. By November 1917, the circulation of *War Pictorial* had reached an astonishing 750,000 copies each month. Moreover, the quality of the magazines received widespread praise from overseas agents although when *The Daily Telegraph* congratulated the government on the publication of *Al Hakikat* and *Cheng Pao* in August 1916, there was considerable embarrassment at the Foreign Office which was keen to maintain the secrecy of the connection between the government and the magazines.[75]

Despite the need for large government subsidies deriving from the high production costs and the low charges to the distributors, or even free distribution in some cases, the illustrated magazines were considered to be an excellent and worthwhile medium of propaganda abroad. Because they concentrated upon the visual image rather than the written word, they were able to overcome the problems of dealing with illiterate audiences in backward countries where newspaper propaganda and pamphlets were effective only among the educated minorities. In India, for example, where the Germans were constantly attempting to encourage Indian nationalism,[76] the visual medium was of particular importance. The photographs used in the magazines were also distributed individually. The Press Bureau had campaigned successfully for the release of official photographs to the press and, in 1915, an official photographer had been despatched to the western front. Continued pressure on the Service Departments gradually led to an increased use of photographic propaganda and, in May 1916, a special pictorial propaganda section was established at Wellington House under the direction of Ivor Nicholson. By the following September, over 4000 photographs had been distributed to the foreign press and to other publications. Wellington House was supplied with a regular stream of high-quality prints both by the official photographers at the front and by the Association of Photographic Press Agencies in London.

Illustrated propaganda was by no means confined to photographs. Lantern slides, picture postcards, cigarette cards and, of course, posters were all produced by Nicholson's department at Wellington House, as well as maps and diagrams, pictures, cartoons and drawings.[77] At Easter 1916, 100,000 postcards were despatched to Russia with greetings messages. Cigarette cards were distributed in China and Japan through arrangements made with the tobacco companies. Lantern slides were provided to speakers who had been granted Foreign Office permission to conduct propaganda tours. As a late-comer to this expanding field, however, Wellington House did encounter some unexpected problems. The Press Bureau had established a measure of control over photographic propaganda through its dealings with the British press and through its censorship functions, but the War Office retained sole authority to dispose of the rights of any photographs taken at the front. Both departments discovered that they could actually sell the rights for commercial gain. The Press Bureau, for example, had negotiated an arrangement with the tobacco companies to distribute 'cigarette stiffeners' and when Wellington House began to consider this particular form of propaganda in accordance with its preference for distributing material through intermediary and unofficial channels, it was informed:

No arrangements to deal with Official Photographs for commercial purposes can be made without the consent of the Press Bureau, and we have already sold certain exclusive rights regarding official pictures taken on the Western Front for large sums, and we intend at the proper time to dispose of such rights as remain.[78]

Those rights had been sold to the *Daily Mail*. Masterman was therefore obliged to seek that newspaper's permission to distribute 'cigarette stiffeners' of official photographs. He was originally told to limit distribution to the Dutch East Indies and to China but when Masterman protested, the *Daily Mail* agreed to allow Wellington House to operate anywhere in the world except in Britain and North America. Similarly, when Wellington House wanted to arrange an exhibition of official photographs in Paris, Masterman again had to seek the permission of the *Daily Mail*. Wellington House had to pay a royalty not only to that newspaper but also to the Press Bureau. Masterman asked the Press Bureau to waive its royalty but in order to secure the permission of the *Daily Mail* he had to promise that any photographs supplied to Wellington House for propaganda purposes would be distributed free and would not be used in the United Kingdom. Although Sir Edward Cook blamed the confusion which resulted from the discovery that propaganda could be lucrative on the number of government departments involved, good propaganda was becoming good business too.

This type of commercial enterprise was not repeated in the use of war paintings. The first 'official war artist' to be allowed at the front was Muirhead Bone, the distinguished painter. In May 1916, Bone had met with A. S. Watt, the literary adviser to Wellington House, who then informed his masters of Bone's impending enlistment in the army and proposed that his talents be put to good use by the propagandists instead. Both Masterman and Gowers proved receptive to the idea. They approached the War Office and it was agreed that Bone would be exempted from military service and granted permission to travel freely at the front making sketches. In December 1916, Masterman invited Bone to paint a series of portraits of Britain's leading military and naval figures. Bone, however, was not confident of his abilities as a portrait artist and suggested that his brother-in-law, Francis Dodd, should be approached instead. Dodd accepted the commission and the result was a series of paintings on 'Generals of the British Army' and another on 'Admirals of the British Navy'. The portraits were widely reproduced in photographic form and they were also used as covers for the *War Pictorial.*

The success of Muirhead Bone and Francis Dodd led to an increase in the number of war artists, including such distinguished figures as Sir John Lavery, Sir William Orpen,[79] C. R. W. Nevison, Eric Kennington, Paul Nash and many others. By the end of the war, some 90 artists had been employed at one time or another and their work was exhibited widely at home and abroad. Lord Beaverbrook shared Masterman's enthusiasm for this particular form of propaganda. As Canadian War Records Officer earlier in the war, he had encouraged Canadian artists to record their impressions on canvas for the Canadian War Memorial which was then being designed as a permanent record of the Canadian contribution to the war effort. When he became Minister of Information in February 1918, Beaverbrook was keen to see that the work of the British war artists was preserved for posterity in what was to become the Imperial War Museum.

The recognition of film as an important medium of official British propaganda also increased as the war progressed. The Foreign Office had recognised its potential, as was so often the case, largely in response to the efforts of the German propagandists. In January 1915, Sir George Barclay, the British ambassador in Bucharest, warned that the Germans were distributing propaganda films in Rumania, one of which demonstrated the British use of dum-dum bullets. As Barclay argued in a later report, 'it is essential to use the cinematograph for propaganda and especially in countries like

Rumania where the number of people who can read and write is very small'.[80] By 1917, it was being claimed that 'the motion picture is the most powerful agent for publicity now in existence'[81] and even a newspaperman of no less significance than Lord Northcliffe stated: 'I hate to confess it, but the motion picture is doing more for the Allied cause than any other means of thought transmission'.[82]

Perhaps Northcliffe was thinking more in terms of films made in the United States because, although Wellington House was quick to recognise the potential for propagandist purposes of what was universally regarded as an entertainment medium, it was not able to actually achieve much in this area during the first half of the war. According to Gowers, Wellington House had proposed to make great use of film propaganda shortly after its creation but the War Office and the Admiralty, in keeping with their early preoccupation with secrecy, had refused to provide the necessary facilities.[83] The reluctance of the Service Departments to permit the making of propaganda films was also encountered by J. Brooke Wilkinson, the Secretary of the British Board of Film Censors and managing director of the Topical Film Company. At a general meeting of film-makers held in March 1915 to discuss the filming of the Football Association Cup Final, Brooke Wilkinson had raised the subject of war films only to discover that hitherto 'the British War Office had flatly refused to grant permission for them to be taken on the western front'.[84]

In fact, the potential of film as propaganda had been recognised by the War Office long before the war. It had even figured in the recruitment campaign. But the War Office had not yet sorted its priorities out as far as film propaganda was concerned. Although it had initially allowed cameramen to accompany the British Expeditionary Force to France, all permits had been cancelled following the British retreat. It was more concerned with the security problems posed by the camera's apparently indiscriminating eye. Even a single frame of a film that had been thoroughly censored might contain something of value to the enemy, whether it contained ammunition markings or a signpost. The War Office therefore preferred films which were features or reconstructions to the actuality footage contained in newsreels. But it always had to balance the possible security aspects of film against its potential value as propaganda. Until 1915, the former invariably outweighed the latter.

In the meantime, the French and German governments had

continued to allow filming to take place. As a result of consistent pressure from Brooke Wilkinson and other leading representatives of the British film industry, the War Office finally relented at a conference held in May 1915. The Film Manufacturer's Association formed a committee to negotiate the appropriate arrangements with the War Office. In July, it was agreed to appoint two operators working under the aegis of the Army Council who would be responsible for the production of two categories of war film: those meant for immediate exhibition and those designed chiefly as historical records. An additional proposal made by Charles Urban of the Kineto Company to use a two-colour film-making process, already widely employed, was rejected by the War Office on the somewhat dubious grounds that there was little evidence of its popular appeal. Final agreement was reached in October 1915. The British film industry agreed to supply the necessary equipment and expertise while running costs and transportation would be provided by the War Office. All negatives and prints, as well as copyright, were to rest with the government. The film-makers were permitted to distribute films only for exhibition in the British Empire, excluding the sensitive areas of India and Egypt. They were to be sold at the rate of $4\frac{1}{2}d$. (2p) per foot, of which the War Office would receive $1d$. ($\frac{1}{2}$p) in royalties, an arrangement which enabled the War Office to donate some of the profits to selected war charities. The right to purchase and distribute films overseas was also retained by the War Office. Two operators were sent to the front, E. C. Tong of Imperial Pictures and G. H. Malins of Gaumont-British, and their footage was sent to London for developing, printing and editing prior to submission to GHQ for censorship. The films were then usually issued in series, one subject being dealt with each week.[85]

In July 1916, at the instigation of Lord Beaverbrook (then Sir Max Aitken), the Canadian government made a similar arrangement. The success of both ventures was considered to be such that the War Office decided to run the entire business of official film propaganda itself. In October 1916, the War Office Cinematograph Committee was formed under Beaverbrook's chairmanship to supervise the arrangements made between the British film industry and the British and Canadian governments. All existing contracts were cancelled in the following month, the War Office having received more than £12,000 in royalties from the previous arrangements. In May 1917, the War Office assumed complete control over the production and distribution of all films taken at the front and purchased a majority of shares (14,782) in the Topical Film Company.[86] It then began to produce its own newsreel, the *War Office Topical News*. The Cinematograph Committee consisted of Beaverbrook, Sir Reginald Brade from the War Office, Sir Graham Greene from the Admiralty and Sir William Jury, the owner of the Imperial Pictures film company. The committee worked in close consultation with the Department of Information in 1917, although it was the Department's policy to produce as few films as possible itself. It preferred to secure the production of propaganda films of a non-military and non-naval character through ordinary commercial channels. In other words, the Department of Information acted largely as a distributing agent for these unofficial films.[87] The Cinematograph Committee continued this policy even after it was absorbed into the Ministry of Information in June 1918 where it functioned as the Cinema Propaganda Department with Jury as its head. The War Office sold its shares in the Topical Film Company in February 1918 in order to protect the commercial appearance of the films.

The change of heart which took place at the War Office during 1915 enabled Wellington House to pursue its plans in so far as film propaganda was concerned. In August 1915, Masterman formed his own Cinema Committee which comprised Brooke Wilkinson, Jury, Charles Urban and T. A. Welsh of Gaumont-British. Its proceedings were kept secret and it dealt almost entirely with film propaganda in allied and neutral countries, the War Office having transferred the rights for those areas to Wellington House. Brooke Wilkinson wrote of this committee's work: 'If it could be described in detail, it would constitute an epic unparalleled in the history of the [British film] industry'.[88] Unfortunately, such a record has not survived. It is known that the committee's first and most famous project involved the making of a film about the armed forces and the British military effort. By November 1915, sufficient footage had been made available by the War Office to produce the compilation film, *Britain Prepared*, which opened on 29 December 1915 at the Empire Theatre in London's Leicester Square. A select audience of influential figures was invited to the première. Music was specially written for the occasion and the film was introduced by Balfour, then First Lord of the Admiralty. The considerable publicity afforded to this event was but the prelude to world-wide distribution and acclaim.

Britain Prepared was especially valuable in portraying the extent of Britain's contribution to the war effort in allied countries. In Russia, the film was distributed by Gaumont. Captain A. C. Bromhead, who had helped to found Gaumont-British in 1898, was selected to accompany the film, provide a short introduction and to answer questions. Bromhead set off for Russia in January 1916 to conduct a fact-finding tour and he arranged an official showing of the film for the Tsar, his chiefs-of-staff and the Petrograd press. The Russian première took place on 5 April 1916 amidst a blaze of publicity at the Marinsky Theatre in Moscow. Nicholas II also attended a screening of the film at the Russian GHQ, whereupon it was agreed to show the film to the troops in the field. Bromhead accordingly arranged for a fleet of cinema lorries to transport the necessary equipment and, in early May, *Britain Prepared* was seen by General Brusilov's armies on the southern front. By 17 May, the mobile cinema vans had travelled the full length of the Austrian front, providing 44 screenings to 100,000 men and 3000 officers. The film was frequently shown within firing range of enemy lines and, on one occasion, when the British national anthem was played at the end by a Russian military band,[89] the Austrians opened fire on the cheering Russian troops.[90] In July 1916, Bromhead accompanied the film to Finland and then, in the following month, to the northern front. For his labours, he was decorated by the Tsar with the Order of St Stanislas (Third Class).

The success of the Russian venture encouraged similar efforts elsewhere. Charles Urban was sent to the United States, T. A. Welsh to France, and Captain Gilbert Frankau, the novelist, to Italy. Their main task was to negotiate contracts for the exhibition of British films on a normal commercial basis and they were under strict instructions not to disclose their connection with the British government. There was to be no question of free distribution. This did create problems in Holland, for example, where the British were forced to compete with lower priced German rates of hire. Wellington House, however, considered that its comparatively high rates provided an incentive for the renter to recoup his costs through wide publicity which meant that British official films tended to be shown more in towns and in cities than in outlying provinces. Yet this did not prevent the propaganda agents from laying the foundations of a vast commercial distribution network which was to undergo further expansion in 1917. The number of requests for British war films received by the Foreign Office continued to increase after the foundation of the Department of Information. That made by the Acting British Consul-General in Rio was typical:

The cinematograph is the most popular form of entertainment in this city. The establishments devoted to it are probably larger and more elaborate than in any other part of the world and its value as a means of propaganda cannot be overestimated.[91]

The Department of Information had established a special section to deal with film propaganda, absorbing the original Cinema Committee established by Masterman at Wellington House in the process. Particular attention was paid to the question of distribution which took place either through the overseas representatives of the Foreign Office or through special agents working for the Department of Information often in collaboration with local propaganda committees. But in all cases, the general principle of commercial distribution remained.[92]

Apart from this general principle, local conditions again tended to determine specific arrangements. In Japan, the British ambassador was made responsible for the distribution of propaganda films. Sir Cunningham Greene began this work by organising a private showing of films for the Imperial family, ministers, ambassadors and bishops, followed by a public exhibition at which the audience was reported to have taken cover every time a British warship appeared on the screen firing a broadside.[93] In September 1917, the Department of Information sent a special representative, Frederick Coleman, to negotiate a commercial cinema contract in Japan. Coleman appointed an agent, Robert Eyre, and formed a committee in Tokyo which comprised the commercial attaché, the President of the local Patriotic League and the head of the Hong Kong-Shanghai Bank in order to supervise the work. Eyre shortly extended his activities into China where he appointed the impresario Maurice Bandman to organise distribution. However, diplomatic and consular officials proved highly critical of Bandman's apparent determination to show official British films for personal gain.[94] B. W. Alston, a counsellor at the British embassy in Peking, wished to see Bandman's work conducted by the propaganda committee which had been established in Shanghai.[95] The Shanghai committee was already in dispute with Bandman over his decision in April 1917 to double the rental charges for the highly successful film, *The Battle of the Somme* (originally entitled *The Great Push* when it first appeared in July 1916). As Miles Lampson, the newly appointed ambassador in China who had been the News Department's film officer, wrote:

Shanghai were perfectly furious with Bandman; they took an entire booking of the film to impress selected Chinese, imagining that the dibs they put up were going to a war charity; afterwards they tumbled to it that the bulk of the proceeds were appropriated by Bandman: so the sickness is great as they swear 'Never again'.[96]

As a result of this and other complaints, the Shanghai committee was given sole control of British film distribution in China in May 1917.

Such local difficulties illustrated the problem of developing a uniform system of world-wide film distribution. In France, the recently organised Maison de la Presse retained overall responsibility for film distribution and the War Office Cinematograph Committee negotiated an exchange agreement with it. In Italy, Captain Frankau was assisted by a specialist to supervise contractual negotiations. In Holland, the Dutch concessionaire was heavily criticised for inefficiency by diplomatic representatives. In Russia, Bromhead worked with a cinema bureau created in August 1917, although this body operated independently of the Anglo-Russian Commission established by Buchanan to supervise the overall conduct of British propaganda in Russia.[97] Both organisations had to be wound up after the Bolshevik revolution when the distribution of British propaganda in Russia was taken over by the secret service. In Siam, the King proved so enthusiastic for British war films that he requested copies for army training purposes. Although he was prepared to pay, the Foreign Office decided to reward his enthusiasm by providing him with free copies of *Britain Prepared* and the *Battle of the Somme*.[98] Conversely, the King of Spain refused to allow the public exhibition of British films and permitted only private showings for British residents in Madrid at the Teatro Benavente after they had been censored by the Spanish authorities.[99]

The Spanish situation appears to have been unusual. Normally, there was little difficulty in securing public exhibition of British war films in foreign countries, provided that the financial arrangements proved satisfactory. And although no detailed analysis seems to have been made concerning the size, composition and reaction of the audiences, reports of packed cinemas and enthusiastic responses abound in the surviving records. Despite the existence of the cinema before the war, it was only after 1914 that the novelty became an established phenomenon. Screened images of the conflict served to personalise the heroism of Allied troops and the horrors of German war-making and contributed towards making the conflict one of total involvement. But if Wellington House had regarded the cinema as the 'bible' of the working classes in most countries,[100] particularly in areas of high illiteracy, the early concentration upon intellectual propaganda meant that its real potential went largely untapped, despite the occasional success. It was only with the advent of Lord Beaverbrook and the establishment of the Ministry of Information that its mass appeal was fully exploited at home and in allied and neutral countries. The Ministry was, for example, responsible for the production of one of the war's most notorious propaganda films, *Once a Hun, Always a Hun*, which played upon popular prejudices about the beastly Germans in a way that had not been done before in this medium.[101]

Apart from the use of the press, pamphlets, films, exhibitions and lectures as part of the sustained campaign, there were also specific propaganda appeals inspired by particular events. The sinking of the *Lusitania* provided one such celebrated occasion. On 12 April 1916, the *Daily Review of the Foreign Press* produced jointly by the War Office and Foreign Office, contained an extract from the *Nieuwe Amsterdammer* published four days earlier which described a bronze medal struck by the German artist Goetz to commemorate the sinking of the passenger liner. The obverse of the medal portrayed the artist's impression of the ship laden with guns beneath the words *Keine Bannware!* ('No Contraband'). On the reverse were the words *Geschäft über alles* ('Business before everything') above a picture of civilians refusing to heed the warnings of the German U-boat campaign while queueing for tickets from a symbolic skeleton sitting in the Cunard office. The Foreign Office managed to obtain a picture of the medal from a Dutch catalogue and Ernest Maxse, the British minister in Holland, managed to obtain an actual copy, despite their limited circulation. Photographs of the medal were sent to the United States and were published in the *New York Tribune* on 7 May 1916. They excited so much attention that Wellington House decided to exploit still further the anti-German feeling generated by the medal in the United States by producing a replica. The idea seems to have originated simultaneously in several quarters. Masterman and Lord Bryce were certainly involved. An almost exact replica was produced, differing from the original only in the spelling of the word 'May' (the original being '5 Mai 1915'), which was distributed in a box containing a leaflet which read in part:

This medal has been struck in Germany with the object of keeping alive in German hearts the recollection of the glorious achievement of the German Navy in deliberately destroying an unarmed passenger ship, together with 1198 non-combatants, men, women and children . . . . This picture seeks apparently to propound the theory that if a murderer warns his victim of his intention, the guilt of the crime will rest with the victim, not with the murderer.

Wellington House assumed responsibility for the production of the first 50,000 replicas but was reluctant to continue thereafter due to the high cost of production. Wishing to maintain the momentum generated by the medal, the Foreign Office arranged for Gordon Selfridge to take over production at the end of July 1916 on a non-profit-making basis. The proceeds earned from sales of the medals were to be donated to the Red Cross. Selfridge calculated that production would rise to 10,000 a week and, in September 1916, a specially appointed committee supervised their distribution throughout the world. Demand for the replicas remained high until the end of the war.[102] What had begun as an attempt by a private German artist working on his own initiative to justify the submarine campaign to his own people became a *cause celèbre* of German barbarism and one of the most effective British propaganda coups of the war.

The propagandists, therefore, were both flexible and opportunistic in their methods, punctuating the sustained campaign with occasional reminders of German barbarity. They also produced ash-trays in the shape of British tanks, gramophone recordings of political speeches and popular songs such as 'Keep the Home Fires Burning',[103] and a wide range of ephemera. Theatrical tours were arranged, Boy Scout movements based upon the British model were promoted abroad, educational exchanges and academic conferences were organised such as that held in Cambridge during August 1916 to promote Slavonic Studies. The Foreign Office also supported Anglo-foreign and anglophile societies abroad or, where none existed, encouraged their foundation, as was the case with the Anglo-Spanish society founded in September 1916. Similarly, the Anglo-Italian Institute founded in Florence in March 1917 was designed to serve a propagandist purpose by the promotion of a better knowledge and understanding of Britain through the teaching of the English language.

The variety of techniques and of distribution methods multiplied as the war progressed, albeit in a somewhat haphazard and disorganised manner at first. Although the Department of Information was founded partly to reduce the overlapping and duplication of effort which inevitably resulted from the manner in which British propaganda was started, it did not introduce any radical change in the distribution and methods employed. Existing arrangements were merely rationalised in an attempt to achieve still greater efficiency. Continuity was maintained by the retention of the same personnel, particularly abroad where the principle was continued that agents with a detailed knowledge of local conditions should serve as the main advisers concerning distribution and methods. The new appointments that were made and the new committees that were established were reflective of the desire to make the existing arrangements more efficient and to strengthen the appearance of a patriotic campaign conducted by people with no ostensible connection with the British government.

The creation of the Ministry of Information in 1918 produced a more discernible change. But the change was more one of emphasis and scale than the introduction of entirely new methods. Pamphlets were much reduced in favour of immediate forms of propaganda, such as films, and the shift in emphasis away from Masterman's literary department reflected this process. In the first three months of the Ministry's existence, only twelve new pamphlets were produced — something like ten per cent of the normal figure. This shift partly stemmed from a controversy which predated the Ministry's foundation. In January 1918, newspaper proprietors had expressed grave concern about the shortage of paper and what they felt to be an enormous waste of this increasingly scarce commodity by the propaganda departments. As a result of mounting criticism, Masterman was asked to reduce the amount of paper used for the pamphlets and illustrated magazines and newspapers produced by Wellington House, despite his insistence that the Department of Information had used only 6000 tons out of an estimated 460,000 tons of available paper, of which 315,000 tons went to the general publishing and printing trade, and the remainder to the government.[104] But the criticisms contained in Robert Donald's second report had gained the support of Lloyd George. The views of the old guard were no longer considered valid; nor were they what either the Prime Minister or Fleet Street wanted to hear. Distribution of the pamphlets was considered wasteful and disproportionate to the results obtained. They represented all that was considered inappropriate in the old regime with its emphasis upon intellectual propaganda. Even the illustrated magazines, which were after all designed to serve a much broader audience than the pamphlets, were criticised on the grounds of excessive duplication. In June 1918, the Ministry of Information withdrew its support from *America Latina*, *O Espelho* and *Hesperia*. The production of *War Pictorial* was also reduced, involving a saving of 4000 tons of paper by July. In the same month, the distribution of photographs was also condemned as being wasteful,[106] and the Ministry adopted a policy of supplying both photographs and pamphlets only on request from overseas agents. Conversely, the production of leaflets was increased dramatically.

The paper shortage was by no means the main reason for the shift away from literary propaganda. Thanks to an astute piece of pre-war business management, Lord Northcliffe, the most vociferous critic of the government's propaganda before 1918 and the newspaper proprietor most feared by Lloyd George, was able to maintain paper supplies to his own newspapers without too much difficulty from Newfoundland rather than from Scandinavia, despite the losses incurred at the hands of the German submarines.[107] Nor was the effect of pamphlets on their intended audience really in question. The entire regime which had been dominated by the Foreign Office before 1918 was the real target. Certain Fleet Street proprietors were determined to wrestle for control over Britain's propaganda and, in 1918, Lloyd George was prepared to award the contest to them. It was not because the system which had developed since 1914 was insufficient to meet the changing demands of war propaganda. There was nothing drastically wrong with it that could not be solved internally. But Beaverbrook and Northcliffe spoke such irresistible phrases as 'popular diplomacy' and 'mass appeal' which merely served to reinforce the Prime Minister's conviction of the role which propaganda could play in the modern world. That such phrases were spoken by powerful newspaper proprietors who shared Lloyd George's dislike for the Foreign Office and for the 'old diplomacy' it represented meant that any criticism of its methods, regardless of its justification, was seized upon as rationalisation for his decision to transfer responsibility for propaganda to them.

Although the Ministry of Information and Crewe House continued to rely heavily upon the diplomatic and consular representatives serving abroad for the distribution of propaganda material, Beaverbrook was keen to reduce the dependence of his organisation upon such officials because he did not feel that they were generally capable of conducting propaganda with a mass appeal. He wrote:

The Foreign Office, both in principle and in practice, refused to recognise this duty of the new Ministry from its inception. It says in effect that the doctrine of popular diplomacy implied a setting up of a second Foreign Office at home with a new set of representatives abroad, and a policy divergent from that of the Foreign Secretary.[108]

Whereas Wellington House and the Foreign Office, followed by the Department of Information, had directed their propaganda initially at an educated and influential audience, the Ministry of Information wanted to by-pass these intermediary opinion-makers and work directly on the opinion itself. This was a newspaperman's view of public opinion, not that of a government official. It was for this reason that Beaverbrook and Northcliffe began a policy of large scale recruitment of journalists from Fleet Street to serve at the higher levels of the propaganda machinery. It was also the reason why the Foreign Office refused to allow the same to happen with regard to the distribution network abroad.

By 1918, however, the question was no longer simply that of a strengthened machinery to conduct a mass campaign. The changing demands of the military and economic situation, particularly after Brest-Litovsk, made a fundamental change in approach necessary. With the failure of more conventional methods of warfare to secure decisive results on the field of battle, alternative methods of breaking the military deadlock were sought. Universal war-weariness, the entry of the United States into the war and the internal instability of the Central Powers convinced many observers that the time had come to shift the emphasis away from propaganda in allied and neutral countries and to launch an all-out psychological offensive against the enemy.[109] Established methods conducted by the Whitehall departments had been tried without any discernible result. The methods adopted by the Foreign Office had been determined during a phase of the war which now seemed remote from the urgent requirements of a country about to enter its fourth year of war. They appeared too cautious, too defensive and too narrowly focused to warrant a further lease of life. What was now required was a resolute and determined propaganda campaign designed to bring the war to a speedy and successful conclusion. Beaverbrook and Northcliffe promised to finish the job that the Foreign Office had started by concentrating their energy upon the most vulnerable areas.

In the case of propaganda against enemy countries, the methods and means of distribution had always been dictated by the nature of the target audience in a way that was not so applicable to propaganda in allied and neutral countries. Attempts to influence the enemy civilian population were conducted on a clandestine basis and usually involved the smuggling of pamphlets and newspapers through adjacent neutral countries such as Holland and Switzerland. More overt methods were used against the front-line soldier. Leaflets, single-sheet newspapers, small pamphlets and books were dropped over enemy lines by aircraft and balloons. The most notable example of a small book was *J'Accuse*, written 'von einem Deutschen', which was 432 pages long and $2\frac{1}{2} \times 6$ inches in size.[110] The War Office, which remained in charge of distributing British propaganda in military zones until 1 September 1918 — more than six months after the creation of Crewe House — also produced a weekly single-sheet newspaper, *Le Courier de l'Air*, which was designed to inform the French and Belgian inhabitants in German occupied areas of events relating to the Allied war effort. Most of the material dropped by air sought to combine words and images in the form of photographs, cartoons or maps showing enemy soldiers the quickest route home. Bruce Bairnsfeather and Frank Reynold were commissioned by the War Office to draw the cartoons.[111] The illustrated newspapers were also dropped; by July 1917, Wellington House was supplying 5000 copies of *War Pictorial* printed in German to the War Office every month.[112] Messages were also relayed by loudspeaker across No Man's Land with musical interludes, and news was often exchanged by informal and strictly unofficial contacts established by the troops themselves.[113]

When, therefore, Beaverbrook and Northcliffe assumed control of propaganda in February 1918, they were able to draw upon the considerable experience which had been gained in the War Office and Foreign Office during the first three years of the war. The changes they did introduce would have been impossible without experimentation in methods, the flexibility of distribution techniques and the continuity in organisation and personnel which had taken place before their appointments. They refined earlier techniques and reduced the emphasis which had been placed upon others. Pamphlets were still used in 1918, just as films and leaflets had been used in 1915. The difference was that there were fewer pamphlets at the end of the war and more leaflets, films and other methods of immediate mass persuasion. They were able to concentrate upon the audience they purported to know best and which they felt would produce a rapid, visible result. They were not forced to operate under conditions of tight secrecy and they were able to focus their material upon government war aims that had not been defined until a comparatively late stage of the war. But it would be an injustice to assume that they succeeded where their predecessors had failed. Rather, the success they did achieve was due largely to the efforts of those early pioneers.

4 The Content of British Propaganda

IMAGES of the bloated 'Prussian Ogre' proudly sporting his pickelhauber, the 'Beastly Hun' with his sabre-belt barely encompassing his enormous girth, busily crucifying soldiers, violating women, mutilating babies, desecrating and looting churches, are firmly implanted in the consciousness of the twentieth century. Evoked repeatedly by Allied propagandists during the First World War, the British stereotype of the 'Hun' or the French stereotype of the 'Boche' came to personify a particular perception of the quintessential immorality of 'Prussian militarism' for causing the war and for its more inhumane excesses. 'Prussian militarism' provided Allied propagandists with the essential focus they required to launch their moral offensive against the enemy at home and abroad, and amongst their own troops. They personified and pictorialised a German society based upon militarist principles in order to bring home the terrifying consequences of defeat and thereby to sustain the will to continue the struggle until victory was secured. Neutral countries would be left in no doubt as to where their sympathies should rest. During the early stage of the war, it was important for British propagandists to apportion blame to the enemy for having caused the conflict and to prove that he had deliberately let loose the dogs of war upon peace-loving nations. The very fact that Belgian neutrality had been violated in the process of the attack upon France, combined with Germany's subsequent admission that she had knowingly flouted international law, provided the British government with the moral *casus belli* it required to justify intervention. For the next four years, official British propagandists exploited this theme ceaselessly and tirelessly and, if not actually fabricating atrocity stories themselves, then encouraging their distribution as a means of sustaining the level of moral condemnation of the enemy.

Herbert Asquith, in his speech of 9 November 1914, identified four main issues upon which the British government insisted as conditions of peace: the restoration of Belgium; the security of France against future German aggression; recognition of the rights of small states; and an end to Prussian military domination of Germany. This statement, which was to remain the government's only real declaration of war aims until 1918, was all that the propagandists had at their disposal to explain and justify British involvement. Although Asquith's statement was reproduced in poster form by the Parliamentary Recruiting Committee,[1] the appeal for volunteers was more usually couched in terms of patriotic duty. The most popular poster of its day and now, of course, the most famous, depicted Lord Kitchener pointing directly at the reader with the words 'Your King and Country Need YOU'. Most of the early recruitment posters were variations on this theme. They were generally straightforward in their imagery and messages, showing a Union Jack or a popular military hero calling for volunteers. However, once recruitment began to dwindle, the posters began to assume a more pressing tone by depicting those who were already fighting and, by implication, suggesting that there were those who were not doing their fair share. Hence the message: 'Who's absent — Is it You?' with John Bull pointing an accusing finger.[2] Other posters contained a simple written message:

> There are three kinds of men;
> Those who hear the call and obey;
> Those who delay,
> And — the others.[3]

The appeal was also directed beyond the potential recruit in order to increase the pressure upon him to enlist and his sense of shame if he did not. In this category came the posters 'Women of Britain Say Go'[4] and 'What did you do in the Great War, Daddy?'[5], both of which exploited male pride in the face of family expectations. Children played a central role in this campaign — several posters depicted boy scouts doing their share for the war effort — which attempted to involve the entire population in the conduct of the war.

As recruiting campaigns revealed, this approach was able to produce a considerable effect. The emphasis placed upon the individual achieving recognition and avoiding social vilification through identification with the majority was maintained until the introduction of conscription in early 1916. Other themes such as the notion of fighting for a just cause received much less attention, although several posters were produced depicting German atrocities in Belgium or other barbarous acts such as the sinking of the *Lusitania* and the bombardment of Scarborough by the German navy. The latter incident provided a reminder to those who believed the war to be a remote issue that the struggle did, in fact, involve the entire population. Yet comparatively few posters dealt with the civilian war effort; the majority, by far, confined themselves to the recruitment of volunteers.

This somewhat narrow approach became increasingly inappropriate in domestic propaganda as the length of the war increased beyond initial expectations and required greater sacrifices on the part of the civilian population. When, therefore, the National War Aims Committee was established in 1917, it was given the particular task of persuading the home front that the war had to be seen through to an uncompromising victory and of explaining that this would require nothing short of total commitment, particularly on the part of British industry. NWAC lectures and publications were accordingly more varied in their themes than those sponsored by the PRC had been. Ironically, however, in view of its nomenclature, war aims did not figure prominently at first because of the government's reluctance to commit itself beyond Asquith's early pronouncement until January 1918. Thus, when the NWAC was founded six months earlier, it found itself explaining less about what the government sought to achieve from its involvement than what was actually taking place.

The lecturers commissioned by the NWAC to tour the country were engaged to speak on all the belligerents involved in the war. Whenever possible, speakers were appointed because of their personal experience of conditions within the various countries, if not during the war itself then at least before its outbreak. Special talks on the causes of the war and on Britain's contribution to the overall Allied effort were prepared, leading to an inevitable consideration of post-war Britain. Lectures were therefore prepared on subjects such as the future of the British Empire and, closer to home, the thorny question of Ireland. It is not clear which lecture topics received particular emphasis at any given time. It does, however, appear that certain subjects were considered more suitable for some areas of the country than for others. Speakers were selected in consideration of local conditions and preferences, although they were free to broaden the debate on their subject in the question-and-answer sessions which usually followed, when considerable emphasis was placed on the need for still further sacrifices on the home front.

The involvement of the civilian population in the war effort was certainly a prominent theme of the written propaganda produced by the NWAC.[7] It was essential to convince the home front that in view of the excessive German peace demands, a negotiated peace on enemy terms was impossible. In his pamphlet, *Those German Peace Offers* (London, 1917), W. S. Sanders attempted to expose the insincerity of recent German peace manoeuvres. Lord Leverhulme argued in *Negotiate Now?* (London, 1917) that a compromise peace was bound to prove unsatisfactory, given the nature of the German leadership and its determination to hold on to territorial gains. This point was also taken up by A. J. Balfour in *Obstacles to Peace* (London, undated but probably 1917). Again, the chief obstacle was said to be 'Prussian militarism'. The nature of Wilhellmine Germany, according to W. S. Sanders in *If the Kaiser Governed Britain* (London, 1918), was tantamount to a police state.[8] The anti-German leadership theme was also stressed repeatedly in *Reality*, a weekly magazine published by the NWAC, which broadly interpreted 'Prussian militarism' as Pan-Germanism and a lust for expansion and world domination. Moreover, it was argued, the German desire for global hegemony could be traced back to the works of its nineteenth century philosophers and the historical determination to spread German *kultur*.

The Germans were allowed to condemn themselves as a consequence of their own words and actions. In *A German on Germans* (London, 1917), Dr Hermann Rosemeier, until September 1914 the political editor of the Berlin *Morgenpost*, attacked the German 'war party' which he argued was determined upon world domination. More popular still was the technique of using direct quotation. One of the *Beacon* series of pamphlets produced by Wellington House was entitled *War for Ever* and consisted of statements by various members of the German General Staff in order to illustrate their aggressive and expansionist political philosophy. German history and the German intellectual tradition were scrutinised to provide further evidence as, for example, in the case of the anonymous pamphlet, *Blood and Brass: Being Glimpses of German Psychology* (London, 1917). Politicians, philosophers, clergymen and, of course, the Kaiser were quoted in order to demonstrate their commitment to German expansion and their belief in the necessity of force in settling international disputes. The writings of Treitschke and Nietzsche provided British propagandists with a rich vein of material which they mined repeatedly. A favourite quotation was taken from Nietzsche's *Beyond Good and Evil*:

One must . . . resist all sentimental weakness: life is in its essence appropriation, injury, the overpowering of whatever is foreign to us and weaker than ourselves, suppression, hardness, the forcing upon others of our own forms, the incorporation of others, or, at the very least and mildest, their exploitation.

The most popular example of this form of propaganda using direct quotation was, perhaps, the 'Calendar of Culture for 1918' based on the German *Abreisskalender*, with a tear-off page for each day of the year. New Year's Day set the tone with a quotation from Frederick the Great's notes made on his copy of Tacitus' works:

No ministers at home, but clerks;
No ministers abroad, but spies;
Form alliances only to sow animosities;
Kindle and prolong war between my neighbours;
Always promise help and never send it;
There is only one person in the kingdom, that is myself.

Another entry for January quoted Houston Stewart Chamberlain's *War Essays* (1914):

The German Army (in which I, of course, include the Navy) is today the greatest institution for moral education in the world.

Values which were therefore held to be sacred within Germany were converted by British propagandists into manifestations of German barbarism.

One of the NWAC's most successful enterprises was the 'German Crimes' calendar which depicted an enemy atrocity for each month of the year with the actual date of each 'crime against humanity' circled in red. Four months featured 'crimes' relating to Belgium: the arrest and imprisonment of Cardinal Mercier; the burning of Louvain; the execution of Nurse Edith Cavell; and the deportation of Belgian and French workers. Five of the months featured U-boat activities, including the sinking of the *Lusitania* and of the *Ancona*, the torpedoing of British hospital ships and the execution of Captain Fryatt, a merchant navy officer who had dared to ram a German submarine. The remaining three months recalled the bombardment of Scarborough, zeppelin raids and the Turkish massacre of Armenians at Bitlis, the latter inferring German guilt by association.

It was not, however, the NWAC which was principally responsible for earning the lurid reputation which British propaganda gained for atrocity stories during the First World War. That dubious honour, at least in so far as the official organisations were concerned, must go to Wellington House. Given that its initial concern was for propaganda in neutral countries, it was natural for Wellington House to exploit the German violation of Belgian neutrality as an atrocious act of war. Such a theme, however, was not inexhaustible. In order to keep the Belgian issue alive, British propagandists sought to exploit any material that would help to sustain the moral condemnation of the enemy. Much of this material related to the actions of the Germans during the initial invasion, but the continued occupation ensured that the issue remained alive throughout the war. The character of the charges levelled against the occupying power was typical of all wars throughout history. The German army was accused of various crimes against the civilian population ranging from the massacre of innocents to the rape of nuns and virgins. One typical pamphlet, *Belgium and Germany: Texts and Documents* (London, 1915), written by Henri Davignon, the Belgian Foreign Minister, dealt with the history of Belgium and the violation of its independence by the Germans, followed by an address by Cardinal Mercier, the Archbishop of Malines and Primate of All Belgium. Then came details of atrocities, complete with illustrations. There was a photograph of an amputated hand and photostats of X-rays revealing the effects of expanding or dum-dum bullets. There were also photographs of the Aerschot 'massacres' and the destruction of various national monuments such as the library at Louvain and the Halles of Ypres. The tone of this hundred-page pamphlet was generally cautious and academic, seeking to present a mass of evidently factual material without recourse to emotional over-statement.

The same technique was used by L. H. Grondys in his pamphlet *The Germans in Belgium* (London, 1915). The case of a sixteen-year-old girl who had been bayonetted to death for daring to resist rape was mentioned, but it was also stated that the offending German soldiers had been punished by their military authorities. Grondys observed that German soldiers were afraid of atrocity accusations and that 'massacres' such as that which had occurred at Aerschot had been carried out in retaliation for crimes allegedly committed by Belgian civilians. This attempt to strive for the appearance of objectivity fully reflected the principles established at Wellington House by Charles Masterman. It was, he felt, essential to ensure a measure of credibility for even the incredible. That meant authoritative accounts written by respected authors on the basis of documentary 'evidence'. When an atrocity was said to have been committed on a Belgian baby and the subject was proposed as an ideal propaganda topic, Masterman replied: 'Find me the name of the hospital where the baby is and get a signed statement from the doctor and I'll listen'.[9] And while it is true that the more sensational and brutal atrocity stories tended to be circulated by the British press without any prompting from the official propagandists, the government cannot be absolved from responsibility because the censors rarely acted to suppress them. Yet a prize offered by Northcliffe for undoctored photographic evidence of a German atrocity was to remain unclaimed even at the end of the war.[10]

Nevertheless, Wellington House continued to circulate 'proven' atrocity stories. The most famous example was the *Report of the Committee on Alleged German Outrages* (London, 1915), better known as the Bryce Report. Costing 1*d*, the price of a newspaper, this 360 page pamphlet contained a 'summary of evidence' and an appendix — of some 300 pages — of selected case histories. These consisted of some 500 depositions chosen from 1200 statements made by Belgian refugees plus extracts from 37 captured German diaries. In his introduction, Lord Bryce confessed to his initial scepticism but, he continued:

this concurrence of testimony, this convergence upon what were substantially the same broad facts, showed itself in hundreds of depositions, and the truth of these broad facts stood out beyond question. The force of the evidence is cumulative.

The report then went on to describe the execution of civilians, the torture and mutilation of Belgian women, the bayonetting of small children and just about every conceivable atrocity that could be committed by German soldiers. The appendix contained particularly explicit descriptions of mutilation, rape and murder. Independent French and Belgian investigations arrived at similar conclusions, although post-war commissions failed to substantiate the allegations.[11]

At the time, however, it was difficult for the Germans to produce an effective counter-argument and, according to one Belgian pamphleteer, Jean Massart in *Belgians Under the German Eagle* (London, 1916), the Germans were victims of their own initiative in so far as they were attempting to justify their actions in Belgium by issuing pamphlets and leaflets describing atrocities committed by Belgian civilians. A common complaint was that German soldiers frequently had their eyes gouged out. Such counter-charges were dismissed outright and provided still further 'proof' of German guilt. If the atrocities had not occurred, then why bother to justify German actions? Moreover, the official and somewhat objective tone of the Bryce report, the credibility of which was enhanced by the fact that the reputable Lord Bryce was himself chairman of the investigatory commission, ensured that it was received favourably both at home and abroad. This was particularly so in the United States, where Bryce was a renowned figure stemming from his period as ambassador in Washington from 1907 to 1913. Bryce had also received several honorary doctorates from German universities and was the recipient of the order of Pour le Mérite, the highest honour the Kaiser could grant. His investigating commission was equally distinguished and reputable: Sir Frederick Pollock, the eminent jurist and constitutional historian; H. A. L. Fisher, historian and vice-chancellor of Sheffield University; Harold Cox, editor of the *Edinburgh Review*; and two lawyers, Sir Edward Clarke, MP, and Sir Alfred Hopkinson, KC. Such a distinguished team enhanced the credibility of their findings which, published as they were only five days after the sinking of the *Lusitania*, generated a wave of anti-German feeling in America and other neutral countries. Its significance as a masterful piece of British propaganda is, perhaps, immeasurable. Its real historical significance lies in the fact that the Bryce Commission did not 'produce a dishonest or fraudulent report in the sense that it reached conclusions which the evidence had shown to be untrue. What it did do was to avoid verifying the evidence'.[12]

'Poor Little Belgium' continued to provide British propagandists with a fertile source of propaganda material until the very end of the war. In 1917, the major issue became the deportation of Belgian workers. Lord Bryce took the lead in raising this subject in *The Last Phase in Belgium* (London, 1917). He not only described the deportations but also took the opportunity of pointing to the failure of the German authorities to reply to his earlier report, which he interpreted as an admission of guilt. Other witnesses of the deportations were Jules Destrée, a Belgian journalist who wrote *The Deportation of Belgian Workers* (London, 1917), and Brand Whitlock, the head of the American delegation in Brussels who indicated in his pamphlet, *The Deportation* (London, 1917), that much of his evidence came from the American Commission for Relief in Belgium, which had been established during America's neutrality period partly as a response to Allied propaganda. Whitlock was also involved in the case of Edith Cavell. Her execution in 1915 for having aided the escape of Allied soldiers might well have been justifiable as a legitimate act of war but it was to prove a disastrous mistake on the part of the Germans. The wave of indignation which followed her death reached world-wide proportions and Wellington House was quick to fan the flames. A best-selling pamphlet was produced immediately by an anonymous author, *The Death of Edith Cavell* (London, 1915), at the price of 1*d.* For the benefit of American readers, particular emphasis was placed upon the role of the American legation in trying to save Nurse Cavell's life and on the failure of the German government to keep the legation fully informed. A year later, James Beck, an American journalist, wrote *The Case of Edith Cavell* (London, 1916), which reprinted his articles first published in the *New York Times* describing the humiliating treatment afforded to Whitlock by the Germans.

It was not just that Nurse Cavell was a woman which presented anti-German propaganda with an ideal opportunity to exploit her execution. The Germans did, after all, prove incapable of exploiting effectively the death of Mata Hari, executed as a spy by the French in 1917. The death of Edith Cavell provoked global indignation because of her role as an 'angel of mercy' (at least that was the way she was presented) and because her execution was set against the broader and emotive background of Belgian violation. By adhering to military justice rigidly, the Germans were merely conforming to the stereotype of them created by the Allied propagandists of Teutonic brutality and ruthless inhumanity encapsulated in the phrase 'Prussian militarism'.

The range of atrocity charges against the Central Powers was limitless. Arnold Toynbee, the distinguished historian and member of Wellington House who became something of a specialist in atrocity propaganda, described and condemned the Turks in

Armenian Atrocities: Murder of a Nation (London, 1915) and *The Murderous Tyranny of the Turks* (London, 1917) while Thomas Masaryk accused the Habsburg government of atrocities in *Austrian Terrorism in Bohemia* (London, 1916). Germany was accused of mistreating prisoners of war in *The Horrors of Wittenberg* (London, 1916) and of exploiting ruthlessly its colonial possessions in *The Black Slaves of Prussia* (London, 1918). In Rumania, they were accused of conducting bacteriological warfare in *Microbe Culture at Bukarest* (London, 1917) which claimed that anthrax had been smuggled into the German legation as a prelude to destroying Rumanian livestock.

Perhaps the most notorious atrocity story of the entire war was the case of the so-called 'corpse-conversion factory'. On 10 April 1917, the *Lokal Anzeiger* of Berlin carried a story of a factory used to convert what appeared to be human corpses into war commodities. A week later, *The Times* accused the Germans of boiling down dead bodies to make soap. Before adopting the story for propaganda purposes, the Foreign Office launched an enquiry. On 1 April, the *Daily Review of the Foreign Press* had contained a report describing the discovery in Holland of a railway carriage loaded with dead German soldiers. The train had been destined for Liège where, it was claimed, the bodies were to be melted down for soap, but the train had been diverted to Holland by mistake. The story had first appeared in a Belgian newspaper, the editor having learned of the incident from a Belgian officer. The Foreign Office was, however, unable to substantiate the story, despite the claim of R. McCleod, MP, that he had received a letter from a senior British officer confirming the accuracy of the story. The Germans, Brigadier Morrison claimed, had been seen removing bodies from Vimy Ridge where there was a noticeable absence of German war graves. From there, the bodies were being taken to the notorious corpse-conversion factory.[13]

Robert Donald, who had reported earlier in the year on what he believed to be the inadequacies of British propaganda, could hardly believe his good fortune. He was a keen advocate of atrocity propaganda and, with the domestic press taking the lead in publicising this latest story, he urged the Department of Information to exploit it overseas. In the literary department, Masterman was more inclined towards caution. He had encountered atrocity stories before which had no factual basis and he wished to ensure that there was sufficient evidence for this latest accusation before it was

publicised by the Department of Information for fear that otherwise
the Germans might expose it as a British concoction. Propaganda in
the domestic press was quite a different matter from that conducted
in neutral countries. If the story was untrue, years of work in building
British credibility might be destroyed. At Wellington House, the
story was initially 'laughed out of court'.[14] But at the Foreign Office,
a number of officials were inclined to believe it. There followed a
considerable debate concerning the use of the word *kadaver* around
which the whole story revolved. Acdemics were called in with their
dictionaries to determine whether the word was used to describe a
human corpse in German because it was more normally used in the
context of animal carcasses. Masterman and others doubted the
likelihood of the German censorship authorities allowing the
publication of a newspaper article admitting that human corpses
were being used in such a way. It was accepted, however, that the
Germans were using available horse flesh in order to lighten the
effects of the Allied blockade. Balfour admitted that the
documentary evidence was inconclusive but, he added:

While it should not be desirable that His Majesty's Government
should take any responsibility as regards the story pending the
receipt of further information, there does not, in view of the many
atrocious actions of which the Germans have been guilty, appear to
be any reason why it should not be true.[15]

It would be too easy to conclude that the Foreign Secretary had
swallowed British propaganda. But the currency of atrocity stories
undoubtedly helped to condition official acceptance of yet one more
example of Prussian barbarism. As a result, Wellington House was
instructed by Montgomery to press ahead with the preparation of
pamphlets in Portuguese, Spanish, Swedish and Dutch. S. A. Guest,
the official in charge of propaganda in Holland and Germany, was
also instructed to gather further information for a German edition.
Masterman went ahead, somewhat reluctantly, with the publication
of the four-page pamphlet entitled *A Corpse-Conversion Factory*
(London, 1917).

   That the story was a complete fabrication was finally exposed in
1925 when it was discussed in the House of Commons.[16] In the years
that followed, Britain's wartime propaganda underwent a critical
and hostile post-mortem, led by Arthur Ponsonby's *Falsehood in*

Wartime, first published in 1928. The popular prejudice generated by these revelations concentrated mainly on Britain's wartime atrocity propaganda. The effect of this hostility, however, was to detract from the value of other forms of propaganda. During the early phase of the war, the presentation of the British case to neutral countries had presented serious problems stemming largely from the Allied blockade. In the United States especially, it was difficult to justify the searching of neutral shipping for material listed by the British as contraband. Initially, the propagandists adopted a defensive stance towards this issue, being more concerned with justifying the right to apply the blockade in terms of international law. In *Great Britain and Neutral Commerce* (London, 1915), two MPs, Leslie Scott, KC, and Alexander Shaw, defended the novel practice of escorting neutral vessels into port for examination rather than the conventional practice of searching ships on the high seas as an indication of Britain's concern for their safety against the German submarine menace. Indeed, it was the persistence of the U-boat campaign which provided British propagandists with the opportunity to shift on to the offensive. As Scott and Shaw pointed out, 'in the exercise of her right to search, Great Britain in the present war has not destroyed a single neutral vessel or caused the loss of a single life'. German methods, by comparison, were portrayed as illegal and inhumane. A similar argument was put forward by the American barrister, Frederic R. Coudert, in *British Trade Restraints and Peace Prospects* (London, 1916). This pamphlet argued that although Britain's blockade policy involved considerable legal complexities regarding the definition of contraband, 'there is no fundamental question of inhumanity or of elementary right involved'. But, the author continued, 'on the other hand the destruction by submarines on the high seas of non-combatant lives is done in defence of elementary principles of humanity'.

In a sense, therefore, German naval warfare became yet another target of British atrocity propaganda. In an almost hysterical pamphlet by Archibald Hurd, *Murder at Sea* (London, 1916), which was unusual among Wellington House pamphlets for its general lack of restraint, the activities of the German U-boats were condemned in highly emotional terms:

It was the Germans . . . who pressed the submarine boat into their service in order to enable them to commit acts of villainy and murder of a character and on a scale which excel any demoniacal scheme which ever entered the brain of a drink-sodden pirate of the past.

The author vowed revenge: 'from every crested wave in every sea the same dirge will continue to rise and fill the ears of men, women and children until such crimes have been punished and expiated in the one and only way'. Hurd returned to this theme in *Submarines and Zeppelins* (London, 1916) when he argued that the Germans were breaking the accepted rules of war. But he was consoled by the thought that, 'in honourable warfare British submarines have at least been successful'. The German navy had murdered neutrals and sunk hospital ships and there was no doubt that 'the fingers of many of its officers and men are dripping with blood of the innocent'.

German propagandists were unable to exploit the 'immorality' of the Allied blockade with the same sort of success largely because to have described its effects upon the German civilian population would have been tantamount to an admission of Prussian vulnerability. Nevertheless, in *The Starvation of Germany* (London, 1917), J. W. Headlam attempted to answer the charge that the blockade was immoral. He described the total nature of modern warfare:

those who remain at home are deliberately working under an organised scheme for the service of the army and the conduct of the war just as much as those away in the field. All food-stuff imported into Germany directly and immediately adds to the combatant power of Germany.

This argument became the accepted rationalisation for the continued use of the economic weapon serving as the fourth arm of defence against the Central Powers in the campaign for neutral sympathy. But it could also be made to apply as a justification for the German submarine campaign, particularly when that campaign was made unrestricted in 1917. The deprivations caused by Germany's attempt to break the blockade led to a re-examination of British propaganda on the home front.

The NWAC had not only to combat war-weariness. It had also to counteract the influence of a movement gaining strength within Britain led by the Union of Democratic Control which sought immediate peace negotiations.[17] Although the NWAC was conceived initially in broad informational terms, there can be little doubt that it was created primarily to combat pacifism, using that word in its broadest sense. Given that the Independent Labour Party had been the only organisation consistently opposed to the war, it was possible for the NWAC to argue that socialism equalled pacifism and that the labour movement in general was vulnerable to pacifist propaganda. The Union of Democratic Control had drawn largely upon disillusioned liberals for its support but, by 1917, it was beginning to make an impact upon the labour movement. Despite the declaration of the Labour Party Conference in January 1917 announcing its support for the continuation of the war, government concern continued to mount and was to be increased substantially when the Bolsheviks secured power in Russia in the following November.

The response of the NWAC to these developments was to publish pamphlets making a direct appeal to the British working classes. In keeping with established practices, however, the appeal was made on behalf of the government by leading figures within the labour movement itself. Ben Tillet, for example, wrote a pamphlet on the origins of the war designed specifically for working men as well as a four-page article in the NWAC's *Searchlight* series entitled *My Message to Labour* (London, undated). W. S. Sanders, the noted Fabian and member of the British labour delegation to Russia, argued in *Germany's Two Voices* (London, 1917) that the interest of German socialists in peace, as expressed in their Reichstag Peace Resolution of July 1917, was misleading because they had always supported the war before and were only now beginning to preach pacifism in an attempt to undermine the commitment of their Allied brethren while still advocating militarism and expansion at home.

Much of the material produced by the NWAC was designed as specific counter-propaganda. With the Bolshevik revolution in Russia and the appearance of subversive propaganda spreading the doctrine of peace, as well as the publication of secret treaties drawn up by the Allies during the war, the NWAC was forced to return to the discussion of war origins and the justification of British wartime policy. The war origins debate was further rejuvenated by the revelations contained in Prince Lichnowsky's memoirs, *My London Mission*.[18] Originally, only eight copies of the book were available when it was first written in July 1917 but, by the beginning of 1918, it was more widely available in printed form. After being serialised in a Swedish newspaper, it was reported in *The Times* on 28 March 1918. The NWAC produced an abridged version and also issued a four-page edition of *Searchlight* entitled *Germany Condemned by Her Own Ambassador* (London,1918).

It was difficult for the NWAC to avoid being negative or defensive. It did, however, manage to strike a more positive note in its material dealing with the British war effort and that of the Allies, particularly after the United States had entered the war. A pamphlet by Winston Churchill on *The Munitions Miracle* (London, 1917) was issued, and another by Herbert Hoover, *Food in War* (London, 1917), dealt specifically with his relief mission in Belgium. The NWAC attempted to stress equally the commitment of all the Allies to winning the war while, at the same time, stressing the essential contribution being made by Britain. The level of that contribution had been the subject of periodic criticism in the French and Russian press during the first half of the war and had prompted the Cabinet in 1915 to widen the brief of Wellington House to include Allied as well as neutral countries in its sphere of operations. In view of Britain's less than total military contribution until the introduction of conscription, particular emphasis was placed upon the extent of her naval and financial commitment while also demonstrating the vast industrial effort being made, especially in the production of munitions. Masterman himself took up the pen in *After Twelve Months of War* (London, 1915), in which he described the achievements of the British economy and emphasised the determination of the British people to see the war through to total victory. In *The British Share in the War* (London, 1915), H. A. L. Fisher wrote in response to domestic criticism of the failure to introduce conscription, while Sir Gilbert Parker in *Is England Apathetic?* (London 1915), which was originally aimed at American opinion,[19] denied accusations of lethargy and charges of seeking American aid. The use of such well-known personalities in this aspect of the propaganda campaign revealed the degree to which the issue of Britain's commitment was taken seriously by the government. This was further revealed by the production of *Britain Prepared*, a film which presented in a straightforward manner the wartime activities of the British armed services, reinforced by scenes of the civilian effort in munitions factories. The film also showed basic military training, trench-digging and trench-fighting techniques (using clods of earth as weapons), as well as the various supporting services such as communications and food supply. Scenes at the Vickers munitions works recorded the contribution of women to the war effort. However, the most striking scenes of the film concerned the Royal Navy. As protector of the British Empire, the navy inspired the most impressive photography, with dramatic scenes of destroyers screening battleships, of submarines firing torpedoes, and of big guns in action. For its day, the film was an impressive production which gave the appearance of British naval supremacy even before the fleet had been tested in battle. And such emphasis did help to alleviate criticism from amongst her Allies that Britain was not pulling her weight sufficiently in the overall war effort against the enemy.

Another method of demonstrating the extent of Britain's commitment was to publicise the Imperial nature of British involvement. British propagandists were anxious to stress the voluntary unity of the Empire, and Wellington House published a series of pamphlets devoted to this theme written by native authors such as Sir Robert Borden, the Canadian Prime Minister, and General Jan Smuts, the South African Minister of Defence who was ultimately to enter the War Cabinet.[20] The overall aim of these publications was to reinforce the argument advanced by H. A. L. Fisher in *The Value of Small States* (London, 1914):[21]

If the British Empire has succeeded in retaining the affections of its scattered members, the result has been due to the wise and easy tolerance which has permitted almost every form of religious, political and social practice to continue unchecked, however greatly they may vary from the established traditions of the English race.

Once national self-determination became a specific war aim of the Allies in 1918, nationalist parties within the Empire were encouraged to believe that their war efforts would be duly rewarded by London on the return of peace. While the war undoubtedly accelerated the transition from Empire to Commonwealth, British propagandists in the meantime conveyed the impression both abroad and towards the Empire that the mother-country enjoyed the full and unquestioned support of all her loyal colonies.

All, however, was not rosy in the British imperial garden. The situation in Ireland required a massive and concerted counter-propaganda campaign to answer Britain's critics, particularly in the United States. Here, British propagandists especially benefited from the absence of any overt or readily identifiable link with the government, and hence official policy. They were therefore able to admit past errors in British policy, a technique which provided their propaganda with a greater element of credibility than a plain whitewashing campaign would have done. In *England, Germany and the Irish Question* (London, 1917), an 'English catholic' freely criticised the British government's record:

Nobody denies that England has treated Ireland with harshness, injustice and stupidity in the past. But that was the old England. The England of modern days has done a great deal to repair the injustice and blunders of the past.

But the author also challenged the right of the Germans to criticise the British government over Ireland in view of their own conduct towards Alsace and Poland: 'There is nothing worse in the whole history of Anglo-Irish relations even at their worst to compare with this onslaught on the Catholic religion of Poland'. Hugh A. Law, an Irish MP, also adopted a frank approach to British policy but his main contention was that because the Allies were the champions of national rights, Ireland should forgive 'England's age-old denial of Irish national rights' in anticipation of future concessions. He noted that 'English foreign policy has often shown itself narrow, cold and selfish' but that Germany had proved herself to be an outright opponent of democracy and nationality. Britain was slowly moving towards these ideals, the argument continued, although:

the old narrow Puritan, self-righteousness is not yet quite gone from her mind, nor the old spirit of ascendancy from her politics; but they move. Her working constitution grows gradually more democratic; her foreign policy less insular, less aggressive. She is making reparation for her one great sin against the principle of nationality.

The Germans, however, counted more than one sin within the British Empire and Wellington House found itself engaged in widespread counter-propaganda in relation to imperial rule, particularly in India.

A number of pamphlets were produced in defence of the British administrative record in India. Again, wherever possible, outside commentators were used as authors. In *The British Administration in India* (London, 1915), a letter from the *Algemein Handelsblad* was reproduced, written by Professor J. Vogel of Leyden University in response to a pamphlet produced by the executive committee of the

Indian National Party which had severely criticised British rule on the sub-continent. The British were charged with atrocities and with forcing Indians to fight in a European war which was of no concern to them. Vogel dismissed the charges as mendacious and defended Britain's record, an exercise repeated by Sir Mancherjee Bhownaggree in *The Verdict of India* (London, 1916) and by Lionel Curtis in his *Letter to the People of India on Responsible Government* (London, 1918). However, the preference for neutral pamphleteers was repeated when an article by an American journalist, Poultney Bigelow, was reprinted from the *New York Times* as *An American Opinion of British Colonial Policy* (London, 1915). In this pamphlet, German claims that Britain exercised a trade monopoly in the colonies were refuted with the argument that Germany herself monopolised her own colonial trade.

Pamphlets tended to have a somewhat limited appeal in this campaign. Visual propaganda produced a wider effect. Exhibitions of war photographs[22] devoted considerable space to portraying the imperial nature of the British war effort with pictures of Indian sepoys and various labour contingents recruited from the colonies. A favourite subject was the Zulu chieftain. But by far the most important medium of visual propaganda was the film. Many British films depicted the multi-national character of the British army, including *South African Labour Contingent, The Egyptian Labour Corps, The Visit of the Canadian Rangers to Ireland* and *Sons of the Empire.* The growing popularity of the medium, however, made film an ideal instrument of propaganda beyond Britain and the Empire. In the age of silent cinema, soundtrack did not pose a problem but footage nonetheless had to be carefully selected in order to project the desired impression without disclosing military or naval secrets. For example, in the film *The King's Visit to the Fleet* made after the battle of Jutland, the written commentary announced H.M.S. Barnham and stated that it 'took a prominent part in the battle of Jutland where she was hit repeatedly' but failed to show the extent of that damage. Instead, the film was devoted to scenes of the investiture of officers and endless marches of men around the decks of their respective ships.

It was not until the second half of the war that films of the army were able to match the dramatic effect of naval scenes when land forces were provided with their own dreadnought in the form of the tank. Various films of the major battles were produced, including the most famous of the tank films, *The Battle of Ancre,* which exploited the 'photogenic' qualities of the tank to the full. Those qualities were also apparent in the photographic exhibitions organised towards the end of the war when the army occupied the central position previously held by the navy. The exhibition catalogues reveal the preponderance of war scenes depicting the trenches, bombardments and, above all, the tanks.[23] One photograph, 'Dreadnoughts of the Battlefield', depicted tanks moving forward into battle and was enlarged to a size of 23½ feet x 17 feet making it, according to the exhibitors, the largest photograph in the world at that time. The aeroplane also received its fair share of attention as the other great 'novel weapon of the war' although the glamour of the Royal Flying Corps, followed by the Royal Air Force, and the publicity afforded in the British press to dogfights and air aces frequently led to concern that the army and navy were not earning their fair share of the credit.

The use of films and photographs for propaganda purposes provided an 'illusion of reality' at a time when it was generally believed that the camera could not lie. The use of film montage techniques might well have been in its infancy but film, whether still or motion, could only depict what the cameraman wanted it to depict. The images presented were, in fact, carefully staged. While there were often several apparently quite realistic camera shots of wounded soldiers at the front, they were usually staged-managed in order to show fatigue being accompanied by cheerfulness. Wounds were always freshly dressed and there were rarely pictures of Allied dead, although dead Germans did feature more often. Only Allied troops in action or Allied victories were exhibited. There were realistic images of the muddy conditions at Ypres in photographic exhibitions, but their theme was symbolised by one exhibit demanding to know 'Where is the pessimist?' among a line of smiling soldiers. The intention of portraying high morale was obvious, namely to convince the civilian population at home, in allied and Imperial countries that their efforts were worthwhile and producing visible effects at the front line.

In their campaigns against pacifism or the effects of bolshevik propaganda at home, against American neutrality or the maintenance of inter-Allied harmony, British propagandists recognised that one of their greatest assets was censorship. If the Press Bureau retained the right to control what appeared in the British press, the War Office remained determined to control the flow of information and the shape of visual images entering and leaving Britain through its work in the cable, postal and cinema censorship offices. It is, however, difficult to evaluate the precise effects of the censorship. It could not, of course, disguise the harsh realities of rationing or military defeats. But it undoubtedly helped to create a false impression of what the war actually signified in terms of fighting at the front. One individual who encountered the controlling hand of the military postal censors was Captain N. C. S. Down, a serving officer in France. Down became increasingly frustrated by the censor's determination to remove not only military information which might prove of value to the enemy from his correspondence but also any reference which might reflect adversely upon the reputation of the British Army. He believed that a reference he had made to a transport ship being a cold-storage vessel had been deleted simply because 'We are a great nation'.[24] A vivid description of the Belgian mud and the ugliness of the Belgian language also invoked censure, and many of his acerbic comments, such as a reference to the instructors in his bombing class not knowing more than the students and an analogy of a farm house to the War Office because 'in it you sleep all day', were also deleted by the censor's blue pencil.[25] Instead, Down was forced to write: 'Why this cottage is called the War Office, I may not divulge'. His propensity for free comment was crushed at every turn. Disparaging remarks about the general staff were obvious victims. A reference to mildewed French rations was removed, presumably in the name of Allied solidarity, as, indeed, was the following attempt to dispel atrocity rumours:

I am sending you another proof of the frightfulness of the Hun. It is a dum-dum bullet. At least it has been turned into one by having the pointed end clipped off with nippers. To be quite honest about it, these horrible instruments of kultur are not all they are made out to be, but are used to smash loop-holes, which they do about three times as effectively as the undoctored kind. Still, of course, if you feel inclined to do so you can turn it into sufficient evidence of the flouting of the Geneva Convention to fill several Blue Books. Another popular myth is the 'explosive bullet'. Any Tommy will give you five or six instances of how his best pal was completely disintegrated by an explosive bullet, complete with the most lurid details of how the big toe of the right foot was found embedded in the left ear at a distance of fifteen feet from where the victim was standing when he was hit. But you never see an explosive bullet. Cos why? Cos there aren't any.[26]

Robert Graves confirmed in *Goodbye To All That* the general contempt in which the front-line soldier held atrocity stories about his foes.[27] Yet civilians did not possess the combat experience of the soldier with which to counteract the influence of propaganda, whether positive in the form of NWAC material or negative in the form of the censorship. It is hardly surprising, therefore, that the best-known novels written about the First World War, regardless of the side to which they refer, comment upon the discomfort of the front-line soldier on his return home on leave who found himself amidst a civilian population infinitely more militant than himself.[28]

The glorification of the British soldier and the vilification of enemy troops through a combination of propaganda and censorship was less obvious in the many examples of war paintings commissioned by the authorities. Indeed, unlike photographic or cinematographic propaganda, it is questionable that the word 'propaganda' is entirely appropriate to describe the activities of the war artists. They were employed not merely for propaganda purposes but also to record the war for posterity. The artist was left largely to his own devices and there is little, if any, evidence that he was instructed by the various propaganda authorities to record anything other than that which he chose to sketch or paint. The main concern was to preserve the visions and impressions of the war artists in a permanent memorial, a function still performed by the Imperial War Museum in London. Paul Nash described how in 1918 he and his brother were 'temporarily seconded and employed by the Ministry of Information to paint pictures for records and propaganda — actually what we like, so long as it is interesting enough under these somewhat vague headings'.[29] Although artists were commissioned to paint pictures with a clear propagandist purpose such, for example, as portraits of leading war figures, the overall impression is one of considerable flexibility. One critic, commenting upon an exhibition of war paintings in the United States, noted with reference to the work of Wyndham Lewis and William P. Roberts:

It is sufficient again to congratulate those in authority upon possessing the salutary eclecticism to choose their interpreters of the war not alone from the approved precincts of the Royal Academy Schools and Burlington House, but also from the Slade and the so-called rebel art centres of Camden Town where freedom alike of idea and expression flourish unabashed.[30]

Vorticism, however did not dominate the works listed in the

catalogue of this particular exhibition. The central works were paintings by Muirhead Bone and Sir William Orpen. The latter's works included many portraits and were largely in the documentary vein recording a variety of different war scenes without the emotional intensity of a Nash landscape which managed to combine commentary with description in artistic form.

Overt propaganda paintings were rare. George Clausen's *Renaissance* took as its theme the revival of Belgium but, in the main, British war paintings were largely descriptive. James McBey's *The Entry of the Allies into Jerusalem, December 11, 1917,* fell into this category although the majority of his works attempted to capture the atmosphere of Palestine and its desert landscapes. Nevertheless, descriptive landscapes on canvas could quite easily be translated into propaganda with the aid of judicious commentary. This was particularly evident in the edition of drawings by Muirhead Bone published in June 1917.[31] Among the drawings are scenes of Peronne accompanied by propagandist text. For example, the accompanying description of the town hall reads:

Before the Germans looted it, the building housed a fine collection of Gallic coins, Roman bronzes, Frankish antiquities, and early printed books. Nothing is left but a few tumbled books.

Similarly, the commentary on a sketch of a ruined church reads:

It may have suffered some damage from Allied shells but its final demolition by the Germans was clearly deliberate for the ruined walls have been blown outward.

In short, the artist's intentions were often irrelevant to the final presentation of his work for propaganda purposes.

The freedom enjoyed by the war artists owed much to the influence of Masterman and his continued presence at Wellington House, even after it was absorbed into the Ministry of Information in 1918. Beaverbrook shared Masterman's view of the war artists although he disagreed with the emphasis which had previously been placed upon pamphlets. With the campaign in the United States fought and won by the time the Ministry was created, Beaverbrook felt that there was less need to concentrate upon intellectual propaganda. Yet it is doubtful whether the changes in organisation affected the actual content of British propaganda. Changes in circumstances, such as the entry of the United States and the departure of Russia, certainly did, but the essential themes — anti-Germanism, inter-Allied solidarity, the need for continued sacrifices at home — remained constant.

A further essential ingredient of the British propaganda campaign was the exploitation of religion. It was a vital feature of the attempt to build a cumulative stereotyped image of the Hun and was also used to demonstrate the correctness of the British cause and to reinforce the Belgian campaign. Wellington House made use of the works of Cardinal Mercier, reprinting his pastoral letters and sermons in small pamphlets and fly-sheets. It also published a collection of his war utterances in *The Voice of Belgium* (London, undated), a book of more than 300 pages. The German treatment of Belgian catholics opened the way for attacks upon Prussian protestantism. Since, however, the historical record of Britain's treatment of catholics was open to criticism, Wellington House began to distribute from 1916 onwards the *Catholic Monthly Letters* which were designed:

to take each department of English Catholic life and to show that Catholicism acts freely and according to its natural function within it, or, at least, that the constant and vital tendency is towards complete liberation so that there will soon be no obstacle to the current of Catholic conviction and aspiration.[32]

This idea was inspired by the appearance of German catholic monthly letters in December 1915, which perhaps helps to explain the defensive nature of the British version. But there was a more positive function:

We shall consider ourselves entitled to go further, and to write in support of our belief that fundamental Catholic doctrines of true liberty of spirit, true justice, order and charity are safeguarded by the Allied cause and imperilled by the Prussian spirit. We shall not even hesitate to declare that Caesarism and militarism for which Prussia professedly stands are in active and open hostility to the Spirit of Christ. Nor will it be in the least difficult to collect evidence from purely German sources to prove that the German conduct of war is in frank defiance of the doctrine of the New Testament, and that the philosophy which prepared and underlies it is in direct descent from the revolutionary and disruptive preaching of Luther.[33]

This was hardly pulling any punches but it is difficult to reconcile this type of argument with that contained in the pamphlet written by James Stalker, Professor of Church History at the United Free

Church College at Aberdeen, entitled *The Lutheran Celebrations, 1517–1917* (London, 1917). Stalker saw Lutheranism as the antithesis of a Prussianised Germany. He was one of several protestant clergymen who wrote pamphlets for the Evangelical Information Committee which were then distributed by Wellington House because they made a special target of the Prussian spirit. They also attacked the Germans through the misdeeds of their allies, especially the Turkish treatment of Christians.

The apparent contradictions between British catholic and protestant propaganda were not as important as they might first appear. Since the pamphlets were published under the heading of their respective information houses and were merely distributed by Wellington House, there was nothing to link them directly to the British government, thus making it difficult for the enemy to counter the arguments by pouncing upon conflicting views. The unofficial source of the material enabled British propagandists to adopt a flexible approach to religious questions, an essential factor in view of the highly sensitive issues surrounding the Irish question. The same sort of latitude was not available on questions of broader policy due to the absence of a comprehensive statement of war aims until January 1918.

The break-up of the Ottoman Empire had long been mooted in Britain and the propagandists had taken their initial cue from the politicians. Arnold Toynbee's pamphlet, *The Murderous Tyranny of The Turks*, took its title from the Allied response to President Wilson's request at the end of 1916 for the belligerents to state their war aims. In other cases, however, the propagandists pre-empted the policy-makers. Lewis Namier, who worked in Wellington House with Toynbee, argued in his pamphlet *Danzig: Poland's Outlet to the Sea* (London, 1917),[34] that the reconstitution of Poland after the war should include the port of Danzig although the British government had yet to establish any firm policy decision on this issue. In an earlier work, *Germany and Eastern Europe* (London, 1915), Namier had argued for the dissolution of the Austro-Hungarian Empire and the reconstruction of the Near East on the basis of nationalistic principles. In an introduction to this pamphlet, H. A. L. Fisher pointed out that although he personally did not agree with Namier's recommendations, the author's immense knowledge of the Slav peoples demanded that his view command respect. In 1917, J. W. Headlam also envisaged the dismemberment of the Dual Monarchy in

The Dead Lands of Europe (London, 1917). Since these pamphlets were written by officials working at Wellington House which, of course, also distributed their work, Namier and Toynbee could either have been working beyond the scrutiny of the Foreign Office or with Foreign Office approval. Given the closeness of the relationship which existed between the News Department and Wellington House, it would appear to be the latter. That the Foreign Office expressed little concern for the views expressed in such works might be explained by the intense secrecy which surrounded the distribution of propaganda material which made it difficult to trace the pamphlets back to an official source.

This issue does, however, raise the question of how material was selected as suitable propaganda. Despite the protestations of the Foreign Office to the contrary, official propaganda material was often inconsistent and contradictory. Many pamphlets distributed by Wellington House were not specifically commissioned by its officials and were therefore originally written from an entirely independent viewpoint. They were selected by virtue of the case which they made on any given issue but do not appear to have been edited or censored or to have had their arguments adjusted to conform to an established set of ideas or policies laid down by the government. This seems also to have been the case with pamphlets which were actually commissioned by Wellington House. However, because the wartime propaganda records have been largely destroyed, it is not possible to reconstruct the exact process by which a pamphlet was commissioned, written or published. As far as it is possible to tell, the Foreign Office does not appear to have been in the habit of dictating the strict content of propaganda pamphlets and Wellington House seems also to have placed few restrictions upon its pamphleteers. It would have been difficult to do so anyway in view of the preference for employing the talents of well-known writers, journalists and academics who would have resisted any signs of unreasonable censorship rather than using unknown writers from within the Civil Service who might not. This is not to suggest that complete academic licence was extended to the pamphleteers. Daily meetings were held at Wellington House to discuss and determine the direction of propaganda and to examine and select pamphlets prior to publication. But it is not known whether these meetings decided to attempt to determine the course of government policy by releasing views on questions which had not been settled at the highest levels.

The result, even so, was the production of material which varied greatly in style, tone and ideas but only marginally varied in its themes.

The freedom seemingly afforded to the pamphleteers, and certainly to the war artists, undoubtedly helped to create the appearance that British writers and painters had managed to retain their liberty to express themselves in wartime conditions. Yet although they often appeared to be operating as private individuals working out of patriotism, they were invariably employed by the British government's propaganda machinery. The wealth of Britain's artistic and creative resources — artists, poets, authors and academics — was mobilised in the service of Britain's propaganda campaign at home and overseas. The cumulative effect of that campaign was the creation of a national stereotype of the German as a 'Beastly Hun' capable of the worst crimes imaginable to civilised man and whose rules of war were barbaric and inhumane. This campaign undoubtedly contributed towards the wave of popular recrimination which greeted the Armistice with calls of 'Hang the Kaiser' and 'Make Germany pay' and the formulation of the infamous 'war-guilt' clause of the Treaty of Versailles. But although the British press must bear the greatest share of the responsibility for distributing atrocity propaganda, the official propaganda machinery was not without guilt. The Ministry of Information's notorious film, *Once a Hun, Always a Hun*, released in 1918, undoubtedly produced an enormous effect in consolidating the stereotype which had been developed during the previous three years. The film portrayed two German soldiers in a ruined French town striking a woman carrying a baby to the ground. The same two soldiers are then portrayed as commercial travellers working in England after the war. One of them enters a village store to sell the shopkeeper a frying pan. He is impressed until his wife enters and exposes the inscription 'Made in Germany'. The final words which appeared on the screen read: 'There can be no trading with these people after the war'.[35]

Such propaganda undoubtedly produced a harmful effect upon British economic recovery on the return of peace when the recovery of Europe as a whole depended to a considerable extent upon the recovery of Germany. It needed a complete re-educational process on the part of people such as Lloyd George and Keynes to drive this point home during the peace negotiations and in the years that followed. In the long-term, the effects were equally tragic. The effect of British atrocity propaganda during the First World War and the failure to substantiate the stories in the years that followed led to a general disinclination in the 1930s and 1940s to believe atrocity stories about the Nazi treatment of the Jews.[36] The distortions of the First World War therefore served to obscure the realities of the Second.

PART THREE

Case Studies

5 British Propaganda in the United States

In September 1914, the Foreign Office and Wellington House were in complete agreement that by far the most important of neutral countries was the United States of America. The reasons for this were obvious. On the outbreak of the First World War, Britain and Germany had lost each other's best customer in economic and commercial terms. It was essential for them both to compensate for this loss by increasing their trade with the rapidly expanding economic might of the United States or, better still, to entice the Americans into joining their cause. For the next two and a half years, British and German propagandists fought an intense and widespread propaganda campaign designed to win American sympathy and all the benefits that entailed. It was a battle only one side could win, if it could be won at all. Both sides held their advantages. The Germans had their considerable share in the American electorate through the organised and intensely patriotic bunds of German emigrés. The British shared a common language and culture and, thanks to the prompt action of the cable ship *Telconia*, they alone enjoyed direct cable communications with the North American continent. It might well have been the case that the British were bound to win. Wellington House was more concerned with not losing. In other words, British propagandists were determined to ensure that if the United States did decide to enter the war, it would not do so on the side of the Central Powers. This was not the same thing as campaigning for America to join the Allies although increasing British dependence upon American finance and supplies as the war unfolded did serve to transform gradually the original negative aim into that same goal.

FROM NEUTRALITY TO BELLIGERENCY

When the question of launching a British propaganda campaign overseas was first discussed by the Cabinet at the end of August 1914, it was the activities of German propagandists in the United States which had prompted the establishment of Wellington House.[1] Masterman decided to create 'a most important special branch' to deal solely with British propaganda in America and appointed the prolific Canadian novelist and MP for Gravesend, Sir Gilbert Parker, as its head.[2] This interest and emphasis was further reinforced by increased British intelligence activities to monitor the internal conditions of that country and to observe the changing moods of American public opinion, much of this work being carried out through the various censorship offices.[3] Thus began the inextricable connection between propaganda and intelligence which was to become an essential feature of the campaign for American sympathies.

From the very beginning, the Foreign Office was determined to avoid swamping the United States with British propaganda material in the same way that the Germans were attempting to do. The majority of British observers in America advised against an overt campaign in view of what were believed to be the counter-productive effects of German methods. The German campaign had merely served to alert most Americans against any attempt by foreign governments to win their sympathies. Arthur Willert, Washington correspondent of *The Times*, warned in November 1914 that 'the contumely with which the German propaganda has been visited shows very clearly that Americans would dislike any machinery for the manipulation of their public opinion'.[4] He considered that British interests would be served best by sympathetic American anglophiles:

What we want are Americans prepared to influence their own localities, with an American organisation in New York as their h.q. [Also] we want to be certain that the work of weeks is not to be undone by official ineptitudes or hysterical diplomacy.[5]

The emphasis, therefore, was to be upon qualitative rather than quantitative propaganda, conducted discreetly by an organisation based in London rather than in the United States in order to avoid arousing suspicion and resentment. The British, French and Belgian ambassadors all agreed that it would be unwise to open a propaganda office on American soil.[6] Moreover, the campaign was to place more emphasis upon personal propaganda than on any other technique of persuasion.

Although the Foreign Office remained determined to ensure that the flow of British material was strictly regulated by Wellington House, it was also keen to avoid any suggestion that the material had, in fact, originated from an official source. Wellington House, therefore operated in strict secrecy and Parker gave the impression that he was operating as a private individual rather than as an official working for the British government's propaganda machinery. He began to compile a mailing list based partly upon his own personal contacts but drawn mainly from entries in the American edition of *Who's Who*. Figures relating to the size of Parker's list vary considerably. According to various sources, by June 1916 material was being despatched to more than 13,000 addresses in America — to lawyers, doctors, businessmen, politicians, scientists, academics and teachers, and to various leading institutions and newspaper offices. By 1917, the list had been increased to 170,000 addresses[7] and it eventually contained 260,000 entries.[8] Parker's audience was an educated élite comprising mainly influential individuals who were in a position to influence much larger numbers of their own people. The material they received from Wellington House was academic in tone, scholarly in approach and was always accompanied by a personal letter from Parker himself without any indication that he was part of an official propaganda campaign.[9] His covering letters were measured and discreet. For example, the following was typical of his approach:

I am well aware that American enterprise has made available reprints of the official papers relating to the present European war; but the original British prints of these publications may not be accessible to those persons of influence who can study them for a true history of the conflict. I am venturing to send to you under another cover several of these official documents. I am sure that you will not consider this an impertinence but will realise that Britishers are deeply anxious that their cause may be judged from authoritative evidence. In common with the great majority of Americans, you have, no doubt, made up your own mind as to what country should be held responsible for this tragedy, but these papers may be found useful for reference, and because they contain the incontrovertible facts, I feel you will probably welcome them in this form.
My long and intimate association with the United States through my writings gives me confidence to approach you, and I trust you will not think me intrusive or misunderstand my motive.[10]

Parker's motive was, however, clearly propagandist. Although, in this particular instance, he was merely sending offical documents in an attempt to let the recipient believe that he was making up his own mind on the basis of 'incontrovertible facts', the distribution of documentary evidence presented in a reasoned manner constituted a vital ingredient of British propaganda. Given the nature of the primary targets of that propaganda, who were felt to be more capable of detecting propaganda when they were confronted by it, the motive had to be carefully disguised. This was achieved partly by distributing information and measured arguments rather than emotional opinions and by disguising the official nature of the source from which the material originated.

It was an approach which produced considerable results. On receiving one grateful letter in November 1915, Parker took the opportunity of following up the goodwill he had already generated:

It is naturally a pleasure to know that the material has proved of service. It does contain the essential facts in the case and it presents them, I think, in that objective scientific form which is alone suitable for serious and impartial study.
I can well understand how the German methods of propaganda are regarded in the United States, and it is encouraging to be told so expressly that your countrymen realise the profound difference in the attitude and policy of the British government in this matter. We have in common with you a tradition of genuine and equitably conducted argument; and I might also add that we and Germany are actually in a very different position. All we desire and require is to present the bare facts and leave the civilised world to draw its own conclusions. But to Germany, on the contrary, the truth is deadly; and she has guided herself with mistaken ingenuity to the task of obscuring what is really happening under a haze of vituperations and special pleadings.[11]

This deliberately restrained approach was based partly upon assumptions concerning American character but it was also a reflection of the considerable advantages which the British enjoyed where the supply of information to the United States was concerned. There was the incalculable benefit of a common language which greatly eased the visit of prominent British figures to the United States and the ready transmission of interviews by such people as Cabinet ministers, leading politicians and the Archbishop of Canterbury.[12] There was also the advantage of direct cable communication following the cutting of the German trans-Atlantic cables which forced the Germans to rely heavily upon other means of communications, particularly wireless. Although they were partly able to surmount the technological limitations of wireless transmissions from Europe by broadcasting from wireless stations at Tuckerton, New Jersey, and at Sayville, Long Island, the former operated under American government censorship regulations from the autumn of 1914 and the latter from August 1915 onwards, thereby limiting the efficacy of the medium.[13]

The British, by comparison, were able to supply the United States with a much broader range of material quite simply because a greater number of communication channels were available to them. Yet because the British were unable to monopolise all the sources of information supplying the Americans, they could ill-afford deliberate distortions. The Germans continued, for example, to supply a considerable amount of news to the United States through South America. But it did mean that British propagandists enjoyed a considerable advantage with the American press. It was Parker's task to persuade American journalists 'to take a right view of the actions of the British government since the commencement of the war'[14] which meant providing them with news which had been censored by the Press Bureau in conjunction with the Service Departments, the Foreign Office and the Neutral Press Committee as the basis for their articles. Parker also supplied some 555 American newspapers with Wellington House material and the cumulative effect, particularly bearing in mind the syndication system operating in America, was such that by August 1916, it was claimed that 'we swept the German news out of the American papers'.[15] Similarly, every effort was made to cater for the needs of the American correspondents in Britain who were among the first to be allowed to visit the front and to be afforded special privileges there; in 1917, two out of the four special châteaux provided by the Allies for foreign journalists and other observers were designed purely for the benefit of American correspondents.

But this campaign of personal propaganda was not simply confined to bringing influential American opinion-makers to Europe. Parker was a regular visitor to the United States where he spoke to many societies, particularly the Society of Pilgrims. Together with Arnold Bennett, who was later appointed Beaverbrook's assistant at the Ministry of Information, Parker was also employed as a writer for the Goldwyn Motion Pictures Corporation.[16] Nor was he unknown in American governmental circles. In June 1915, Parker was granted an audience with Colonel

House, President Wilson's most intimate aide, to whom he explained his work in North America. House was much impressed with a speech by Parker made on Lincoln Day comparing Wilson with the founder of the Union and recorded that Sir Gilbert had asked 'if I had ever spoken to Mr Balfour and other members of the Cabinet concerning his work'. House replied that:

until today I did not know the extent of it, but I had mentioned time and time again, to Grey, Balfour, Asquith and others, the admirable manner in which they had refrained from publishing things which they must have felt like publishing and which the Germans had, in similar circumstances, published to their undoing.[17]

Such comments would appear to represent yet another vindication of Parker's approach. His preference for personal contact between persuader and target, his avoidance of the barnstorming German techniques by the provision of accurate information and measured arguments to influential Americans, and the absence of any overt connection between propaganda material and the British government all helped to create the illusion that Wellington House was not, in fact, operating in the United States. Americans were led to believe that they were making up their own minds when they were really being directed gently towards a pre-determined set of opinions in favour of the Allies. Parker was supported in this approach by Sir Cecil Spring-Rice, the British ambassador in Washington, and by the Foreign Office. The News Department reinforced his work by supplying news, views and facilities which enabled American journalists to write their own articles, books and pamphlets rather than spoonfeeding them with blatant propaganda. The British censorship not only removed any unwarranted criticism or adverse comments from any cable or postal communications between Britain and the United States but also regulated the correspondence between American correspondents working in Germany and their newspaper offices. Moreover, it was official policy to commission whenever possible neutral, and preferably American, writers such as Morton Prince, author of *The Psychology of the Kaiser* (New York, 1915), to produce material for pamphlets relating to such issues as the violation of Belgian neutrality, the British contribution to the Allied war effort and other propaganda subjects.

This was particularly important with regard to an issue of intense sensitivity in the United States, namely the blockade. British propaganda was initially defensive on this highly delicate question, being more concerned with defending and justifying the British position chiefly through legalistic arguments relating to Allied interference with American shipping and American mail. C. Noble Gregory, for example, Chairman of the Standing Committee on International Law of the American Bar Association, accepted the legitimacy of the principles which lay behind the blockade in *Neutrality and Arms Shipments* (London, 1915).[18] Despite such efforts, however, British propagandists were forced to tread warily on this issue. They were able to shift on to the offensive only when the German submarines provided them with suitable opportunities to exploit the 'barbarism' of enemy activities, as on the celebrated occasion of the sinking of the *Lusitania* in May 1915. Even so, as Arthur Willert noted at the time, 'I suppose since the *Lusitania* sank I have read several hundred leaders from newspapers all over the country. Virtually none of them demands war'.[19] Yet German submarine warfare continued to be depicted as a violation of the rules of international warfare and was thus classified as an atrocity. The Germans were, of course, able to reply that because the blockade was attempting to starve the civilian population of the Central Powers into submission, it too constituted an act of atrocity warfare, although this could not be done without actually admitting in the process that the blockade was producing a damaging effect upon their morale. The sinking of the *Lusitania*, combined with the sinking of the *Arabic* in August 1915 and the torpedoing of the *Sussex* without warning in March 1916, the intensification of German U-boat activity in October 1916 and its extension to unrestricted submarine warfare at the end of January 1917, enabled the British to sustain the propaganda offensive over the war at sea even in adverse circumstances.

During the first eighteen months of the war, British propaganda in the United States was generally cautious and defensive. Wellington House and the Foreign Office followed the near unanimous advice of informed observers in not establishing an organisation on American soil which would suggest that the British government was attempting to win over American sympathies. Opportunities were taken to exploit German mistakes in an attempt to demonstrate the 'barbarism' of the enemy as, for example, on the occasion of the Bryce Report which was published within a few days of the *Lusitania* incident. These incidents undoubtedly helped to consolidate the impression already created by the German invasion of Belgium and France that the German military regime was aggressive and ruthless. But British propaganda offensives in the United States were episodic. In general, the aim was, as Lord Cecil wrote, 'to do good by stealth' not as a means of persuading Americans to join the Allied side but rather to ensure that they at least remained neutral. The presentation of Germany as an unattractive potential ally was achieved partly by letting the 'facts' speak for themselves and partly by presenting those 'facts' in such an apparently reasonable and objective manner that British actions stood out in sharp contrast to the harsh and brutal behaviour of the Central Powers.

1916, however, saw a renewed British propaganda campaign in the United States. The growth of anti-British sentiment arising from the suppression of the Easter rebellion in Ireland, continued British interference with the trans-Atlantic mails and the blacklisting in July of American business firms suspected of trading with the Central Powers threatened to create the impression that the British at war were no more civilised than the Germans were alleged to be. These developments, coming as they did in an American election year, forced the newly rationalised propaganda machinery to launch a massive counter-propaganda campaign designed to improve Britain's image. This was essential at a time when British financial and economic dependence upon the United States was increasing. Matters were not helped by President Wilson's peace initiative in December 1916 which 'actually helped to stimulate a desire for more propaganda'[20] because of its suggestion that the war aims of the belligerents were effectively the same.

The publication of the Lusitania medal details by the American press in May 1916 came at a fortuitous moment. Following the abortive Easter rising in Ireland and the subsequent execution of its leaders, there developed considerable sympathy in the United States for the martyrs of the rebellion. Moreover, the trial and sentencing of Sir Roger Casement provided American Irish — and the American press — with an immediate focus of anti-British attention and with an ideal opportunity for a retrospective condemnation of previous British activities. The sympathy generated for the Irish by these events alarmed the British government which immediately began to consider means of redressing the propaganda balance. The Lusitania medal was one such attempt; by publicising the details of this celebration of German naval warfare, and by reproducing the medal itself for widespread circulation in America, the British were attempting to demonstrate the gloating inhumanity of 'Prussian militarism'. Yet the harsh suppression of the Easter rising threatened to force British propagandists back on to the defensive. They responded by launching an attack upon Casement's moral reputation. This response appears to have been initiated by Basil Thomson, head of the CID at Scotland Yard, who held the disputed Casement diaries. On 23 April 1916, following the publication of several favourable articles on the Irish rebels in the American press, Thomson had made copies of extracts from the Casement diaries depicting homosexual activities. He then showed the extracts to Walter Page, the American ambassador in London, whose reaction was reported to be after a page and a half of reading:

Forgive me, but I have a luncheon engagement today and, if I read any more, my host and his other guests will think that I have been taken suddenly ill! One needs a strong stomach to eat anything after reading this. Still I suppose that it will be my duty to send it to the State Department.[21]

Copies also appear to have reached members of the Cabinet, Foreign Office and the Admiralty. Although there was considerable disagreement as to whether such unpalatable material should be released to the American authorities, various individuals decided to take the matter into their own hands. For example, Lord Newton, head of the Foreign Office News Department, recalled:

The papers were in the custody of my Department, and when the time came for the despatch of the diplomatic bag, without waiting for further instructions from the government, I took the responsibility of sending the necessary documents to America.[22]

The Director of Naval Intelligence since November 1914, Admiral Sir Reginald 'Blinker' Hall, also made an independent decision to pass on the extracts to Captain (later Admiral) Guy Gaunt, the naval attaché at the Washington embassy. It was Gaunt who released the extracts to the American press which quickly gave them considerable publicity. In addition, Hall showed the extracts to Ben Allen of the Associated Press after one of his weekly press conferences with foreign journalists.[23] The ruling of Sir Edward Grey on 30 June 1916 that no further copying of the diaries should take place[24] came too late to prevent the widespread circulation of the story although it did prevent the full details from becoming widely known.

It is not easy to ascertain the effects of the Casement diary extracts as propaganda. Public sympathy for Casement persisted in America and, in July 1916, the Senate sought to pass a resolution expressing regret at the death sentence passed upon him. The motion did, however, prove too extreme for the Foreign Relations Committee and a more moderate version, calling upon the British government to exercise clemency for political prisoners, was sent to the White House for transmission. The resolution was then 'unaccountably' held up for several hours before it was sent and it arrived in London a few hours after Casement's execution had taken place.[25] It might well be that the diary extracts had some bearing on this delay. Although it is difficult to accept Newton's statement that, once the extracts had been published in America, 'nothing more was heard of the pro-Casement agitation',[26] it is possible that they did serve to neutralise the initial hostile reaction of various leading American officials towards the British government's Irish policy while, at the same time, disarming the effects of German propaganda which had been quick to exploit the issue.

The policy of forcing Germany onto the defensive was greatly aided by the cartoons of Louis Raemakers. A Dutchman of part German extraction (on his mother's side) and a persistent critic of the German government, Raemakers had regularly published his cartoons in one of Holland's leading newspapers, the Amsterdam *Telegraaf*. British propagandists decided to use his cartoons not simply because of their virulence or popularity but mainly because of Raemakers' neutral status and background. Exhibitions of originals and facsimiles were organised on the continent, where they were also sold in book form or as postcards and reproduced in neutral newspapers. In May 1916, John Buchan suggested that the cartoons should also be distributed in the United States and, in July, Wellington House sent J. Murray Allison to prepare the ground. Contracts were negotiated with Doubleday and Page, the Stern Advertising Company and with the Curtis Publishing Company to reproduce the cartoons in America, and arrangements were also made to secure syndication of any new cartoons amongst the American press. But when Allison returned to England in October 1916, he discovered that nothing had been done to publish the cartoons in America. It seemed that many newspapers were reluctant to reproduce the cartoons and few were prepared to authorise the exhibition of what was felt to be blatant anti-German propaganda of the kind most disliked in the United States. German pressure groups had been especially active in certain regions, notably in the mid-west, by threatening to withdraw advertising revenues from newspapers which published the cartoons. The first exhibition of Raemakers' work, held in Chicago, was a disaster. Only three out of an invited audience of 2000 turned up. Yet Allison retained his faith in Raemakers and was able to make the essential breakthrough by persuading the *Boston Transcript*, the *Philadelphia Ledger* and the *Chicago Tribune*, all members of the Public Ledger Syndicate, to print the cartoons. Thereafter, they continued to attract attention and wider publication. By the end of December 1916, fourteen journals were publishing Raemakers' work and although the figure fluctuated between eight and twenty-five until the United States entered the war in April 1917, by the following November some 2255 American newspapers had reproduced 2224 cartoons.[27] Allison's attempts to organise exhibitions continued to be met with opposition from some quarters during the period of American neutrality, but he was able to display the cartoons first in New York and Boston before returning to Chicago more successfully, and thereafter in most major American cities.[28]

The virulence of Raemakers' work meant that to some extent the British were taking a risk in the United States where propaganda conducted by Wellington House had been much less blatant. This risk was offset considerably by the fact that Raemakers himself was a neutral citizen and by utilising people other than Englishmen to promote and distribute the cartoons. Those British writers whose material was distributed in America had to appear to be motivated by individual initiative and patriotism, but if they became too outspoken, as in the case of Cecil Chesterton writing in the American press in 1915, they were repudiated immediately by the British government.[29] But the brutal style of Raemakers' cartoons often provided the shock treatment that was required to bring home to many Americans the horrible and brutal deeds of 'Prussian militarism'. Nevertheless, although they undoubtedly helped to consolidate the particular stereotype which the British were attempting to construct about the Germans, they only became a massive success once Germany became an enemy of the United States. Before then, their circulation was comparatively limited.

Whenever possible, therefore, British propagandists began to depart from the initial policy of defensive propaganda in the United States. They did this chiefly by increasing the amount of counter-propaganda on specific issues, although Sir Gilbert Parker and his colleagues continued their sustained campaign of gentle persuasion amongst influential groups. Attacks were launched upon Germany's colonial policy in East Africa as a means of defending Britain's imperial record in India, Ireland and elsewhere. A similar strategy was adopted towards Britain's allies. In view of the influential Jewish community in the United States, British propagandists were anxious to draw attention away from the anti-semitic excesses of Russia's policy of persecution of the Jews and to concentrate instead upon the Armenian massacres conducted by Germany's ally, Turkey, and indeed by the Germans themselves. The predominant themes used in America were generally typical of British propaganda directed at neutral countries. But the United States was always regarded as a special area requiring special attention. It was perhaps more important to avoid alienating American opinion than it was to actually win over American support, a factor which gave British propaganda in the United States its essentially cautious and defensive appearance. In fact, the campaign was clandestine, subtle and persistent. As in the case of propaganda directed against enemy opinion, sheer force of circumstance necessitated a definite link between propaganda work and secret intelligence.

Two of the most significant intelligence figures in the propaganda campaign were 'Blinker' Hall and Guy Gaunt. As a result of Hall's inventiveness and tendency towards taking the initiative and exceeding his authority, and as a consequence of Gaunt's own initiatives in his role as naval attaché in Washington, the Admiralty assumed a central position in the organisation of British propaganda. Both Hall and Gaunt agreed that propaganda constituted an integral part of the work of an intelligence agent. An essential feature of Gaunt's work involved the observation and combating of German espionage activities. Where those activities involved a threat of any kind to American neutrality, counter-espionage provided a fertile field for propaganda. But it was essential that the methods employed in exposing enemy activities were kept secret if they were to be used again.

It would appear that the development of this work owed as much to chance as it did to design. Gaunt was able nonetheless to build up a substantial network of agents. The initial opportunity for this development was provided by Emmanuel Voska who worked with Thomas Masaryk and who, by way of Wickham Steed and Lord Northcliffe, had been given an introduction to the British embassy in Washington where he encountered Gaunt.[30] The naval attaché informed Voska that he was unable to pay him for his services, but Voska agreed to work for him regardless.[31] Working through an organisation known as the Bohemian National Alliance, Voska maintained contact with a wide variety of agents and information sources throughout the United States. This network he now placed at Gaunt's disposal. It was a case of combining forces against a common enemy. Voska and his agents were able to provide detailed reports on German and Austro-Hungarian activities in the United States but they lacked the facilities to publicise them. Here Gaunt was able to utilise his personal contacts with the publicity world. He contacted an old Australian friend, John Rathom, the editor of the *Provincial Journal*, who had connections with the *New York Times*. Voska, Gaunt and Rathom formed a triumvirate which was to collaborate until February 1917.[32] As Voska recalled:

Gaunt and I realised already that our best counter-propaganda would be in the news. One provable case of a German agent plotting to blow up a ship or to arm an expedition against Canada, we felt, would outweigh a ton of pamphlets.[33]

Voska reassured Gaunt and Spring-Rice that all his agents saw themselves as American citizens who would act within the confines of United States law. Gaunt, for his part, was quick to recognise their significance. At various times, Voska had four agents placed in the Austrian consulate in New York, one in the German embassy in Washington and another working as a wireless operator at the Sayville radio station used by the Germans on Long Island. Even the superintendent at the building where a group of Hindu revolutionaries met was one of Voska's men.[34]

The role of British Naval Intelligence in these operations was extremely active. Gaunt's secret organisation in the United States was supported by the genius of Hall and the code-breakers of Room 40 who had broken the German ciphers, thereby providing British intelligence with a significant advantage over the Central Powers.[35] Gaunt himself was perfectly positioned within the Washington embassy to play a multiple role. He assisted in the American distribution of Wellington House literature and he also collaborated with Charles Urban when he was sent to America to arrange for the distribution of official British films. Gaunt acknowledged and reaffirmed the principles of the British campaign in the United States. Because propaganda was still in its infancy, he felt that 'by leaving everything to American common sense, I would achieve all that was possible'.[36] Besides, this was the ruling of Spring-Rice with whom Gaunt was in regular contact. The British ambassador used the naval attaché as his liaison officer with Colonel House. Through regular meetings, Gaunt became friendly with House which enabled him to advance the British case directly and frankly. In December 1915, House recorded that he had spoken with Gaunt 'of German propaganda in this country and of the naval end of the war. He tells me quite frankly what he is doing and gives me all the information he has'.[37] House was also informed of Hall's work and he was sufficiently impressed to commend both of them to the King.[38] In May 1916, he recorded that it was his intention 'to suggest to the British government that they handsomely recognize Gaunt's services during the war'[39] and later that year he informed Balfour:

. . . I want to express my high regard and appreciation of Captain Gaunt. I doubt whether you can realize the great service he has rendered our two countries. His outlook is so broad and he is so self-contained and fairminded that I have been able to go to him at all times to discuss, very much as I would with you, the problems that have arisen. I feel it is due to him to let you know this and I hope you will not keep him too long on the other side and it is important for him to be here in these critical times.[40]

During Gaunt's absence, however, House came into contact with another British intelligence officer and propagandist, William Wiseman, who had been acting as a temporary replacement during Gaunt's visit to England. They first met on 17 December 1916. House took an immediate liking to Wiseman who lost no time in presenting himself as Gaunt's replacement.[41] The President's personal adviser soon began to confide in Wiseman and by 19 January 1917 was writing:

Wiseman and I discussed Spring-Rice's temperamental defects, giving him praise where praise was due. The question came up as to what was best to be done when Captain Gaunt returned which will be in the next few days. I do not want to hurt Gaunt's sensibilities, and yet I feel that it is more profitable to work with Wiseman. He has more aptitude for the kind of work to be done as liaison officer between the British Government and myself.[42]

When Gaunt did return, House found himself dealing with both men and friction soon began to develop. House left them to sort the matter out between themselves but, when the United States finally entered the war in April 1917, it was decided to arrange direct contact between House and Balfour through Wiseman.[43]

Gaunt bitterly resented the way in which he had been ousted and, in his memoirs, devoted much space to minimising Wiseman's work. He particularly resented Wiseman's description as head of British intelligence in the United States and, on the title page of his memoirs, described himself as holding that position during the war.[44] According to Arthur Willert, Wiseman appears to have acquired that title when asked by Frank Polk, the influential Counsellor in the State Department, who exactly was head of the British secret service in America. Wiseman replied that there was officially no such position but, in so far as any one man could be so described, it was himself.[45] In fact, Wiseman was head of military intelligence in the United States and Gaunt was head of naval intelligence, two quite separate organisations.[46] Following a war wound which had rendered him unfit for further active service, Wiseman had encountered Captain Mansfield Cumming (known as 'C') in December 1915.[47] When Cumming complained about the American section of military intelligence, Wiseman offered his services and was promptly sent to the United States as head of the British Purchasing Committee with Norman Thwaites serving as his deputy.[48] Wiseman arrived in January 1916 and began to operate in a similar manner to that of Gaunt. He continued to work in the office of the British military attaché until the arrival of the Balfour Mission in April 1917 when Colonel Dansey assumed control over military intelligence in the United States.

Wiseman's functions, as Gaunt's had been, were chiefly concerned with counter-espionage in general but also, more specifically, with combating German-sponsored Irish and Hindu sedition in the United States. For the latter purpose, Wiseman worked with the India Office and he also benefited from the services of Voska with whom he had made contact in London through Masaryk. In June 1918, Wiseman informed Arthur Murray (later Lord Elibank) at the Foreign Office that he had worked closely with the chief organiser of the Bohemian National Alliance for the past two years.[49] Voska, however, made no reference in his memoirs to Wiseman although he did acknowledge his partnership with Gaunt. Indeed, Voska's memoirs make hardly any suggestion of a working relationship between the two British intelligence officers.[50] But in fact, Wiseman and Gaunt were in regular contact and, by the middle of 1917, the latter was expressing his concern at the anomalies which had arisen in the arrangements: 'I respectfully submit that unless some definite orders are sent placing all the naval matters on this side under one head bad blunders are sure to occur'.[51] Gaunt appears to have already mooted to Hall the idea of closer co-operation, suggesting that he leave the New York Consulate and set up office with Wiseman in Washington in order to unite the coding arrangements,[52] but all that came from this was the offer by Wiseman of additional cable facilities. The two intelligence departments remained quite separate.

The role of the intelligence services in the propaganda campaign fought on American soil is difficult to assess in any precise terms. Hall, in particular, played a significant part as, indeed, did the code-breakers of Room 40 who were able to supply British propagandists with information which not only enabled them to identify and counteract the efforts of their German counterparts but also enabled them to expose publicly German agents in the United States, thereby serving to denigrate the German cause in the process. Hall's main objective was to discredit diplomatic representatives of the Central Powers stationed in America. In August 1915, a German official was obliged to leave the country after a briefcase containing incriminating documents had been seized from him by the American secret service. Although it is not certain that the British were involved in this incident,[53] the documents implicated various officials at the German embassy, including ambassador Bernstorff, in a variety of propaganda activities which represented interference in the internal affairs of the country, at least in American eyes. Together with Voska, Hall was able to keep this issue alive following the interception of an American subject, J. F. J. Archibald, on a Dutch ship docked in Falmouth. Archibald was acting as messenger between the Austrian ambassador in Washington, Constantin Dumba, and the German Foreign Office. The papers seized from Archibald were shown to the London correspondent of the *New York World* which, on 5 September 1915, exposed Dumba as having been involved in plans to prevent the manufacture of armaments at various American munitions plants.[54] Dumba was consequently obliged to leave the country in October and, before the year was over, the German naval attaché, Captain K. Boy-Ed, and the military attaché, Captain Fritz von Papen (the future German Chancellor), had also been invited to leave the United States as a result of the furore created by the publication of the Dumba documents.[55] On his return home, von Papen was intercepted at Falmouth by Hall who, through an examination of Papen's cheque book stubs, was able to expose the activities of yet another German saboteur, Horst van der Goltz.[56] British propagandists took full advantage of these episodes, releasing information to the press and circulating official White Papers. In 1916, they even managed to discredit Bernstorff when Norman Thwaites, while attending a weekend party, appropriated a photograph of the German ambassador with a bathing belle standing on each side of him. The photograph in question was then released to the American press. As Thwaites recalled:

As a piece of anti-enemy propaganda, I have no hesitation in saying that this incident was more effective than pages of editorial matter which the British were alleged to inspire in the United States.[57]

Although this was perhaps overstating the case somewhat, there was undoubtedly a cumulative effect produced by various acts of adverse publicity of this kind from which the Germans were unable to recover completely. The circulation of atrocity stories, the publicity afforded to the German submarine campaign, the exposure of enemy espionage activities in the United States, all helped to develop an image of the criminal inhumanity of the Central Powers which no amount of counter-propaganda concerning the blockade or Ireland was able to dispel. The successful British alliance of propaganda and intelligence activities in the United States ensured a low profile for the British campaign, punctuated by sensational exposures which appeared not to have any connection with the British government. Yet the crowning achievement of this cumulative process was unquestionably the timely release of the famous Zimmermann telegram which was one of the final contributory factors resulting in the decision of the American government to enter the war against Germany.

Shortly after the outbreak of war in August 1914, two Russian cruisers had encountered the German ship *Magdeburg* laying mines in the Baltic. The captain had ordered his signalman to destroy the German code book but was killed in the process of doing so. His body was recovered with the code book still clutched to his chest. Thus, by an extraordinary piece of good fortune, the Allies acquired the ability to break the German naval ciphers at an early stage of the war. The Russians dutifully passed the book on to the British Admiralty where Room 40 set about cracking the codes. This feat, combined with the severance of the direct German trans-Atlantic cables, provided the British with an incalculable advantage over their adversaries in monitoring the flow of information between Germany and the United States. Good fortune was followed by the courageous actions of a young Austrian radio expert, Alexander Szek, in obtaining the German diplomatic ciphers. Szek, who was half English and anti-German, managed to obtain the code which enabled Room 40 to decipher the telegram sent by the German Foreign Minister to his Washington embassy on 16 January 1917. The Zimmermann telegram read as follows:

We intend to begin unrestricted submarine warfare on the first of February. We shall endeavour in spite of this to keep the United States neutral. In the event of this not succeeding, we make Mexico a proposal of alliance on the following basis: make war together, make peace together, generous financial support, and an understanding on our part that Mexico is to reconquer the lost territory in Texas, New Mexico and Arizona. The settlement in detail is left to you.
You will inform the President [of Mexico] of the above most secretly as soon as the outbreak of war with the United States is certain and add the suggestion that he should, on his own initiative, invite Japan to immediate adherence and at the same time mediate between Japan and ourselves.
Please call the President's attention to the fact that the unrestricted employment of our submarines now offers the prospect of compelling England to make peace within a few months. Acknowledge receipt.[58]

The message was transmitted by three separate routes: by wireless from Nauen to Sayville; by cable via Sweden; and through the American State Department Cable. Room 40 intercepted all three routes and immediately set about deciphering the message.

The collection of information is merely one aspect of secret intelligence work. To assess its significance accurately and to take the correct course of action is perhaps more important, if equally difficult. But although Nigel de Grey and the Reverend

W. Montgomery, the experts in Room 40 who deciphered the Zimmermann telegram, were unable to crack the entire message, it was obvious that they had uncovered a potential propaganda bombshell. Hall passed the message on to the Foreign Office and, after a six week period in which the telegram was fully deciphered, its authenticity confirmed and active attempts made to convince the Americans that it was genuine, the story was published by the press on 1 March 1917. Publication caused an immediate sensation in the United States. The reaction of public opinion which had voted for an isolationist platform barely six months earlier was everything that British propagandists could have wished for. The combination of the sensitive Mexican issue with unrestricted submarine warfare, which had finally forced President Wilson to break off diplomatic relations with Germany on 3 February, coming as it did after a series of incidents such as the sinking of the *Lusitania* and other passenger liners, provided the final inducement for the American government to 'take the right view' of the issues at stake in the war.

PROPAGANDA AND THE ANGLO-AMERICAN ENTENTE

With the entry of the United States into the war on 6 April 1917, the first phase of the British propaganda campaign in that country came to a successful close. Indeed, by November 1917, one official doubted the value of continuing the work at all.[59] The principal rationale of Gilbert Parker's section at Wellington House had seemingly disappeared and Parker had himself resigned earlier in the year. Yet because anti-British propaganda did not cease, it was decided to continue his work, and Professor Macneile Dixon, Parker's assistant since 1916, took over the American section. Masterman felt that British policy required explanation in the United States in the same way as propaganda had been required in France and Russia from the start.[60] Masterman's view was widely shared amongst his fellow propagandists who believed that the American entry into the war had merely served to create a new set of priorities in so far as their work was concerned, particularly with regard to the question of operational methods. It was now possible to conduct propaganda in the United States openly and directly in a way that had not been advisable before.

Speculations concerning the need for a change in propaganda policy towards America had begun as early as February 1917 when the Department of Information was being established. Indeed, the departure of Gilbert Parker at the beginning of the year provided an indication that changes were under consideration, as Geoffrey Dawson, the editor of *The Times*, indicated to Willert.[61] Willert, who had definite opinions of his own on this issue, had replied:

So far as the United States is concerned, we have got the skeleton of a good organisation. The salient thing about our plan is that it will involve purely unofficial machinery. Its central feature here would be a small unofficial committee consisting of Englishmen whose business it is to keep in touch with American opinion and some of whom have practical journalistic experience. Its membership would probably be Wiseman, the head of the intelligence people here; Norman Thwaites, one of his assistants; Murray Allison, Ian Beith, myself and perhaps Granville Barker.[62]

Willert felt that increased co-ordination was essential if the newly reorganised machinery in London were to prove successful. His proposed committee would place particular emphasis upon personal propaganda with newspapermen and other influential figures and would require the appointment of a special official in London, such as Geoffrey Butler of the News Department, although the committee would be free from direct official control.

In his capacity as Washington correspondent of *The Times*, Willert had become interested in propaganda from an early stage in the war and he had undertaken several tasks on behalf of the British ambassador, especially in helping to distribute propaganda material in America, despite his initial conviction that 'publicity work of any kind goes against the grain . . . .'[63] By 1917, he was much less reticent and he approached both Spring-Rice and Frank Polk at the State Department to discuss his proposals for the establishment of an overt American propaganda organisation. In an attempt to secure support at home for the scheme, Willert approached Philip Kerr (later Lord Lothian), a member of Lloyd George's 'garden suburb' who had aided the distribution of propaganda in the United States through the Round Table organisation. Willert informed Kerr that Polk was 'not averse to our having a decent propaganda'.[64]

However, while Willert was formulating his own proposals, official steps were being taken to investigate the propaganda situation in America. Lord Northcliffe had persuaded the recently appointed Prime Minister, Lloyd George, to despatch to the United States Pomeroy Burton, a former news editor on *Pulitzer's World* and currently serving as general manager of Northcliffe's newspaper empire, in order to assess the existing propaganda arrangements and report to John Buchan, head of the Department of Information. In January 1917, Burton had written a forceful critique in which he had argued that 'the whole English so-called "propaganda scheme" as practised to date is wrong' and that it was now important 'for the first time to be able to tell the people of America the truth, the whole truth, about the war'.[65] He felt that although there had been adequate general propaganda material — books, pamphlets, pictures and films — there was insufficient attention paid to immediate publicity in the press. This view ran counter to the findings of the first Donald report which concluded that too much emphasis had been placed upon press propaganda and it is difficult to reconcile the two diametrically opposing set of conclusions. They merely serve to cast further doubt upon the validity of investigations conducted by newspapermen into the official propaganda machinery. Yet even Willert was unaware of Burton's appointment and was surprised to discover that he was being sent to America.[66]

Burton's investigations unearthed considerable American disquiet with the existing British propaganda arrangements. As he telegraphed to Buchan on 1 April 1917:

No possible doubt that energetic publicity campaign needed here . . . . There is overwhelming evidence that such publicity work as has been done here by the British has been badly done . . . . The simple fact is that the Masterman bureau has not succeeded in making the slightest impression on the American public while the German propaganda with its direct wireless news service, its constant contact with newspapers small and great and in all languages throughout the country, its organised driving power showing in a 100 different ways, though resented by the more intelligent classes still has had cumulative effect even among these classes while among the masses of working people there is no possible doubt that its effect has been very great and far reaching.[67]

It would appear that 'Burton spent more time investigating the German propaganda campaign in the United States. His findings generally were incompatible with the facts and impressions that had been previously gathered; they took little account of the advantage held by the British in trans-Atlantic communications, although Burton did reserve his main criticisms for that favourite American hobbyhorse, the censorship; they paid little attention to the work of the intelligence and counter-espionage activities of Wiseman, Gaunt, Thwaites and Voska, the full extent of which was probably kept from him; they failed to recognise the significance of the cumulative effects of individual triumphs such as the Bryce Report, the Lusitania medal and the Zimmermann telegram; and they failed to appreciate the wisdom of directing propaganda mainly at the influential classes. In short, his criticisms appear to have taken little account of the fact that the United States was about to enter the war on the side of the Allies.

Burton's telegram caused considerable confusion in London. Northcliffe even instructed him to confine his investigations to British propaganda.[68] But when he produced his final report on 20 April 1917, he remained critical of the way in which the British propaganda in the United States had been conducted hitherto. He wrote:

Lack of touch with England has been the most serious handicap which those who have tried to help the United States understand this war and the British share in it have had to endure. They have laboured under ignorance as to what London really wanted to be said in regard to specific events, they have never been forewarned of important events for which American public opinion ought to have been prepared and they have felt the lack of someone to whom suggestions could be made as to the kind of publicity they ought to have put out from London, and they have nobody to whom they could appeal when it was a case of having important American correspondents and special writers well looked after. They have, in fact, been left almost entirely adrift.[69]

Burton, like Willert before him, therefore proposed the appointment of a special director in London and a committee in the United States consisting largely of experienced journalists who would supervise the distribution of propaganda material such as pamphlets. 'A great deal of energy', wrote Burton, 'has been wasted in this direction. No real effort has been made to do more than convince people already convinced'. He felt that, 'in order to make the United States an effective factor in winning the war, the American people must be aroused to the full significance of what the war means — particularly what it means to them'. One of the basic mistakes so far had been to neglect propaganda among the American masses whereas the Germans had spent millions of dollars on this area with the result that 'immense numbers of people who are pro-Ally even now suspect

England of forcing the States into the war for her own purposes'. Burton then cited the opinion of one observer who had claimed:

The 'let-our-case-speak-for-itself' policy which in the main we have hitherto followed in the USA and which has had the approval of many educated Americans, especially in the Eastern States, has not been a success so far as the masses (or roughly speaking, the working class) are concerned. Travelling through the country one discovers an extraordinary ignorance and confusion of thought about the war prevailing in the masses; and to the existence of these conditions plenty of testimony is forthcoming from purely American sources.[70]

To this, Burton added:

First, the actual *news* requirements of the situation have not been studied and have in no sense been met; second, the general propaganda work, excellent though some of it has been in character . . . has practically all been wasted because it has been expended among the exclusive circles of New York, Boston and other large cities, and the people who need the truth and who are largely misinformed about the basic facts of the war have never heard a word of them or their messages.
The scattered work done here in the direction of distribution of pamphlets, special articles, exhibitions and lectures, has really made no impression, and so far as Wellington House, the War Office, the Foreign Office and the Admiralty (the four branches in London which have up to now regulated all publicity matters here) are concerned, they might have saved a lot of money by doing nothing — the results would have been the same.[71]

In the light of the emphasis which American politicians and historians were subsequently to place upon the significant role played by British propaganda in helping the American government to abandon its neutrality in April 1917, it is curious that Burton should so completely dismiss the efforts of British propagandists at the very moment that the United States had entered the war. It is more curious still that his conclusions met with little contemporary challenge. This may well have been because Wellington House and the machinery responsible for conducting the work since 1914 was already in disgrace as a result of the first Donald report, even though that report had contained little criticism of the way in which propaganda in America had been performed. In addition, Burton was also a Northcliffe man. Few were prepared to challenge Northcliffe's views at a time when he was fast becoming the champion of Lloyd George's campaign to remove control of

Britain's propaganda from the hands of the Foreign Office. Another Northcliffe employee, Arthur Willert, found the Burton report 'quite excellent': 'the only suggestion that I would make is that it would be better for us here to form our advisory commission ourselves than to allow London a chance of butting in'.[72] Yet Burton had proposed closer collaboration with London. Willert later informed his editor that Wiseman and Thwaites were responsible for 'all that was best' in the Burton report,[73] and it is possible that Willert was entertaining hopes of becoming head of the new organisation in America. He informed Dawson:

There seems to be a curious but general view that I ought to try to run the organisation. Wiseman and Thwaites, Gaunt, the naval attaché and I had thought that I could do this in conjunction with my *Times* work and with benefit to it.[74]

Although he had yet to discuss this matter with Balfour, who had recently arrived in the United States at the head of the British War Mission which was designed to explain the state of war and to obtain further war loans, Willert suggested that Dawson 'ought to lend me to the Foreign Office to become a regular Director of American publicity under Buchan'.[75] However, Geoffrey Butler, who accompanied the Balfour mission as its publicity officer, informed Willert that such an appointment would prove difficult because of the 'jealousy of Northcliffe in London'.[76]

On 16 May 1917, with still no decision made about the new American propaganda organisation, Butler informed Willert that the Foreign Secretary had suggested that if Burton's scheme was not implemented soon, he would appoint Willert as a temporary head in New York 'with power to proceed in the same direction but with more caution as befits the somewhat delicate situation with which we are going to be faced'.[77] The matter was left for Buchan to decide. Undoubtedly influenced by the Foreign Office, Buchan chose to appoint Butler as head of a new British Bureau of Information in New York which would supervise propaganda in America and improve the supply of information to the press.[78] Willert was to assist Butler in this work while also serving as liaison officer with George Creel, the head of the newly established American propaganda organisation known as the Committee on Public Information (CPI).

The British Bureau of Information was housed at the offices of the War Mission on New York's Fifth Avenue and was made directly responsible to the American section of the Department of Information, formerly developed at Wellington House, thereby ensuring a considerable measure of organisational continuity. Burton's proposals were, in the main, rejected although Burton himself remained in America to pursue another scheme for developing British publicity through the press. On 17 May, he approached Colonel House who agreed to refer him to several leading editors, but by August Butler informed House that he was unhappy with Burton and wanted no part in his schemes.[79] This was prompted by recent press reports of a speech Burton had delivered to the American Luncheon Club in which the President had been criticised. On receiving an official complaint, Northcliffe replied that the press report which had appeared in the *New York Tribune* was a concoction,[80] but Burton attempted to put matters right himself by explaining to House in October what exactly he had meant when he said of Wilson:

Since he had worked so hard and so earnestly to keep the country out of the war it was quite natural that great masses of people in various sections should be slow to awaken to the urgency of the present situation.[81]

But Burton had become an embarrassment, even to Northcliffe,[82] and he was eventually removed to Paris where he became French representative of the British War Mission. Burton had learnt a lesson in diplomacy, but his publicity schemes — as House admitted to Butler — had been allowed to lapse by default.[83]

That Burton was able to remain in America for so long was due largely to the influence of Northcliffe who was also convinced of the need for an all-out campaign in the United States to explain the true extent of the British contribution to the war. At the end of May 1917, Northcliffe was provided with an ideal opportunity to do precisely that when he was appointed Balfour's successor as head of the British War Mission. Northcliffe's task was to co-ordinate the work of the various missions operating in America and to prevent conflict of interests and loss of effort, to determine priority and to maintain friendly relations both with Allied representatives in the United States and with the United States authorities themselves.[84] These terms of reference left considerable room for manoeuvre. Certainly, when Wiseman was asked by the Cabinet for his opinion of Northcliffe's appointment, he commented:

Mr Balfour's mission has done excellent work, but it is strongly felt that much still remains to be done, especially with a view to bringing home to the United States Government the realities of the present war situation, and the necessity of immediate, active and strenuous co-operation in the war with the least possible delay.[85]

This was exactly how Northcliffe saw his appointment. He considered his main task to be propaganda.

Northcliffe's determination to drive home his message to the American people alarmed both Wiseman and Willert. The latter subsequently noted that 'Northcliffe's self-appointment as British propagandist-in-chief was personal, unofficial and irregular'.[86] Both men were anxious to confine his activities to Washington and became alarmed at his forays to New York, his desire to avoid the British embassy in Washington and the frank manner in which he dealt with the American press. There was also the fear that he would try to dominate the work of Butler and the Bureau of Information. Northcliffe's biographers considered that 'as a journalist and newspaper owner, he had a far better appreciation than the diplomats of what could be done by publicity, above all to America'.[87] Yet, as in London at that time, permanent officials did not agree and were not prepared to lose their control over propaganda without a struggle. When, therefore, Northcliffe attempted to absorb the work of the bureau into his War Mission and to implement the Pomeroy Burton proposals, he was faced with considerable opposition.

Northcliffe was obsessed with the issue of propaganda in the United States. He considered that the work done since the beginning of the war had been lamentable[88] and, in the reports of his discussions with Colonel House, Northcliffe referred constantly to propaganda as the single most important reason for his visit. He alleged that House believed the Allies had been completely outwitted by the Germans in the war of words, particularly in Russia, and that if sufficient money had been made available earlier, the conflict would by now have been well over. Northcliffe wrote:

I do not know how far House speaks for the President on this matter of propaganda but in the course of our interviews he referred to it again and again. He said the war was being fought without imagination; that where the Germans had spent millions we have spent only thousands and that ours was poor matter at that.[89]

The House diaries are, however, quite silent on this issue and reveal none of the emphasis which Northcliffe claimed he placed upon propaganda. Whether House was a master of saying what he thought people wanted to hear without attaching too much significance to what he himself said, or whether Northcliffe's reports were the product of an over-active imagination is not clear. But House was soon in communication with Balfour concerning Northcliffe, particularly with regard to his strained relations with Spring-Rice. House noted: 'Northcliffe does not realize how he is being moved on the chess board [by Lloyd George] and how he is being watched to keep him from making mistakes'.[90] By October 1917, House was discussing Northcliffe's indiscretions with Wiseman. An article had been published at that time in *Current Opinion*, in which Northcliffe stated that America had joined the war for self-preservation rather than to make the world safe for democracy, which was likely to antagonise the President if he happened to see it.[91] Wiseman refused to believe that Northcliffe had personally written the article but he was more critical of his other publicity ventures. Although he admired Northcliffe's 'singleness of purpose' he was concerned by the fact:

that he cannot keep his hands off propaganda, and is even now engaged in writing a series of articles for American magazines which criticise the President and have given some offence in that quarter. He is convinced that he is doing it in the best interests of the country, and simply cannot see that no British official ought to write articles of any kind, still less of a controversial nature.[92]

Willert agreed. He informed Dawson in September 1917 that Northcliffe was making a huge mistake in trying to utilise the American press,[93] although he was to argue later that the good work performed by Northcliffe far outweighed the 'unbridled and damaging publicity' he conducted.[94]

British propagandists working in the United States did not have to endure Northcliffe for much longer. He had already demonstrated that he was uncomfortable with financial matters and he wanted either Lord Reading or Bonar Law to take over the negotiations for further loans and supplies.[95] At the same time, Northcliffe was anxious to return to England because he suspected that Lloyd George had appointed him merely to get him out of the way; Frank Polk recorded that Northcliffe had told him this and later threatened to resign.[96] Finally, in November 1917, Northcliffe did return to

England to direct the British War Mission from its London headquarters. He continued to entertain notions of conducting an open propaganda campaign on a broad basis in America until he gradually became subsumed in the creation of an Enemy Propaganda Department in February 1918. Meanwhile, the work in the United States continued unabated. The transformation of the United States from a neutral to an allied country enabled British propagandists to operate on a much more open and active basis, partially reflecting the urgency for American financial aid. Yet even before the creation of the British Bureau of Information in New York, there had begun a discernible trend away from the early emphasis upon academic propaganda to methods more applicable to a mass campaign.

The most obvious example of this development lay in the use of film. In his report, Pomeroy Burton had justly criticised the arrangements for the distribution of British films prior to 1917. That film propaganda had not been fully exploited in the United States was due largely to the fact that Charles Urban, whose task it had been to arrange distribution on behalf of the government, had encountered serious problems in arranging satisfactory contracts because of his instructions not to reveal his connection with the official British propaganda machinery. Nevertheless, he was able to lay the foundations required for the expansion which took place in 1917. The Department of Information distributed a memorandum in October for the benefit of its cinema agents throughout the world based upon the successful methods of film publicity used experimentally in Omaha.[97] After a preliminary press and poster campaign, a mass parade had been organised there in a manner familiar to Americans, complete with bands and cheerleaders. The film of *The Tanks of Ancre* was shown nightly to specific groups such as the Masons or the Knights of Columbus. Moreover, in October 1917, the War Office Cinematograph Committee maintained the principle of using Americans wherever possible by commissioning D. W. Griffith to make *Hearts of the World* which first opened in London in June 1918.

Another method which was used to an increasing degree was that of the bazaar or exhibition. The first of these had been proposed in July 1916. Norman Thwaites had returned from a visit to England with a collection of war trophies which were not only meant to be shown as part of a series of Allied bazaars[98] but which were also designed to promote the sale of British goods. By 1917, similar ventures were organised on a vast scale. In one bazaar, for example, a full-scale replica of the celebrated London restaurant, the Cheshire Cheese, was constructed. British tanks were also sent for exhibition and, in October 1917, a captured German U-boat was actually sent — although a burst water main very nearly submerged the vessel in a New York street after the truck carrying the submarine had collapsed through the road![99]

The American entry into the war also enabled the British to arrange a personal tour by Raemakers to the United States in June 1917. His tour greatly stimulated the circulation of his cartoons and, by October, they had been reproduced in more than 2000 newspapers with a combined circulation of just under 250 million readers. As a result, 'Raemakers' cartoons have received greater prominence than any other six cartoonists in this country and far greater publicity than in all the European papers put together'.[100] All such work was co-ordinated by Geoffrey Butler at the British Bureau of Information although both Wiseman and Thwaites continued their involvement in propaganda through their military intelligence organisation known as Section V.

Wiseman has provided a detailed description of Section V's work once the United States had entered the war.[101] The work was divided into three types of activity: counter-espionage and secret intelligence gathering in direct collaboration with London; similar work done in conjunction with local British organisations in the United States and with the American authorities; and miscellaneous activities. The first branch investigated issues requested by the War Office and provided information concerning enemy aliens, anarchists, Irish revolution-aries and any other hostile or disloyal elements. It also acted as the liaison between the military intelligence services of both countries and occasionally organised the sending of agents from the United States to enemy and neutral countries. The second branch of Section V acted as a sort of information bureau for the benefit of the Washington embassy, particularly the Indian department, the British War Mission and the British Recruiting Mission. It also worked with the Canadian police and military authorities, and with various American government departments, dealing with such matters as smuggling, the arrest of Irish revolutionaries and the interception of undesirable aliens. Leon Trotsky, for example, was arrested on 3 April 1917 at Halifax following a tip from Voska.[102] It further compiled a list of British subjects living in America and had the task of tracing any deserters from the British armed forces. Wiseman stated that the department's 'miscellaneous' functions included propaganda work, 'but we have done little or nothing in this line recently'.[103] However, by serving as a central information service, Section V maintained its involvement in propaganda, as indeed it did through its provision of facilities for visiting official parties. Section V was also responsible for cable communications on behalf of the British War Mission in New York, although it ceased to monitor foreign shipping in American ports after April 1917.

The system of propaganda that existed in the United States during the last eighteen months of the war, therefore, retained many of the features of the organisation which had operated clandestinely before 1917. But there were fundamental differences, the most obvious and important of which was the British Bureau of Information in New York which was rechristened the British Pictorial Service on 24 July 1918. Even so, its head, Geoffrey Butler, who was himself a former News Department official, maintained his connection with the Foreign Office through the Department of Information, under whose aegis he ostensibly functioned. Wiseman and Gaunt retained their links with the propaganda organisation through Willert, who became Butler's special representative in Washington as the work of the Bureau was extended. Branch offices were also opened in Chicago and San Francisco, employing a total of 96 officials.

Wiseman became increasingly preoccupied with his role as liaison officer between Balfour and Colonel House, for which purpose he was provided with a direct cable link to London in April 1917.[104] The War Cabinet formalised his position in the following December.[105] In terms of influence with the American administration, Wiseman was perhaps the most significant British official working in the United States. He communicated regularly with Sir Eric Drummond, Balfour's private secretary, and with Arthur Murray, head of the American section of the Political Intelligence Department of the Foreign Office.[106] Wiseman looked to the Foreign Office rather than to his intelligence chiefs at the War Office for policy decisions relating to propaganda. In August 1917, for example, he asked Drummond whether he should distribute material he had received from Buchan relating to the question of war aims and possible peace terms: 'Am I safe in accepting anything he sends as representing unofficially and quite broadly the views of the F.O.?'[107] Drummond replied that because the material on this occasion consisted of special reports prepared by the Department of Information which were largely of a factual nature, 'no inferences are drawn in them and they must not . . . be taken as representing in any way the policy of the Foreign Office'.[108] In other words, so long as the Foreign Office was able to maintain its control over the Department of Information, conflicts arising between foreign policy and propaganda could be minimised. But when the Ministry of Information was created and the Foreign Office was forced to renounce its control over propaganda, this proved more difficult.

The incompatibility of propaganda conducted by Beaverbrook and his 'press gang' at the Ministry of Information and the diplomacy conducted by the Foreign Office was vividly illustrated by one incident which concerned propaganda in the United States. In September 1918, Murray informed Wiseman that the Foreign Office had arranged 'a better scheme for looking after and entertainment of distinguished Americans than is at present being carried out by the Ministry of Information'.[109] Lord Reading, who had replaced Northcliffe as head of the British War Mission in America, and Balfour had felt for some time that the hospitality arrangements made by the Overseas Press Centre at the Ministry were inadequate and they had agreed to establish privately a more satisfactory scheme. Murray was anxious not to antagonise the Ministry and requested Wiseman to discuss the matter 'very confidentially' with Butler:

One has to remember of course that he is [now] an official of the Ministry of Information and that it is important that the Ministry at this end should not be appraised of the scheme for they would probably take distorted views regarding it.[110]

Nothing was to come of this scheme because the war ended. But the problems of co-ordinating foreign policy and propaganda had clearly been exacerbated by the reorganisation that had taken place earlier in the year. Given the tension which existed between the Ministry of Information and the Foreign Office throughout 1918, the position of officials who for three and a half years had worked under the latter, only to now find themselves with a new set of masters, often proved difficult in the extreme.

Even Willert's position was a delicate one. His Washington office for the British Bureau of Information was situated next to *The Times* building. Willert was not excluded from the criticism which followed the appointment of newspapermen to leading positions within the official propaganda machinery. When Willert learned of North-cliffe's appointment as Director of Propaganda in Enemy Countries, he wrote to his employer:

I am hoping since reading of the new propaganda task that you have taken over that it may be possible to supplement it in the sense of acting as your representative here. The Americans ought to do a lot in enemy countries and I am sure that they would second your efforts enthusiastically . . . I am on quite good terms with Creel and the others and I need not say that your ideas on propaganda are sure to be listened to more than anyone else's.[111]

Perhaps so, but Willert's ambition to become responsible for some form of official propaganda was not to be realised until after the war when he resigned his position as Washington correspondent of *The Times* and joined the Foreign Office as a News Department official in 1921.

As in the case of organisation, changes in the content of British propaganda in America can largely be explained by the change in circumstances which prevailed after April 1917 and not by sudden revelations of past incompetence. The transformation from being a neutral power to that of an associated power rather than as a full ally demonstrated American determination to retain their independence while adhering to the common aim of defeating the Central Powers. As Wiseman indicated, there was a need at governmental level to promote full agreement on the questions of war aims and peace terms and, on all levels, 'to assist and encourage the United States to bring the full might of power to bear as soon and effectively as possible'.[112] He was keen to emphasise the role being played by Britain since it was the task of American propaganda agencies to arouse their own people for the efforts that total war demanded. As Pomeroy Burton had discovered to his cost, British officials needed to be extremely cautious in this work. Nevertheless, because they had suitable material ready at hand, British propagandists in the United States were able to feed public curiosity about the nature of the war without offending the American administration. This was reflected in the exhibitions of photographs and paintings, the bazaars and in the press and cinema. In other words, the work could now be conducted on a much broader scale than previously. The overall aim was to convey a vivid impression of modern war and, by implication, to suggest to Americans the effort that was now required of them by the Allied cause. To some extent, the British had to contradict their earlier messages which had emphasised the value of investing in British industry since it was bound to ensure victory because, by 1917, there was a more urgent need to convince the American government and people that the Allies needed urgent financial aid.

On the other hand, there was less need to vilify the enemy once it became generally accepted that the Allies were fighting 'Prussian militarism'. However, atrocity propaganda persisted, as indeed did the exposure of German 'misdemeanours' in the United States. In September 1917, the Von Igel papers, which had been seized by the American secret service in April 1916, were published revealing German involvement in Irish and Indian subversive activities. At the same time, the British exposed the Luxburg telegrams which had been intercepted in Room 40.[113] Count Luxburg, the German minister in the Argentine, had transmitted messages via the Swedish embassy concerning unrestricted submarine warfare and the possibility of exempting Argentinian vessels from German attacks. The news was released to the American press on 8 September 1917.[114] In March 1918, Section V was responsible for providing evidence against a group of Hindu revolutionaries who were on trial in San Francisco.[115] Irish activities were also under constant investigation. The always sensitive Irish question became particularly difficult following the British government's attempt to extend military conscription to the Irish in March 1918. Irish resistance led to the arrest of several Sinn Fein leaders on charges of conspiring with the enemy. Hall, who possessed incriminating material dating from an early part of the war, was prepared to pass it on to the prosecuting authorities. When Hall was asked for further evidence, he was reluctant to provide it because by releasing such material he would reveal that his code-breakers had cracked the German ciphers, thus prompting the enemy to develop a new code.[116]

Although as late as April 1918, the War Cabinet recognised that there was 'an entire absence of any organised system of propaganda in Ireland',[117] the British worked hard to improve their image concerning Ireland in the United States. *The Times History of the Irish Rebellion* became a popular seller.[118] Particular attention was paid to propaganda directed at American catholics, especially during the period of the Vatican's peace manoeuvres. Both Butler and Willert monitored catholic opinion and sent detailed reports to the Foreign Office with proposals for action.[119] The Jews, also, were an influential religious community requiring careful attention, particularly after the Balfour Declaration of 8 November 1917 promising a Jewish homeland in Palestine. Balfour himself fully recognised the enormous propaganda value of his declaration,[120] which was followed up in the United States by a campaign to explain Zionism. Wiseman made contact with Justice Brandeis, one of the leaders of the Zionist movement in America,[121] and a report to MI5 further stressed the growing importance of Jewish affairs,[122] particularly in the Eastern states. The British were, moreover, able to abandon their somewhat defensive tone concerning the Russian treatment of the Jews following the March revolution. However, the instability of the Provisional Government, combined with mounting German propaganda on the eastern front, prompted Wiseman and Voska to organise a campaign designed to combat pacifism in Russia and to keep her in the war.[123] Wiseman secured American support for his plan and asked Voska to repeat the methods he had used in the United States while serving as secretary of the Bohemian National Alliance and latterly as head of the new Slav Press Bureau.[124] W. Somerset Maugham was sent as Wiseman's agent to Russia to prepare the ground[125] but, shortly before the Bolshevik revolution, Maugham reported that 'the situation in Russia was entirely out of hand and that no propaganda or organised support undertaken by the Allies could possibly stem [the] rising tide of Bolshevism'.[126] Lenin's success in November merely served to increase the problem for British propagandists. Much of the anti-pacifist material produced by the National War Aims Committee was sent to the United States, especially that which emphasised the commitment of British workers to total victory, in an attempt to combat the subversive influence of Bolshevik propaganda.

Still more problematical was the publication by the Bolsheviks of the secret treaties made by the tsarist government with the Allies which exposed the contradictory nature of the promises made by the British government to the Italians and to the southern Slavs, amongst others. Pamphlets were issued defending the Italians, such as Anthony Hope's *Why Italy is with the Allies* (London, 1917), but mostly the British preferred to adopt a more positive stance in support of the principle of national self-determination for all peoples, particularly after the declaration of war aims by Lloyd

George and Woodrow Wilson in January 1918. Although it had not been established policy before, various pamphlets advocating self-determination amongst the subject nationalities of Eastern Europe had been distributed by Wellington House during the early years of the war, most notably the work of Lewis Namier. Moreover, the work of Voska in the United States had served to enhance the prestige and significance of the Bohemian National Alliance. Anglo-American support for this body and for the Polish International Committee enabled both governments to utilise their members as intelligence agents in Austria and Germany.[127] Voska himself became a captain in American intelligence.

These developments, combined with the Anglo-American negotiations on the League of Nations, would appear to suggest that a high level of co-operation existed between Britain and the United States over propaganda. Yet this relationship became somewhat strained over the issue of Russia. In September 1918, George Creel decided to release the so-called Sisson documents to the press. These documents had been obtained six months earlier by Edgar Sisson, a former editor of *Cosmopolitan Magazine* now attached to the CPI, and purported to show that the Bolsheviks were merely the pliant tools of the German government. Creel and Sisson managed to convince President Wilson of their authenticity and, according to House, they went ahead with their plans to publish without consulting the State Department.[128] Nor did Creel bother to consult the British authorities and became most upset when they proved reluctant to publish the documents in Britain. The papers received a mixed reception in America and the British were convinced that they were forgeries.[129] Even a report by the National Board for Historical Service which stated that the documents were genuine failed to satisfy many American newspapers.[130] For this reason, the British not surprisingly held back from publication. Willert urged his government to support Creel:

As to the authenticity of the documents, it is admitted that there may be doubts in some cases; but who, it is asked, would question it save discredited Bolshevists and worse discredited Junkers.[131]

Willert produced an article which somehow managed to slip past the censors and helped to compensate for Creel's disappointment at the British delay in publication.[132] But, by then, the British had decided to follow the American lead. Wiseman informed Polk that he had received a message from Balfour to the effect that although the British considered the Sisson documents to be forgeries, the government would go ahead with publication if the American government still wished it to do so.[133] Willert was charged with the task of explaining to Creel:

that at the time of their appearance in the United States it was considered inexpedient to arouse in Great Britain by these or similar publications an embittered agitation against the Bolsheviki government which might endanger the lives of British officials whose exchange for M. Litvinoff and his party was at that time in process of negotiation.
When these officials had left Russian territory objection to publication of the documents was thereby removed.[134]

Co-operation was therefore maintained. Given that the documents were accepted by the British to be forgeries, largely correctly, the only major casualty was the truth.

The Sisson documents affair provided an indication that Bolshevism was beginning to replace Prussian militarism as the major enemy. The Germans were, by that time, on the verge of physical exhaustion and incapable of sustaining the fight for much longer. British propagandists were more concerned with preserving Allied unity in readiness for the forthcoming peace conference. For the victorious coalition was by no means the monolithic combination it might have appeared. Held together by little more than the desire to defeat a common enemy, once that goal had been achieved the cement of the combination was removed. Yet there could be no return to pre-1914 conditions. Europe's financial debt to the United States would have to be repaid and the map of Europe completely redrawn. Continued American co-operation was therefore essential to the reconstruction of Europe in a way it had not been before.

The effect of Britain's propaganda campaign in the United States during the First World War was cumulative. The British began their campaign with certain 'natural' advantages, such as linguistic and cultural affinity and the so-called 'special relationship' that has eluded precise definition, which they proceeded to exploit to the full. The Germans were the aggressors in Belgium and France, a fact which forced them on to the defensive over propaganda. In an early report, it was noted that American newspapers were, in general, favourable to the Allied cause and that pro-German sentiment was slight and confined largely to areas such as the mid-west.[135] Moreover, because they controlled a significant proportion of the communications channels between Europe and North America, the British were able to regulate the flow of news and views about the war to suit their image. The Germans were thus forced to maintain the aggressive propaganda which had characterised their initial campaign. Through skilful and successful intelligence operations, the British were also able to expose acts of German espionage on American soil while preserving the secrecy of their own intelligence operations. Again, the Germans were consequently forced back on to the defensive. The establishment of the blockade against the Central Powers, of supplies as of information, and the reluctance of the American government to impose an embargo on trade, meant that the Allies became the natural purchasers of American goods. In seeking to undermine that trade, the Germans were forced to resort to sabotage and submarine warfare, the effects of which were fully exploited by British propaganda.

Before 1917, the work of Gilbert Parker, Guy Gaunt and William Wiseman was probably made easier by the fact that, overall, the British government made fewer diplomatic mistakes than the Germans. The British were able to exploit a series of moral issues ranging from the German invasion of Belgium and the shooting of Nurse Cavell to the sinking of the *Lusitania* and the Zimmermann telegram. Conversely, the Germans were unable to sustain a similar campaign, partly because of Britain's control over the channels of direct communication and partly because their propagandists lacked subtlety and imagination. But the main reason was that they were unable to present their cause as just and right. They failed to portray the British blockade in the same light as the British portrayed the campaign of unrestricted submarine warfare. They were more successful in exploiting the Irish issue, but not sufficiently to prevent British propagandists from recovering.

Above all, the British remained acutely aware of American sensitivity to manipulation by foreign propaganda. American resentment was easily aroused by foreign governments telling them how to think or how they should behave. British propagandists did not tell the American people that they should abandon their neutrality and join the Allied cause. They merely presented the enemy in such a light as to make it impossible for the majority of decent, peace-loving Americans to consider joining the Central Powers.

In this respect, the criticisms made by Pomeroy Burton were largely misplaced. Parker and Masterman did provide a coherent and logical policy from Wellington House, while the Foreign Office was constantly striving to limit the activities of over-enthusiastic self-appointed propagandists, including Burton himself. Both the War Office and Wellington House provided detailed analyses of American newspaper opinion which permitted a rapid response to any unfavourable propaganda while at the same time providing an indication of how widely British news and opinions were being spread.

There is, in fact, very little evidence to suggest that British propaganda was consistently poor, as Pomeroy Burton maintained. His report must be seen in the same light as the investigations of Robert Donald. They were the views of newspapermen who considered that they were better suited to conduct propaganda than the permanent officials who had been placed in charge of the work on the outbreak of war. It is also noticeable that Donald did not share Burton's view of the work in the United States. He maintained that 'it could not have been handled more successfully than it has been'.[136] The selection of an educated and influential audience as the primary targets of British propaganda in America, as elsewhere, was deliberate and logical. Propaganda directed at a mass audience was purposely eschewed. It was the financiers and Treasury officials who made the loans, the journalists who wrote the newspapers, the teachers who educated the students and the lawyers who made the laws. Direct interference from the outside was likely to arouse immediate suspicion and resentment. The British felt that it was better to convince influential Americans to convince in turn their own people than to attempt a direct mass campaign similar to that of the Germans. In London, there was complete agreement on this approach which had been recommended by all sympathetic observers on the spot. As early as September 1914, Willert wrote to his editor:

Possibly I am too cautious but I am more than ever impressed with the desirability of not making too vociferous a bid for American support. We have got the support now and as I said last week, American correspondents are doing all the special pleading that can be wanted.[137]

In view of this opinion, which Willert retained, it is curious to find him strongly supporting Burton's findings three years later. Since Willert was quite prepared in his subsequent writings to praise the work of the early propagandists, it would appear that in 1917 his attitudes were determined by personal ambition. He knew that Burton enjoyed the backing of Northcliffe and that Northcliffe was feared by Lloyd George. He also wanted to direct propaganda in the United States himself.

Both Willert and Wiseman demonstrated that they retained their belief that American opinion should be dealt with cautiously during Northcliffe's War Mission to the United States. Willert's own scheme, on closer scrutiny, was in fact relatively subdued. If, as most authorities emphasised, British propaganda should avoid the appearance of preaching to the Americans, why then should their entry into the war have suddenly required the need for a radical change — especially as there had been sufficient opposition to the decision to suggest that many still opposed belligerency? After April 1917, it certainly made sense to try to reach a broader audience more directly than had been the case before. But there remained a need to be cautious. Right to the very end of the war and beyond, Wiseman stressed this point. He informed William Tyrrell in March 1919:

There are many people who believe that the aggressive method is the only effective one and would like to see Anglo-American societies organized all over the United States, with public demonstrations and meetings, and even go so far as to recommend a big advertising campaign through the Press, posters and leaflets with a view to educating the American people to understand the advantages of an Anglo-American entente.[138]

But he maintained:

I can only say that I consider such a method would be disastrous and produce exactly the reverse effect to that which its advocates contemplate.[139]

Wiseman preferred a discreet approach, even to the extent of avoiding any ostensible connection with the British government:

When people ask whether British propaganda should be official or not, consider for a moment H.M. Government entering into a controversy with Mr. Hearst over the merits of British rule in Egypt. It is unthinkable.[140]

He also warned of the dangers of becoming involved in American party politics. Propaganda, in his view, should be apolitical and he favoured the cultural approach involving educational exchanges, lecture tours, visits by influential public figures and an increased interchange of news. Such methods would not appeal to the mass of the population although Wiseman recognised that 'British propaganda supported by those who live on Fifth Avenue will always be regarded with deep suspicion by the mass of the American public'.[141]

Because of his role in the diplomacy of Anglo-American relations during the war, Wiseman tended to regard propaganda as the servant rather than the master of foreign policy. In this respect, he was operating in the same tradition as the officials in Wellington House and the Foreign Office. The journalists who were called in to take over the propaganda machinery in 1918 saw matters differently. Northcliffe, in particular, saw propaganda as an alternative to diplomacy. Arthur Willert had a foot in both camps. He recognised Northcliffe's qualities as a propagandist but considered that blatant activities were self-defeating in the American context. Even in espousing rationalisation of the British propaganda machinery in the United States during early 1917 to conduct a more open campaign, his approach was still consistent with Wiseman's view that propaganda should only become aggressive when the need to counteract misleading enemy statements occurred or when there was a need to eliminate areas of misunderstanding between Britain and America.[142] Willert paid tribute to Wiseman's excellence at this form of propaganda.[143] Both men felt that a constant campaign of direct and blatant propaganda was unacceptable to the American tradition.

Wiseman's retrospective analysis was not that of Great Britain's 'Commander-in-Chief' for propaganda in America, as George Viereck described him,[144] but that of a man who had played a central role in the campaign first as an intelligence officer and then as a key figure in the diplomatic conduct of the war. Considerable credit must also be given to Wellington House and to Gilbert Parker for initiating the campaign and to Geoffrey Butler who completed it. By recognising that propaganda must be subordinate to diplomacy, and that German actions often spoke louder than British words, all these men played a considerable role in capitalising upon the fundamental advantages which Britain enjoyed over Germany in the battle for American allegiance. But it was not just a question of avoiding actions or propaganda which would offend the Americans, although that certainly played an important part, from which the Germans would have profited had they learned the lesson of their early campaign. There was also the more positive aspect of the British campaign which served to foster a particular stereotype of the Central Powers as cruel, tyrannical regimes bent on world domination and, as such, were anathema to the democratic ideals cherished in Britain, France and America. The manner in which the battle was fought, whether on the western front, at sea or in the hearts and minds of the American public ensured that British propaganda would make a positive contribution towards the decision of the United States government to join the Allied cause. Once that decision had been made, the task of British propaganda was made considerably easier although it remained important to ensure that the past experience provided the basis upon which the future of inter-allied co-operation was maintained.

6 British Propaganda in Enemy Countries

In 1932, a German spy who had worked undetected in the War Office censorship organisation for the entirety of the First World War wrote:

Even today the poison is still working that Britain instilled into her terrible anti-German propaganda campaign, undermining our reputation and turning every nation of the world against us. We were branded as peace-breakers, mad with the lust for conquest and power, and the blood-guilt of the War was fastened on us .... While Germany was still theorising as to whether propaganda was ethical or not, America had developed it into a practical science and England into a great art.[1]

Such a view was by no means uncommon in Weimar Germany. Perhaps its most famous exponent was Adolf Hitler who stated in *Mein Kampf*:

In the year 1915, the enemy started his propaganda among our soldiers. From 1916 it steadily became more intensive, and at the beginning of 1918, it had swollen into a storm cloud. One could now see the effects of this gradual seduction. Our soldiers learned to think the way the enemy wanted them to think.[2]

But if Hitler was keen to stress the cumulative effect of the work before the creation of the Enemy Propaganda Department at Crewe House in February 1918, the work of Lord Northcliffe during the final nine months of the war has tended to attract a disproportionate amount of historical attention in relation to the overall propaganda effort conducted by the British government between 1914 and 1918. While much of its work was undoubtedly effective, the reputation which Crewe House has earned for its successful role in helping to defeat the Central Powers has not only been exaggerated but it has also tended to devalue the efforts made in the sphere of psychological warfare before 1918. It must be remembered that there was a great deal of political mileage to be gained in Weimar Germany from praising British propaganda. By maintaining that the German army had not been defeated on the field of battle but had been forced to submit due to the disintegration of morale from within, a process which had been accelerated by skilful British propaganda, Hitler was providing historical legitimacy for his 'stab-in-the-back' theory. For propaganda reasons of his own, therefore, Hitler was quite prepared to pay tribute to what he described as the 'very real genius' of Britain's war propaganda.

This was by no means an original thesis. Hitler's former military commanders, Generals Ludendorff and Hindenburg, had been equally prepared to praise the effectiveness of British propaganda emanating from Crewe House as a rationalisation for their inadequacies on the field of battle. In his memoirs, Ludendorff stressed the combined role played by the Allied blockade and British propaganda in precipitating a serious decline in the morale of both the civilian population and the troops serving at the front. He wrote:

In wide quarters a certain decay of bodily and mental powers of resistance was noticeable, resulting in an unmanly and hysterical state of mind which under the spell of enemy propaganda encouraged the pacifist leanings of many Germans.[3]

Moreover, he continued, the British campaign:

now turned its attention directly to the man at the front, who by this time was ready to give it a hearing. Blockade and propaganda began gradually to undermine our moral resolution and shake the belief in ultimate victory.[4]

Ludendorff then went on to describe a campaign of considerable proportions during the last months of the war, mounted from a variety of sources, particularly from neutral Holland and Switzerland, which bombarded the German army and civilian populace with material designed to destroy the will to continue fighting. He also expressed his frustration at the apparent inability of the German government to combat effectively this campaign and, he concluded:

We were hypnotised by the enemy propaganda as a rabbit is by a snake. It was exceptionally clever and conceived on a great scale. It worked by strong mass-suggestion, kept in the closest touch with the military situation and was unscrupulous as to the means it used.[5]

The result was that 'many people could no longer distinguish between enemy propaganda and their own sentiments'.[6]

Although Hindenburg's memoirs reflect little of the obsession with the effects of British propaganda demonstrated by Ludendorff,[7] contemporary accounts do reveal a similar concern: 'His airmen throw, besides bombs which kill the body, leaflets which are intended to kill the soul'.[8] Another claim stated in July 1918 that 'a cloud of anger, hopelessness and doubt spreads further and further over the German people, due, to no small extent, to the Northcliffe propaganda'.[9] A German army order of 29 August 1918 stated that the British government had 'founded for this purpose a special ministry, "The Ministry for the Destruction of the German Confidence", at the head of which he [i.e. the enemy] has put the most thoroughgoing rascal of all the Entente, Lord Northcliffe'.[10] However, as Robert Donald pointed out shortly after the war, the Germans had been too quick to see Northcliffe as the sole villain of the piece:

Some time ago Hindenburg raised a great cry of distress and said Lord Northcliffe was demoralising his army and his people. He was a little premature, because at that time Lord Northcliffe and his Committee had not begun operations in Germany.[11]

In fact, Crewe House had directed its initial efforts against Austria-Hungary which, in view of its heterogeneous population, was felt to offer more immediate prospects of a propaganda success. Moreover, the leaflets to which Hindenburg referred as being dropped in increasing numbers over the German lines during the early summer of 1918 were actually prepared and distributed by MI7(b)4 at the War Office. It was not until the end of August 1918 that Crewe House assumed responsibility for directing this work, by which time MI7(b)4 had handled nearly 26 million leaflets, prisoner-of-war letters and cartoons.[12]

If Hindenburg was therefore guilty of failing to appreciate the work of Northcliffe's predecessors, so also was Robert Donald who had been a constant critic of the system which had been controlled by the established Whitehall departments and who, indeed, had been largely responsible for initiating the transfer of that control into Northcliffe's hands. In other words, the focus of contemporary and historical attention on the work of Crewe House has served to obscure recognition of the activities of both British and French propagandists before 1918. In the words of two former French officials:

A partir du moment où le nom de Lord Northcliffe leur fut jeté en pâture, ils ne voulurent plus connaître que lui et lui attribuèrent la responsibilité de toute l'oeuvre accomplie depuis deux ans et demi.[13]

Although the work of Crewe House was undoubtedly effective, largely by virtue of the scale on which it was conducted and the prevailing circumstances of 1918 which provided the prerequisite for a successful psychological offensive, it owed much of its efficacy to the cumulative process begun during an earlier part of the war.

The concept of psychological warfare was first practised by the Germans who initiated the business of dropping leaflets over Allied troops in Nancy during the battle of Grande-Couronne in September 1914.[14] Some leaflets even appear to have been dropped over Paris.[15] By October 1914, the Germans were publishing the *Gazette des Ardennes* for the benefit of French troops. At first, the War Office was reluctant to respond. When Lord Northcliffe suggested in September 1914 first to Sir John French and then to General Wilson that facsimile letters should be dropped over German lines by aeroplane, the latter replied that propaganda was 'a minor matter — the thing was to kill Germans'.[16] But when, in response to the Nancy venture, Sir Ernest Swinton suggested that the Royal Flying Corps should initiate leaflet-dropping raids over the German lines, it was decided to experiment with this form of warfare. By March 1915, there had been developed a full-scale 'paper war' supervised by the Directorate of Special Intelligence under Cockerill.[17] The War Office remained in charge of this task until 1 September 1918.

Not only did the British prepare their own material but also undertook the distribution of French propaganda. In August 1915, the French established their own Service de la Propagande Aérienne which compiled *La Voix du Pays*, a newspaper designed for occupied France.[18] The French asked the British to undertake aerial distribution of their material in the area occupied by British forces such as Lille. According to one French account:

Il ne nous était pas possible, naturellement, d'exercer aucun contrôle sur eux. Pourtant nous avions l'impression que le commandement britannique avait pris très du sérieux cette question de lancement de journaux. Nous ne pouvions exiger de lui, commes nous le faisions des unités françaises, les comptes rendus de lancement. Mais, de lui-meme, il nous renseignait sur les efforts faits et sur les résultats obtenus.[19]

This arrangement was to continue uninterrupted until the end of 1917 when the aerial distribution of propaganda by aeroplane was brought to an end. This was because of an official German announcement in May 1917 that the dropping of inflammatory literature, particularly that directed against the Kaiser, would henceforth be considered a violation of international law. Consequently, on 17 October 1917, four British airmen were arrested and tried by court martial 'for having distributed pamphlets containing insults against the German army and Government among German troops in the Western Theatre of War'.[20] Although two of the accused were acquitted due to lack of evidence, and although the court questioned the ruling concerning violations of international law, Lieutenants Scholtz and Wookey were nonetheless sentenced to ten years imprisonment. In the meantime, the British went ahead with plans to initiate a more active campaign of aerial propaganda on the western front. On 20 December, GHQ in France suggested that a good deal more should be done in view of the results of German propaganda in Russia and France but also because of the apparent fear of the Germans concerning the impact of British propaganda. As a result, on 9 January 1918, the War Office approved an intensification of aerial distribution but, instead of dropping French newspapers, which were considered to be too provocative, it was decided to drop their own paper, *Le Courier de l'Air* (first published in April 1917), over the occupied zones. However, on 28 January 1918, the German wireless broadcasts contained news of the punishments meted out to Lieutenants Scholtz and Wookey. The War Office ordered the immediate suspension of aircraft distribution of propaganda material over enemy lines. The British government took up the issue with the Germans and eventually threatened reprisals. This threat produced the desired effect. On 11 March 1918, on the eve of the reprisals, the Dutch government informed His Majesty's government that the two British pilots were to be pardoned, returned to their camps and would be treated as normal prisoners of war.[21] Even so, the Air Ministry did not wish to risk any more of its officers or machines[22] and the order to suspend aircraft distribution remained in force until the end of October 1918, despite the appeals of Beaverbrook and Northcliffe to reverse the decision[23] (although Northcliffe did come to accept the Air Ministry's case[24]).

Instead, the British chose to rely upon distribution by balloon. Once this method had been introduced on a large scale in 1918, Colonel Onslow of the General Staff suggested that the distribution of French newspapers should be resumed.[25] This made it all the more important for *Le Courier de l' Air* to be continued in order to provide an alternative viewpoint in the occupied areas. As Colonel Fisher informed Onslow:

Personally, I think in view of what the French papers are now saying and their general tone it is desirable that the inhabitants of occupied territory should also be informed of our point of view. If the French include in their material for aerial distribution some of the articles appearing in their press I should think that the Germans will gladly use them for propaganda purposes on their own account.[26]

Nevertheless, co-operation between the two countries did continue and, by September 1918, *La Voix du Pays* was being distributed daily over the German lines by balloon, 'surtout par les soins de l'Aéronautique Britannique qui a bien voulu se charger de ce service, c'est à dire au Nord de la Somme'.[27] Various experiments were conducted which often bordered on the absurd. Chalmers Mitchell, for example, deduced that:

For any piece of paper, folded or unfolded, the theoretical wind driftage in miles from a point vertically under the point of liberation from the balloon to the point on the ground where the paper falls is given by the formula:-

$$\text{wind speed in mph} \times \frac{\text{number of minutes paper would take to fall}^{28}}{60}$$

In other words, a leaflet which took 20 minutes to fall from a height of 5000 feet in a wind speed of 15 miles per hour would drift $15 \times {}^{20}\!/_{60} = 5$ miles. The Directorate of Military Intelligence believed that with a wind speed of 50 miles per hour, the balloons could reach Germany,[29] but 'the bulk of the propaganda was distributed over an area of from 10 to 50 miles behind the enemy lines'.[30] This has led one historian recently to challenge the alleged efficacy of balloon propaganda:

Leaflets could thus only have reached German civilians by the occasional freak balloon, by being brought back by soldiers on leave and by such surreptitious channels as being slipped inside neutral books and papers sent into Germany. It is hard to believe this was how a revolution was set off.[31]

Aircraft distribution was, indeed, a more effective means of reaching the German civilian population, as Beaverbrook always maintained,[32] and it was in fact resumed during those critical days in early November. By then, the cumulative effect of a campaign which had been fought for the past three years was beginning to produce visible results.

The British and French had worked together on other aspects of propaganda work, stemming initially from their common censorship functions which led to an exchange of general information through the *Bureau Central Inter-Allié*, established in September 1915 to ensure close liaison between the Allied General Staffs.[33] The information exchanged derived either from censorship activities or from other sources categorised as 'special intelligence'. And it was the intelligence aspect of the War Office's functions which led to another significant aspect of British propaganda directed against enemy countries. Although the precise nature of the relationship between propaganda and secret service work remains unclear,[34] it does appear from the limited evidence available that the distribution of propaganda material was an integral function of the work of intelligence agents operating in neutral countries adjacent to Germany, particularly Denmark, Holland and Switzerland. Their task was not simply confined to the gathering of information about German military and civilian affairs but also included the smuggling into enemy territory of propaganda designed to undermine German morale and thereby to weaken the capacity of the enemy to continue the war. It also appears that these agents attempted to foster and promote revolutionary elements within Germany and the Dual Monarchy.

In Switzerland, the French took the lead in organising subversive propaganda against the German government, led by attaché Frouville and Professor Emile Haguenin.[35] The American propaganda representatives made contact with Haguenin in July 1918[36] while the British, though playing a subordinate role, had links with the French through their consulate at Zurich and their established agents in Basle and Berne. The chief British organising agent was Leo Wolfsohn, alias Mandelbaum, a Russian by birth who became a naturalised Swiss. He developed a network of agents who smuggled propaganda into Germany by various routes, chiefly across Lake Constance. When exposed by the Swiss police in June 1917, they were said to have had nearly 60,000 leaflets in their possession.[37] In common with his French counterpart, Wolfsohn enjoyed links with various German socialists and anarchists, most notably with those producing the social democratic newspaper, *Freie Zeitung*, which was printed in Berne and smuggled into Germany by secret critics of the 'military regime'. There was also a high ranking British officer in Berne, often presumed to be a Colonel Sawyer, whose organisation:

ausdrücklich mit der Erregung revolutionärer Stimmung in deutschen Volke betraut sei und Mittelsleute zu diesem Zwecke nach Deutschland schicke.[38]

The connection between these British agents and the avowedly republican group which issued the *Freie Zeitung* proved invaluable. Both the British and French were able to utilise its German members as couriers and as informants on the internal condition of Germany. The group also provided them with several successful pamphleteers including Hermann Rosemeier and Dr Richard Grelling who wrote *J'Accuse* (London, 1916). A wide variety of methods was used to smuggle the material into Germany, including bottles floated down the Rhine, literature carried across the border by schoolchildren or workers and hidden inside books and newspapers. In 1917, the Foreign Office was informed that some 2500 copies of the *Freie Zeitung* had been smuggled into Germany wrapped up in other newspapers,[39] much of this having been organised by the French.

In Holland, it was the British who took the lead: 'Was die Schweiz für Frankreich bedeutete, bedeuteten die Niederlande für England'.[40] The key figure here was Captain Tinsley who held the post of director of the Uranian Steamship Company which had its main offices in Rotterdam. Tinsley's organisation, according to one source, employed over 300 agents.[41] He sub-divided his work into four sections dealing with naval, military and industrial espionage and with press propaganda. There were, in addition, five branch offices throughout Holland serving both intelligence and propaganda functions, including the dissemination of Reuters news. Tinsley enjoyed a wide range of influential friends, especially war correspondents such as Leonhard Kooyper of the *Nieuwe*

Rotterdamsche Courant who travelled freely inside Germany and at the German front lines, dutifully reporting all he had seen to Tinsley on his return. Tinsley also worked with another journalist in Holland, Carl Minster, a committed opponent of the German regime who had fled his country in March 1917 to evade military service and who had settled in Holland from where he continued to produce *Kampf*, a radical weekly paper which he had founded in Duisburg in July 1916. *Kampf* was smuggled into Germany in newspaper and tobacco shipments and it was also distributed by French airmen.[42] In an attempt to promote insurrectionary movements within Germany, Minster established contact with the *Freie Zeitung* group in Switzerland. According to Hans Thimme, Minster then approached the American government for support and was in turn passed on to the British who proved more receptive to his schemes. It also appears that Tinsley agreed to help subsidise *Kampf*. However, 'Ein strikter Nachweis für diese Vorgänge hat sich niemals erbringen lassen'.[43] After the war, the Dutch social democratic party defended Minster against charges that he had been employed as a British agent. Although the evidence is inconclusive, there was nothing unusual in the British government subsidising a foreign newspaper for wartime propaganda purposes. Tinsley was, in fact, head of British intelligence in Holland and Germany,[44] and he worked closely with G. F. Steward who supervised British propaganda in the Netherlands during the last two years of the war. Steward operated through the Limited Liability Company in Rotterdam, ostensibly a normal commercial enterprise.[45] Steward was answerable directly to Ernest Maxse, the British Consul-General in Holland, but his operations were largely directed by S. A. Guest from Wellington House, a connection which the Germans unearthed in October 1917 when letters from Guest to Maxse were intercepted.[46]

Guest was the most important figure in Britain's propaganda campaign in enemy countries before Lord Northcliffe's appointment in February 1918. He was responsible for the Dutch section at Wellington House where his work drew him increasingly into a consideration of propaganda in Germany. Guest worked through Steward in order to utilise Tinsley's intelligence network for distributing propaganda material into Germany through Holland.[47] Sir George Aston stated in 1930 that he could not:

recall an example of a practice adopted in some foreign countries in the war, and in Russia at the present time, of using Secret Services to undermine the authority of foreign governments and to incite internecine strife, class hatred and rebellion.[48]

Such claims must be treated with extreme scepticism. In January 1918, Maxse stated that 'Our only chance of influencing German opinion at the present minute is to try and open the eyes of the German Socialist Party to what the real aims of the Allies are'.[49] By that time, British contacts with German socialist revolutionary groups were well established. Guest had begun to develop these links as early as 1916, initially through his contacts with Dr Terwagne, the head of Belgian propaganda in Holland who was in touch with Dutch socialist groups smuggling material to their German comrades.[50] On 5 June 1916, *The Times* referred to a statement by the German Chancellor, Bethmann-Hollweg, concerning the effects of British pamphlets being circulated inside Germany. Guest did not know for certain whether the material referred to had originated in Wellington House but in October he reported that 'our efforts to circulate pamphlets in Germany have accordingly been redoubled and the total number exported directly to that country must now amount to a very considerable quantity'.[51] The pamphlets were printed in German by the Payot company of Switzerland and among the requests which poured into the Foreign Office for such material came one from Tinsley.[52]

The liaison between Wellington House, the Foreign Office and the War Office enabled British propagandists to co-ordinate their efforts against the enemy as early as 1916, a development which has been generally overlooked in later accounts with their emphasis upon the work of Crewe House. However, inter-departmental rivalry and jealousies jeopardised the effectiveness of that co-ordination. The profusion of propaganda bodies undoubtedly created considerable friction but the bureaucratic struggle at home was not necessarily reflected in the field, as the success of Guest's operations indicate. In fact, enemy propaganda work was relatively well co-ordinated and the arrangements made for the exchange of information between the War Office and the Foreign Office did ensure some consistency in the preparation of Wellington House material.[53]

The content of the material designed for enemy opinion was conceived in relation to the campaign in allied and neutral countries. This was greatly facilitated by S. A. Guest's position at Wellington House where much of the material used in Holland was also sent into

Germany. The German edition of *War Pictorial, Der Krieg im Bilde*, was dropped over the German lines and contained such universal themes as the efficiency of the British army, the global nature of the war effort and the total allied commitment that this involved. Depictions of the humane treatment which prisoners of war received were used in all target areas but received particular emphasis in material dropped over enemy lines in an attempt to reassure enemy soldiers that they would be well-treated, contrary to the claims of German propaganda. The prisoner of war theme was pursued strongly by the War Office propagandists who prepared leaflets and cartoons for aerial distribution. Though they worked independently of Wellington House, an examination of the material produced in 1918 reveals close liaison and similarity of aims.[54]

Of necessity, the War Office produced mainly flysheets. These consisted mostly of photographs with short written commentaries and slogans or cartoons. The photographs were normally obtained either from Wellington House or from the War Office's own considerable collection. A popular device, apart from the obvious pictures of German prisoners of war having a thoroughly good time in British camps, was the production of facsimile letters written by prisoners describing the comforts of their situation or condemning the war, especially if they were deserters. German prisoners were provided with special letter sheets and instructions for their guidance and, in those camps which were selected as sources of propaganda, the inmates were especially well fed.[55] Intercepted letters from German soldiers at the front to their families were also reproduced alongside letters home from British troops in order to contrast conditions on either side of the lines. Information obtained through the intelligence services concerning the price of food in Germany prompted the production of menus and shopping lists comparing how much cheaper food was in Britain in an attempt to reveal the supposed failure of the U-boat campaign and the corresponding success of the blockade.

The reproduction of prisoners' letters testifying to German failure could, of course, be dismissed simply as the work of forgers and traitors. The British therefore stressed the accuracy of such statements made by Germans in captivity. Moreover, in order to enhance the credibility of the notion that German soldiers had done the honourable thing by surrendering, there was an attempt to drive a wedge between the German soldier and his government. Many leaflets were therefore directed against the evils of the German government through caricatures of the Kaiser or attacks upon Prussian militarism and German imperialism. One cartoon, entitled 'A Place in the Sun' portrayed the German donkey being tempted with a carrot against the background of a graveyard. There were also derogatory quotations extracted from statements made by the German royal family with particular emphasis on the sacrifices they were demanding from their troops in order to pursue questionable aims, as in the case of the leaflet entitled '"Just for the Fun of it" — the Crown Prince'. The German government was further accused of resisting genuine peace efforts, notably those made by the Papacy.

The emphasis upon Prussian militarism, as distinct from the normal instincts and habits of the average German, was quite deliberate. On the one hand, it provided a useful catch-phrase for propaganda in allied and neutral countries while, on the other, the British were attempting to exploit separatist tendencies within a German federation which was, after all, both young and vulnerable. Accordingly, leaflets were dropped which were specific appeals to the various regional groups such as the Saxons and the Bavarians ('Prussia-Bavaria' and 'Are the Bavarians a Free People?'). In June 1918, it was decided to increase the number of direct appeals to the Poles under German domination, a reflection of the influence of Crewe House.[56] An additional dimension to this particular approach was the attack upon the Prussian 'industrial-military complex', namely war profiteers whose interests were bound up with continuing the war. This particular line of attack became merged with the appeal to German socialists which involved the distribution of socialist newspapers printed in Germany and appeals to proletarian soldiers. One leaflet, for example, contained extracts from Karl Kautsky's condemnation of the Brest-Litovsk treaty. In short, Guest, Tinsley and the War Office were exploiting a specifically German situation, just as in England the NWAC attempted to combat socialism and pacifism. However, although the NWAC was attempting to suppress precisely those elements at home which British propagandists were attempting to encourage within Germany, no contradiction was admitted because, as some leaflets revealed, the British worker was fighting for the right cause!

The effect of any propaganda designed to undermine the morale of the enemy invariably depends, to a considerable extent, upon the fortunes of war. Victorious troops tend to have high morale because they are victorious, regardless of any hardships which they might have to endure. They are, perhaps, most vulnerable to propaganda in the aftermath of a great offensive which has failed to bring decisive results even if it has not actually resulted in military defeat. Thus, when the great German offensive of Spring 1918 had been contained, British propaganda was provided with a genuinely fertile field in which it could operate. It is in this light that the impact of the considerable expansion in the number of leaflets dropped during 1918 must be seen, and not simply in terms of organisational changes. The very fact of being able to drop large numbers of leaflets over enemy lines with relative impunity was itself an indication of the changing fortunes of war. It is, for example, noticeable that the documents reproduced in Lutz's *Fall of the German Empire* (1932) relating to the orders issued to the German troops not to read or distribute the leaflets dropped by the British and French are dated in August 1918, after the Allied breakthrough.[57] It was at this time that leaflets appeared describing the collapse of Germany's allies and the arrival of the 'First Million' Americans. Moreover, the failure of the German spring offensive, the impact of the blockade, German submarine losses and military defeats were driven home in leaflets depicting German dead and the pointlessness of the sacrifice. The death skull, a prominent Gothic symbol, made regular appearances in which death toasted its latest recruits. The revelations of Prince Lichnowsky, from which 'proof' of aggressive German diplomacy could be extrapolated,[58] were equally exploited to such effect that Ludendorff later claimed that 'Prince Lichnowsky shares the gruesome distinction of having undermined the discipline of the Army with the Bolsheviks and many others'.[59]

Britain's enemy propaganda, therefore, clearly benefited from the immediacy of its themes and content, particularly when it was directed at the enemy soldier on the western front. Yet it was also assumed that he would somehow relay home his increasing disillusionment, usually in the form of letters. Balloons could also be used by the Allies to reach the civilian population, although they were an unreliable method of distribution. However, they were able to reach the crucially important assembly areas where units which had been withdrawn from the lines were able to mix with troops being returned to the trenches and from where soldiers departed for home on leave or sick-leave. It was mainly in the assembly areas rather than in the trenches that disciplinary problems surfaced in the form of mutinies or other, less serious, troubles. It was, moreover, the function of agents working in neutral countries bordering on German soil to smuggle material directly to the civilian population. This was regarded as a long-term campaign that had begun as early as the beginning of 1916; the intensification of balloon distribution in 1918 greatly reinforced the cumulative effect of that work.

Despite the considerable co-ordination which did occur in the enemy propaganda campaign before the creation of Crewe House, it would be wrong to assume that all the departments involved pursued a common policy in complete harmony. Early in 1917, for example, S. A. Guest proposed a special coupon scheme involving leaflets depicting well-fed German prisoners together with a coupon which any enemy soldier could surrender in exchange for one mark's worth of food. The coupon would expire after a period of seven days and could be used only once. Guest further suggested that similar coupons might be distributed among the civilian population and that slight variations in the printing could enable their movement inside Germany to be monitored.[60] The Department of Information supported the scheme but GHQ opposed it on the grounds that 'Germans, by reproducing coupons in large numbers and giving one to every German in the line, would succeed in mulcting us for extra chocolate for every prisoner'.[61] The military authorities disliked the idea of bribing hungry soldiers to desert their country and the scheme was rejected. But the episode does at least reveal the degree of communication between the various departments concerned, including the French propaganda authorities.[62]

Co-ordination of effort has been stressed in order to evaluate more accurately the true significance of the creation of the Enemy Propaganda Department in February 1918. Continuity was certainly maintained in the person of S. A. Guest, with whom Wickham Steed made contact at an early date. Steed felt that parts of Guest's work in Holland and Switzerland were 'excellent' and that 'one of his Swiss channels might be used by us to get our stuff into Austria'.[63] Even so, he felt that Guest's work 'hitherto has been of a mild "poison gas" type . . . . Our methods will have to be more of the "high explosive" type if they are to produce any tangible results in time to affect the Austrian offensive'.[64] On the one hand, Steed's comments reveal both the willingness and the need of the new department to draw upon established practices and personnel. The War Office did, after all, continue to produce propaganda for military zones until

1 September 1918 and remained in charge of its distribution until the end of the war under the supervision of Chalmers Mitchell at MI7(b)4. Guest also continued his work in Holland and Switzerland until he was eventually transferred to Crewe House in October. On the other hand, Crewe House represented a new mood of aggressive propaganda in response to the changed conditions prevailing after nearly four years of war. Although its creation might appear to represent a condemnation of past methods, as indeed it was seen in some quarters, this was not in fact the case. Lord Northcliffe's appointment as Director of Propaganda in Enemy Countries was merely the culmination of an interest he had shown throughout the war, an appointment made possible by the advent of Lloyd George as Prime Minister and the winds of change. Just as Northcliffe believed in his own power to influence government through the power of the printed word, so also did he believe in the power of propaganda to influence radically the course of the war, as he felt he had demonstrated in America. He was joined in this belief by Wickham Steed who was largely responsible for introducing what was perhaps the most novel feature of the work conducted in 1918, namely the campaign directed against Austria—Hungary. The considerable degree to which the Dual Monarchy came to dominate the work of Crewe House was due mainly to Steed's influence and, indeed, according to one of his colleagues, 'Wickham Steed was the heart and soul of Crewe House'.[65]

Steed was the natural choice to run the Austro-Hungarian section of the new Enemy Propaganda Department. As diplomatic correspondent of *The Times* in Vienna between 1902 and 1913, he had acquired a wide knowledge and profound understanding of the Habsburg Monarchy. When war broke out in August 1914, Steed was then foreign editor of *The Times* and immediately began to devote his energies to the cause of national self-determination on behalf of the oppressed nationalities of the Austro-Hungarian empire in collaboration with a former colleague, Robert Seton-Watson. In March 1916, Steed devised a 'programme for peace' calling for the creation of a Yugoslavian state, 'a self-governing Poland and an autonomous Bohemia'.[66] Together with Seton-Watson, Thomas Masaryk, Sir A. F. White and Dr Ronald Burrows, Steed was instrumental in the foundation of *The New Europe,* the foremost aim of which was 'to further consolidate that entente cordiale of allied publicists, which must accompany the wider political entente, if the Allies are to think and act in harmony, and to help towards the formation of a sane and well-informed body of public opinion upon all subjects affecting the future of Europe'.[67] When Crewe House was formed, Steed was able to secure the services of Seton-Watson as his assistant as a direct result of the struggle which took place in February 1918 between the Foreign Office and the Ministry of Information over the Political Intelligence Department.[68]

In July 1917, Seton-Watson had drawn up a memorandum which argued that seven points should be stressed in Allied propaganda directed against Austria-Hungary: the complex and artificial character of the dualistic structure of Habsburg government; the absolutist treatment of certain parts of the empire before 1914; the foreign policy of the Vienna cabinet, particularly in the Balkans; the racist ideology and practices of the Magyar governing oligarchy; the wartime atrocities inflicted upon the smaller national communities; the growth of patriotic movements for freedom; and the issue of Bosnia-Herzegovina, especially the desire of the Yugoslavs to amalgamate with Serbia. However, until the British government decided to issue a clear statement of policy concerning Austria-Hungary, Seton-Watson felt, it would be 'far safer and wiser to refrain from all propaganda' which would raise 'false hopes whose realisation there is no intention of assisting'.[69] Firm policy declarations were, in other words, essential to an effective propaganda campaign. Following the Bolshevik revolution and the Russian departure from the war, the situation in Germany appeared to offer no more prospect of an early propaganda success than the situation in Austria-Hungary where mass strikes broke out in January 1918. Morale in Bulgaria also seemed to be holding firm. Wickham Steed felt that:

The futility of British propaganda hitherto has been due to its divorce from policy. It is no good dumping down literature in various parts of the world explaining what noble people we are and how immense has been our contribution to the war. That does not interest people. You have got to make up your mind where and how hard you can hit the enemy hardest and then to get to work and do it without talking about it. For that there must be a policy; and once it has been laid down and sanctioned it must be carried out by every available means.[70]

He was quite clear in his own mind concerning the direction which that policy should take. The Austrian Germans and the Magyars upon whom the Germans chiefly relied for stability within the Habsburg Monarchy had been neglected as targets for British propaganda. So too had the non-German and non-Austrian peoples of this heterogeneous empire despite the fact that they were largely anti-German if not entirely pro-Ally. President Wilson had led the way on 8 January 1918 when he proclaimed his Fourteen Points calling, amongst other things, for a readjustment of Italy's frontiers on lines of nationality, autonomous development for the peoples of Austria-Hungary and the restoration of Rumania, Serbia and Montenegro. Steed believed that if the 'oppressed nationalities' could be convinced of Allied sincerity and the certainty of Allied victory, the influence of the Austrians and Hungarians would be undermined thereby weakening the striking power of the Habsburg armies. In short, he believed that the primary objective of Crewe House was to foster the disintegration of the Dual Monarchy through the promotion of internal disaffection and even insurrection among the subject races which would, in turn, weaken Germany's capacity to sustain the fight.

Northcliffe provided Steed and Seton-Watson with his complete backing and while he sought Cabinet approval for their programme, Steed set about the difficult task of reconciling the various interests whose co-operation was a precondition of the propaganda campaign which he wished to see launched from the Italian front. A constant problem was that Steed was a representative of Crewe House and not of the Foreign Office but his greatest obstacle derived from the existence of the 1915 Treaty of London, recently published by the Bolsheviks, by which Britain, France and Russia had promised Italy certain territories occupied by the Yugoslavs. On the one hand the Allies appeared to be advocating 'the liberation of peoples on the principle of nationality while on the other hand they had violated this principle themselves in the Treaty of London with Italy'.[71] Moreover, recognition of the subject races in Austria-Hungary raised the thorny questions of the Sinn Fein in Ireland and the British position in India and Egypt. Steed, however, was more immediately concerned with convincing the Yugoslavs of Allied friendship and sincerity. Ever since the Southern Slav Unitary Declaration of June 1917 and the Declaration of Corfu the following month, the Yugoslavs had been joined by the Serbs, Croats and the Slovenes in a common desire to reject foreign domination and to unite their peoples. The effect of these declarations among the Slav regiments of the Habsburg armies caused considerable concern among the German military authorities and hastened their decision to assume direct control over the Austro-Hungarian forces in October 1917 before routing the Italians at Caporetto. It was only a temporary respite. The wave of industrial strikes in January 1918 revealed considerable political and economic dislocation within Austria-Hungary, 'often fanned by returning prisoners of war from Russia' which forced the government to retain seven combat divisions for internal security purposes.[72] This situation provided the signal for Steed and Seton-Watson to redouble their efforts to find a solution to the Italo-Yugoslav question. Caporetto had served to make the Italians more flexible in their attitude to the subject nationalities while Wilson's Fourteen Points made them more amenable to Allied pressure. A series of conferences was held in London at which considerable progress was made to reach an Italo-Yugoslav *rapprochment* before the so-called Pact of Rome was signed on 7 March 1918 recognising the 'imprescriptible right to full political and economic independence' for the Southern Slavs and acknowledging the 'vital mutual interest' of their unity.[73] This was followed up by the Rome Congress in April which broadened the terms of the Rome agreement so as to include all the nationalist groups. The Congress, however, was not official. The Italian government did not send an official representative and expressed only sympathy for its aims. The British government adopted a similar position. Moreover, the congress only concerned nationality groups in exile; it remained to be seen how far it affected the Habsburg armies. Yet Steed took every opportunity of co-ordinating efforts to initiate the propaganda campaign. The Italo-Yugoslav reconciliation provided the necessary precondition to any successful attempt to undermine the morale of the Austro-Hungarian armies,[74] although the real differences between the Italians and the Southern Slavs remained unresolved.[75]

Meanwhile, Northcliffe had been busy in London to secure approval for the actions of his officials in Europe. This was a delicate issue because the Foreign Office interpreted the work of Steed and Seton-Watson as direct interference in the foreign policy-making process for which it had been traditionally responsible at a time when the influence of the Foreign Office was already being undermined by the actions of Lloyd George. Besides, 'the Foreign Office was anything but convinced of the success of a disruptive policy'.[76] Relying heavily upon a memorandum drafted by Wickham Steed,[77] Northcliffe informed Balfour on 24 February 1918 that a decision on Austria-Hungary was required before Crewe House could begin its work. There were two possibilities. Either the British could work for a separate peace with the Habsburg government or they could promote its disintegration by encouraging the subject races. Because attempts to work for a separate peace had failed, Northcliffe argued, the time had come 'to try to break the power of Austria-Hungary, as the weakest link in the chain of enemy states, by supporting and encouraging all anti-German and pro-Ally peoples and tendencies'.[78] The aim was not to foster the creation of a series of small disjointed states but to form a non-German confederation of Central European and Danubian states. Balfour's reply was cautious. He did not feel that the two policies outlined in Northcliffe's letter were mutually exclusive because by encouraging the subject races Emperor Charles might be forced to sue for a separate peace.[79] The Foreign Office was, in fact, reluctant to disclose to such newspapermen plans relating to the Smuts mission to Geneva to discuss secretly with Count Mensdorff conditions for a separate peace.[80] Northcliffe, however, was anxious 'to move as rapidly as possible' in view of what was believed to be an impending Austrian offensive against Italy and he again reiterated Steed's proposal to promote disintegration from within.[81] There is no record of the Foreign Office's reply although it is known that the Foreign Office was far from convinced of the wisdom of promoting internal disintegration within Austria-Hungary.

Cabinet approval was granted to Northcliffe on 5 March 1918 with the proviso that 'no promise should be made to the subject races in Austria which we could not redeem' and that Northcliffe should remain in close contact with the Foreign Office and with the General Staff.[82] Final authority was, however, withheld pending the outcome of the secret negotiations for a separate peace with Austria-Hungary which were finally abandoned in April 1918.[83] On 18 April, the British ambassador in Rome, Rennell Rodd, expressed the view of the British government to Baron Sonnino, the Italian Foreign Minister, that it was prepared:

to recognise proclamations of independence made by the subject nationalities in Austria-Hungary, though they cannot pledge themselves to secure such independence. We also approve of giving assurances to the troops belonging to those nationalities that in the event of their coming over to the allies, they would be treated not as prisoners of war but as friends and would be allowed to fight on our side.[84]

However, because of Italian intransigence, the Allied governments were forced to express merely 'sympathy' but not necessarily actual recognition of the Czechs and Yugoslavs. The British government left its options open. Yet, 'while a decision to use the nationalities to destroy Austria-Hungary was never taken, a host of less significant decisions, when combined in their historical context, had the same effect'.[85]

The propaganda campaign against Austria-Hungary was launched on 8 April 1918 to coincide with the opening of the Rome Congress of Oppressed Nationalities. Steed was able to initiate the full-scale distribution of leaflets by using methods which had been pioneered by the French and Italians who had long been co-ordinating their efforts. He was not hampered by restrictions on distribution of propaganda material by aeroplane which existed on the western front. Basing his conclusions on evidence gathered from Austrian sources and from British intelligence reports, Steed believed that the combination of the Rome Congress, which was a major propaganda event in its own right because of its proclamation calling for 'full political and economic independence' for *all* the subject nationalities, and the actual timing of the propaganda campaign itself led to the withdrawal of Slav troops from the front line by the Austro-Hungarian high command.[86]

Thereafter, the campaign was supervised by the Central Inter-Allied Propaganda Commission (often known as the Central Committee for Propaganda to the Enemy) attached to the Italian high command at Padua. This body began work on 18 April 1918 and maintained the psychological offensive until Austria signed the armistice. It was a joint Anglo-French-Italian venture assisted by representatives of each of the subject nationalities. The Commission published a weekly newspaper in Czech, Polish, Serbo-Croat and Rumanian which was dropped by aeroplane over enemy lines. Leaflets were also fired at the enemy by means of rockets and rifle grenades.[87] Between May and October 1918, some 60 million copies of 643 leaflets in eight languages and some 10 million copies of 112 newspapers in four languages were distributed in Austria-Hungary.[88] Other direct methods included the use of gramophone records and loudspeakers in No Man's Land and the formation of contact patrols, composed mainly of deserters, which were 'wonderfully successful' in distributing material to their comrades in the Habsburg regiments.[89] Closely involved in this work was Emmanuel Victor Voska, the Czech agent in the United States who had recently been made a captain in American intelligence. Voska was immediately sent to Europe where he worked from the centres at Padua, Chaumont, in Holland and in Switzerland in his efforts to make contact with enemy troops. At one point, Voska even managed to cross No Man's Land and confirm the existence of widespread disaffection amongst the troops he had met.[90] By October 1918, desertions were taking place on a massive scale and, Voska claimed, hundreds of thousands of Slav troops had surrendered without a fight.[91] Campbell Stuart also stressed the high number of desertions as well as the considerable amount of sabotage that was taking place behind the Austrian lines.[92] Many deserters were found to be carrying propaganda leaflets, despite heavy penalties for doing so if they had been caught by the Austrian authorities. Crewe House was convinced that its propaganda had been instrumental in helping to stem the Austrian offensive on the Piave in June 1918, when Italy recaptured much of the territory it had lost at Caporetto. Deserters had provided the Allies with invaluable military information and many carried propaganda leaflets; 800 were found on 350 prisoners of war in a single day.[93]

Results thereafter were generally less satisfying, perhaps due, in part, to the reluctance of the British government to follow up its earlier declarations. Blame was placed upon the Italians, at least until 16 October when Emperor Charles, in anticipation of certain defeat, conceded to the nationalities the right to form their own states. Crewe House claimed that:

As against Austria-Hungary, our propaganda contributed to the defeat of the Austrians in the Piave in June,[94] and had our efforts not been thwarted in a hundred ways by political intrigue on the part of the Italian authorities, it is certain that much greater headway would have been made and that the Italian armies would now have been in a much more favourable position.[95]

This was perhaps expecting too much of propaganda. It was certainly expecting too much of the Italian government with its reluctance to commit itself wholeheartedly to the principle of national self-determination for the Southern Slavs, particularly after the earlier

Allied promises. It proved equally reluctant to recognise the other subject races for fear of creating a precedent for the Yugoslavs. Northcliffe felt that the Italians were jeopardising the entire success of Steed's attempts to broaden the gap between oppressor and oppressed within the Dual Monarchy. But he might have looked much closer to home for a further reason. Successful propaganda presupposes a clear policy. Despite its relatively clear attitude towards the Poles and the Czechs, the British government did not in fact have a clear policy towards the Yugoslavs because of a desire to maintain inter-allied harmony with the Italians.

Propaganda, by itself, could not defeat the enemy. Actions on the field of battle or in the political arena counted for much more. One official wrote after the war that 'the effect of the propaganda carried out against Austria-Hungary conclusively proved the accuracy of the conception upon which the work of this Department was grounded from the first—i.e. that propaganda is comparatively useless unless it is based on a sound policy and unless it works definitely as an agency for the application of that policy'.[96] But although he recognised that propaganda 'must be inspired by policy' he also felt that 'its varying needs also suggest policy'.[97] The British government's reluctance to make a categorical statement concerning the Yugoslavs eventually meant that events overtook Crewe House when the question of Yugoslavia 'was decided by the Southern Slav people themselves, before the British had come to any decision in their favour . . . . Yugoslavia, despite all the British sympathy for it, had never become a declared British war aim'.[98] Even so, Wickham Steed, Seton-Watson and Northcliffe were able to push the government further than it might otherwise have gone in providing Crewe House with a clarity of purpose where Austria-Hungary was concerned. Steed could therefore justifiably claim credit for Crewe House 'not for the actual breaking-up, but for very materially accelerating the break-up of Austria'.[99] The combination of propaganda and Allied promises to the Slavs, particularly at the time of the Rome Congress, had a noticeable effect upon the morale of the Austro-Hungarian army and population. The Austrian official history states: 'An extraordinarily dangerous weapon, used to perfection, threatened the morale of the Austro-Hungarian army from the time of the Rome Congress'.[100] Vienna even asked Berlin to retaliate by organising a congress of Indian, Irish and Egyptian nationalities,[101] itself an indication of the impact which British propaganda, as distinct from the undoubtedly effective propaganda emanating from Bolshevik Russia,[102] was producing.

The Austrian experiment therefore demonstrated what could be done by propaganda in conjunction with even limited policy declarations. On 16 May 1918, Lloyd George wrote to Northcliffe:

> It seems to me that you have organised valuable work in your Austrian propaganda . . . . I trust that you will soon turn your attention towards German propaganda along the French and British fronts. I feel sure that much can be done to disintegrate the *moral* [sic] of the German army along the same line as we appear to have adopted with great success in the Austro-Hungarian army.[103]

This statement would appear to devalue the work that Chalmers Mitchell at MI7(b)4 and S. A. Guest had been doing. In fact, it was less of a condemnation of past efforts than a recognition of the need for a new formula which appeared to be producing dramatic results in Austria-Hungary.

As in the campaign against the Dual Monarchy, inter-allied co-operation was essential to the propaganda campaign against Germany. The British and French had established an element of co-operation in propaganda matters at an early stage of the war. After the entry of the Italians in 1915, the French were quick to co-ordinate their activities with those of their new ally. Indeed, it was the Italian Ministry of the Interior which initiated the proposal for closer inter-allied co-operation in the war of words. In July 1917, Gallenga Stuart, head of the Italian propaganda organisation, proposed to the French that the work of the various Allied propaganda departments be more closely co-ordinated.[104] The initial French reaction was cautious and only became more sympathetic over the next six months.[105] Gallenga Stuart's proposals were, in the meantime, also forwarded to the British. His main concern was with the work of the three countries in neutral territories not only as a means of demonstrating Allied unity but also to effect greater efficiency in the distribution of propaganda material. For these purposes, he proposed joint co-operation in the making of propaganda films, co-ordinated action with the press, and a more efficient distribution process. Gallenga Stuart therefore proposed that the various heads of the allied propaganda departments should meet to discuss his proposals in greater detail.[106]

No sooner had Northcliffe been appointed in February 1918 than he was approached by Gallenga Stuart and Franklin Bouillon of the French propaganda organisation.[107] Northcliffe was delighted with their proposals, not least because of the plans for an allied propaganda campaign against Austria-Hungary. Northcliffe therefore arranged a preliminary conference of allied propaganda representatives in March. Gallenga Stuart represented Italy, while Franklin Bouillon and Henri Moysset, who worked for the French Ministry of Marine, represented France. Because the French were currently in the process of reorganising the Maison de la Presse, there was some confusion concerning the appointment of the French representatives. Before long, however, Lieutenant Tonnelat, who had been directing French aerial propaganda, was invited to attend the conference, as indeed was the American propaganda agent for Northern Europe, Robinette.

The conference did not prove to be a great success, although it did help to pave the way for Wickham Steed's visit to Italy for the Rome Congress. The Italians were not just worried about Austria-Hungary but were also concerned with the internal political situation within Italy itself.[108] But the conference did little to improve inter-allied co-operation. Moysset did not at that time enjoy the backing of his government which was generally opposed to greater Anglo-Italian co-operation. Indeed, on his way to Italy, Wickham Steed decided to visit Clemenceau on 21 March in an attempt to clear up any misunderstandings. However, because of the concentration on Austria-Hungary and given that the new French propaganda organisation, the Commissariat General de la Propaganda under A. Klobukowski, did not emerge until May 1918, it was not found possible to convene a full inter-allied propaganda conference in London until 14 August.

The conference was held in Crewe House and was attended by members of all the allied propaganda departments, including the various British organisations.[109] It opened with an address by Northcliffe which was followed by discussions in four committees dealing with policy, distribution (both civil and military), 'material' and prisoners of war. Klobukowski, the chairman of the political committee, felt that Northcliffe's opening address had 'toute l'ampleur d'un exposé ministériel'[110] and he also regarded Steed, who served with him on the political committee, as the leading spirit of Crewe House:

auquel il a insofflé toute l'ardeur de ses convictions et de ses sentiments anti-autrichiens en même temps que les dispositions les plus favorables à notre pays.[111]

Steed pressed the need to concentrate upon taking the Austrians out of the war before concentrating fully on Germany. This required the promotion of Yugoslavian independence and confirmation of the agreements made at the Rome Congress. He was supported by the Italian representative, Borgese, who produced a plan — which Klobukowski considered to be the work of Orlando — designed as part of a political campaign to undermine Sonnino's position within Italy. Why else would the Italians, after pursuing a policy of obstruction for so long, now suddenly reverse their position with regard to Yugoslavia?[112] The American representative was none other than Walter Lippmann, then a captain serving in the psychological sub-section of the United States army, who stressed that he was only an observer but who nonetheless stated that he saw few problems in transmitting the Borgese plan to President Wilson who was sympathetic to the plight of small nations. Klobukowski also stressed that he was merely attending the conference to listen and report back to the French government but he accepted Steed's resolutions in principle with the exception of making the liberation of Czechoslovakia an Allied war aim.

Steed also reported on the work that had been done in Bulgaria. Bulgarian agents in Switzerland had made contact with the Allies but their proposal to replace the Bulgarian monarch with an English prince was not being considered seriously. The agents had, however, been asked to generate discontent within Bulgaria as an indication of their sincerity. But as the United States had not declared war against Bulgaria at the time of the conference, this was not felt to be an area suitable for genuine inter-allied co-operation. Crewe House instead chose to launch its own unilateral campaign. On 29 July 1918, the Foreign Office had received a memorandum by Wickham Steed, Seton-Watson, Alan Leeper and Captain Heard which emphasised the need for an Allied decision in favour of Southern Slav, Rumanian and Greek unity as a preliminary for any arrangement with Bulgaria. The documents also called for the expulsion of King Ferdinand and his family, a complete rupture with Germany, the establishment of a democratic government and the orientation of Bulgarian policy in the direction of a Balkan Confederation under the aegis of the Allies.[113] The Foreign Office replied that 'until Bulgaria had given proof that a complete reversal of her policy had actually been brought about, we are not prepared to entertain any suggestions from her'.[114] In his autobiography, Steed stated that British propaganda towards Bulgaria was somewhat negative in view of the dangers of making contradictory promises which would upset Serbia and Greece.[115] Bulgaria was not, in fact, regarded as important as Austria-Hungary or Germany and little effort was therefore devoted to reconciling inter-allied differences. At the propaganda conference, Steed said very little about Turkey which was the responsibility of the Ministry of Information and not Crewe House. Nor, much to Klobukowski's surprise, did he say much about Germany.

The British and French were not in full agreement about Poland. Both the British and the Italians were opposed to the Polish National Committee which enjoyed French support. Klobukowski, however, opposed the idea that a League of Free Nations could be converted into an economic alliance for peace because, he argued, such co-operation already existed between the Allies and it was this fact which should be emphasised in any propaganda campaign. There was universal agreement on the continued need to stress anti-militarism and anti-imperialism in Allied propaganda directed against Germany. After four days, the committee closed by agreeing upon future allied co-operation through a four-man body comprising representatives of Britain, France, Italy and the United States which would meet at Crewe House.

The political committee was undoubtedly the most significant of the four but the conference was also important for bringing together the various propaganda experts of each Allied country, especially in the distribution committee where the men behind the Dutch and Swiss campaigns against Germany met together, namely S. A. Guest and E. Haguenin. G. H. Mair also attended to report on the situation in Spain. Mair was joined by Haguenin in opposing the Italian representative, Captain Pallavicino, who proposed closer co-operation between the diplomatic services and propaganda agents of the various countries. More significant, however, was an agreement made by Guest and Haguenin to strengthen their contacts and to improve their co-ordination in reaching enemy opinion through the allied and neutral press. Haguenin stressed the importance of influencing pacifist elements in Germany through various publications issued from Switzerland and of exploiting the relationship between the neutral press and the German democrats. Although there was nothing very new in this, the general air of co-operation was strengthened at an important stage of the war with the prospect of continued mutual help in the future.[116] In the opinion of the American propaganda representative in Switzerland, Vera Whitehouse, the 'very idea of concerted Allied action had so great an effect that one of the strongly-entrenched cinema-house companies, supposedly German controlled, offered for immediate sale its whole string of houses'.[117]

The overall level of inter-allied co-operation in propaganda matters was, however, disappointing. When the Americans became involved in the Austrian campaign, albeit late in the day, their immediate impression of the Inter-Allied Commission at Padua, which was the first joint venture, was one of dissension between the British, French and Italians. Franco-Italian tension revolved around the question of the Yugoslav legion which the Italians wished to see employed on their own front while the French wanted to see it used in the Balkans.[118] The British and the Italians continued to squabble over the entire Southern Slav question. Professor G. H. Edgell, head of the American propaganda team in Italy, was convinced that Steed, Seton-Watson and Campbell Stuart were decidedly anti-Italian[119] and that Steed in particular was 'quite inimical to the Italians'.[120] For their part, the Italians 'almost universally believe that Northcliffe and Stead [sic] are their sworn enemies'.[121] Herber Blankenhorn, head of the psychological sub-division of American military intelligence, reported from Paris in August 1918:

We expected to find three organized and working Inter-Allied Propaganda Boards, one in Paris, one in London and one in Padua, which would be landmarks in the field, with which we would have to deal and to which we could immediately designate liaison officers. These Boards are ghosts. This afternoon we sat in at a session of the so-called Board here. It is essentially the new French Army Board for propaganda into enemy countries headed by Commandant Chaix and international only by virtue of the fact that an Italian, and Englishman, three Belgians and three Americans (Hugh Gibson, Lippmann and I) were present to hear what the French had done and were planning.[122]

Blankenhorn therefore felt that the American government should develop its own organisation. He was perhaps expecting too much of inter-allied co-operation. A supreme military commander at the western front, Marshall Foch, had only been appointed in March 1918. But although there was little high-level co-operation in propaganda matters, the Americans were able to draw upon a vast amount of experience at the lower levels where there was an impressive store of knowledge about methods, distribution and content from which the Americans could, and did, draw. Vera Whitehouse, for example, reported that 'The French Bureau de la Press have at last taken me into their very center — Haguenin has discovered that I can be helpful'.[123] There was thus no need for the appointment of a liaison officer between the French and the American governments 'in view of the fact that Mr Haguenin and I are in constant and easy communication'.[124] However, since most Allied countries were still seeking to resolve internal dissensions and structural anomalies within their national propaganda organisations, it is hardly surprising that a fully integrated inter-allied propaganda campaign was difficult to obtain, particularly when the attempts of Crewe House to co-ordinate the work came so late in the war.

The German section of Crewe House had initially been placed under the direction of H. G. Wells who was assisted by J. W. Headlam-Morley. With the Austrian precedent very much in mind, the first task to which they devoted themselves was the formulation of a coherent policy. There was, however, little sign of the type of harmony evident in Wickham Steed's relationship with Northcliffe. On 27 May 1918, Wells had written a memorandum which attempted to define Britain's policy towards Germany. He began:

The real war aim of the Allies is not only to beat the enemy, but to establish a world peace that shall preclude the resumption of war. Successful propaganda in Germany presupposes the clear definition of the kind of world-settlement which the Allies are determined to secure and place of the Germans in it.[125]

Wells had then gone on to state that the Germans should be convinced of Allied determination to continue the war until victory was secured or until Germany was prepared to accept Allied peace terms. Those terms included the creation of 'a practical League of Free Nations' based upon the existing Allied combination. Moreover, he continued:

It should be pointed out that nothing stands between the enemy peoples and a lasting peace except the predatory designs of their ruling dynasties and military and economic castes; that the design of the Allies is not to crush any people, but to assure the freedom of all on a basis of self-determination to be exercised under definite guarantees of justice and fair play; that, unless enemy peoples accept the Allied conception of a world peace settlement, it will be impossible for them to repair the havoc of the present war, to avert utter financial ruin, and to save themselves from prolonged misery; and that the longer the struggle lasts the deeper will become the hatred of everything German in the non-German world, and the heavier the social and economic handicap under which the enemy peoples will labour, even after their admission into a League of Nations.

In short:

The primary aim of the Allies thus becomes the changing of Germany, not only in the interest of the Allied League, but in that of the German people itself . . . . Germany has, therefore, to choose between her own permanent ruin by adhering to her present system of government and policy and the prospect of economic and political redemption by overthrowing her militarist system so as to be able to join honestly in the Allied scheme of world organisation.

It was therefore essential to announce Allied war aims and to inform the Germans of their destiny once the war was over. Wells went on to elaborate his scheme in greater detail before turning to what he termed '*the* primary war aim for the Allies', namely the changing of Germany:

How Germany is to be changed is a complex question. The word *Revolution* is, perhaps, to be deprecated. We do not, for instance, desire a Bolshevik breakdown in Germany, which would make her economically useless to mankind. We look, therefore, not so much to the German peasant and labourer as to the ordinary, fairly well-educated mediocre German for co-operation in the reinstatement of civilisation. Change there *must* be in Germany; in the spirit in which the Government is conducted, in the persons who exercise the control, and in the relative influence of different classes in the country. The sharpest distinction, therefore, has to be drawn between Germany and its present Government in all our propaganda and public utterances; and a constant appeal has to be made by the statesmen of the Alliance, and by a frank and open propaganda through the Germans of the United States of America and of Switzerland, through neutral countries and by every possible means, from Germany Junker to Germany sober. We may be inclined to believe that every German is something of a Junker, we have to remember he is also potentially a reasonable man.[126]

In other words, Wells was appealing for the removal of the stereotype which had been exploited by British propaganda throughout the war in any assessment of Germany's future. Yet, such was the potency of the stereotype, that even Wells was unable to escape entirely its effect.

Northcliffe submitted Wells' proposals to Balfour on 10 June 1918.[127] The Foreign Secretary again feared the interference of propagandists in the formulation of policy although he did declare himself to be 'in general agreement with the line of thought'.[128] Although no public declaration was made, the Wells memorandum did, in fact, provide the basis for Crewe House's propaganda campaign against Germany.[129] Wells, however, became increasingly alarmed at the line taken by the Northcliffe press which maintained that 'nothing would serve but the extermination of the German people'.[130] The discrepancy between this line of thought and the policy adopted by Crewe House, added to friction with Campbell Stuart,[131] precipitated Wells' resignation on 17 July 1918. He was replaced as head of the German section by a loyal Northcliffe supporter, Hamilton Fyfe, who immediately began to set about converting Wells' theories into practice.

Hamilton Fyfe secured the transfer of Chalmers Mitchell from the War Office and, at the end of August 1918, Crewe House assumed responsibility from MI7(b)4 for the production of propaganda leaflets. But although Crewe House became the chief production agency for this material, producing its first leaflet on 4 September, the War Office remained in charge of their distribution at the front until the end of the war. According to Campbell Stuart, the numbers of leaflets dropped over and behind German lines by balloon totalled 1,689,457 in June and 2,172,794 in July. Hindenburg testified to their successful distribution: 'Our soldiers have delivered to the authorities the following number of hostile handbills: in May, 34,000; in June, 120,000; in July, 300,000'.[132] The number of leaflets handed in, therefore, was but a fraction of those which were not. During August, an average figure of 100,000 leaflets a day were being despatched, totalling 3,958,116. The precision of these figures is startling. Once Crewe House took over the work from the War Office, the figures became less exact but even more impressive. In September, the total dropped slightly to 3,715,000 but increased to 5,360,000 in October. During the last ten days of the war, 1,400,000 leaflets were dropped by balloon and by aeroplane.[133] After the war it was claimed that:

The unrest in Germany, with the spreading of wild rumours to which unrest always gives birth, were caused indeed by British propaganda; this propaganda used as its ammunition, however, not lies but solely the truth. It was because they began to realise the truth that the German people felt nervous and depressed. It was because the failure of the U-boats and the coming of the Americans and the solidarity of the Allies and the weakening of their own military power were now revealed to them, in spite of their leaders' efforts to keep them still in ignorance. It was because of their enlightenment of these and other matters that the Germans were seized with panic, a panic which culminated towards the end of October in complete collapse and, during the first days of November, in Revolution.[134]

Thus, by the time that Crewe House took charge of the work from the War Office, these processes were already well under way. British propaganda did not create the conditions which led to the German collapse in November 1918. But it did exploit and accelerate the process of defeat.

For inter-allied co-operation, events had overtaken developments in London. The problem centred around the relationship between propaganda and policy. It proved even more difficult to combine the two when it came to Allied interests than it had been to find an adequate solution to the tension which existed between Crewe House and the Ministry of Information on the one hand and the Foreign Office on the other. Until the very end of the war, Foreign Office officials proved highly sensitive to what they saw as attempts by propagandists to determine foreign policy, whether it concerned Germany or Austria-Hungary. Northcliffe recognised the inseparable link between propaganda and policy: 'I think it indispensable that I should be kept fully informed of, and consulted about, anything that the Government may think of doing in regard to Austria'.[135] This, at least, was the theory. But Northcliffe, in seeking to secure Cabinet approval for the proposals of Wickham Steed or H. G. Wells, was also attempting to shape government policy, a process which the Foreign Office was not prepared to tolerate. Balfour clung to the principle that it was the traditional right of the Foreign Office to advise the government on foreign policy matters more, perhaps, with a view to the return of peace which the temporary wartime departments were unlikely to survive. Lloyd

George, however, generally avoided any kind of ruling concerning the respective roles of the Foreign Office and of Crewe House which merely served to perpetuate the confusion. French and Italian propagandists seem to have suffered from similar ambiguities deriving from the confusion caused by wartime expedients in a traditional environment. At the inter-allied conference held at Crewe House in August, they were anxious to stress that any agreements made about the content and nature of propaganda would in no sense automatically bind their governments to any decisions which might affect their foreign policy.

The clearest indication of this condition was made by Klobukowski when he reported the observations of his foreign minister, Pichon, to Northcliffe in October 1918.[136] Northcliffe was informed that any communications to the Yugoslav or Polish National Committees should be made by the diplomatic representatives of each country, not by the propagandists. Cambon, the French ambassador in London, had been instructed to convey this point to the British government. Northcliffe, in other words, was being reminded that statements about Slav independence were purely a function of diplomacy and beyond the competence of propaganda representatives. Similarly, any proposals made to the Polish National Committee concerning Polish independence were strictly a matter for the Foreign Offices. Klobukowski insisted that the powers of the inter-allied propaganda committee be clarified:

Pour les mesures d'exécution, l'organe permanent pourrait avoir de pouvoirs assez étendus, mais il ne peut être en aucune manière, question de l'autoriser à donner des directions générals qui ne peuvent émaner que des gouvernments. C'est pourquoi, en cas notamment de désaccords entre les réprésentants respectifs des alliés à cet organe permanent motivés par le différence de leurs instructions, c'est aux gouvernments qu'il appartient de se concerter entre eux par la voix diplomatique pour réaliser l'entente.[137]

Northcliffe also encountered resistance when he sought to play an influential role in the forthcoming peace settlement. Once the extent of the German collapse became clear in October 1918, he immediately proposed allied co-operation in conducting a co-ordinated propaganda campaign relating to the peace terms. Lord Onslow was appointed to serve as Crewe House's representative in Paris while at home arrangements were made to convene an inter-departmental committee which would draw up a peace programme.[138] Steed believed that Crewe House could be converted into 'an agency for enlightenment on both sides, and might help to find a "common denominator". Otherwise the conclusion of peace would be followed by a dangerous period of ignorance and misunderstanding'.[139] Northcliffe preferred a more ambitious scheme of 'enabling the German people to see why Germany had lost the war, and to understand the force of the moral ideas which had ranged practically the whole world against her'.[140]

On 26 October 1918, the secretary of Crewe House informed James Keeley, the American propaganda representative in London, that the programme 'has been sanctioned by the government as a confidential document to be used as the basis for British propaganda at home and abroad'.[141] What authority he had for making this claim is unknown. On 3 November, Northcliffe wrote to Lloyd George:

in view of the urgency of the matter, I request that I be given, with the least possible delay, authority as Chairman of the British War Mission to undertake this peace terms propaganda in the closest collaboration with the various departments of state until the final peace settlement has been concluded.[142]

It was not the best moment for Northcliffe to make such a request. The erratic relationship between the two men was fast deteriorating. Having resisted earlier inducements to join the Cabinet, Northcliffe was now suspected of trying to wangle an official appointment at the forthcoming peace negotiations.[143] Lloyd George thought the suggestion 'dangerous in the extreme . . . . Indirectly it would have given him great power in the direction and control of our policy . . . . I curtly told him to go to Hades'.[144] In view of the storm which had erupted over the appointments of Beaverbrook and Northcliffe nine months earlier, Lloyd George had to be extremely careful in his relationship with Fleet Street, particularly on the eve of peace and a general election. The publication on the following day (4 November) of Northcliffe's infamous article, 'From Peace to War' in both *The Times* and the *Daily Mail* made the breach virtually irreparable. Northcliffe resigned his post as Director of Propaganda in Enemy Countries on 12 November.

Both Wickham Steed and Northcliffe believed that the publication of the peace programme had a considerable influence upon the final German collapse. Steed maintained that 'it certainly helped to hasten the collapse of German resistance. In fact, it was the crowning achievement of Crewe House propaganda'.[145] Campbell Stuart pointed out that 'it was widely reproduced by German newspapers and it had the effect of producing a state of mind which culminated in the complete collapse of German resistance'.[146] Yet these were impressionistic conclusions. The evidence to support them was, at best, circumstantial. Northcliffe's own assessment of the work of Crewe House in 1918 was more moderate. 'We have', he said, 'to some extent hastened the end'.[147]

Northcliffe's influence at Crewe House was, in fact, more limited than is often assumed. Chalmers Mitchell believed that he was not the principal figure, merely a figure-head, and that Steed was the real 'ideas man' and Campbell Stuart the 'organisation man'.[148] Hamilton Fyfe has confirmed this impression: 'The whole effect of Crewe House propaganda was due to Stuart. Northcliffe hardly came there'.[149] Northcliffe was certainly not a well man for long periods in 1918. He was quite prepared to leave the day to day running of the Enemy Propaganda Department to his deputies, in whom, he had every confidence. But it was Northcliffe whom Lloyd George feared and it was Northcliffe's support for people such as Wickham Steed and H. G. Wells that enabled Crewe House to push the Foreign Office much further than it might otherwise have preferred into policy statements concerning the Central Powers and the subject nationalities. Lloyd George rarely interfered, preferring to let the Foreign Office sort out its own troubles with the propagandists at Crewe House and the Ministry of Information. In such a situation, the Foreign Office resorted to the only weapon left in its armoury, namely the existence of overseas diplomatic and consular representatives serving as agents for the distribution of propaganda material. It held on to all it had, resisted any further attempts to undermine its traditional role or status and did all it could to irritate the work of the propagandists. In this, the Foreign Office was frequently successful, forcing Northcliffe to threaten resignation on several occasions. However, there was little the Foreign Office could do about Wickham Steed's mission to Italy to attend the Rome Congress or indeed other such 'unofficial' activities on the part of the propagandists. Crewe House was therefore able to establish an albeit vague policy line that was just sufficient to enable it to saturate the Austro-Hungarians and the Germans with the sort of material required to shake their resolve. Yet when Northcliffe tried to repeat this process on the return of peace, Lloyd George did decide to act to prevent him. This could only have confirmed Foreign Office suspicions that, in fact, the real aim of the Prime Minister's decision had been to transfer responsibility for propaganda into the hands of Beaverbrook and Northcliffe.

Wickham Steed undoubtedly enjoyed considerable influence at Crewe House, a factor which partially explains the decision to concentrate initially upon Austria-Hungary. Although Northcliffe had expressed considerable interest in propaganda against Germany during his discussions with Colonel House in 1917,[150] when the opportunity presented itself for him to convert his ideas into practice, he chose not to appoint a head of Crewe House's German section until May 1918. The man chosen for that position, H. G. Wells, soon found himself at odds with Northcliffe over the issue of distinguishing between the German government and the German people. Wells was alarmed at both the NWAC's campaign of vilification against all Germans and by Northcliffe's newspapers which echoed similar sentiments. He wrote:

This campaign to insult and repudiate everything German grows and grows . . . . I do not see how Crewe House can be anything but ineffective and a little absurd until the War Aims Committee and the section of the press that goes beyond it, are made to toe the line we have drawn.[151]

Northcliffe was unresponsive to Wells' complaints, particularly with regard to his own newspapers with whose policy he fully agreed: 'I have not wandered about Prussia for two years without learning something, and if you will wait you will find that I will unearth much sinister and active Prussianism in England'.[152] Wells believed that his assistant had been sacked by Campbell Stuart because he was believed to be of German origin,[153] and he finally decided to resign. Northcliffe's hatred of 'Prussianism' was undoubtedly genuine. Yet he was always sensitive to charges that his official appointments were largely designs on Lloyd George's part to see him muzzled which might help to explain the discrepancies which frequently occurred between the views expressed in his newspapers and the generally less extreme material produced by Crewe House. To be seen to be pursuing a newspaper line different from that pursued in his official capacity might have been sufficient to ease Northcliffe's sensitivity.

The campaign against Austria-Hungary was probably Crewe House's greatest achievement. Although Italy managed to avoid making any firm diplomatic commitments to the subject nationalities, she was still anxious to maintain a propaganda offensive against what may be described as the soft underbelly of the enemy coalition.[154] By championing Steed's proposals, Northcliffe did help to influence the War Cabinet to accept the break-up of the Austro-Hungarian Empire. He provided Steed with ministerial representation for his views but found himself unable to support wholeheartedly the more moderate proposals of H. G. Wells towards Germany. To Northcliffe, all Germans were Prussians although he recognised the logic of trying to separate the bulk of the German people from their Prussian leaders as the most profitable course of action for British propaganda to take. It had worked in Austria and it was to work in Germany. It was something which Northcliffe had wanted to see even before he was given the opportunity of carrying it out. In August 1916, for example, he had proposed various schemes to General Charteris which were designed to encourage desertion among the German armies. He suggested that vast amounts of leaflets should be scattered over the German lines depicting the favourable treatment afforded to prisoners of war, and so on. He wrote:

After reading a number of German soldiers' letters given to me by the Germans themselves in No. 4 Hospital, Versailles, at the end of Sept. 1914, I sent this scheme to Lord French through Colonel Swinton but nothing came of it. Later, I put it before General Henry Wilson, but he told me after all it was a minor matter — the thing was to kill Germans, with which I agreed; and he also told me that the French would break through the German lines last June; so that his calculations regarding an early victory may also have led him wrong in his conclusions regarding enemy propaganda.[155]

. Charteris' reply pointed out that such measures were already being taken but it was presumably this type of letter which prompted Northcliffe's biographers to accredit him with responsibility for initiating the leaflet campaign.[156] This was not the case. The psychological offensive against Germany began in 1915 and, as Northcliffe himself realised, it was pointless to expect quick results of a decisive nature from propaganda. It was a cumulative process begun by the War Office and finished by Crewe House. In July 1918, Colonel House informed Northcliffe that he had received reports from neighbouring neutral countries testifying to the concern which the German authorities felt for the 'propaganda which Lord

Northcliffe is directing against us. The English are doing more to defeat us in this way than the armies in the field'.[157] Yet this was written before Crewe House assumed responsibility for the work from the War Office.

As is apt to happen, 'the new brooms get public credit for what they did by conveniently obscuring what had been done before'.[158] Those who were engaged in propaganda before 1918 'worked with tied hands and were hampered sorely by lack of funds. It speaks well for their perseverance that they were able to accomplish anything at all'.[159] Even Northcliffe admitted in December 1918:

I do not think I was quite fair to Mr Guest in suggesting that he should receive a Commandership of the Order of the British Empire. I was not fully aware that Mr Guest had been engaged in this propaganda for more than three years and the culminating success was considerably due to the routes and methods he had devised.[160]

If, therefore, the balance of historical judgement invariably tends to rest with those who finished the campaign, due credit must be given to those who began it.

The major difference between the work of Crewe House and that conducted by its predecessors was that of scale and, crucially, timing. After the failure of the German spring offensive, more leaflets were dropped than ever before. Given that the majority of those leaflets were scattered over enemy lines by balloons and not by aeroplanes, this was a most remarkable achievement. Even so, according to Chalmers Mitchell, it was not until Armistice Day itself that an efficient method of packing the leaflets so that they would scatter effectively over a wide area was devised.[161] This type of detail has led to at least one revisionist evaluation of the effectiveness of Crewe House propaganda.[162] Yet, while it is surely appropriate to challenge the reputation which has surrounded the work of Lord Northcliffe and of Crewe House for nearly half a century, the temptation to move too far in the opposite direction must also be resisted. The work may not have been an unqualified success but it was still, nonetheless, a success. After the war, one official wrote that: 'if what our enemies said was true, we may congratulate ourselves upon our share in bringing about the defeat of Prussianism'.[163] German military figures and Weimar politicians admittedly had good reasons for explaining away Germany's defeat in 1918 by testifying to the success of British propaganda rather than admitting to the inadequacies of their armed forces. But, after four years of war, Germany was ripe for a psychological offensive. With the gradual impact of the Allied blockade, the corresponding failure of the German U-boat campaign to starve Britain into submission, the failure of the spring offensive and the loss of her allies, the German people generally were hard pressed to envisage the possibility of victory. Similarly, in Austria-Hungary, where 'the energy of the centrifugal forces within the Austrian Empire was vastly increased and given more definite direction' by British propaganda,[164] Crewe House was exploiting the cumulative effect of the political, military and economic circumstances which prevailed after four years of war. British propaganda did not create those circumstances. It simply intensified their effect and exploited their implications.

Conclusion

Oɴ the return of peace in 1918, the British government chose to dismantle the machinery it had created during the course of the war for the manipulation of public opinion at home and abroad. Many of those who had been directly involved in the work seriously doubted the wisdom of such a decision. During the closing stages of the conflict, several officials had given serious consideration to the question of continuing their work in peacetime. On 16 October 1918, for example, Lord Beaverbrook had drawn up a memorandum in which he argued the need for preserving the Ministry of Information at least until a peace treaty had been signed because 'public opinion throughout the world will be a vital object to His Majesty's Government during the intervening period'.[1] While recognising that his organisation would need to undergo 'considerable modification' in order to meet the new requirements of peacetime conditions, he nonetheless felt that it was essential to continue the work so that allied solidarity could be preserved and to secure 'public support in all foreign countries for the view of the Imperial Government and to give reasons why the Imperial Government is justified in adopting a certain attitude towards the problems before the Conference'.[2] It might also be necessary, he continued, 'to dwell on the efforts Great Britain has made during the war' and he therefore sought Cabinet authority to convert the Ministry into an agency for peacetime enlightenment.

Similar schemes were formulated in Crewe House. Campbell Stuart argued that 'the maintenance of British prestige demanded that our position in regard to the peace should be explained and justified by the widespread dissemination of news and views, both before and during the Peace Conference'.[3] Wickham Steed, who was to the philosophy of Crewe House what Campbell Stuart was to its administration, believed that the Enemy Propaganda Department could serve an invaluable peacetime role, particularly with regard to Anglo-German relations. Steed argued that by the promotion of international understanding through a free exchange of news and views, propaganda could enable the people of one country to understand better the actions and policies of the other.[4] Northcliffe, too, harboured desires to continue by converting Crewe House into an agency for the re-education of Germany.[5] However, mounting tension with Lloyd George, particularly after the publication of Northcliffe's peace programme in *The Times* and *Daily Mail* on 4 November, meant that post-war schemes relating to the continuation of propaganda became submerged beneath more immediate issues. Northcliffe resigned his position a week later. Beaverbrook had already resigned on 21 October for reasons of ill-health and his scheme was not considered by the Cabinet until two days after the Armistice had been signed. By that time, it lacked a sufficiently powerful champion, despite the support of John Buchan who was appointed official liquidator of the Ministry of Information.[6] Campbell Stuart was appointed Acting Chairman of the British War Mission with instructions to close down Crewe House by the end of the year.

Buchan's latest appointment was not without its irony. On Lord Milner's suggestion, he had been placed in charge of the Department of Information in February 1917 but he soon came under attack from the Northcliffe press for his close association with the Foreign Office. In the wake of the second Donald report, Lloyd George had decided to replace Buchan with Fleet Street representatives who had been most critical of Britain's propaganda. Beaverbrook may well have been appointed because of his successful record in organising Canadian propaganda but Northcliffe was almost certainly offered his position because Lloyd George wanted to draw his teeth while at the same time undermining the influence of the Foreign Office in the conduct of both propaganda and foreign policy-making. Admittedly, Northcliffe had expressed an active interest in propaganda from an early stage of the war — he had suggested leaflet-dropping raids to the War Office as early as September 1914 — but it was his self-appointed role as keeper of the government's conscience which concerned Lloyd George more. When Northcliffe resumed his role as one of the government's severest critics in November 1918 by launching an attack upon Lord Milner, the Prime Minister's choice of Buchan as the man responsible for dismantling the machinery of which Northcliffe was so proud might be interpreted as another act of effrontery on Lloyd George's part.

Buchan chose to dismantle the wartime propaganda machinery

almost in its entirety. Most of the work was terminated immediately but, where this proved impossible, instructions were issued to begin its gradual cessation. Buchan further decided to return the responsibility for any remaining work, about which he was either uncertain or which he considered desirable to maintain, back into the hands of the Foreign Office for that department's deliberation and decision. Both the Ministry of Information and Crewe House were officially closed down on 31 December 1918, although the process of liquidation did, in fact, take less time than Buchan had originally anticipated and the Foreign Office inherited the remnants some weeks earlier.[7] Considerable support within the Foreign Office — and, to a lesser extent, from without — was to ensure that the News Department was recreated to conduct propaganda abroad in peacetime, albeit on a much reduced scale.[8] The various other wartime creations were less fortunate. The National War Aims Committee was abolished with the Armistice and the Press Bureau was closed down on 30 April 1919.[9]

In view of the alleged success of Britain's wartime propaganda experiment, it might seem a little curious that the government should prove so eager to forfeit the considerable lead it had established on the return of peace. The various decisions relating to the dismemberment of the official propaganda machinery appear more curious still in view of the fact that the return of peace was accompanied not by disarmament in the war of words but rather by an increase in the use of national propaganda by foreign governments over and above even wartime levels.[10] Although the wisdom of the British government's attempt to return to pre-war conditions in which propaganda had played a relatively minor role in international affairs soon came to be seriously questioned, finally forcing Britain during the inter-war years to re-enter the field she had done so much to pioneer, when viewed in the context of the years 1918-19 the causes are entirely explicable. Quite apart from the question of peacetime propaganda becoming subsumed in the Lloyd George-Northcliffe dispute, the reputation which the British government earned for the successful employment of propaganda was not one of which many contemporaries felt proud. Propaganda was regarded as a necessary evil of war. It was associated with subversion and secrecy dating from the early days of the war, a somehow 'un-English' activity made necessary only by the activities of the enemy. Robert Donald undoubtedly echoed the sentiments of many of his contemporaries when he claimed that propaganda was 'utterly repugnant to our feelings and contrary to our traditions'.[11] Regardless of the role it had played either in helping to bring the United States into the war on the Allied side in 1917 or in bringing the Central Powers to their knees during the following year, there was felt to be little need for British propaganda in the post-war world. As another observer noted:

That the State should advertise itself was an idea which occurred to few before the war and which, had it been brought before the notice of the general public, would have seemed to them repellent: advertisement, apart from commercial advertisement, which through lapse of time had acquired respectability, was thought to be the work of the vulgarian; it was also thought useless.[12]

Despite enlightened appeals from various sources not to 'sink back into the old lethargy that regarded foreigners as inferior and self-advertisement as either vulgar or unnecessary',[13] the prevailing official attitude towards propaganda remained unfavourable. During the only major wartime debate on the subject in August 1918, the attitude of the House of Commons had been overwhelmingly hostile.[14] From a political point of view, the Ministry of Information had been disliked because of its direct accountability to the Prime Minister rather than to the Treasury or to Parliament, thereby giving it the appearance of being an extra-parliamentary power. The appointments of Lord Beaverbrook and Lord Northcliffe were regarded with deep suspicion, not least because of the belief that Lloyd George was attempting to influence the press in his favour,[15] a suspicion which the Prime Minister did much to encourage by his involvement in purchasing the *Daily Chronicle* in 1918.[16] It was not beyond the imagination of many of his opponents to suspect that the official wartime propaganda machinery could be used by an unscrupulous government as a means of sustaining political power. With an impending general election, few were prepared to champion the cause of propaganda in peacetime with the kind of commitment required to see through schemes for the re-education of Germany or the dissemination of the British point of view at the Paris Peace Conference. Moreover, once Lloyd George had seen the war through to its successful conclusion, albeit with the aid of the 'press gang', he was determined to ensure that the Cabinet retained its control over the formulation of government policies. Northcliffe and other representatives of Fleet Street who had worked in the official propaganda machinery posed too great a threat to that position.

Nevertheless, the reason why the use of a weapon which attempted to persuade the enemy to lay down its arms and return to his home instead of killing his opponent should be regarded with as much, if not greater, distaste than more conventional weapons of destruction was essentially fear of the unknown. The power of propaganda was not widely understood at a time when psychology and other attempts to explain the workings of the human mind were still in their infancy. Arthur Ponsonby explained that 'the injection of the poison of hatred into men's minds by means of falsehood is a greater evil in wartime than the actual loss of life. The defilement of the human soul is worse than the destruction of the human body'.[17] It was generally agreed that British propaganda had played an important role in determining the final result, but precisely how this had been done was not fully understood. The tributes which gushed forth from the mouths of the vanquished were paraded as 'proof' of its impact without serious challenge. The flood of memoirs which appeared after the war by former participants such as Campbell Stuart, E. T. Cook, Douglas Brownrigg and Wickham Steed all served to perpetuate the reputation for success without really questioning the assumptions which lay behind German praise. In many respects, those writers were themselves victims of a skilful German propaganda campaign which attempted to demonstrate that the German army had not been defeated on the field of battle but had been forced to submit because it had been 'stabbed-in-the-back'.[18] It is no coincidence that the leading exponents of this view—Ludendorff, Hindenburg and, slightly later, Adolf Hitler—were members of the German army that had been defeated in 1918.

The German High Command undoubtedly had good reason to fear British propaganda, particularly during the final year of the war. After four years of stalemate and the failure of the last great German push in July, the preconditions of Germany's internal collapse were fast becoming evident. Despite the momentary triumph of Brest-Litovsk, the unrestricted submarine campaign that had done so much to provoke American entry into the war ultimately failed to force the Allies into submission. Food shortages caused by the blockade, socialist-pacifist propaganda inspired by Russia and the arrival of American troops on the western front all seriously affected the will to fight, let alone win, of the German army and people by the late summer of 1918. The collapse of Austria-Hungary was a further blow to the camel's back. Thus, when Crewe House assumed control from the War Office over Britain's propaganda against Germany at the end of August, having already contributed materially to the Habsburg collapse, the internal cohesion of the country was already beginning to disintegrate. The question that has to be asked is would Germany have collapsed without any encouragement from British propaganda? The answer is: probably, but not quite so quickly. Crewe House therefore began its work against Germany at a critically important time and accelerated the collapse that was already under way.

Even so, the German High Command's fear of British propaganda pre-dated the creation of Crewe House. This was illustrated by the decision to impose severe penalties on Allied pilots captured during leaflet-dropping raids over German lines. Those caught dropping bombs continued to be treated as honourable prisoners of war. The German argument that leaflet-dropping by aeroplane was contrary to the rules of war was eventually dismissed in 1923 by the Hague Commission of International Jurists. Article 21 of the Code of Rules for Aerial Warfare stated that 'the use of aircraft for the purposes of disseminating propaganda shall not be treated as an illegitimate means of warfare. Members of the crews of such aircraft must not be deprived of their rights as prisoners of war on the charge that they have committed such an act'.[19] Yet, during the final winter of the war, the German announcement had produced the desired effect. The British government called a halt to aeroplane distribution of propaganda material on the western front, although this highly efficient means of distribution was continued on the Italian front. If the Habsburg government had issued a similar warning, it too would have secured an important propaganda victory in its own right. Fieldmarshall Conrad, however, remained sceptical concerning the real impact of propaganda,[20] an attitude which he came to regret.

How effective, then, was British wartime propaganda? It must be remembered that the campaign was fought at home and in allied, neutral and enemy countries from an early stage of the war. In Wellington House it was appreciated that the initial aims of British propaganda must necessarily be modest:

It is in the nature of such work as this that its results should be difficult to estimate. It was not to be desired that all converts to the British point of view should proclaim their conversion: the object to be aimed at is rather to secure that opinion in neutral countries shall not be based on imperfect or distorted information regarding the nature of the British case.[21]

Until 1917, at least, Wellington House could hardly be expected to do much more in view of the absence of any coherent statement of war aims which meant that British propaganda was largely defensive in its sustained campaign and was only able spasmodically to move on to the offensive when individual events presented an opportunity to do so. Even Lord Cecil recognised that 'as long as the military situation is, at any rate superficially, unfavourable to the Entente, it will be difficult to construct out of it effective propaganda'.[22] Cecil Spring-Rice agreed: 'The real propaganda is facts and results'.[23]

Propaganda, as John Buchan recognised in December 1917, 'cannot work miracles':

Its aim is to state honestly and fully the different aspects of Britain's achievement in the war, to circulate in the popular mind the main principles of Allied policy and its justification, and to inform the world accurately of the atrocities and claims of our opponents.[24]

Buchan did, after all, have more to work with as far as war aims were concerned than his predecessors had ever had. But, as he correctly recognised:

it is a perpetual struggle . . . . The most active propaganda cannot undo the effect of an enemy victory or explain away an Allied check. No propaganda of ours can really counteract Socialist and pacifist appeals in a country where the Government itself makes no attempt to counteract or suppress them. If the powerful war parties in Italy and Russia failed to stem the tide of anti-war propaganda, it is hard to see how the efforts of a foreign government could have succeeded.[25]

Buchan was, in many respects, apologising for a situation which no amount of propaganda could have changed radically. If the National War Aims Committee found it difficult to combat pacifism inside Britain, epitomised by the Lansdowne letter, then the Department of Information could hardly be expected to compensate for the harsh military realities of Caporetto or the consequences of the Bolshevik revolution. Yet even that most ardent of critics, Robert Donald, while recognising that 'it is a grave defect that no adequate means exist for testing the efficiency of our various propaganda efforts abroad', was nonetheless forced to admit that 'the results which we have obtained from our somewhat haphazard methods have been more effective in some parts of the world than those of the enemy, despite his stupendous world organisation, scientifically planned many years before the war, and well directed. His clumsiness sometimes defeats itself, for his methods are not seldom clumsy and crude'.[26]

This somewhat negative tribute to the efficacy of British propaganda before the advent of Beaverbrook and Northcliffe was echoed by at least one MP during the Commons debate of August 1918 in relation to the role played by British propaganda during the first three years of the war. He maintained:

After all is said and done, it was not our propaganda that influenced opinion in America. It was enemy propaganda that did that . . . . The German touch is not a delicate one, and the propaganda which they carried out in the United States did far more to discredit the German case in the United States than anything our Department of Propaganda did.[27]

There may indeed be something in the argument that British propaganda was effective because German propaganda was not, or even that British propagandists succeeded because they avoided the same mistakes made by their German counterparts. However, the argument that British propaganda succeeded in the United States almost by default rests upon the assumption that had the government done little or nothing to influence American opinion between 1914 and 1917, the final result would have been the same. The critics of Wellington House may not have been in full possession of the details concerning its work because of the intense secrecy which surrounded its campaign, but the fact remains that the sinking of the *Lusitania* and other passenger liners, the introduction of submarine warfare and the Zimmermann telegram were undoubtedly significant episodes in President Wilson's decision to abandon American neutrality in favour of the Allied cause. Yet without control over the trans-Atlantic cables, the Zimmermann telegram would never have been intercepted by British naval intelligence. Moreover, without the ability to decipher the German codes and without some appreciation of the role propaganda could play in influencing American opinion, the telegram would never have been publicised. British propaganda, therefore, not only benefited from the various inherent advantages of the so-called 'special relationship' but it also capitalised upon any opportunities which the Germans presented to it while, at the same time, sustaining a persistent but low-key campaign among those sectors of the American community that mattered most. By not undoing the work of diplomacy, Wellington House was able to overcome the periodic outbursts of anti-British sentiment over such issues as the blockade, censorship and Ireland, and was eventually able to overcome the nation's predisposition towards neutrality as expressed in the 1916 election. Moreover, by exploiting a particular stereotype of the Germans and their ways of warfare through the presentation of seemingly objective atrocity propaganda, Wellington House was able to undermine the credibility of the German case in such a way as to make it appear barbaric and inhuman in the eyes of neutral observers. Because this work was conducted quietly and discreetly, often in conjunction with the British intelligence services, it received little credit from contemporaries. Even Beaverbrook accepted the need for secrecy[28] although it was, of course, a different matter when it came to propaganda in enemy countries. But after the war, when many of the details of the campaign in the United States came to light for the first time, the argument that the country had somehow been 'duped' into involvement in 1917 by subversive propaganda emanating from Wellington House was seized upon by those 'isolationist' elements as a further reason for American withdrawal from the devious machinations of the Old World. This sensitivity to the existence of foreign propaganda in the United States was to culminate in 1938 with the passing of the Foreign Agents Registration Act, requiring all foreign propagandists operating on American soil to register with the United States government. As in Germany, Britain's wartime success in the field of propaganda was used as a factor in a post-war counter-propagandist campaign.

As Beaverbrook readily admitted, the conduct of national propaganda overseas involved the direct interference by one government in the internal affairs of another country. This type of activity ran counter to British tradition but was essential if the Great War was to be fought to the maximum of the nation's resources. Morale, both at home and abroad, had become a military asset. Beaverbrook wrote:

Propaganda is the task of creating and directing public opinion. In other wars this work has not been a function of the Government, but has been left to the enterprise of the private citizen, since it is the traditional British plan to do nothing by official channels which can possibly be done outside them. But it was soon evident that in a struggle which was not one of armies but of nations, and which tended to attract every people on the globe, this aloofness could not be maintained. Since strength for the purposes of war was the total strength of each belligerent nation, public opinion was as significant as fleets and armies.[29]

The emergence of propaganda as the chief instrument of control over public opinion by 1918 was the inevitable consequence of 'total war'. At home, it became the fifth arm of defence; abroad, it provided another means of combating the enemy in a struggle for neutral sympathy and for launching a psychological offensive against the enemy himself. In short, propaganda became an indispensable part of the equipment of the modern state at war.

Although considerable research remains to be done, there appears to be little reason for challenging the assumption that British propaganda directed against Austria-Hungary was anything but successful in helping to accelerate the internal collapse of the Dual Monarchy, not least because of the role played by Crewe House officials in helping to determine the government's policy — if policy it can be called — towards the subject nationalities. Virtually all of the available evidence suggests that without Allied help, whether in the form of President Wilson's Fourteen Points or the propaganda conducted by the Inter-Allied Commission at Padua, the subject nationalities would not have succumbed to Allied promises. Their aspirations for national self-determination would have remained aspirations had it not been for the efforts of people like Wickham Steed to let propaganda requirements dictate policy. The dangers of this line of action became apparent at the Paris Peace Conference when the problems of keeping promises, whether declared or implied, were to provide serious headaches for the peacemakers when it came to the creation of Yugoslavia, Rumania and Czechoslovakia. Indeed, the Foreign Office had warned of the dangers of allowing propaganda to dictate policy, rather than vice versa. But in 1918, when the principal object of the British government was to win the war as quickly as possible by any and every means available, short-term considerations tended to receive priority. In this respect, Crewe House was successful in pursuing a line of policy without securing from the government anything more than a series of vague declarations. Its propaganda enabled those declarations to become known amongst troops normally denied access to enemy information. The methods employed on the Italian front in achieving this result were thus critically important in exploiting the aspirations of the various subject nationalities by promising something which Crewe House was not really authorised to give. For Lloyd George, who had been personally responsible for the creation of Crewe House in February 1918, the implications of his expediency were to be felt by him at Paris in 1919.

There remains the question of the impact of British propaganda in Germany. One of the earliest claims made for the effect being produced was that of General Charteris in August 1916. He wrote from GHQ in France:

We are getting on with the dropping of letters and pamphlets on the German side of the line; quite possibly in consequence of that, although not certainly, we have had the biggest batch of deserters coming over together since the beginning of the war. It is not very big, only ten in all, but they came together and therefore is encouraging.[30]

Most claims do, however, relate to the final year of the war. In November 1917, one German press article lamented the failure to combat British propaganda in the campaign for neutral sympathy:

Reuter rules the market, not Wolff; London makes foreign opinion not Berlin. We Germans have remained despite all our exertions as regards impressing foreign opinion, the same bunglers we always were . . . . Where Reuters indulges in rapid and skilful swordplay, we bring up our heavy artillery.[31]

Again, in July 1918, came the often quoted tribute from a German official: 'More powerful than the English fleet, more dangerous than the English army, are Reuter and the English news-propaganda'. Clearly, the Germans felt that they were losing the war of words. But how did this affect the fighting spirit of the men in the trenches?

In 1918, the War Office began to compile information from a wide variety of sources as to whether prisoners it had interrogated claimed that they had been influenced by Allied propaganda. Many were found to have propaganda literature on their person when captured. Moreover, of the 48 reports compiled between 13 May and 17 October 1918 on the effectiveness of balloon propaganda, only one contained an adverse comment by a German prisoner of war. Statements made by deserters revealed that the leaflets had been received with considerable enthusiasm. On occasion, they had even been exchanged for money and, in a few cases, they had contributed materially to the eventual decision to surrender.[32] Some prisoners referred to the orders issued by the German High Command forbidding the troops to read or distribute enemy literature which was also said to have caused a considerable response among German troops of Polish origin. Despite a considerable discrepancy between the British and American figures reporting the number of prisoners found carrying leaflets when captured — the American figure was 80 per cent, the British 12 per cent[33] — some of the material was clearly making an impact, a conclusion confirmed by French military intelligence reports of interrogated prisoners and deserters which also stated that the German High Command was becoming increasingly preoccupied with seizing the material for destruction.[34] However, although some attempt was made to assess the effectiveness of propaganda among the German troops by examining the connection with desertions, the investigations were not taken much further. In short, the evidence was left to speak for itself on the assumption that a direct connection between propaganda and desertion did exist within the German army.

As subsequent investigations were to reveal, this assumption rested on highly dubious foundations. During the Second World War, when the investigation of prisoners was placed upon a systematic basis, many of the findings relating to the psychology of desertion did serve to cast new light upon the effectiveness of propaganda. Psychologists ascertained that statements made by captured prisoners could not be taken at their face value; there was always the possibility that a prisoner would say merely what he believed his captors wished to hear. Casting blame upon external influences such as propaganda might also prove to be simply a convenient rationalisation for his current predicament. Moreover, possession of propaganda literature did not necessarily mean that it had actually been read and, even when it had been, it could not be proved beyond all reasonable doubt that it had directly influenced his behaviour. In other words, the decision of soldiers to surrender or desert in large numbers could not be directly attributed to enemy propaganda. What keeps a soldier fighting is largely his membership of an identifiable primary group, usually small units within the army which provide him with a sense of identification and loyalty. Propaganda directed at the self-interest of the individual, therefore, is unlikely to produce a significant effect unless the primary group structure has begun to disintegrate as a consequence of military reversals or defeat.[35] Thus, the 'legendary success of Allied propaganda against the German army at the end of the First World War' helped to create 'erroneous views concerning the omnicompetence of propaganda' in the Second.[36]

Even the Germans were unable to sustain their own argument. In the early 1930s, Hans Thimme conducted an investigation into the state of morale within the German Sixth Army in September 1918 involving the analysis of some 54,000 letters written by soldiers. Although Thimme listed propaganda as one of nine factors contributing to the collapse of morale, he attempted to explain away the paucity of references to propaganda as a determinant of subversive or revolutionary activity against the State by arguing that the letters examined were written by nationally-minded people who were immune to enemy influence and that anyway revolutionaries or mutineers do not normally speak their real minds in letters![37] It would therefore seem difficult to support such extreme claims as that made by *The Times* at the end of October 1918: 'Good propaganda probably saved a year of war, and this meant the saving of thousands of millions of money and probably at least a million lives'.[38]

However, given the nature of propaganda, combined with the absence of quantifiable evidence, it is perhaps impossible to assess in any precise terms the impact of British propaganda in the First World War. Perhaps too much has been expected of it as an instrument of modern war. But although *The Times* was a victim of this type of over-expectation, it remains difficult to refute the evidence which points to its successful impact. The vulnerability of the target, the pertinence of the views expressed to the situation of that target, and the actual success of the material in reaching its audience at the right moment are undoubtedly important factors. Yet, as one official noted:

Mere propaganda cannot do everything: unsupported by military and naval victories any propaganda organisation tends to become a sounding brass. On the one hand the causes and significance of victories do not soak in of their own accord: if left alone the average man dispenses praise and blame according to his individual prejudices and animosities. The business of propaganda is to make the wheels of victory run smoothly.[39]

Accordingly, if British propaganda was at all successful during the First World War, it was because events favoured its conduct. If the British had lost, would it still have been so universally praised?

Nevertheless, the American conversion from neutrality to belligerency, the growth of discontent within the Central Powers after four years of total war and the desire to maintain Allied solidarity until victory was achieved were all pounced upon by British propagandists who did not create the preconditions of success but who did display a masterly capacity to identify and exploit any opportunities and advantages which came their way. This was a cumulative process requiring infinite patience as well as an instinctive capacity to throw a left-handed punch to an opponent who was about to fall to his knees following a right hook. Northcliffe was thus being more realistic than modest when he claimed that 'we have to some extent hastened the end'.

An essential element in this process was the organisation of British propaganda. Because, in many respects, the work was begun reluctantly, the organisation was initially tentative and exploratory. Its real significance was realised only gradually with the recognition that the war required the mobilisation of the nation's entire resources. This factor partially explains the various changes which took place in the organisation of Britain's propaganda. A further explanation, as Beaverbrook indicated in 1918, lay in the nature of propaganda itself:

It is not a static thing and can never be standardised. It is a business of infinite small details, involving a day-to-day study of foreign affairs. Policies change, and methods must be changed to meet them; what is the centre of gravity today is not the centre of gravity tomorrow; and a method which was fruitful in the first year of the war might well be superfluous in the third. Clearly the constitution of any propaganda department must be adapted to so fluctuating a subject matter, drawing in here and expanding there.[40]

It was largely because Wellington House and the Foreign Office, followed by the Department of Information, proved inflexible in the eyes of their critics to proposals for change that control over British official propaganda was transferred into the hands of Beaverbrook and Northcliffe. Although the Foreign Office retained a vested interest in the conduct of propaganda through its continued involvement in the policy-making process, it had been deprived of actual responsibility for it because Fleet Street enjoyed the support of the Prime Minister. It was not just the appointment of powerful newspapermen which created a public outcry in February 1918; journalists had been employed in the official propaganda machinery from an early stage of the war, George Mair, E. T. Cook and Arthur Willert being the most obvious examples. It was the appointment of influential proprietors to controlling positions that raised fears that the traditional demarcation lines between government and the press were being blurred. The appointments of Beaverbrook and Northcliffe were partly the result of Lloyd George's desire to undermine the influence of the Foreign Office in the foreign policy-making process by transferring responsibility for propaganda into the hands of those who were criticising the government most vociferously over this issue.

Although the Ministry of Information — but not Crewe House — did reflect the influence of the second Donald Report, its establishment has too often been interpreted as a condemnation of previous arrangements. The Ministry was founded upon the experience of its predecessors. Lord Beaverbrook's newspaper admitted as much in an article written in the *Sunday Express* in 1919:

Lord Beaverbrook, when he became Minister for Information at the beginning of 1918, only took over and developed an organisation which already existed and which, though discouraged by Ministers and too often attacked by the Press, was doing the work which extorted the admiration of the Prussian leader. For the work of the old department Mr Masterman and Colonel John Buchan can claim the credit. They laboured diligently to convert the neutrals of which America was the most important, and according to hostile evidence they succeeded. The difficulty of this original department was that it had too little power and practically no direct access to the Cabinet.[41]

In fact, the changes that did take place in organisational terms were more apparent than real. In theory, an independent organisation had been created to supervise the conduct of all British official propaganda from under one roof. In practice, however, the system remained as diverse as it had ever been. The National War Aims Committee remained in charge of domestic propaganda, the Press Bureau retained its control over censorship whereas a separate department was created to deal with propaganda in enemy countries. The War Office remained in charge of distribution of propaganda material in military zones while the diplomatic and consular officials serving 'on the spot' remained the most important distribution agents overseas. In effect, the Ministry of Information was only responsible for British propaganda in allied and neutral countries and in one enemy country, Turkey. The arguments which had long been presented concerning the creation of a single unified organisation responsible for all propaganda were never realised.

Nevertheless, there were several significant changes, which perhaps would be more accurately described as modifications. The centre of gravity was shifted away from the literary production department at Wellington House and much less pamphlet material was produced in the final year of war resulting in a one-sixth reduction in the use of paper. The need for this and other rationalisations had been emphasised at a conference between John Buchan and the Newspaper Proprietors' Association on 16 January 1918. A subsequent enquiry conducted by the Ministry of Information confirmed the findings of Robert Donald and Arthur Spurgeon on this particular type of propaganda. It stated: 'the work of Wellington House has, owing to a number of causes, been carried on in a machine-like groove, with regular output and too great a similarity in character and distribution. Wellington House has wrongfully become more of a great publishing institution than an effective propaganda agency'.[42] The emphasis on intellectual propaganda, as reflected in the use of pamphlets, was also modified by the Ministry of Information in favour of a wider appeal. Masterman admitted in December 1917 that 'we have hitherto done very little from the central office in England to produce on a large scale popular leaflets for the working classes in foreign countries'. He continued:

The appeal to the popular crowd has been in the main (in addition to newspapers) the production of pictorial matter which is welcomed in cafes, barbers' shops and in shop window display, whereas leaflets awaken no similar response.[43]

Instead Wellington House had produced pamphlets 'which we consider suitable for the *leaders* of the working class'. Masterman remained convinced that 'neither in the preparation nor the distribution of such leaflets can very much be done from England for foreign lands'.[44]

Neither Beaverbrook nor Northcliffe agreed. The Bolshevik revolution in Russia and its subsequent international appeals to the working classes to end the 'capitalist' war provided them with powerful evidence to support their argument that British propaganda should be conceived in mass terms. Sir Edward Carson had recognised the need to broaden its appeal from the opinion-makers to the opinion itself. He wrote in October 1917:

If the maker of shells could see the ammunition dumps at the front, if the maker of guns could visit camouflaged batteries, if both could witness the burst of shells over German lines, they would return to the factory with a spirit more braced to continued effort, and more determined to see the war through, than would be gained from endless speech-making or pamphlet reading.[45]

Equally, the continued importance of censorship as a form of negative propaganda was illustrated by the Cabinet's decision at the end of November 1917 to suppress the publication of Bolshevik appeals in the British press because they were 'appeals to the people as against their Governments, and were in many respects of a violent character'.[46] Yet this was precisely what Beaverbrook and Northcliffe were to do on behalf of the British government in 1918 when the appeal was launched to the subject nationalities of Austria-Hungary to stop fighting for the Habsburg cause in return for national self-determination. Similarly, in Germany, British propaganda emphasised that the war was being fought not against the German people but against their Prussian leaders. If those leaders could somehow be overthrown and replaced by a more reasonable and less barbaric governing regime, the German people could expect fair treatment in any peace settlement. This direct appeal to a mass audience was perhaps the most significant innovation of the Ministry of Information and of Crewe House. The decline in the importance of written material and the corresponding increase in the use of visual media, particularly film, was symptomatic of a radically different view of 'public opinion' to that held generally in the Foreign Office and Whitehall at the time.

Beaverbrook was undoubtedly correct when he wrote that 'the munitions of the mind become not less vital for victory than fleets or armies; for it is the frame of mind in which the world is found at the close of the war which will determine the world's future'.[47] It is, of course, difficult to generalise about the state of world opinion and the role played by British propaganda in shaping that opinion on the return of peace. In November 1917, Roderick Jones explained about the work of Reuters during the war:

The principle observed in shaping this service is a simple one. While bearing in mind that the proper presentation of the Allies' point of view is the main object of the Service, the fact is not forgotten that this object can best be attained by a candid and exact description of events as they occur. A military operation, for instance, in which the Allies have not been successful, is not ignored but is set out soberly in its proper perspective. Nor are Allied successes made the subject of paeans of enthusiasm. They are recorded in measured language, neither detracting from their value nor exaggerating their extent. Many years' experience in the handling of news has shown that these methods provide the best means of creating that intangible atmosphere of confidence which is indispensible if the service is to be trusted by people at home and abroad and is therefore to be of value.[48]

However, such reassurances failed to dispel the overall impression of Britain's wartime propaganda deriving from the German label of 'All-lies' and the abundance of crude atrocity stories which circulated during the conflict. The ferocity of atrocity propaganda was most marked in the British press where much of it originated. Crewe House maintained that:

A point was made of telling the enemy only the truth. The truth was being concealed from them by their leaders. Nothing could be more effective in depressing their spirits than a daily dose of unpleasant fact.[49]

Such assertions must be treated with some degree of scepticism. British propaganda was indeed news-based and factual in character but it rarely assumed the proportions of the whole truth. It was further argued:

If this task of enlightenment had not been entrusted to a department created for the special purpose, it would have rightly formed part of the duties of the Ministry of Education. Ours was a task of education and its effect will endure far beyond the war.[50]

And so it proved. In the short-term, the wartime exploitation of stereotypes concerning the 'Beastly Hun' and the 'Prussian Ogre' almost certainly contributed towards the insertion of the 'War Guilt Clause' into the Treaty of Versailles and the calls to 'Hang the Kaiser'. In 1919, the Foreign Office was keen to stress that, in its plans to conduct propaganda in the post-war world, it had no intention of conducting propaganda of 'the "Corpse Factory" type'[51] and that its conception of propaganda was nearer to the original meaning rather than the debasement of the activity that had taken place during the course of the war. Nevertheless, the sensational propaganda brought discredit on all other forms of activity. The exposure of wartime atrocity stories after the war, notably by Arthur Ponsonby's *Falsehood in Wartime*, served to further undermine the respectability of the wartime experiment. No official history was ever commissioned or written.[52] The continued association of propaganda with lies and atrocity stories was largely responsible for the view in Britain that propaganda was discreditable work and the absence of an authoritative contemporary appraisal merely served to perpetuate this image. The type of propaganda conducted by the majority of official British propagandists went unexplained and unfairly maligned.

One Wellington House official wrote after the war: 'Personally, I cannot recall an occasion when we circulated a deliberate untruth, and infinite pains were taken to sift information'.[53] Despite such disclaimers, however, official propagandists did not disassociate themselves from atrocity stories, even if it is difficult to ascertain whether they were actually involved in their fabrication. Wellington House, for example, did translate and distribute the Bryce Report on German atrocities and also circulated Raemakers cartoons depicting the German manufacture of glycerine from human corpses. The Press Bureau could have prevented the publication of atrocity stories in the British press, but did not. The Ministry of Information was responsible for the sensational film, *Once a Hun, Always a Hun*. Moreover, the infamous 'Corpse-Conversion Factory' story was exploited by the Department of Information. Such stories and their exposure after the war merely served to inoculate many intelligent observers against the atrocity stories which began to emerge from Nazi Germany during the 1930s. There was, of course, nothing new in the wartime circulation of atrocity stories and they were a proven method of rousing popular sentiment against the enemy and of rousing hatred against him among the troops. But their widespread distribution during the First World War was greatly facilitated by the new means and media of communication which served to create a lasting impression. Yet as one apologist has stated: 'Lying is an act of conscious deception. Much of British atrocity propaganda was unconscious deception built upon erroneous reports and impressions'.[54]

Perhaps the most serious consequence of the British government's attempt to return to normalcy after the war was the loss of an important British initiative in the conduct of international relations. The use of propaganda by foreign governments increased dramatically on the return of peace. The British had demonstrated its power in war; Soviet Russia and Nazi Germany were to utilise the lessons of the British wartime experiment and combine them with technological advancements in such areas as radio and film in order to mould propaganda into a powerful weapon of peacetime expansion. There could be no return to the period before 1914 when propaganda had played a relatively minor role in national and international affairs. However much British officials might have lamented such a development, the fact remains that it was the British government itself which, between 1914 and 1918, had demonstrated to the world the enormous power of propaganda.

Appendices

The Organisation of Official British Propaganda
1914-1916

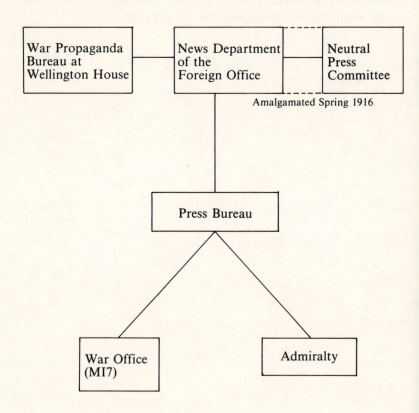

War Propaganda Bureau at Wellington House

News Department of the Foreign Office

Neutral Press Committee

Amalgamated Spring 1916

Press Bureau

War Office (MI7)

Admiralty

APPENDIX 2

The Department of Information, 1917

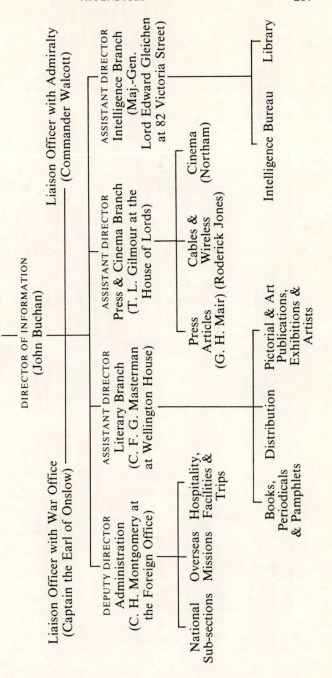

APPENDIX 3

The Organisation of Official British Propaganda
1917

Sir Edward Carson

FOREIGN PROPAGANDA
(The Department of Information)

John Buchan

- Administration
- Literary Production
- Press & Cinema
- Intelligence

PROPAGANDA IN MILITARY ZONES & PRODUCTION OF PROPAGANDA MATERIAL ON MILITARY SUBJECTS
(MI7 at the War Office)

Col. Fisher

Lord Onslow

- MI7(c) Visits to military centres at home & abroad
- MI7(d) Analysis of British & foreign press

MI7(b): Propaganda

- MI7(b)1 Preparation of special military articles
- MI7(b)2 Preparation of historical & technical military articles
- MI7(b)3 Military news for Dominions; Military artists
- MI7(b)4 Analysis of German Propaganda; Aerial propaganda at front
- MI7(b)5 Analysis of German cables & wireless; Collection of news concerning military operations

HOME PROPAGANDA
(The National War Aims Committee)

Frederick Guest

Joint Committee: Col. Sanders (Chairman) plus representatives of Ministries of Food, National Service and Munitions, and War Savings Committee

- Meetings Department
- Publicity Department

Appendix 4

The Ministry of Information, 1918

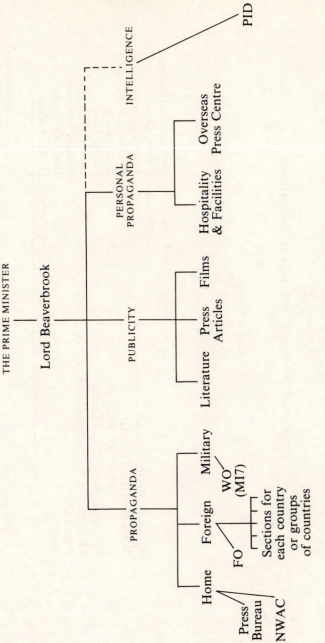

APPENDIX 5

The Department of Enemy Propaganda at Crewe House
1918

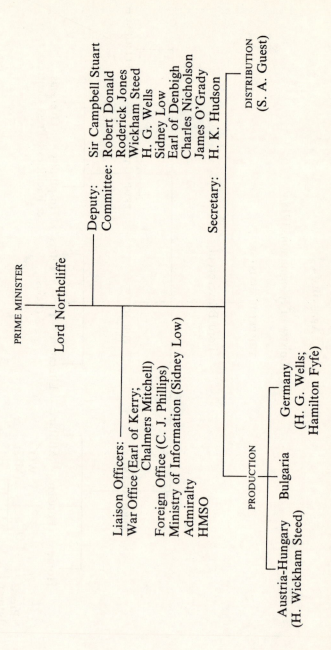

PRIME MINISTER

Lord Northcliffe

Deputy: Sir Campbell Stuart
Committee: Robert Donald
Roderick Jones
Wickham Steed
H. G. Wells
Sidney Low
Earl of Denbigh
Charles Nicholson
James O'Grady
Secretary: H. K. Hudson

Liaison Officers:
War Office (Earl of Kerry; Chalmers Mitchell)
Foreign Office (C. J. Phillips)
Ministry of Information (Sidney Low)
Admiralty
HMSO

PRODUCTION

Austria-Hungary
(H. Wickham Steed)

Bulgaria

Germany
(H. G. Wells;
Hamilton Fyfe)

DISTRIBUTION
(S. A. Guest)

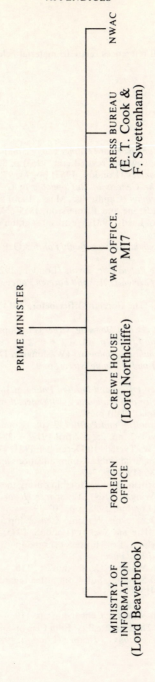

APPENDIX 6

The Organisation of Official British Propaganda, 1918

PRIME MINISTER

- MINISTRY OF INFORMATION (Lord Beaverbrook)
- FOREIGN OFFICE
- CREWE HOUSE (Lord Northcliffe)
- WAR OFFICE, MI7
- PRESS BUREAU (E. T. Cook & F. Swettenham)
- NWAC

Notes

Unless otherwise stated, all references relate to material held in the Public Records Office, Kew, London.

INTRODUCTION

1. K. Martin, *The Triumph of Lord Palmerston: A Study of Public Opinion before the Crimean War* (London, new and revised edn, 1963) p. 82.
2. H. Nicolson, *Diplomacy* (London, 1963) pp. 73, 97.
3. J. H. Gleason, *The Genesis of Russophobia in Great Britain: A Study of interaction of policy and opinion* (Cambridge, Mass., 1950) p. 190ff.
4. E. D. Steele, 'Gladstone and Palmerston, 1855-65', an unpublished paper delivered at the University of Leeds, 1981. We are most grateful to Dr Steele for letting us see a copy of this paper.
5. E. H. Carr, *Propaganda in International Politics* (Oxford pamphlets on World Affairs, no. 16, 1939).
6. J. A. Spender, *The Public Life*, 2 vols (London, 1925) II, p. 40
7. Z. S. Steiner, *The Foreign Office and Foreign Policy, 1898-1914* (Cambridge, 1969) p. 172.
8. Cf. R. Langhorne, 'The Foreign Office before 1914', *Historical Journal*, 16. (1973) 4, 857.
9. K. Jones, *Fleet Street and Downing Street* (London, 1920) pp. 98-100.
10. Spender, *The Public Life*, II, p. 40.
11. B. Akzin, *Propaganda by Diplomats* (Washington D. C., 1936) pp. 1-3.
12. Jones, *Fleet Street and Downing Street*, p. 95.
13. Ibid., p. 97.
14. Steiner, *The Foreign Office and Foreign Policy*, p.36.
15. O. J. Hale, *Publicity and Diplomacy, with special reference to England and Germany, 1890-1914* (Virginia, 1940) p. 38.
16. Spender, *Life, Journalism and Politics*, 2 vols (London, 1926) I, p. 186.
17. *The New Europe*, vol. 2, no. 25, 5 April 1917, p. 384.
18. Memorandum by W. Tyrrell, 10 December 1921, FO 800/329.
19. P. M. Kennedy, 'Imperial Cable Communications and Strategy, 1870-1914', *English Historical Review*, 86 (1971) p. 747.
20. Colin Lovelace, 'British press censorship during the First World War' in G. Boyce, J. Curran and P. Wingate (eds), *Newspaper History: from the seventeenth century to the present day* (London, 1978) pp. 307-19.
21. P. Towle, 'The Debate on Wartime Censorship in Britain, 1902-14', in B. Bond and I. Roy (eds), *War and Society* (London, 1975) pp. 103-16.
22. Ibid., p. 109; Lovelace, 'British press censorship', p. 308.
23. Hale, *Publicity and Diplomacy*.
24. Towle, 'Debate on Wartime Censorship', p. 110.
25. Report of the CID Standing Sub-Committee regarding press censorship in time of war, 31 January 1913, CAB 16/27.
26. Ibid.
27. Towle, 'Debate on Wartime Censorship', p. 110.
28. Nicholas Pronay, 'The First Reality: Film Censorship in Liberal England' in K. R. M. Short (ed.), *Feature Films as History* (London, 1981) pp. 113-37.

29.   D. Hopkin, 'Domestic Censorship in the First World War', *Journal of Contemporary History*, 5 (1970) 4, 151-69.

30.   D. French, 'Spy Fever in Britain, 1900-15', *Historical Journal*, 21 (1978) 2, 355-70.

31.   Cmd. 7680 (1914-16) vol. 39.

32.   For further details see WO 106/1516.

33.   J. H. Ferguson, *American Diplomacy and the Boer War* (Philadelphia, 1939) p. 176.

34.   G. P. Gooch and H. Temperley, *Documents on the Origins of the War, 1898-1914* (London, 1927) I, no. 298, p. 241.

35.   Ibid., II, no. 231, p. 203.

36.   Hansard, 5th series (Commons), vol. 132, 3 November 1911, col. 564.

37.   Steiner, *The Foreign Office and Foreign Policy*, p.167.

38.   Memorandum by G. B. Beak, 2 December 1918, FO 395/301.

39.   G. Barraclough, *An Introduction to Contemporary History* (London, 1966) p. 19.

40.   R. Albrecht-Carrié, *The Meaning of the First World War* (New Jersey, 1956) p.64.

1. THE ORGANISATION OF OFFICIAL BRITISH PROPAGANDA, 1914-1916

1.   George H. Cassar, *Kitchener: Architect of Victory* (London, 1977) p. 204.

2.   Cate Haste, *Keep the Home Fires Burning* (London, 1977) pp. 49-52.

3.   Report by R. H. Davies on the work of the PRC, Treasury paper 154, WO 106/367.

4.   J. D. Squires, *British Propaganda at Home and in the United States from 1914 to 1917* (Cambridge, Mass., 1935) pp. 16-25.

5.   C. Hazlehurst, *Politicians at War* (London, 1971) pp. 140-2.

6.   Report of the publications sub-department of the PRC, WO 106/367.

7.   Report of the meetings sub-department of the National War Aims Committee, 25 September 1917. T 102/16. For the broader picture see R. J. Q. Adams, *Arms and the Wizard: Lloyd George and the Ministry of Munitions, 1915-16* (London, 1978).

8.   Ibid.

9.   Barbara W. Tuchman, *The Zimmerman Telegram* (London, 1959) p.11.

10.   P. M. Kennedy, 'Imperial Cable Communications and Strategy, 1870-1914', *English Historical Review*, 86 (1971) pp. 728-52.

11.   T. F. Jaras, 'Promoters and Public Servants: The Role of the British Government in the Expansion of Submarine Telegraphy, 1860-70' (Georgetown University, unpublished Ph.D. thesis, 1975).

12.   Michael Palmer, 'The British press and international news, 1851-99: of agencies and newspapers' in G. Boyce, James Curran and Pauline Wingate (eds), *Newspaper History: From the 17th Century to the present day* (London, 1978) 205-19.

13.   Kennedy, 'Imperial Cable Communications', p. 747.

14.   Earl of Birkenhead, *F. E., The Life of F. E. Smith* (London, 1965) p. 244.

15.   Hansard, 5th series (Commons), vol. 65, col. 2155, 7 August 1914.

16.   Hansard, 5th series (Commons), vol. 66, col. 150, 27 August 1914.

17.   Colin Lovelace, 'British press censorship during the First World War', in Boyce, Curran & Wingate, *Newspaper History*, p. 310.

18.   For further details see WO 106/1516. See also the account by J. C. Silber, a German spy working in the War Office censorship department, *The Invisible Weapons* (London, 1932).

19.   E. T. Cook, *The Press in Wartime* (London, 1920), ch. 4.

20.   'The Censor's Uneven Hand', *Daily Chronicle*, 18 January 1915.

21.   As argued by Cate Haste in *Keep the Home Fires Burning* which does, however, fail to distinguish adequately between press propaganda and government propaganda conducted through the medium of the press.

22.   Rear-Admiral Sir Douglas Brownrigg, *Indiscretions of the Naval Censor* (London, 1920) p. 6.

23.   Cited in Haste, *Keep the Home Fires Burning*, p. 33.

24.   P. Knightley, *The First Casualty: The War Correspondent as Hero, Propagandist and Myth Maker from the Crimea to Vietnam* (London, 1975) ch. 5.

25.   D. Hopkin, 'Domestic Censorship in the First World War', *Journal of Contemporary History*, 5 (1970) 4, 155.

26.   History of The Times, *The 150th Anniversary and Beyond* (London, 1952) vol. 4, Part I, p. 222ff.

27.   Knightley, *The First Casualty*, pp. 89-92; R. Pound & G. Harmsworth, *Northcliffe* (London, 1959) p. 469.

28.   History of The Times, p. 227.

29.   Haste, *Keep the Home Fires Burning*, p. 51.

30.   Pound & Harmsworth, *Northcliffe*, p. 469ff.

31.   P. Towle, 'The Debate on Wartime Censorship in Britain, 1902-14' in B. Bond & I. Roy (eds.) *War and Society* (London, 1975) cited p. 113.

32.   Lord Riddell, *War Diary 1914-18* (London, 1933) p. 79.

33.   See the Cabinet discussions on Repington's activities: CAB 23/5, 342 (16) and 343, 11 February 1918; CAB 23/5, 344 (1 & 2) 12 February 1918.

34.   Brownrigg, *Indiscretions of the Naval Censor*, p. 13.

35.   Pound & Harmsworth, *Northcliffe*, p. 470.

36.   Cited in the 'Memorandum on the Official Press Bureau', Cmd. 7680 (1915).

37.   Unsigned memorandum, 27 October 1914, FO 371/2555.

38.   Buckmaster to editors of the British press, 17 November 1914, FO 371/2217.

39.   History of The Times, cited p. 234.

40.   Ibid.

41.   Robinson (i.e. Geoffrey Dawson) to Arthur Willert, 31 December 1914. Willert MS. The Times Archive (TTA).

42.   Interview given by Sir Edward Cook to the Associated Press, April 1916, FO 371/2844.

43.   Memorandum by R. Cecil, 16 October 1915, FO 371/2577.

44.   Steed to Cecil, 11 August 1915, FO 371/2571.

45.   See Hopkin, 'Domestic Censorship', and Lovelace, 'British Press Censorship'.

46.   'General Notes on Propaganda', undated, unsigned, INF 4/1B.

47.   H. O. Lee, 'British Propaganda during the Great War, 1914-18', INF 4/4A.

48.   Minute by Cecil, 22 December 1915, FO 371/2579; see also the memorandum by J. A. Simon, 27 October 1915, CAB 37/136/34.

49.   Cited in the enclosure in S. G. Tallents to Sir A. Cadogan, 6 July 1938, CAB 16/127, MIC 13.

50.   Brownrigg, *Indiscretions of the Naval Censor*, ch. 3.

51.   Minute by Cecil, 22 December 1915, FO 371/2579.

52.   For an example of the proceedings of one such conference see F/191/3/2, Lloyd George papers.

53.   Northcliffe to Bonar Law, 4 February 1915, Northcliffe papers, vol. ii, 1581, British Library (BL).

54.   N. Lytton, *The Press and the General Staff* (London, 1921).

55.   H. O. Lee, 'British propaganda during the Great War', INF 4/4A.

56.   Ibid.

57.   A. Ponsonby, *Falsehood in Wartime* (London, 1928).

58.   F/191/3/2, Lloyd George papers.
59.   Knightley, *The First Casualty*, p. 107.
60.   For further details see FO 395/140.
61.   CAB 23/2, 119 (24) 16 April 1917.
62.   HO 45/10787/297549.
63.   Cited in E. Blackwell to Foreign Office, 7 December 1916, HO 45/10786/297549; see also the Cabinet discussion on this issue in CAB 23/4, 274 (17) 15 November 1917.
64.   CAB 23/2, 136 (13) 11 May 1917.
65.   CAB 23/2, 145 (4) 24 May 1917.
66.   Cook, *The Press in Wartime*, p. 44.
67.   Donald to Lloyd George, 9 January 1917, INF 4/4B.
68.   Memorandum by Simon, 'The Neutral Press Committee', 8 October 1915, CAB 37/135/14.
69.   G. H. Mair, 'Report of propaganda of the Neutral Press Organisation' undated, FO 371/2555.
70.   Memorandum by Simon, 8 October 1915, CAB 37/135/14.
71.   Undated minute by J. D. Gregory on C. Spring-Rice to F. D. Acland, 29 January 1915, FO 371/2556.
72.   Foreign Office memorandum, 'British propaganda in Allied and Neutral Countries', 20 December 1916, CAB 24/3, G 102.
73.   Lee, 'British propaganda during the Great War', INF 4/4A.
74.   Minute by E. Percy, 27 October 1914, FO 371/2211.
75.   Memorandum by L. W. 'Mr Hearst and the International News Service' 30 August 1917, FO 800/223,Pp/1.
76.   Lee, 'British propaganda during the Great War', INF 4/4A.
77.   Foreign Office memorandum, 20 December 1916, CAB 24/3, G 102.
78.   Ibid.
79.   Unsigned memorandum on the News Department, 29 January 1915, FO 371/2555.
80.   Foreign Office memorandum, 20 December 1916, CAB 24/3, G 102.
81.   Ibid.
82.   Lee, 'British propaganda during the Great War', INF 4/4A.
83.   Ibid.
84.   Sir Roderick Jones, *A Life in Reuters* (London, 1951) pp. 187-9.
85.   Memorandum by R. Jones, 10 November 1917, CAB 27/17, OPC 3.
86.   Unsigned memorandum on the News Department, 29 January 1915, FO 371/2555.
87.   Donald to Lloyd George, 9 January 1917, INF 4/4B.
88.   G. Storey, *Reuters Century* (London, 1951) p. 160.
89.   Memorandum by Jones, 10 November 1917, CAB 27/17, OPC 3.
90.   Storey, *Reuters Century*, p. 148ff.
91.   Donald to Lloyd George, 9 January 1917, INF 4/4B.
92.   Memorandum by Jones, 10 November 1917, CAB 27/17, OPC 3.
93.   Foreign Office memorandum, 20 December 1916, CAB 24/3, G 102.
94.   Donald to Lloyd George, 9 January 1917, INF 4/4B.
95.   Memorandum by Jones, 10 November 1917, CAB 27/17, OPC 3.
96.   Sir James Rennell Rodd, *Social and Diplomatic Memories* (London, 1925) p. 309.
97.   H. H. Asquith to the King, 31 August 1914, CAB 41/35/38.
98.   His most notable book was *The Condition of England* (London, 1909) and he had written for *The Daily News*, *Independent Review*, *The Pilot*, *The Nation* and the *Daily Chronicle*.

99. Sir Fife Clark, *The Central Office of Information* (London, 1970) p. 23.
100. FO 371/2209.
101. Conference with representatives of the London press, summoned by C. F. G. Masterman, held at Wellington House, Buckingham Gate on 7 September 1914, FO 371/2209.
102. F. D. Acland to Masterman, 9 September 1914, FO 371/2209.
103. A. Toynbee, *Experiences* (Oxford, 1969).
104. N. Rose, *Lewis Namier and Zionism* (Oxford, 1980).
105. A. Headlam-Morley, R. Bryant and A. Cienciala (eds), *Sir James Headlam-Morley: A Memoir of the Paris Peace Conference, 1919* (London, 1963).
106. There is a photograph of 'the moot' in Lucy Masterman's biography of her husband, *C. F. G. Masterman: A Biography* (London, 1939) facing p. 304.
107. H. C. Peterson, *Propaganda for War* (New York, 1939) p. 16.
108. Enclosed memorandum dated 2 December 1914 in Gowers to Montgomery, 18 December 1914, FO 371/2207.
109. Schuster to Grey, 4 December 1914, FO 371/2213.
110. First report on the work of Wellington House, 7 June 1915, INF 4/5.
111. Ibid.
112. J. D. Squires, *British Propaganda*, p. 16ff.
113. Montgomery to Cust, 23 November 1914, FO 371/2207.
114. Cecil to Cust, 2 August 1915, FO 371/2561.
115. Second report on the work of Wellington House, February 1916, INF 4/5.
116. Donald to Lloyd George, 9 January 1917, INF 4/4B.
117. Cited in 'A history of the work of MI7, 1914-19', INF 4/1B.
118. Sir R. Brade to Foreign Office, 10 December 1915, FO 371/2579.
119. Ibid.
120. Minute by Montgomery, 10 December 1915, FO 371/2579.
121. Schuster to Montgomery, 13 December 1915, FO 371/2579.
122. Schuster to Sir Edward Troup, 13 December 1915, FO 371/2579.
123. Ibid.
124. Ibid.
125. See Montgomery's proposals of 2 and 6 October 1915, FO 371/2579.
126. Maurice de Bunsen to War Office, 14 December 1915, FO 371/2579.
127. Ibid.
128. 'A History of the work of MI7, 1914-19', INF 4/1B.
129. Memorandum by Montgomery, 6 December 1915, enclosed in Montgomery to S. W. Harris, 16 December 1915, FO 371/2579.
130. Simon to Cecil, 20 December 1915, FO 371/2579.
131. Ibid.
132. Cecil to Simon, 22 December 1915, FO 371/2579.
133. Ibid.
134. Ibid.
135. Report of proceedings of a conference held at the Home Office, 26 January 1916, INF 4/9.
136. Masterman to Cecil, 31 January 1916, FO 371/2835.
137. Memorandum by Cecil, 28 January 1916, FO 371/2835.
138. Minutes by Cecil, 6 and 7 February 1916, FO 371/2835.
139. E. T. Cook to Montgomery, 31 January 1916; Montgomery to Cook, 1 February 1916, FO 371/2835.
140. Masterman to Cecil, 31 January 1916, FO 371/2835.
141. Ibid.
142. Lord Newton, *Retrospection* (London, 1941) p. 218.
143. J. D. Squires, *British Propaganda*, p. 33.

144. It is from this point that the administrative records of the News Department begin, FO 395.
145. Memorandum by Montgomery, 7 March 1916, FO 395/51.
146. FO 371/2833.
147. Note by Cecil, 29 December 1916, CAB 24/3, G 102.
148. 'A History of the work of MI7, 1914-19', INF 4/1B.
149. Cockerill to Montgomery, 11 July 1916, FO 371/2835.
150. 'A History of the work of MI7, 1914-19', INF 4/1B; see also the memorandum by Cockerill, 6 November 1917, CAB 27/17, OPC 3.

2   THE ORGANISATION OF OFFICIAL BRITISH PROPAGANDA, 1916-1918

1. War Office memorandum on press propaganda, 1 February 1916, INF 4/9.
2. Ibid.
3. Brownrigg, *Indiscretions of the Naval Censor*, p. 79.
4. Cockerill to Montgomery, 11 July 1916, FO 371/2835.
5. Brigadier-General John Charteris, *At GHQ* (London, 1931) diary entry for 22 July 1916.
6. Ibid., diary entry for 2 August 1916.
7. Ibid., diary entry for 19 September 1916.
8. Ibid., p. 166.
9. Lampson to Montgomery, 28 July 1916, FO 371/2835.
10. Minute by Montgomery, undated, FO 371/2835.
11. See the memorandum by Buchan of August 1916, the undated War Office memorandum enclosed in Macdonagh to Newton, 14 September 1916, and Newton's reply (not sent) of 18 September 1916, FO 371/2835.
12. CAB 23/1, 1 (4), 9 December 1916.
13. 'British propaganda in allied and neutral countries; Admiralty notes on the use of the press in the United States of America', 20 December 1916, CAB 24/3, G 101.
14. 'Note by the General Staff on the organisation of propaganda', 23 December 1916, CAB 24/3, G 103.
15. Foreign Office memorandum, 'British propaganda in allied and neutral countries', 20 December 1916, CAB 24/3, G 102.
16. Ibid.
17. Note by Cecil, 29 December 1916, CAB 24/3, G 102.
18. CAB 23/1, 43 (37).
19. CAB 23/1, 29 (9), 2 January 1917.
20. Lloyd George to Donald, 1 January 1917, INF 4/4B.
21. Donald to Lloyd George, 9 January 1917, INF 4/4B.
22. 'German propaganda in 1917', INF 1/715.
23. Donald to Lloyd George, 9 January 1917, INF 4/4B.
24. Newton was also head of the Foreign Office's prisoners of war department.
25. Donald to Lloyd George, 9 January 1917, INF 4/4B.
26. Ibid.
27. Ibid.
28. CAB 23/1, 43 (7), 24 January 1917.
29. Donald to Scott, 29 May 1917, INF 4/7.
30. Milner to Lloyd George, 17 January 1917, Lloyd George Papers (LGp), F 38/2/2.
31. CAB 23/1, 43 (7).
32. Note by Montgomery, 3 February 1917, FO 800/384.
33. Drummond to Balfour, 3 February 1917; Drummond to Cecil, 4 February 1917, FO 800/384.
34. Note by Balfour, undated, CAB 24/6, GT 2.

35. Memorandum by Buchan, 'Propaganda—a department of information', 3 February 1917, CAB 24/3, GT 128.
36. Ibid.
37. Memorandum by T. L. Gilmour, 13 October 1917, CAB 27/17, OPC 4.
38. Memorandum by Buchan, 3 February 1917, CAB 24/3, GT 128.
39. Memorandum by the Department of Information, 31 October 1917, CAB 27/17, OPC 1.
40. CAB 23/1, 75 (13).
41. Memorandum by Buchan, 3 February 1917, CAB 23/3, GT 128.
42. CAB 23/1, 43 (7).
43. Buchan's report to the Prime Minister on the Organisation and establishment of the Department of Information, 18 May 1917, CAB 24/13, GT 774.
44. CAB 23/2, 109 (3).
45. Buchan's report to the Prime Minister, 18 May 1917, CAB 24/13, GT 774.
46. Ibid.
47. CAB 23/2, 149 (2)
48. CAB 23/3, 154 (22), 5 June 1917.
49. T 102/18.
50. Report by the NWAC on home publicity during the Great War, INF 4/4A.
51. The Times, 6 August 1917.
52. NWAC instructions to speakers, 8 December 1917, T 102/18.
53. Report of NWAC meetings department, 10 October 1917, T 102/16.
54. CAB 23/3, 187 (19), 16 July 1917.
55. CAB 23/3, 220 (2).
56. CAB 23/3, 221 (13), 21 August 1917.
57. CAB 23/4, 245, 4 October 1917.
58. Memorandum by Carson, October 1917, CAB 24/48, GT 2268.
59. M. L. Sanders, 'Official British Propaganda in Allied and Neutral Countries during the First World War, with special reference to organisation and methods' (University of London M.Phil. thesis, 1972).
60. F. E. Guest to Sir William Grey Wilson, 27 July 1917, T 102/3.
61. Grey Wilson to Gratton Doyle, 2 August 1917, T 102/3.
62. Memorandum by F. E. Guest, 28 February 1918, CAB 24/43, GT 3757.
63. Ibid., p. 32.
64. Carson reporting on finance of NWAC, 5 October 1917, CAB 24/
65. Memorandum by Fiennes, 21 January 1918, CAB 24/40, GT 3412.
66. Donald to C. P. Scott, 29 May 1917, INF 4/7.
67. Scott to Donald, 29 May 1917; Burnham to Donald, 30 May 1917, INF 4/7.
68. Burnham to Donald, 30 May 1917, INF 4/7.
69. Lloyd George to Donald, 6 June 1917, INF 4/7.
70. J. A. Smith, John Buchan (London, 1965) cited p. 209.
71. Burnham to Donald, 31 July 1917, INF 4/7.
72. The Times, 7 August 1917.
73. Smith, John Buchan, p. 209.
74. CAB 23/4, 230 (15).
75. Lord Beaverbrook, Men and Power (London, 1956) p. 266.
76. CAB 23/4, 245 (20).
77. The files of this committee are in CAB 27/17, OPC series.
78. Lloyd George to Donald, 19 October 1917, INF 4/4B; see also H. A. Taylor, Robert Donald (London, n.d.) pp. 156-7.
79. Robert Donald, 'Inquiry into the extent and efficiency of propaganda: reports on various branches of propaganda, and recommendations', 4 December 1917, INF 4/4B.

80.   Memorandum by Donald on the Department of Information, enclosed in Donald to Carson, 25 October 1917, INF 4/4B.
81.   Robert Donald, 'Inquiry into the extent and efficiency of propaganda', 4 December 1917, INF 4/4B.
82.   Arthur Spurgeon, 'Report on the operations at Wellington House: reports on various branches of propaganda, and recommendations', 14 November 1917, INF 4/4B.
83.   Smith, *John Buchan*, p. 209.
84.   Reply by Masterman to reports on the Department of Information, Appendix II, 29 December 1917, INF 4/5.
85.   Ibid.
86.   Buchan to Carson, 28 December 1917, INF 4/5.
87.   Memorandum by Buchan, 1 December 1917, FO 395/235.
88.   Buchan to Carson, 28 December 1917, INF 4/5.
89.   Memorandum by Buchan, 1 December 1917, FO 395/235.
90.   Buchan's comments on the reports by Donald and Spurgeon, 21 December 1917, INF 4/1B.
91.   Buchan to Carson, 28 December 1917, INF 4/5.
92.   Memorandum by Montgomery, 18 December 1917, FO 395/235.
93.   Smith, *John Buchan*, cited p. 211.
94.   Note by the Department of Information, 4 January 1918, CAB 24/38, GT 3226.
95.   H. O. Lee, 'British propaganda during the Great War, 1914-18', INF 4/4A.
96.   Beaverbrook, *Men and Power*, p. 267.
97.   J. M. McEwen, 'The Press and the fall of Asquith', *Historical Journal*, 21, 4 (1978) 863-83.
98.   A. J. P. Taylor, *Beaverbrook* (London, 1972) p. 137.
99.   H. O. Lee, 'British propaganda during the Great War, 1914-18', INF 4/4A.
100.   Memorandum by F. E. Guest, 28 February 1918, CAB 24/43, GT 3757.
101.   Minutes of a conference held in General Smuts' room on 5 March 1918, CAB 24/44, GT 3823.
102.   Memorandum by Lord Rhondda, 4 March 1918, CAB 24/44, GT 3809.
103.   Memorandum by J. C. Smuts, 3 May 1918, CAB 24/50, GT 4444.
104.   Donald to Carson, 25 October 1917, INF 4/4B.
105.   Memorandum by Buchan, 6 November 1917, INF 4/9, see also the discussion of this issue at the second meeting of the committee on Overlapping and Distribution of Propaganda, CAB 27/17.
106.   Minute by Montgomery, 24 November 1917, FO 395/235.
107.   Memorandum by Balfour, 5 February 1918, CAB 24/41, GT 3547.
108.   CAB 23/5, 349 (11).
109.   Memorandum by Beaverbrook, 'The need for an intelligence department of the Department of Information', 20 February 1918, CAB 24/43, GT 3702.
110.   Balfour to Sir Eric Geddes, 11 April 1918 and the First Lord's reply, with enclosure, FO 800/207.
111.   Memorandum by Balfour, 28 February 1918, CAB 24/43, GT 3788.
112.   Foreign Office memorandum, undated, unsigned (but probably Hardinge), enclosed in CAB 24/43, GT 3788.
113.   CAB 23/5, 349 (11), 29 February 1918.
114.   Minutes of a conference held in General Smuts' room on 5 March 1918, CAB 24/44, GT 3823.
115.   Minutes of a conference held in General Smuts' room on 13 March 1918, CAB 24/45, GT 3942.
116.   R. A. Leeper to his father, 12 March 1918. We are grateful to Miss

V. A. Leeper for sending copies of family letters from Australia, and for permission to quote from them.

117. Hugh and Christopher Seton-Watson, *The Making of a New Europe: R. W. Seton-Watson and the last years of Austria-Hungary* (London, 1981) pp.252-4.

118. FO 366/787.

119. K. J. Calder, *Britain and the Origins of the New Europe, 1914-18* (Cambridge, 1976).

120. Rex Leeper to his sister, 28 March 1918.

121. Roberta Warman, 'The erosion of Foreign Office influence in the making of foreign policy, 1916-18', *Historical Journal*, 15, 1 (1972) 113-59.

122. Beaverbrook to Lloyd George, 24 June 1918, enclosed in Northcliffe to Balfour, 7 July 1918, FO 800/212.

123. Enclosure in Balfour to Geddes, 11 April 1918, FO 800/207.

124. Beaverbrook, *Men and Power*, p. 290.

125. A. J. P. Taylor, *Beaverbrook*, cited p. 145.

126. Beaverbrook to Balfour, 21 May 1918, FO 800/207.

127. Northcliffe to Balfour, 7 July 1918, Northcliffe papers, Balfour correspondence, BL.

128. Balfour to Northcliffe, 9 July 1918, Northcliffe papers, Balfour correspondence, BL.

129. Beaverbrook to Lloyd George, 13 June 1918, LGp, F 4/5/21.

130. Memorandum by Beaverbrook, 13 June 1918, LGp, F 4/5/21.

131. Ibid.

132. Beaverbrook to Lloyd George, 13 June 1918, LGp, F 4/5/21.

133. Memorandum by Beaverbrook, 13 June 1918, LGp, F 4/5/21.

134. Ibid.

135. Ibid.

136. Beaverbrook to Lloyd George, 18 June 1918, LGp, F 2/268.

137. Memorandum by Lloyd George, 9 July 1918, LGp, F 2/200.

138. Balfour to Lloyd George, 12 July 1918, FO 800/212.

139. Beaverbrook to Bonar Law, 28 August 1918, Bonar Law papers.

140. Kerr to Beaverbrook, 23 July 1918, FO 800/212.

141. Balfour to Kerr, 24 July 1918, FO 800/212.

142. See for example, Beaverbrook to Cecil, 25 June 1918, LGp, F 2/268.

143. Cecil to Balfour, 29 July 1918, FO 800/212.

144. Balfour to Lloyd George, 31 July 1918, FO 800/212.

145. Balfour to Lloyd George, 13 August 1918, FO 800/212.

146. Ibid.

147. Lloyd George to Balfour, 27 August 1918, FO 800/212.

148. For further details, see Beaverbrook, *Men and Power*, p. 291ff.

149. Minute by Lloyd George, 11 September 1918, LGp, F 2a/1/2.

150. As defined by C. P. Robertson in a memorandum written on 12 September 1935, CAB 16/129, MIC (CC) 2.

151. Memorandum by Northcliffe, 28 February 1918, Northcliffe papers, TTA.

152. H. Wickham Steed, *The Fifth Arm* (London, 1940) p. 14; Steed, *Through Thirty Years* (2 vols, London 1924) II, pp. 185-6.

153. Hansard, 5th series, vol. 103, col. 656ff.

154. Austen Chamberlain to Lords Curzon and Milner, 21 February 1918, Austen Chamberlain papers, 15/7/7, Birmingham University Library.

155. K. O. Morgan, *Consensus and Disunity* (Oxford 1979).

156. Sir Campbell Stuart, *Secrets of Crewe House* (London 1920).

157. Northcliffe to Balfour, 24 February 1918, FO 899/4, no. 764.

158. Ibid.

159. Balfour to Northcliffe, 26 February 1918, FO 899/4, no. 764.
160. Northcliffe to Balfour, 6 June 1918, CAB 24/75, GT 6839.
161. Balfour to Northcliffe, 8 June 1918, CAB 24/75, GT 6839.
162. Steed, *Fifth Arm*, p. 15.
163. K. J. Calder, *Britain and the Origins of the New Europe*, p. 177.
164. Steed, *Through Thirty Years*, ii, p. 222.
165. See Northcliffe to Balfour, 10 June 1918, FO 899/4; Balfour to Northcliffe, 11 June 1918, CAB 24/75, GT 6839; Northcliffe to Balfour, 13 June 1918, CAB 24/75, GT 6839.
166. Northcliffe to C. J. Phillips, 12 July 1918, cited in Pound and Harmsworth, *Northcliffe*, p.653.
167. For a detailed discussion of this affair see C. Hazlehurst, *Politicians at War*, p. 202ff.
168. Reginald Pound, *Arnold Bennett* (London, 1952) cited p. 270.
169. T. Wilson (ed.), *The Political Diaries of C. P. Scott, 1911-28* (London, 1970) entry for 4 March 1918.
170. Ibid.
171. Stephen Roskill, *Hankey: Man of Secrets* (London, 1970) I, p. 390.
172. Wilson, *Political Diaries of C. P. Scott.*
173. Beaverbrook to Lloyd George, 24 June 1918, FO 800/212.

3 THE METHODS AND DISTRIBUTION OF BRITISH PROPAGANDA

1. Schuster to Robinson, 3 December 1914, INF 4/1B.
2. Ibid.
3. Unsigned memorandum, 2 December 1914 enclosed in Gowers to Montgomery, 18 December 1914, FO 371/2207.
4. Memorandum by Buchan, 1 December 1917, FO 395/235.
5. Schuster to Robinson, 3 December 1914, INF 4/1B.
6. Confidential report of the PRC meetings sub-department, 25 May 1916, WO 106/367.
7. R. Douglas, 'Voluntary Enlistment in the First World War and the work of the Parliamentary Recruiting Committee', *Journal of Contemporary History*, 42 (1970) 564-85.
8. Confidential report of the PRC meetings sub-department, 25 May 1916, WO 106/367.
9. Ibid.
10. Ibid.
11. Maurice Rickards, *Posters of the First World War* (London, 1968); Max Gallo, *The Poster in History* (New York, 1974); Bevis Hillier, *Posters* (New York, 1969); Harold Hutchinson, *The Poster: An Illustrated History since 1860* (New York, 1968); Barbara Jones and Bill Howell, *Popular Arts of the First World War* (New York, 1972); Irvine Metzl, *The Poster: Its History and its Art* (New York, 1963).
12. Confidential report of the PRC Meetings sub-department, 25 May 1916, WO 106/367.
13. Ibid.
14. Confidential report of the PRC householders' returns committee, 25 May 1916, WO 106/367.
15. Report of Meetings department of NWAC, T 102/16 and Records of meetings, T 102/17.
16. The collection of speakers' daily reports is in T 102/22-24.
17. NWAC to J. Cabourn, 29 July 1918, T 102/1, file 1.
18. For further details see T 102/20.

19. See the letter on behalf of W. H. Smith, 22 October 1917, T 102/16.
20. Unsigned letter to Bell, 8 November 1918, T 102/10.
21. For further details see T 102/2, files 1 and 2.
22. NWAC correspondence, 10 October 1918, T 102/8.
23. Thomas Cameron to NWAC, 4 June 1918, T 102/2, file 1.
24. For further details see T 102/2, file 1 and T 102/9.
25. T. Hollins, 'The Conservative Party and Film Propaganda between the wars', *English Historical Review*, 96 (1981) pp. 359-69.
26. First report on the work of Wellington House, INF 4/5.
27. Second report on the work of Wellington House, INF 4/5.
28. H. C. Peterson, *Propaganda for War: The Campaign Against American Neutrality, 1914-17* (New York, 1939) p. 17.
29. Second report on the work of Wellington House, INF 4/5.
30. Brigadier-General G. Cockerill, *What Fools We Were* (London, 1944) p. 63.
31. Philip M. Taylor, *The Projection of Britain: British Overseas Publicity and Propaganda, 1919-39* (Cambridge, 1981) ch. 3.
32. Report of the Newbolt Committee, 9 April 1918, INF 4/5.
33. Ibid.
34. Correspondence between Geoffrey Williams and the Foreign Office in FO 395/44.
35. Rennell Rodd to Foreign Office, 15 May 1916, FO 395/44.
36. First report on the work of Wellington House, INF 4/5.
37. Unsigned memorandum, 4 August 1915; Buchan to Foreign Office, 3 August 1915, FO 371/2566.
38. See FO 371/2824.
39. First report on the work of Wellington House, INF 4/5.
40. Ibid.
41. Minute by Alston, 5 November 1915 on Jordan to Grey, 4 November 1914, FO 371/1950.
42. H. O. Lee, 'British propaganda during the Great War, 1914-18', INF 4/4A.
43. For further details see FO 371/2825.
44. Foreign Office minutes, 10 April 1916, FO 371/2829.
45. CAB 23/4, 253 (4), 22 October 1917.
46. H. O. Lee, 'British propaganda during the Great War, 1914-18', INF 4/4A.
47. Ibid.
48. Ibid.
49. Esmé Howard to Foreign Office, 10 September 1915, FO 371/2562.
50. Grant Duff to Montgomery, 27 August 1915, FO 371/2562.
51. Memorandum by A. W. G. Randall, 13 October 1917, FO 395/124.
52. See 'La Propagande pendant la Guerre' an extract from the General Budget Account of the Ministry of Foreign Affairs, 1920, used as an introduction to the documents of the Maison de la Presse, 1914-28, MAE, Paris.
53. Fisher's report to the Foreign Office, 6 April 1916, FO 371/2842.
54. 'The Foreign Office appear to have decided to leave to me the entire direction of English propaganda in France. They are going to put permanently at my disposal a new, English assistant, whose salary will be paid by them and who will help me with every aspect of this part of my work.' General report on the Section Anglaise by Captain Millet, July 1916, *Papiers d'Agents*, Phillipe Berthelot, *Propagande Grande-Brétagne, 1916-17, Ministère des Affaires Étrangères*, Paris.
55. See correspondence with the English propaganda services in vol. 34, *Grande-Brétagne, VI, Information, Propagande, Ministère des Affaires Étrangères*, Paris.
56. Bertie to Foreign Office, 26 July 1916, FO 395/19.
57. For further details see FO 395/94.

58.   For further details see FO 395/25. See also K. Neilson, '"Joy Rides"?: British Intelligence and Propaganda in Russia, 1914-17', *Historical Journal*, 24 (1981) 885-906.

59.   Foreign Office minutes, 9 November 1915, FO 371/2579.

60.   Hardinge to Bertie, 4 August 1916, FO 395/19.

61.   Rodd to Foreign Office, 2 September 1916, FO 395/20.

62.   Robertson Scott to Montgomery, 23 April 1916, FO 395/17.

63.   Robertson Scott to Foreign Office, 12 February 1917, FO 395/91.

64.   See FO 395/74.

65.   Elliot to Foreign Office, 28 March, 1917, FO 395/87.

66.   Maxse to Foreign Office, 23 March 1917, FO 395/100.

67.   Steward to Foreign Office, 13 December 1917, FO 395/100.

68.   Report on the propaganda of the Neutral Press Organisation, undated, unsigned, FO 371/2555.

69.   G. H. Mair to Foreign Office, 11 September 1916, FO 371/2562.

70.   Second report on the work of Wellington House, INF 4/5.

71.   Third report on the work of Wellington House, September 1916, FO 371/2837.

72.   See the correspondence between R. W. Perks and Lord Newton, March 1916, FO 395/41.

73.   Ibid.

74.   Bertie to Montgomery, 1 July 1916, FO 395/18.

75.   Foreign Office minutes, 14 August 1916, FO 395/55.

76.   Thomas Fraser, 'Germany and the Indian Revolution, 1914-18', *Journal of Contemporary History*, 12 (1977) 255-72.

77.   Ivor Nicholson, 'An Aspect of British Official Wartime Propaganda', *Cornhill Magazine*, 71 (1931) 593-606.

78.   Mitchell to Masterman, 21 September 1916, FO 395/36.

79.   Bruce Arnold, *Orpen: Mirror to an Age* (London, 1981).

80.   Barclay to Foreign Office, 10 September 1915, FO 371/2577.

81.   Minute by T. L. Gilmour, 'The Cinema Industry and its Relation to the Government', 13 October 1917, CAB 27/17, OPC 4.

82.   Cited in ibid.

83.   Gowers to Foreign Office, 29 May 1916, FO 395/37.

84.   J. Brooke Wilkinson, *Film and Censorship in England*, ch. XI: 'The War Years', undated copy in INF 4 /2.

85.   Rachel Low, *The History of the British Film, 1914-18* (London, 1950); see also N. Reeves, 'British Official Film Propaganda in the First World War' (University of London, PhD. thesis, 1981).

86.   First report of the War Office Cinematograph Committee, September 1918, INF 4/1B; see also F. Thorpe and N. Pronay, *British Official Films in the Second World War* (Oxford, 1980) p. 14ff.

87.   Minute by T. L. Gilmour, 'The Cinema Industry and its Relation to the Government', 13 October 1917, CAB 27/17, OPC 4.

88.   Brooke Wilkinson, *Film and Censorship in England*.

89.   The Russian bands had gone to considerable lengths to learn the national anthem, although they were often uncertain as to whether they should play 'God Save the King' or 'Rule Britannia'. They solved the problem by playing both.

90.   Report by Captain Bromhead to the Cinema Committee, June 1916, FO 395/25; see also FO 371/2825.

91.   F. E. Drummond-Hay to the Board of Trade, 19 February 1916, FO 371/2831.

92.   Unsigned memorandum on cinematograph propaganda, 12 April 1917, FO 395/66.

93. Greene to Foreign Office, 2 January 1917, FO 395/92.
94. Alston to Foreign Office, 2 February 1917, FO 395/72.
95. Ibid.
96. Lampson to Foreign Office, 26 February 1917, FO 395/92.
97. For further details see FO 395/107.
98. Dering to Foreign Office, 9 April 1917, FO 395/92.
99. W. Pryde Hughes, 'First General Report on Film Propaganda in Spain', 19 October 1917, FO 395/120.
100. Second report on the work of Wellington House, INF 4/5.
101. For further details see A. Marwick, *The Deluge* (London, 1965) p. 230.
102. File on the Lusitania medal, FO 395/42; see also Colin Simpson, *Lusitania* (London, 1972).
103. Lt Col. Wade to Foreign Office, 15 August 1917, FO 395/113.
104. Report of a conference held on 19 January 1918, FO 395/252.
105. Report by Major-General A. D. McRae, 1 July 1918, Beaverbrook papers, F/2/307.
106. Ibid.
107. Pound and Harmsworth, *Northcliffe*, pp. 293, 384, 446.
108. Beaverbrook to Lloyd George, 24 June 1918, FO 800/212.
109. Memorandum by M. P. A. Hankey and covering note by Sir E. Carson, 'A Psychological Offensive against Germany', 11 December 1917, CAB 24/35, GT 2941.
110. For further details see WO 32/5140.
111. Comments on enemy propaganda, INF 4/4A.
112. War Office report, 10 July 1917, WO 32/5140.
113. Emmanuel Victor Voska and Will Irwin, *Spy and Counter-Spy* (New York, 1940) p. 271ff.

4 THE CONTENT OF BRITISH PROPAGANDA

1. Poster number 110 in the collection of PRC posters held in the Imperial War Museum. (IWM).
2. Poster no. 125, PRC collection, IWM.
3. Poster no. 103, PRC collection, IWM.
4. Poster no. 75, PRC collection, IWM.
5. Poster no. 79, PRC collection, IWM.
6. For details of NWAC lectures see T 102/1.
7. See the list of publications issued by the NWAC, October 1918, T 102/20.
8. This pamphlet was based upon his articles in the *Glasgow Evening News* published during January 1918.
9. Lucy Masterman, *C. F. G. Masterman: A Biography* (London, 1939) p. 274.
10. Pound and Harmsworth, *Northcliffe*, p. 669.
11. James Morgan Read, *Atrocity Propaganda, 1914-19* (New York, 1972) pp. 201-8.
12. Trevor Wilson, 'Lord Bryce's Investigation into Alleged German Atrocities in Belgium, 1914-15', *Journal of Contemporary History*, 14 (1979) 369-81.
13. See the 'Kadaver' file, FO 395/147.
14. Lucy Masterman, *C. F. G. Masterman*, p. 295.
15. Minute by Balfour, 26 April 1917, FO 395/147.
16. Hansard, 5th series, vol. 188, 24 November 1925; see also Arthur Ponsonby, *Falsehood in Wartime* (London, 1928) pp. 102-20; 'Kadaver' *The Nation*, 38 (1925) 171-2.
17. Marvin Swartz, *The Union of Democratic Control in British Politics during the First World War* (Oxford, 1971); M. Ceadel, *Pacifism in Britain, 1914-45* (Oxford, 1981); K. Robbins, *The Abolition of War* (Cardiff, 1976).

18. See Harry F. Young, *Prince Lichnowsky and the Great War* (Athens, 1970).
19. Originally published in the *New York Times* on the first anniversary of the war.
20. Sir Robert Borden and Lt Col. J. C. Smuts, *The Voice of the Dominions* (London, 1917) and Sir Robert Borden, *The War and the Future* (London, 1917).
21. No. 17 in the Oxford Pamphlet series.
22. Souvenir of the First Exhibition of British Battle Photographs in Colour, 22 April 1918, and Catalogue of British War Photographs in Colour, 4 March—27 April 1918, Ministry of Information library, Box 1, Hoover Institute on War, Revolution and Peace (HIWRP).
23. Ibid.
24. See the account of the censorship in his book, *Temporary Heroes*, which was a contemporary account of his war experiences, PP/MCR/101, IWM.
25. Ibid.
26. Ibid.
27. R. Graves, *Goodbye to All That* (New York, 1957) p. 182ff.
28. Ibid., p. 228ff; see also Erich Maria Remarque, *All Quiet on the Western Front* (New York, 1928) pp. 102ff.
29. Claud Colleer Abbott & Anthony Bertram, *Poet and Painter – Correspondence between Gordon Bottomley and Paul Nash* (London, 1955) p. 98. However, Orpen, for example, did experience problems with the censor. For further details see Bruce Arnold, *Orpen: Mirror of an Age*, p. 313ff.
30. Christian Brinton in his introduction to *War Paintings and Drawings by British artists exhibited under the auspices of the Ministry of Information* (1919) HIWRP.
31. *The Western Front-Drawings by Muirhead Bone*, vol. 2, part 1, June 1917.
32. Father C. C. Martindale, 'English Catholics to their Fellow Catholics', *Catholic Monthly Letters*, no. 1, p. 1.
33. Ibid., p. 16.
34. Reprinted from the *Nineteenth Century and After* (February 1917).
35. A. Marwick, *The Deluge* (London, 1965) p. 230.
36. See I. McLaine, *Ministry of Morale* (London, 1978) p. 168; W. Laqueur, 'Hitler's Holocaust. Who Knew What, When and How?', *Encounter*, 60 (981) 1, 6-25.

5 BRITISH PROPAGANDA IN THE UNITED STATES

1. H. H. Asquith to the King, 31 August 1914, CAB 41/35/38.
2. First report on the work of Wellington House, 7 June 1915, INF 4/5.
3. J. C. Silber, *The Invisible Weapons* (London, 1932) p. 87, p. 139.
4. A. Willert to G. Robinson, 20 November 1914, Willert MS. TTA.
5. Willert to Robinson, 31 December 1914, Willert MS. TTA.
6. Willert, *Washington and Other Memories* (Boston, 1972) p. 72.
7. H. O. Lee, 'British propaganda during the Great War, 1914-18', INF 4/4A.
8. H. C. Peterson, *Propaganda for War: The Campaign Against American Neutrality, 1914-17* (New York, 1939) p. 16; *The Times History of the War* (London, 1920) vol. 21.
9. See Gilbert Parker's despatch list in FO 395/3 and Parker's own account of his activities, 'The United States and the War', *Harper's Monthly Magazine*, vol. 134 (March 1918) no. 814, pp. 521-31.
10. Letter from Parker, 16 March 1915, Box 1, Great Britain, Foreign Office: Wellington House, Hoover Archives, HIWRP, Stanford; see also the reprint of a similar letter in Peterson, *Propaganda for War*, facing p. 52.
11. Parker to Sellers, 10 November 1915, Box 1, Great Britain, Foreign Office: Wellington House, Hoover Archives, HIWRP, Stanford.
12. Parker, 'The United States and the War'.

13.   Albert Russell Buchanan, 'European Propaganda and American Public Opinion, 1914-17' (Stanford University, PhD. thesis, 1935) HIWRP, Stanford, pp. 32ff and p. 331.
14.   First report on the work of Wellington House, 7 June 1915, INF 4/5.
15.   Memorandum by G. Butler, 3 August 1916, FO 395/3.
16.   Winifred Johnston, *Memo on the Movies: War Propaganda, 1914-39* (New York, 1939) p. 15.
17.   House Diaries, entry for 4 June 1915, series II, 3/1, vol. VI, p. 160. Yale University Library (hereafter YUL).
18.   Esther Sprott, 'A Survey of British Wartime Propaganda in America Issued by Wellington House' (Stanford University, Masters thesis, 1921) HIWRP, p. 32.
19.   Willert to Robinson, 24 May 1915, Arthur Willert papers (AWP) series I, Box 2, f. 57, YUL.
20.   S. Kernek, 'Distractions of Peace During War: The Lloyd George Government's Reactions to Woodrow Wilson, December 1916—November 1918', *Transactions of the American Philosophical Society*, vol. 65, part 2 (1975) 5-114.
21.   Basil Thomson, *The Scene Changes* (New York, 1937) p. 297.
22.   Lord Newton, *Retrospection*, p. 226. The documents were despatched on 29 June 1916.
23.   Admiral Sir William James, *The Code Breakers of Room 40* (New York, 1956) p. 114.
24.   FO 395/43 (Casement file).
25.   A. J. Ward, *Ireland and Anglo-American Relations, 1899-1921* (London, 1969) p. 101ff.
26.   Newton, *Retrospection*, p. 226.
27.   Statistics of circulation of Raemakers cartoons in USA, FO 395/131.
28.   Allison to Foreign Office, October 1917, FO 395/66.
29.   Buchanan, 'European Propaganda and American Public Opinion', p. 244ff.
30.   Emmanuel Victor Voska and Will Irwin, *Spy and Counter Spy* (New York, 1940) p. 10 & p. 21ff.
31.   Admiral Sir Guy Gaunt, *The Yield of the Years* (London, 1940) p. 167.
32.   Voska and Irwin, *Spy and Counter-Spy*, p. 24.
33.   Ibid.
34.   Ibid., p. 32ff.
35.   For further details see James, *The Code Breakers of Room 40*.
36.   Gaunt, *The Yield of the Years*, p. 137.
37.   House Diaries, entry for 16 December 1915, series II, 3/1, vol. VII, YUL.
38.   Ibid., entry for 14 January 1916, series II, 3/1.
39.   Ibid., entry for 6 May 1916, series II, 3/1, vol. XI.
40.   House to Balfour, 23 November 1916, House papers, 466/1/10/285, YUL.
41.   For a detailed account of the role of Sir William Wiseman see W. B. Fowler, *British-American Relations, 1917-18: The Role of Sir William Wiseman* (Princeton, 1969).
42.   House Diaries, entry for 19 January 1917, series II, 3/1, vol. X, YUL.
43.   Ibid., entry for 22 April 1917.
44.   Gaunt, *The Yield of the Years*.
45.   A. Willert, *The Road to Safety* (New York, 1953) p. 26.
46.   F. H. Hinsley *et al*, *British Intelligence in the Second World War* (London, 1979) I, p. 16 & note p. 20.
47.   R. Deacon, *A History of the British Secret Service* (New York, 1969) p. 175; Willert, *Road to Safety*, p. 19.
48.   Lt Col. Norman Thwaites, *Velvet and Vinegar* (London, 1932) p. 119.

49. Wiseman to Murray, 8 June 1918, William Wiseman Papers (WWP) Group 666, Box 3, 91/85, YUL.
50. Voska and Irwin, *Spy and Counterspy.*
51. Gaunt to Wiseman, 2 August 1917, Group 666, Box 6 (Gaunt file) WWP, YUL.
52. Gaunt to Hall, 8 February 1917, Group 666, Box 6 (Gaunt file) WWP, YUL.
53. Voska and Irwin, *Spy and Counterspy*, p. 95.
54. Buchanan, 'European Propaganda and American Public Opinion', p. 342ff.
55. Franz Von Papen, *Memoirs* (London, 1952) ch. 3 and 4.
56. James, *The Code Breakers of Room 40*, p. 98.
57. Thwaites, *Velvet and Vinegar*, p. 155ff.
58. B. Tuchman, *The Zimmermann Telegram* (London, 1959) p. 146.
59. Reports on Various Branches of Propaganda Work and Recommendations; Report on the Operations of Wellington House, by Arthur Spurgeon, 19 November 1917, INF 4/4B.
60. Reply by Masterman to reports on the Department of Information, Appendix II, 29 December 1917, INF 4/5.
61. Dawson to Willert, 23 January 1917, AWP, 720/1/2/65, YUL.
62. Willert to Dawson, 13 February 1917, AWP, 720/1/2/65, YUL.
63. Willert to Dawson, 4 December 1914, AWP, 720/1/2/54, YUL.
64. Willert to Kerr, 14 February 1917, AWP, 720/1/3/103, YUL.
65. Memorandum by Pomeroy Burton, 'War Intelligence Department or Special War News Service', 29 January 1917, enclosed in Burton to Northcliffe, 30 January 1917, Northcliffe papers, vol. II, Burton file, BL.
66. Willert to Dawson, 23 February 1917, AWP 720/1/2/65, YUL.
67. Burton to Buchan, 1 April 1917, Northcliffe papers, vol. II, Burton file, BL.
68. Northcliffe to Burton, 11 April 1917, Northcliffe papers, vol. II, Burton file, BL.
69. Pomeroy Burton's Report on British Propaganda in the United States, 20 April 1917, AWP, 720/1/13/27, YUL.
70. Ibid.
71. Ibid.
72 Willert to Burton, 17 April 1917, AWP, 720/1/1, YUL.
73. Willert to Dawson, 28 April 1917, AWP, 720/1/2/65, YUL.
74. Ibid.
75. Ibid.
76. Ibid.
77. Memorandum by Willert on British Propaganda, 24 June 1917, AWP, 720/1/14/63, YUL.
78. Butler to Montgomery, 6 July 1917, FO 395/79.
79. House Diaries, series II, 3/1, vol. XI, entry for 17 May 1917, YUL; Butler to House, 4 August 1917, House Papers, 466/1/23/714, YUL.
80. Northcliffe to House, 13 August 1917, House Papers, 466/1/83a/2871, YUL.
81. Burton to House, 1 October 1917, House Papers, 466/1/23/711, YUL.
82. Burton to Northcliffe, 22 December 1917, Northcliffe papers, vol. II, Burton file, BL.
83. House to Butler, 11 August 1917, House Papers, 466/1/23/714, YUL.
84. CAB 23/2, 152 (1) and 153 (Appendix II) 31 May 1917.
85. Wiseman to War Cabinet, 31 May 1917, WWP, 666/1/90/4, YUL.
86. Willert, *Washington and Other Memories*, p. 103.
87. Pound and Harmsworth, *Northcliffe*, p. 550.
88. Northcliffe to Lloyd George, 8 August 1917, WWP, 666/3/91/91, YUL.
89. Northcliffe to Phillips, 15 August 1917, WWP, 666/3/91/91, YUL.

90. House Diaries, series II, 3/1, vol. XI, entry for 30 June 1917, YUL.
91. Ibid., series II, 3/1, vol. XII, entry for 1 October 1917, YUL.
92. Wiseman to Drummond, 4 October 1917, WWP, 666/2/90/42, YUL.
93. Willert to Dawson, 19 September 1917, AWP, 720/1/2/66, YUL.
94. Willert, *Washington and Other Memories*, p. 105.
95. Northcliffe to War Cabinet, 21 August 1917, WWP, 666/3/91/91, YUL.
96. Frank L. Polk Diary, entry for 4 August 1917, film no. Hist. MSS 47, Reel 1, YUL.
97. Memorandum by Department of Information, 4 October 1917, FO 395/78.
98. Supplementary memorandum on the work of Section V, 3 October 1918, WWP, 666/6, YUL.
99. Report to Foreign Office, 22 October 1917, FO 395/82.
100. Allison to Foreign Office, October 1917 and Allison to Foreign Office, February 1917, FO 395/66.
101. Report on the work of Section V, 11 December 1917, WWP, 666/6, YUL.
102. Voska and Irwin, *Spy and Counterspy*, p. 213.
103. Report on the work of Section V, 11 December 1917, WWP, 666/6, YUL.
104. Fowler, *British-American Relations*, p. 14.
105. Balfour to Wiseman, 19 December 1917, WWP, 666/1/90/42, YUL.
106. Lt Col. Arthur Murray, *At Close Quarters: A Sidelight on Anglo-American Relations* (London, 1946) p. 13.
107. Wiseman to Drummond, 22 August 1917, WWP, 666/2/90/42, YUL.
108. Drummond to Wiseman, 24 August 1917, WWP, 666/2/90/42, YUL.
109. Murray to Wiseman, 19 September 1918, WWP, 666/3/91/88, YUL.
110. Ibid.
111. Willert to Northcliffe, 22 February 1918, AWP, 720/1/4/140, YUL.
112. Memorandum on Anglo-American relations, August 1917, WWP, 666/1/90/4. YUL.
113. Fowler, *British-American Relations*, p. 91; James, *The Code Breakers of Room 40*, p. 156ff.
114. Fowler, *British-American Relations*, p. 156ff.
115. Memorandum by General McLachlan and Colonel Pakenham to MI5, 28 March 1918, WWP, 666/6, YUL.
116. Thomson, *The Scene Changes*, p. 406ff.
117. CAB 23/6, 398 (10), 24 April 1918.
118. Gaunt to Montgomery, 29 March 1917, WWP, 666/6, YUL.
119. Thomas E. Hachey, 'British War Propaganda and American Catholics in 1918', *Catholic Historical Review*, 61 (1975) 48-66.
120. CAB 23/4, 261 (12), 31 October 1917.
121. Wiseman to Lt Ascherson, 7 July 1918, WWP, 666/6, YUL.
122. Memorandum by McLachlan and Pakenham, 28 March 1918, WWP, 666/6, YUL.
123. See Wiseman papers 666/4/91/112 and 666/4/91/113, YUL.
124. K. J. Calder, *Britain and the Origins of the New Europe, 1914-18*, p.131ff.
125. W. Somerset Maugham, *The Summing Up* (London, 1938); see also his novel *Ashenden or The British Agent* (New York, 1927).
126. Report on Intelligence and Propaganda work in Russia, July-December 1917, WWP, 666/4/91/113, YUL.
127. Memorandum for Gordon Auchinloss, 4 November 1917, WWP, 666/3/91/106, YUL.
128. House Diaries, series II, 3/1, vol. XIV, entry for 24 September 1918, YUL.
129. See clippings relating to the Sisson documents, Box 322, CPI 17 D/1. National Archives, Washington. See also George Kennan, 'The Sisson Documents',

Journal of Modern History, 28 (1956) 130-54.
130. For the activities of American historians in the case see George T. Blakey, *Historians on the Home Front: American Propagandists for the Great War* (Kentucky, 1970) p. 98ff.
131. Willert to Murray, 4 October 1918, AWP, 720/1/3/130, YUL.
132. Willert, *Washington and Other Memories*, p. 111.
133. Frank L. Polk Diary, entry for 4 October 1918, film no. Hist. MSS 47, Reel 1, YUL.
134. Willert to Creel, 23 October 1918, Box 30, folder 39, CPI A1, National Archives, Washington.
135. Buchanan, 'European Propaganda and American Public Opinion', p. 19ff.
136. Report by Robert Donald on Propaganda Arrangements, 9 January 1917, INF 4/4B.
137. Willert to Dawson, 14 September 1914, AWP, 720/1/2, YUL.
138. Wiseman to Tyrrell, 4 March 1919, WWP, 666/1/90/4, YUL.
139. Ibid.
140. Ibid.
141. Ibid.
142. Ibid.
143. Memorandum on British Propaganda, 24 June 1917, AWP, 720/1/14/63, YUL.
144. George Viereck, *Spreading Germs of Hate* (New York, 1930) p. 26.

6 BRITISH PROPAGANDA IN ENEMY COUNTRIES

1. Silber, *The Invisible Weapons*, pp. 138-64.
2. Adolf Hitler, *Mein Kampf* (London, 1939: trans. by James Murphey) p. 163.
3. General Erich von Ludendorff, *My War Memories, 1914-18*, 2 vols (London, 1919) I, p. 349.
4. Ibid., p. 360.
5. Ibid., p. 361.
6. Ibid., p. 368.
7. Marshal von Hindenburg, *Out of My Life* (London and New York, 1921).
8. Manifesto to the German people, 2 September 1918 (from *Norddeutsche Allgemeine Zeite*, 5 September 1918) cited in R. Lutz, *The Fall of the German Empire, 1914-18*, vol. I (Stanford, 1932) p. 163.
9. Enclosure in Northcliffe to J. T. Davies, 18 July 1918, FO 800/213.
10. General order of the 18th Army, 29 August 1918, cited in Lutz, *The Fall of the German Empire*, p. 162.
11. As reported in *The Times*, 15 November 1918.
12. History of the Work of MI7, INF 4/1B.
13. 'From the moment that the name of Lord Northcliffe was put before them, they recognised only him and attributed responsibility to him for all the work accomplished in the previous two and a half years.' Hansi et Tonnelat, *À Travers Les Lignes Ennemies*, p. 160.
14. Ibid., p. 10.
15. J. M. Spaight, *Air Power and War Rights* (London, 1924) p. 124.
16. Pound and Harmsworth, *Northcliffe*, p. 468.
17. Cockerill, *What Fools We Were*, pp. 62-3.
18. Hansi et Tonnelat, *À Travers Les Lignes Ennemies*, p. 13.
19. 'It was not possible for us, naturally, to exercise any control over them. However, it was our impression that the British officers in charge had taken the matter of dropping newspapers by air very seriously. We were not able to require from them,

as we did the French units, reports on the distribution. But, of their own accord, they informed us of all their work and the results achieved.' Ibid., p. 105.

20.   MI6 Report, 'The legal aspect of the distribution of propaganda by aeroplane', 12 April 1918, WO 32/5140; see also Spaight, *Air Power*, p. 305ff.

21.   MI6 Report.

22.   Memorandum by W. A. Robinson, 3 August 1918, CAB 24/58, GT 5323.

23.   Memorandum by Beaverbrook, 12 July 1918, CAB 24/57, GT 5100.

24.   CAB 23/7, 455(22), 7 August 1918.

25.   Onslow to Fisher, 4 May 1918, WO 32/5141.

26.   Fisher to Onslow, 11 May 1918, WO 32/5141.

27.   'Especially through the good offices of the British Air Service who are specifically responsible for undertaking this work, that is to say north of the Somme.' President of the Council, Minister of War to C-in-C Armies of North and North East, 14 September 1918. Propagande Aérienne 1917-18, 16 N 1569, Service Historique de l'Armée, Château de Vincennes, Paris.

28.   Memorandum by Chalmers Mitchell, 'Wind driftage of paper', 16 June 1918, WO 32/5140.

29.   CAB 23/7, 447(8), 17 July 1918.

30.   Campbell Stuart, *Secrets of Crewe House*, p. 60.

31.   M. Balfour, *Propaganda in War*, (London, 1979) p. 4.

32.   Memorandum by Beaverbrook, 12 July 1918, CAB 24/57, GT 5100.

33.   Cockerill, *What Fools We Were*, p. 40ff.

34.   R. Deacon, *A History of the British Secret Service* (London, 1969) p. 203.

35.   Wilhelm Ernst, *Die Antideutsche Propaganda durch das Schweizer Gebiet im Weltkrieg Speziell die Propaganda in Bayern* (Munich, 1933) p. 4.

36.   Vera Whitehouse to James Kerney, 22 July 1918, Committee on Public Information (CPI) 21 A1, Box 360, National Archives, Washington.

37.   Ernst, *Die Antideutsche Propaganda*, p. 3ff.

38.   'Was expressly charged with the task of arousing a revolutionary mood amongst the German people and with sending agents into Germany for this purpose.' Report of 31 May 1918 in Bavarian War Archives. Cited in Ernst, *Die Antideutsche Propaganda*.

39.   Horace Rumbold to H. Montgomery, 15 May 1917, FO 395/123.

40.   'What Switzerland signified for France, the Netherlands signified for England.' Oberst W. Nicolai, *Geheime Mächte: Internationale Spionage und ihre Kämpfung im Weltkrieg und Heute* (Leipzig, 1924) p. 64ff.

41.   Ibid.

42.   Hans Thimme, *Weltkrieg Ohne Waffen: Die Propaganda der Westmächte gegen Deutschland ihre Wirkung und ihre Abwehr* (Stuttgart & Berlin, 1932) p. 111.

43.   'Firmer evidence of these facts has never been furnished.' Ibid.

44.   B. Thomson, *The Scene Changes*, pp. 335, 398.

45.   Ministry of Information report on British propaganda in Holland, 31 March 1918, FO 395/180.

46.   Thimme, *Weltkrieg Ohne Waffen*, p. 16.

47.   FO 395/180.

48.   Sir George Aston, *Secret Service* (London, 1930) p. 293.

49.   Maxse to Gaselee, 25 January 1918, FO 395/179.

50.   Guest's report on his visit to Holland, 31 January 1916, FO 371/2825.

51.   Memorandum by Guest, October 1916, FO 395/22.

52.   See FO 395/22.

53.   Cockerill, *What Fools We Were*, p. 63ff.

54.   Selection of Crewe House material in WO 32/5143.

55. G. C. Bruntz, *Allied Propaganda and the Collapse of the German Empire in 1918*, p. 55.

56. Second report on the distribution of propaganda, WO 32/5143.

57. Lutz, *The Fall of the German Empire*, p. 161ff.

58. Harry F. Young, *Prince Lichnowsky and the War*.

59. Ludendorff, *My War Memories*, ii, p. 641.

60. Coupon scheme, WO 32/5140.

61. MI7(b) to Buchan, 26 May 1917, WO 32/5140.

62. Report by Major Austin Lee on English propaganda, 2 January 1918, Propagande Aérienne 1917-18, 16 N 1571, Service Historique de l'Armée, Château de Vincennes, Paris (Major Lee's papers are listed in the Imperial War Museum catalogue but have been lost or destroyed by fire).

63. Steed to Northcliffe, 7 March 1918, Wickham Steed MS, File 1914-18, TTA.

64. Ibid.

65. Sir Peter Chalmers Mitchell, *My Fill of Days* (London, 1937) p. 296.

66. From a document attributed to E. H. Carr, Wickham Steed MS, File 1914-18, TTA.

67. *The New Europe*, vol. 1, no. 1, 19 October 1916, p. 1.

68. Steed to Northcliffe, 7 March 1918, Northcliffe papers, vol. xciv, BL. Seton-Watson was technically under the orders of the War Office and thus did not take part in the transfers affecting the PID described in chapter 2.

69. A. J. May, *The Passing of the Habsburg Monarchy, 1914-18*, 2 vols (Philadelphia, 1966) ii, cited p. 605.

70. H. Wickham Steed, *Through Thirty Years, 1892-1922*, 2 vols (London, 1924) ii, p. 186.

71. W. Fest, *Peace or Partition* (London, 1978) p. 209.

72. Gunther E. Rothenburg, 'The Habsburg Army in the First World War' in R. A. Kann, B. K. Kiraly and P. S. Fichtner (eds), *The Habsburg Empire in World War One* (Boulder, 1977) pp. 73-86.

73. Fest, *Peace or Partition*, p. 214.

74. Steed, *Through Thirty Years*, ii, p. 204ff.

75. K. J. Calder, *Britain and the Origins of the New Europe, 1914-18*, p. 181.

76. Fest, *Peace or Partition*, p. 216.

77. Steed, *Through Thirty Years*, ii, pp. 187-9.

78. Northcliffe to Balfour, 24 February 1918, FO 899/4, no. 764.

79. Balfour to Northcliffe, 26 February 1918, FO 899/4, no. 764.

80. Hugh and Christopher Seton-Watson, *The Making of the New Europe: R. W. Seton-Watson and the last years of Austria-Hungary*, p. 259ff.

81. Northcliffe to Balfour, 27 February 1918, FO 899/4, no. 764.

82. CAB 23/5, 359(6).

83. S. Kernek, 'Distractions of Peace During War', *Transactions of the American Philosophical Society*, vol. 65, part 2 (1975) pp. 77-84.

84. Leo Valiani, *The End of Austria-Hungary* (London, 1973) p. 241.

85. Calder, *Britain and the Origins of the New Europe*, p. 175.

86. Steed, *Through Thirty Years*, ii, p. 197.

87. Campbell Stuart, *Secrets of Crewe House*, p. 37ff.

88. Valiani, *The End of Austria-Hungary*, p. 245.

89. Campbell Stuart, *Secrets of Crewe House*, p. 37ff.

90. Voska and Irwin, *Spy and Counterspy*, p. 271ff.

91. Ibid., p. 290ff.

92. Campbell Stuart, *Secrets of Crewe House*, p. 44.

93. Valiani, *The End of Austria-Hungary*, p. 246.

94. Cf. Rennell Rodd, *Social and Diplomatic Memories*, iii, pp. 353-7.

95. Minutes of Crewe House Committee, 15 October 1918, Northcliffe papers, vol. x, BL.
96. CAB 24/75, GT 6839.
97. Ibid.
98. Fest, *Peace or Partition*, p. 244.
99. Minutes of Crewe House Committee, 29 October 1918, Northcliffe papers, vol. x, BL.
100. Cited in Valiani, *The End of Austria-Hungary*, p. 434.
101. Ibid.
102. May, *The Passing of the Habsburg Monarchy*, II, pp. 622-3. 653.
103. Campbell Stuart, *Secrets of Crewe House*, p. 50.
104. Note sur le projet de M. Gallenga, Correspondence E. Kann, Grande Brétagne, v, vol. 33, Maison de la Presse 1914-28. Ministère des Affaires Étrangères, Paris.
105. Camille Barrère to Quai d'Orsay, 23 December 1917, ibid.
106. Copy of document attached to above.
107. Minutes of Crewe House committee, Northcliffe's letter to, 14 May 1918. Northcliffe papers, vol. x, BL.
108. Klobukowski papers. Papiers D'Agents, Papiers 95. Ministère des Affaires Étrangères, Paris.
109. Steed, *Through Thirty Years*, II, p. 241ff.
110. 'With all the weight of a ministerial statement.' Report to Pichon on Inter-Allied Conference, 23 August 1918. Klobukowski papers, Papiers D'Agents, Papiers 95, Ministère des Affaires Étrangères, Paris.
111. 'Into which he has breathed all the ardour of his anti-Austrian beliefs and feelings while at the same time creating the most favourable attitudes of mind towards our country.' Ibid.
112. Steed, *Through Thirty Years*, II, p. 241ff.
113. CAB 24/75, GT 6839.
114. Ibid.
115. Steed, *Through Thirty Years*, II, pp. 228-9.
116. Comert to Klobukowski, September 1918, Dossier Général, Grande-Brétagne, vol. 29, Maison de la Presse 1914-28, Ministère des Affaires Étrangères, Paris.
117. Vera B. Whitehouse, *A Year as a Government Agent* (New York, 1920) p. 153.
118. Merriam to Sisson, 2 October 1918, CPI 17/A1, Box 258, National Archives, Washington.
119. Edgell to Sisson, 11 November 1918, CPI 17/A2, Box 259, National Archives, Washington.
120. Edgell to Merriam, 18 November 1918, CPI 17/A2, Box 259, National Archives, Washington.
121. Ibid.
122. Capt. Blankenhorn to Col. Marlborough Churchill, 1 August 1918, CPI 17/A1, Box 237, National Archives, Washington.
123. Whitehouse to Creel, 24th February 1918, CPI 1/A1, Box 23, folder 21, National Archives, Washington.
124. Whitehouse to James Kerney, 22 July 1918, CPI 21/A1, Box 360, National Archives, Washington.
125. Campbell Stuart, *Secrets of Crewe House*, p. 62.
126. Ibid., p. 80.
127. Northcliffe to Balfour, 10 June 1918, FO 899/4.
128. Balfour to Northcliffe, 11 June 1918, CAB 24/75, GT 6839.
129. Steed, *Through Thirty Years*, II, p. 224.

130. Bruntz, *Allied Propaganda and the Collapse of the German Empire*, p. 28.

131. Balfour, *Propaganda in War*, p. 6.

132. L. M. Salmon, *The Newspaper and Authority* (New York, 1923) cited p. 349; see also Steed, *Through Thirty Years*, II, pp. 226-7.

133. Campbell Stuart, *Secrets of Crewe House*, p. 93.

134. CAB 24/75, GT 6839.

135. Northcliffe to Lloyd George, 26 April 1918, Northcliffe papers, vol. v, BL.

136. Klobukowski to Northcliffe, 1 October 1918, Klobukowski papers, Papiers D'Agents, Papiers 95, Ministère des Affaires Étrangères, Paris.

137. 'For carrying out measures, the permanent organisation would be able to have fairly extensive powers but there can be no question of it being authorised to lay down general lines of policy which may only emanate from governments. This is why, in particular cases where disagreements among the respective representatives of the allies on this permanent body are caused by differences between their instructions, it is the responsibility of the governments to reach agreement amongst themselves through diplomatic channels in order to achieve harmony.' Ibid.

138. Campbell Stuart, *Secrets of Crewe House*, p. 199ff; Steed, *Through Thirty Years*, II, p. 242ff.

139. Wickham Steed, *The Fifth Arm*, p. 41.

140. Steed, *Through Thirty Years*, II, p. 248.

141. 26 October 1918, House papers, Group 466, series 1, Box 83A, file 2871, YUL.

142. History of The Times, *The 150th Anniversary and Beyond, 1912-48*, part I (London, 1952) pp. 385-6.

143. Lord Riddell, *An Intimate Diary of the Peace Conference and After* (London, 1933) p. 3.

144. D. Lloyd George, *Memoirs of the Peace Conference*, 2 vols (New Haven, 1939) I, p. 176.

145. Steed, *Through Thirty Years*, II, p. 249.

146. Campbell Stuart, *Secrets of Crewe House*, p. 230.

147. Pound and Harmsworth, *Northcliffe*, p. 670.

148. Chalmers Mitchell, *My Fill of Days*, p. 295.

149. Hamilton Fyfe, *My Seven Selves* (London, 1935) p. 228.

150. Stanley Morison, 'Personality and Diplomacy in Anglo-American Relations, 1917' in R. Pares and A. J. P. Taylor, *Essays Presented to Lewis Namier* (London, 1956) p. 460.

151. Wells to Northcliffe, 27 June 1918, Northcliffe papers, vol. IX, BL.

152. Northcliffe to Wells, 16 July 1918, Northcliffe papers, vol. IX, BL.

153. Wells to Northcliffe, 18 July 1918, Northcliffe papers, vol. IX, BL.

154. Harry Hanak, *Great Britain and Austria-Hungary during the First World War* (London, 1962); Calder, *Britain and the Origins of the New Europe*.

155. Northcliffe to Charteris, 6 August 1916, Northcliffe papers, vol. VII, BL.

156. Pound and Harmsworth, *Northcliffe*, p. 656.

157. House to Northcliffe, 18 July 1918, House papers 466/1/83a/2872, YUL.

158. Balfour, *Propaganda in War*, p. 4.

159. CAB 24/75, GT 6839.

160. Northcliffe to J. T. Davies, 5 December 1918, Northcliffe papers, vol. v, BL.

161. Chalmers Mitchell, *My Fill of Days*, p. 294.

162. See Michael Balfour's chapter entitled 'The Demythologisation of Crewe House' in his *Propaganda in War*.

163. CAB 24/75, GT 6839.

164. Ibid.

CONCLUSION

1.   Memorandum by Lord Beaverbrook, 'Functions of the Ministry of Information on the cessation of hostilities', 16 October 1918, CAB 24/67, GT 6007.
2.   Ibid.
3.   Campbell Stuart, *Secrets of Crewe House*, p. 202.
4.   H. Wickham Steed, *The Fifth Arm*, p. 41.
5.   Steed, *Through Thirty Years*, ii, p. 248.
6.   CAB 23/8, 501 (11), 13 November 1918.
7.   Minute by Sir H. Newbolt, 17 January 1919, FO 395/301.
8.   For further details see Philip M. Taylor, *The Projection of Britain: British
Overseas Publicity and Propaganda, 1919-39* (Cambridge, 1981).
9.   CAB 24/77, GT 7062.
10.   See A. J. Mackenzie, *Propaganda Boom* (London, 1938).
11.   *The Times*, 22 February 1918.
12.   H. O. Lee, 'British propaganda during the Great War, 1914-18', INF 4/4A.
13.   M. T. H. Sadler, 'The Meaning and Need of Cultural Propaganda', *The New
Europe*, vol. 7, no. 84, 23 May 1918.
14.   Hansard, 5th series, vol. 109, cols 947-1035.
15.   Philip M. Taylor, 'Publicity and Diplomacy: The Impact of the First World
War upon Foreign Office attitudes towards the press' in D. N. Dilks (ed.) *Retreat from
Power*, 2 vols (London, 1981) i, pp. 42-63.
16.   H. A. Taylor, *Robert Donald* (London, n.d.).
17.   A. Ponsonby, *Falsehood in Wartime*, p. 18.
18.,   L. Fraser, *Germany between two wars: A study of propaganda and war guilt*
(London, 1943).
19.   Cited in the memorandum by S. G. Tallents, 7 November 1938, CAB 16/127,
MIC 15.
20.   Oskar Regele, *Fieldmarshal Conrad*, pp. 481-6.
21.   Unsigned memorandum, 2 December 1914, enclosed in Gowers to
Montgomery, 18 December 1914, FO 371/2207.
22.   Cecil to Spring-Rice, 12 May 1916, Spring-Rice papers, FO 800/242.
23.   Spring-Rice to Cecil, 2 June 1916, Spring-Rice papers, FO 800/242.
24.   Memorandum by Buchan, 1 December 1917, FO 395/235.
25.   Ibid.
26.   Donald to Lloyd George, 9 January 1917, INF 4/4B.
27.   Hansard, 5th series, vol. 109, 5 August 1918.
28.   Lord Beaverbrook, 'The Organisation and Functions of the Ministry of
Information', September 1918, Cmd 9161 (not issued), INF 4/5.
29.   Ibid.
30.   Charteris to Northcliffe, 19 August 1916, Northcliffe papers, vol. vii, BL.
31.   Cited in the memorandum by Roderick Jones, 10 November 1917, CAB
27/17, OPC 3.
32.   Summary of reports received on effects of balloon propaganda, WO 32/5141.
33.   Minutes of Crewe House committee, 15 October 1918, Northcliffe papers,
vol. x, BL.
34.   Lt Col. Toutain, 'Note for Army Groups' (2eme bureau), Propagande
Aérienne, 1917-18, 16 N 15 69, Service Historique de l'Armée, Château de Vincennes,
Paris.
35.   Shils and Jonowitz, 'Cohesion and Disintegration in the Wehrmacht' in
D. Katz, D. Cartwright, S. Eldersveld and A. McClung Lee (eds), *Propaganda in War
and Crisis* (New York, 1954) p. 554ff.
36.   Ibid., pp. 581-2.

37.   Thimme, *Weltkrieg Ohne Waffen*, p. 162.

38.   Cited in Bruntz, *Allied Propaganda and the Collapse of the German Empire in 1918*, p. 220.

39.   Lee, 'British propaganda during the Great War, 1914-18', INF 4/4A.

40.   Beaverbrook, 'The Organisation and Functions of the Ministry of Information', September 1918, INF 4/5.

41.   Lucy Masterman, *C. F. G. Masterman*, cited p. 300.

42.   Report by Major-General A. D. McRae, 1 July 1918, Beaverbrook papers, F/2/307.

43.   Memorandum by Masterman, 'Leaflets for working men', 13 December 1917, FO 395/236, Part 1.

44.   Ibid.

45.   Memorandum by Carson, 12 October 1917, CAB 24/28, GT 226.

46.   CAB 23/4, 286 (8), 29 November 1917; see also CAB 23/4, 288 (8), 30 November 1917 and the memorandum by G. H. Roberts, 'Use of the Press for Propaganda Purposes', 15 January 1918, CAB 24/39, GT 3360.

47.   Beaverbrook, 'The Organisation and Functions of the Ministry of Information', September 1918, INF 4/5.

48.   Memorandum by Jones, 10 November 1917, CAB 27/17, OPC 3.

49.   CAB 24/75, GT 6839.

50.   Ibid.

51.   Note of proceedings of a conference held at the Treasury, 14 May 1919, FO 395/297.

52.   However, the 'Report of the Work of the Department of Propaganda in Enemy History', undated, unsigned in CAB 24/75, GT 6839 bears a striking resemblance to Campbell Stuart's *Secrets of Crewe House.*

53.   Ivor Nicholson, 'An aspect of British wartime propaganda', *Cornhill Magazine* (1931) 593-606.

54.   James Morgan Read, *Atrocity Propaganda*, p. 187.

Select Bibliography

I UNPUBLISHED PRIMARY SOURCES

A   Administrative and Departmental records

(1) *London*, Public Records Office, Kew (PRO).

Cabinet papers, 1910-16.
Cabinet minutes and memoranda, 1916-20.
Foreign Office general correspondence, 1914-19.
Foreign Office News Department, 1916-19.
Home Office, 1914-19.
Ministry of Information (War of 1914-18).
Treasury, 1914-18.
War Office, 1914-18.

(2) *Paris*, Archives du Ministère des Affaires Étrangères (MAE).

La Maison de la Presse, 1914-28.

(3) *Vincennes*, Archives du Service Historique de l'Armée.

Cabinet du ministre (5N).
Cabinet ministériels — cabinet Clemenceau (6N).
GQG and 2e bureau (16N).

(4) *Washington*, National Archives.

Committee on Public Information.

(5) *Stanford*, Hoover Institute on War, Revolution and
Peace (HIWRP).

Great Britain — Director of Propaganda in Enemy Countries.
Great Britain — Foreign Office (Wellington House).
Great Britain — Ministry of Information.

B   Private Papers

(1) *Great Britain*

Balfour, A. J. (PRO, London).
Beaverbrook, Lord (House of Lords Record Office, London).

Bonar Law, Andrew (House of Lords Record Office, London).
Bryce, Lord (PRO, London & Bodleian Library, Oxford).
Cecil, Lord Robert (PRO, London).
Chamberlain, Austen (Birmingham University Library).
Fisher, H. A. L. (Bodleian Library, Oxford).
Grey, Viscount (PRO, London).
Kitchener, Lord (PRO, London).
Lloyd George, D. (House of Lords Record Office, London).
Northcliffe, Lord (The Times Archive & British Library, London).
Spring-Rice, Sir Cecil (PRO, London).
Stuart, Sir Campbell (Imperial War Museum, London).
Wickham Steed, H. (The Times Archive, London).
Willert, Sir Arthur (The Times Archive, London).

(2) *France*

Barrère, Camille (Papiers d'Agents, MAE, Paris).
Berthelot, Philippe (Papiers d'Agents, MAE, Paris).
Cambon, Paul (Papiers d'Agents, MAE, Paris).
Klobukowski, Antony (Papiers d'Agents, MAE, Paris).

(3) *United States of America*

Casement, Sir Roger (HIWRP, Stanford).
House, Colonel E. M. (Yale University Library, Connecticut).
Lutz, Ralph (HIWRP, Stanford).
Polk, Frank L. (Yale University Library, Connecticut).
Raemakers, Louis (HIWRP, Stanford).
Squires, J. D. (HIWRP, Stanford).
Willert, Sir Arthur (Yale University Library, Connecticut).
Wiseman, Sir William (Yale University Library, Connecticut).

(4) *Australia*

Correspondence between Rex and Allen Leeper and their family. We are grateful to Miss V. A. Leeper for sending copies of these letters from Australia.

C *Miscellaneous*

Material relating to propaganda (films, paintings, pamphlets and other published material, photographs and posters) held at the Imperial War Museum in London and the Hoover Institute on War, Revolution and Peace in Stanford.

II PUBLISHED PRIMARY SOURCES

A   Official documents

Hansard (Parliamentary Debates, Commons) 5th series, 1910-25.
6th report of the Select Committee on National Expenditure, *Reports from Committees*, vol. 2 (1918).
Gooch, G. P. and Temperley, H. W., *British Documents on the Origin of the War, 1898-1914* (London, 1927).
Mitchell, Peter Chalmers, *Report on the Propaganda Library*, 3 vols (London, 1917).
Temperley, H. W. and Penson, L. M., *A Century of Diplomatic Blue Books, 1814-1914* (Cambridge, 1938).

B   Command papers, 1914-18.

C   Newspapers

The Times, 1914-18.
The New Europe, 1916-18.

III CONTEMPORARY PAMPHLETS

Place of publication is London unless otherwise indicated.

ANDLER, C. H., *Pan-Germanism* (Paris, 1915).
ARCHER, WILLIAM, *Colour Blind Neutrality* (1916).
————, *501 Gems of German Thought* (1917).
————, *The Pirate's Progress: A short history of the U-boat* (1918).
————, *The Thirteen Days* (1915).
BALFOUR, A. J., *Obstacles to Peace* (n.d.).
————, *The Freedom of the Seas* (1916).
————, *The Navy and the War* (1915).
BARKER, ERNEST, *Ireland in the Last 50 years* (1916).
BEAVERBROOK, LORD, *Canada in Flanders*, 2 vols (1916-17).
BECK, JAMES, *The Case of Edith Cavell* (1916).
BEDIER, T., *German atrocities from German evidence* (1915).
BENSON, E. F., *Crescent and Iron Cross* (1918).
BEVAN, EDWYN, *Germany's Future* (1918).
————, *The Pan-German Programme* (n.d.).
BHOWNAGGREE, SIR M., *The Verdict of India* (1916).
BIGELOW, POULTNEY, *An American Opinion of British Colonial Policy* (1915).

BONE, MUIRHEAD, *Western Front Drawings* (1917).

BORDEN, SIR ROBERT, *The War and the Future* (1917).

_____ , *The Voice of the Dominions* (with J. C. Smuts, 1917).

BORSA, MARIE, *England and her critics* (1917).

BRYCE, LORD, *Report of the Committee on Alleged German Outrages* (1915).

_____ , *The Attitude of Great Britain in the present war* (1916).

_____ , *The Last Phase in Belgium* (1917).

BUCHAN, JOHN, *Battle of the Somme* (1916).

BUTLER, GEOFFREY, *International Law and autocracy* (1917).

CAIRNS, D. S., *Christianity and Macht-Politik* (1918).

CAMMAERTS, EMILE, *Through the Iron Bars* (1917).

CARTER, HENRY, *The Control of the drink trade* (1918).

CECIL, LORD ROBERT, *Black List and Blockade* (1918).

CHAPMAN, S. J., *Labour and Capital after the War* (1918).

CHESTERTON, G. K., *How to help Annexation* (1918).

_____ , *Letters to an Old Garibaldian* (1914).

CHURCHILL, WINSTON S, *The Munitions Miracle* (1917).

CLARKE, G. H., *Why the United States of America entered the war* (n.d.).

CLEARY, REVEREND, *Prussian militarism at work* (1917).

COHEN, ISRAEL, *Anti-semitism in Germany* (1918).

_____ , *The Turkish persecution of the Jews* (1918).

COOK, SIR EDWARD, *Britain and Turkey: the cause of the rupture* (1914).

_____ , *The Press Censorship* (1916).

CORBETT, SIR JULIAN, *The League of Peace and a Free State* (1917).

COUDERT, FREDERIC, *British Trade Restraints and Peace Prospects* (1916).

CROOKES, WILL, *The British Workman defends his home* (1917).

CURTIS, LIONEL, *Letters of the People of India on Responsible Government* (1918).

D'ALVIELLA, COUNT GOBLET, *The True and False Pacifism* (1917).

DAVIES, E. F., *British and German finance* (1915).

DAVIGNON, HENRI, *Belgium and Germany* (1915).

DESTRÉE, JULES, *The Deportation of Belgian Workers* (1917).

DODD, FRANCIS, *An Atlas of the World War* (1918).

_____ , *Generals of the British Army* (1917).

DONALD, ROBERT, *Trade Control in War* (1916).

DOYLE, SIR ARTHUR CONAN, *A Visit to Three Fronts* (1916).

_____ , *The Outlook on the War* (1915).

——————, *To Arms* (1914).

DRYSDALE, A. M., *Canada to Ireland* (1917).

EL-GHUSEIM, FAIZ, *Martyred Armenia* (1917).

FISHER, H. A. L., *The British Share in the War* (1915).

——————, *The Value of Small States* (1914).

GALACINO, ALVARO, *The Truth about the War* (1915).

GOSCHEN, SIR EDWARD, *The One Condition of Peace* (1916).

GOSLING, HARRY, *Peace: How to get and keep it* (1916).

GRAY, ALEXANDER, *The New Leviathan* (1915).

——————, *The True Pastime* (1915).

GREGORY, CHARLES NOBLE, *Neutrality and Arms Shipments* (1915).

GRELLING, DR RICHARD, *J'Accuse* (1916).

GREY, VISCOUNT, *Great Britain's measures against German trade* (1916).

——————, *The League of Nations* (1918).

GRONDYS, L. H., *The Germans in Belgium* (1915).

GWATKIN, H. M., *Britain's case against Germany* (1917).

HARD, WILLIAM, *How the English take the War* (1917).

HEADLAM, J. W., *Belgium and Greece* (1917).

——————, *England, Germany and Europe* (1914).

——————, *The Dead Lands of Europe* (1917).

——————, *The Starvation of Germany* (1917).

HENDERSON, ARTHUR, *The League of Nations and Labour* (1918).

HIGGINS, A. PEARCE, *Armed Merchant Ships* (1914).

——————, *Defensively Armed Merchant Ships and Submarine Warfare* (1917).

HOOVER, HERBERT, *Food in war* (1917).

HOPE, ANTHONY, *Militarism, German and British* (1915).

——————, *The New (German) Testament* (1915).

——————, *Why Italy is with the Allies* (1917).

HURD, ARCHIBALD, *Defence of the British Empire* (1915).

——————, *Murder at Sea* (1916).

——————, *New Prospects in 1917* (1917).

——————, *Outlawry at Sea* (1915).

——————, *Submarines and Zeppelins* (1916).

KERR, P., *What the Irish Regiments have done* (1916).

LAW, HUGH A., *Why is Ireland at War?* (1916).

LEVERHULME, LORD, *Negotiate Now?* (1917).

LICHNOWSKY, PRINCE, *My London Mission* (1918).

LLOYD GEORGE, D., *British War Aims* (1918).

LETI, P., *The Trail of the Barbarians* (1917).

LOW, A. MAURICE, *The Law of the Blockade* (1916).

MACDONAGH, M., *The Irish at the Front* (1916).

—————, *The Irish at the Somme* (1917).

MACLEAN, F., *Germany's Colonial Failure* (1918).

MARTINDALE, C. C. (ed.), *Catholic Monthly Letters* (1916-18).

MASARYK, T. G., *Austrian Terrorism in Bohemia* (1916).

MASSART, JEAN, *Belgians under the German Eagle* (1916).

MASSINGHAM, H. W., *Why we came to help Belgium* (1914).

MASTERMAN, C. F. G., *After Twelve Months of War* (1915).

—————, *The Triumph of the Fleet* (1915).

MEARS, E. G., *The Destruction of Belgium* (1916).

MERCIER, CARDINAL, *The Voice of Belgium* (n.d.).

MITRANY, D., *Greater Rumania* (1917).

MURRAY, GILBERT, *Ethical problems of the war* (1915).

—————, *Faith, War and Policy* (1918).

—————, *The Foreign Policy of Sir Edward Grey, 1906-15* (Oxford, 1915).

—————, *The League of Nations and the Democratic Idea* (1918).

NAMIER, L. B., *Danzig: Poland's Outlet to the Sea* (1917).

—————, *Germany and Eastern Europe* (1915).

NASH, PAUL, *British Artists at the Front* (1918).

NEVINSON, C. R. W., *The Roads of France* (n.d.).

NEWBOLT, HENRY, *A Note on the history of Submarine War* (1918).

NIPPOLD, O., *Dangerous Optimism* (1918).

—————, *The Awakening of the German People* (1918).

PARKER, SIR GILBERT, *Is England Apathetic?* (1915).

—————, *What is the matter with England?* (1915).

PASSELECQ, FERNAND, *Truth and Travesty* (1916).

PRINCE, MORTON, *The American versus the German view of the war* (1915).

—————, *The Psychology of the Kaiser* (1915).

PROTHERO, G. W., *A Lasting Peace* (1917).

READE, ARTHUR, *Russia under Nicholas II* (1917).

REDMOND, JOHN, *Ireland and the War* (1915).

—————, *Mr. Redmond's Visit to the Front* (1915).

—————, *The Voice of Ireland* (1916).

REVELSTOKE, LORD, *Britain's Staying Power* (1916).

ROBERTS, MAJ. CHARLES D., *Canada in Flanders*, vol. 3 (1918).

ROLLESTON, T. W., *Ireland and Poland* (1917).

Rose, J. Holland, *Why we carry on* (1918).

Rosemeier, Hermann, *A German on Germans* (1917).

Sanday, W., *When should the war end?* (1917).

Sanders, W. S., *Germany's Two Voices* (1917).

——————, *If the Kaiser Governed Britain* (1918).

——————, *Those German Peace Offers* (1917).

Scott, Leslie and Shaw, A., *Great Britain and Neutral Commerce* (1915).

Seddon, J. A., *Why British Labour Supports the war* (1917).

Selbe, W., *Christian Nationalism* (1917).

Sloss, R., *Some Facts about India* (1917).

Stalker, James, *The Lutheran Celebrations, 1517-1917* (1917).

Tillett, Ben, *My Message to Labour* (n.d.).

——————, *Who is Responsible for the War?* (1917).

Torras, Valentin, *Spanish Prisoner in a German camp* (1917).

Toynbee, A. J., *Armenian Atrocities: Murder of a Nation* (1915).

——————, *Murderous Tyranny of the Turks* (1917).

Trevelyan, G., *The Servians and Austria* (1915).

Vogel, Prof. J., *The British Administration in India* (1915).

Wallace, Sir D. M., *Our Russian Ally* (1914).

Wedgewood, Josiah, *With Machine-guns in Gallipoli* (1915).

Weiss, Andre, *The Violation by Germany of the Neutrality of Belgium and Luxembourg* (Paris, 1915).

Weston, E. F., *The Black Slaves of Prussia* (1918).

White, J. William, *America's Arraignment of Germany* (1915).

Whitlock, Brand, *The Deportation* (1917).

Wile, Frederick William, *Explaining the Britishers* (1918).

Willson, Beckles, *In the Ypres Salient* (1918).

Anonymous and Miscellaneous

Blood and Brass: Being Glimpses of German Psychology (1917).

Blood and Treasure: Facts and Figures of Britain's Effort, 1914-17 (1918).

British civilian prisoners in German East Africa (Rumanian official documents, 1918).

British Universities in the War (1917).

Catalogue of British Official War Photographs in Colour (1918).

A Corpse-Conversion Factory (1917).

Disclosures of a German Staff Officer (1918).

England, Germany and the Irish question (1917).

Germany condemned by her own Ambassador (1918).
Microbe culture at Bukarest (1917).
Russia and her Allies (1917).
Souvenir of the first exhibition of British Battle Photographs in Colour (1918).
The Death of Edith Cavell (1915).
The deportation of women and girls from Lille (n.d.).
The Horrors of Wittenburg (1916).
War paintings and drawings by British war artists exhibited under the auspices of the Ministry of Information (USA, 1919).

IV SECONDARY SOURCES

A   Autobiographies, diaries, memoirs etc.

ABBOTT, CLAUDE COLLEER AND BERTRAM, ANTHONY, *Poet and Painter: Correspondence between Gordon Bottomley and Paul Nash* (London, 1955).
BEAVERBROOK, LORD, *Politicians and the War, 1914-16* (London, 1928).
————, *Men and Power, 1917-18* (London, 1956).
————, *Politicians and the Press* (London, 1926).
BERNSTORFF, COUNT, *Memoirs* (New York, 1936).
————, *My Three Years in America* (London, 1920).
BERTIE OF THAME, LORD, *Diary, 1914-18*, 2 vols (London, 1924).
BLAKE, ROBERT, *The Private Papers of Douglas Haig, 1914-18* (London, 1952).
BLANKENHORN, HEBER, *Adventures in propaganda: letters from an Intelligence Officer in France* (Boston and New York, 1919).
BROMHEAD, A. C., *Russian diaries, 1916-17* (London, 1972).
BROWNRIGG, SIR DOUGLAS, *Indiscretions of the Naval Censor* (London, 1920).
BUCHANAN, SIR GEORGE, *My Mission to Russia and other Diplomatic memories*, 2 vols (London, 1935).
CHARTERIS, JOHN, *At G.H.Q.* (London, 1931).
CHURCHILL, WINSTON S., *The World Crisis, 1911-18*, 4 vols. (London, 1923-29).
COCKERILL, SIR GEORGE, *What Fools We Were* (London, 1944).
COOK, SIR EDWARD, *The Press in Wartime, with some account of the Official Press Bureau* (London, 1920).
DUMBA, CONSTANTIN, *Memoirs of a Diplomat* (Boston, 1932).

FYFE, HAMILTON, *My Seven Selves* (London, 1935).

—————, *Sixty Years of Fleet Street* (London, 1949).

GAUNT, SIR GUY, *The Yield of the Years* (London, 1940).

GRAVES, ROBERT, *Goodbye to All That* (New York, 1957).

GREGORY, J. D., *On the Edge of Diplomacy: Rambles and Reflections, 1902-28* (London, 1928).

GREY OF FALLODEN, VISCOUNT, *Twenty Five Years, 1892-1916*, 2 vols (London, 1925).

—————, *Speeches on Foreign Affairs, 1904-14* (London, 1931).

HANKEY, LORD, *The Supreme Command, 1914-18*, 2 vols (London, 1961).

HENDRICK, BURTON J., *The Life and Letters of Walter H. Page*, 3 vols (New York, 1926).

HINDENBURG, MARSHAL VON, *Out of My Life* (London and New York, 1931).

JONES, KENNEDY, *Fleet Street and Downing Street* (London, 1920).

JONES, SIR RODERICK, *A Life in Reuters* (London, 1951).

LEIGH, THOMAS WODEHOUSE (LORD NEWTON), *Retrospection* (London, 1941).

LLOYD GEORGE, D., *War Memoirs*, 2 vols (London, 1933-7).

—————, *Memoirs of the Peace Conference*, 2 vols (New Haven, 1939).

LUDENDORFF, GENERAL ERICH VON, *My War Memories*, 2 vols (London, 1919).

LYTTON, N., *The Press and the General Staff* (London, 1921).

MAUGHAM, W. SOMERSET, *The Summing Up* (London, 1938).

MITCHELL, SIR PETER CHALMERS, *My Fill of Days* (London, 1937).

MURRAY, LT COL. A., *At Close Quarters: A Sidelight on Anglo-American Relations* (London, 1946).

NASH, PAUL, *An Outline* (London, 1949).

NORTHCLIFFE, LORD, *At the War* (London, 1916).

PAPEN, FRANZ VON, *Memoirs* (London, 1953).

REPINGTON, COLONEL, *The First World War*, 2 vols (London, 1920).

RIDDELL, LORD, *War Diary, 1914-18* (London, 1933).

RINTELEN, CAPTAIN VON, *The Dark Invader* (London, 1933).

—————, *The Return of the Dark Invader* (London, 1935).

RODD, SIR RENNELL, *Social and Diplomatic Memories, 1902-19* (London, 1925).

SEYMOUR, CHARLES, *The Intimate Papers of Colonel House*, 4 vols (Boston and New York, 1926).

SPENDER, J. A., *The Public Life*, 2 vols (London, 1925).

——————, *Life, Journalism and Politics*, 2 vols (London, 1928).

STEED, H. WICKHAM, *Through Thirty Years*, 2 vols (London, 1924).

STUART, SIR CAMPBELL, *The Secrets of Crewe House* (London, 1920).

SWINTON, SIR ERNEST D., *Eyewitness* (London, 1932).

THOMSON, BASIL, *My Experiences at Scotland Yard* (New York, 1923).

——————, *The Scene Changes* (London, 1937).

THWAITES, LT. COL. NORMAN, *Velvet and Vinegar* (London, 1932).

VOSKA, E. V. AND IRWIN, W., *Spy and Counter Spy* (New York, 1940).

WELLS, H. G., *An Experiment in Autobiography*, 2 vols (London, 1934).

WHITEHOUSE, VERA B., *A Year as a Government Agent* (New York, 1920).

WILLERT, SIR ARTHUR, *The Road to Safety: A Study in Anglo-American Relations* (London, 1953).

——————, *Washington and Other Memories* (Boston, 1972).

WILSON, T. (ed.), *The Political Diaries of C. P. Scott, 1911-28* (London, 1970).

WRENCH, J. E., *Struggle, 1914-20* (London, 1935).

B Other books

ALBIG, W., *Public Opinion* (London, 1939).

ARNOLD, BRUCE, *Orpen: Mirror to an Age* (London, 1981).

ASPINALL, A., *Politics and the Press, c. 1780-1850* (London, 1949).

ASTON, SIR GEORGE, *Secret Service* (London, 1930).

BALFOUR, MICHAEL, *Propaganda in War, 1939-45* (London, 1978).

BARTLETT, F. C., *Political Propaganda* (Cambridge, 1940).

BERTRAM, ANTHONY, *Paul Nash* (London, 1955).

BIRKENHEAD, THE EARL OF, *F. E. : The Life of F. E. Smith* (London, 1965).

BISHOP, S., *The Administration of British Foreign Policy* (Syracuse, New York, 1961).

BLAKEY, GEORGE T., *Historians on the Home Front: American Propagandists for the Great War* (Kentucky, 1970).

BOND, B., AND ROY, I. (eds.), *War and Society* (London, 1975).

BOYCE, G., CURRAN, J. AND WINGATE, PAULINE, *Newspaper History: From the seventeenth century to the present day* (London, 1978).

BROWN, J. A. C., *Techniques of Persuasion* (Harmondsworth, 1963).

BRUNTZ, GEORGE C., *Allied Propaganda and the Collapse of the German Empire in 1918* (Stanford 1938).

CALDER, K. J., *Britain and the Origins of the New Europe, 1914-18* (Cambridge, 1976).

CALDER, R. L., *W. Somerset Maugham and the quest for freedom* (London, 1972).

CARR, E. H., *Propaganda in International Politics* (Oxford pamphlets on world affairs, no. 16, 1939).

CHAMBERS, FRANK P., *The War behind the War, 1914-18: A History of the political and civilian fronts* (London, 1939).

CHAPMAN, GUY, *Vain Glory* (London, 1968).

CLARK, SIR FIFE, *The Central Office of Information* (London, 1970).

COLLINS, DOREEN, *Aspects of British Politics, 1904-19* (London, 1965).

COLVIN, I. AND MARJORIBANKS, E., *The Life of Lord Carson*, 3 vols (London, 1932-6).

CREEL, GEORGE, *How we advertised America* (New York, 1920).

CROSS, J. A., *Sir Samuel Hoare: A Political Biography* (London, 1977).

DAVIES, J., *The Prime Minister's Secretariat, 1916-20* (London, 1951).

DEACON, R., *A History of the British Secret Service* (London, 1969).

DEARLE, N. B., *A Dictionary of Wartime Organisations* (Oxford 1924).

DEMARTIAL, GEORGES, *La Guerre de 1914: Comment on mobilisa les consciences* (Paris, 1922).

DOOB, L. W., *Public Opinion and Propaganda* (New York, 1948).

DUFF, CHARLES, *Six Days to Shake an Empire* (London, 1966).

DUGDALE, B., *Arthur James Balfour*, 2 vols (London, 1936).

ELLUL, JACQUES, *Propaganda* (New York, 1973).

ERNST, WILHELM, *Die Antideutsche Propaganda durch das Schweizer Gebiet im Weltkrieg, Speziell die Propaganda in Bayern* (Munich, 1933).

FAY, SIR SAM, *The War Office at War* (London, 1973).

FERGUSON, J. H., *American Diplomacy and the Boer War* (Philadelphia, 1939).

FEST, W., *Peace or Partition* (London, 1978).

FOWLER, W. B., *British-American Relations, 1917-18: The Role of Sir William Wiseman* (Princeton, New Jersey, 1969).

FRASER, LINDLEY, *Propaganda* (London, 1957).

————, *Germany between two wars* (London, 1944).

FUSSELL, PAUL, *The Great War and Modern Memory* (New York, 1975).

FYFE, HAMILTON, *Northcliffe* (London, 1930).

GALLO, MAX, *The Poster in History* (New York, 1974).

GLEASON, J. H., *The Genesis of Russophobia in Great Britain: A study of the interaction of policy and opinion* (Cambridge, Mass., 1950).

GOLLIN, A. M., *Proconsul in Politics: A Study of Lord Milner in Opposition and in Power* (London, 1964).

GOSSE, F., *The Management of British foreign policy before the First World War* (London, 1948).

GUINN, PAUL, *British strategy and politics, 1914-18* (Oxford, 1965).

GWATKIN, F. T. ASHTON, *The British Foreign Service* (Syracuse, New York, 1950).

HALE, O. J., *Publicity and Diplomacy, with special reference to England and Germany, 1890-1914* (Gloucester, Mass., 1964).

HANAK, HARRY, *Great Britain and Austria-Hungary during the First World War* (London, 1962).

HANCOCK, W. K., *Smuts: The Sanguine Years, 1870-1919* (Cambridge, 1961).

HANSI (WALTZ, JEAN JACQUES) AND TONNELAT, HENRI, *À Travers Les Lignes Ennemies* (Paris, 1922).

HARDACH, GERD, *The First World War, 1914-18* (London, 1977).

HART-DAVIS, R., *Hugh Walpole: A Biography* (London, 1952).

HASTE, CATE, *Keep the Home Fires Burning* (London, 1977).

HAZLEHURST, CAMERON, *Politicians at War: July 1914 to May 1915* (London, 1971).

HEINDEL, R. H., *The American Impact on Great Britain, 1898-1914* (Philadelphia, 1940).

HILLIER, BEVIS, *Posters* (New York, 1969).

HINSLEY, F. H., (ed.), *British foreign policy under Sir Edward Grey* (Cambridge, 1977).

————, *British Intelligence in the Second World War* (London, 1979).

HUBER, DR GEORG, *Die Französische Propaganda im Weltkrieg gegen Deutschland, 1914-18* (Munich, 1928).

HUTCHINSON, HAROLD, *The Poster: An illustrated history since 1860* (New York, 1968).

JAMES, ADMIRAL SIR WILLIAM, *The Code Breakers of Room 40* (New York, 1956).

JOHNSTON, WINIFRED, *Memo on the Movies: War Propaganda, 1914-39* (Norman, 1939).

JOLL, JAMES, *Europe since 1870* (New York, 1973).

JONES, B. AND HOWELL, B. H., *Popular Arts of the First World War* (New York, 1972).

KANN, R. A., KIRALY, B. K. AND FICHTNER, P. S. (eds) *The Habsburg Empire in World War One* (Boulder, 1977).

KATZ, D., CARTRIGHT, D., EELDERSVELD, S. AND MCCLUNG A. (eds) *Popular Opinion and Propaganda* (New York, 1954).

KENNEDY, P. M., *The Rise of Anglo-German Antagonism* (London, 1980).

KNIGHTLEY, P., *The First Casualty: The War Correspondent as Hero, Propagandist and Myth Maker from the Crimea to Vietnam* (London, 1975).

KOSS, S., *The Rise and Fall of the Political Press in Britain: the Nineteenth Century* (London, 1981).

LAUREN, PAUL GORDON, *Diplomats and Bureaucrats: The First Institutional Responses to Twentieth century diplomacy in France and Germany* (Stanford, 1976).

LASSWELL, H. D., *Propaganda Technique in the World War* (London, 1927).

LERNER, D. (ed.), *Propaganda in War and Crisis* (New York, 1972).

LUEBKE, FREDERICK C., *Bonds of Loyalty: German Americans and World War One* (DeKalb, 1974).

LUTZ, R., *The Fall of the German Empire 1914-18*, 2 vols (Stanford, 1932).

MARRETT, SIR ROBERT, *Through the Back Door: An Inside View of British Overseas Information Services* (London, 1968).

MARTIN, KINGSLEY, *The Triumph of Lord Palmerston: A Study of Public Opinion in England before the Crimean War* (London, 1963).

MARWICK, A., *The Deluge: British Society and the First World War* (London, 1965).

MASTERMAN, LUCY, *C. F. G. Masterman: A Biography* (London, 1939).

MAUGHAM, W. SOMERSET, *Ashenden or the British Agent* (London, 1927).

MAY, ARTHUR J., *The Passing of the Habsburg Monarchy, 1914-18*, 2 vols (Philadelphia, 1966).

MAY, ERNEST R., *The World War and American Isolation, 1914-17* (Cambridge, Mass., 1959).

METZL, IRVINE, *The Poster: Its History and its Art* (New York, 1963).

MOCK, J. R. AND LARSON, C., *Words that Won the War* (Princeton, 1939).

MORGAN, K. O., *Consensus and Disunity* (Oxford, 1979).

MORGAN, T., *Maugham: A Biography* (New York, 1980).

MUSA, FARAJ, *Diplomate Contemporaine Guide Bibliographique* (Geneva, 1964).

NICOLAI, WALTER, *Geheime Mächte: Internationale Spionage und ihre Kämpfung im Weltkrieg unde Heut* (Leipzig, 1924).

NICOLSON, H., *Diplomacy* (London, 1963).

ORWELL, GEORGE AND REYNOLDS, REGINALD, *British Pamphleteers*, 2 vols (London, 1948).

PARSONS, I. M., *Men who marched away: Poems of the First World War* (London, 1965).

PETERSON, H. C., *Propaganda for War: The Campaign against American neutrality, 1914-17* (Norman, 1939).

PLAYNE, CAROLINE E., *Society at War, 1914-16* (London, 1931).

PONSONBY, ARTHUR, *Falsehood in Wartime* (London, 1928).

POOLMAN, KENNETH, *Zeppelins over England* (London, 1975).

POUND, REGINALD, *Arnold Bennett* (London, 1952).

POUND, REGINALD AND HARMSWORTH, G., *Northcliffe* (London, 1959).

PRONAY, N. AND SPRING, D. W. (eds), *Propaganda, Politics and Film, 1918-45* (London, 1982).

RAPPAPORT, ARMIN, *The British Press and Wilsonian Neutrality* (London, 1951).

READ, JAMES MORGAN, *Atrocity Propaganda, 1914-19* (Yale, 1941).

REMARQUE, ERICH MARIA, *All Quiet on the Western Front* (New York, 1958).

RICKARDS, MAURICE, *Posters of the First World War* (London, 1968).

ROBBINS, KEITH, *The Abolition of War* (Cardiff, 1976).

—————, *Sir Edward Grey* (Cassell, 1971).

ROETTER, CHARLES, *Psychological Warfare* (London, 1974).

ROGERSON, S., *Propaganda in the Next War* (London, 1938).

ROSKILL, S., *Hankey: Man of Secrets*, vol I, *1877-1918* (London, 1970).

ROTHWELL, V. H., *British War Aims and Peace Diplomacy, 1914-18* (Oxford, 1971).

SHORT, K. R. M. (ed.), *Feature Films as History* (London, 1981).

SETON-WATSON, H AND C., *The Making of the New Europe: R. W. Seton-Watson and the last years of Austria-Hungary* (London, 1981).

SILBER, J. C., *The Invisible Weapons* (London, 1932).

SINGLETON-GATES AND GIRODIAS MAURICE, *The Black Diaries: The Life and Times of Sir Roger Casement* (Paris, 1959).

SMITH, J. A., *John Buchan* (London, 1965).

SPAIGHT, J. M., *Air Power and War Rights* (London, 1924).

SQUIRES, J. D., *British propaganda at home and in the United States from 1914 to 1917* (Cambridge, Mass., 1935).

STEED, H. WICKHAM, *The Fifth Arm* (London, 1940).

STEINER, Z. S., *The Foreign Office and Foreign Policy 1898-1914* (Cambridge, 1969).

STOREY, G., *Reuters Century, 1851-1951* (London, 1951).

SWARTZ, M., *The Union of Democratic Control in British Politics during the First World War* (Oxford, 1971).

TAYLOR, A. J. P., *Beaverbrook* (London, 1971).

————, *The Trouble Makers* (London, 1969).

TAYLOR, PHILIP M., *The Projection of Britain: British Overseas Publicity and Propaganda, 1919-39* (Cambridge, 1981).

TEMPERLEY, H. W. V., *A History of the Peace Conference of Paris*, 6 vols (London, 1920).

TERRAINE, JOHN, *Impacts of War, 1914 and 1918* (London, 1970).

————, *Mons: The Retreat to Victory* (London, 1960).

————, *The Smoke and the Fire: Myths and Anti-myths of war, 1861-1945* (London, 1980).

THIMME, HANS, *Weltkrieg ohne Waffen: Die Propaganda der Westmächte gegen Deutschland: Ihre Wirkung und ihre Abwehr* (Stuttgart and Berlin, 1932).

TILLEY, SIR JOHN, AND GASELEE, SIR STEPHEN, *The Foreign Office* (London, 1932).

TIMES, THE, *History of The Times: The 150th Anniversary and Beyond*, part I, *1912-1920* (London, 1952).

TUCHMAN, BARBARA, *The Zimmermann Telegram* (London, 1959).

VALIANI, LEO, *The End of Austria-Hungary* (London, 1973).

VIERECK, GEORGE, *Spreading Germs of Hate* (New York, 1930).

WANDERSCHECK, HERMANN, *Bibliographie zur Englischen Propaganda im Weltkrieg* (Stuttgart, 1935).

WARD, A. J., *Ireland and Anglo-American Relations, 1899-1921* (London, 1969).

WATT, D. C. (ed.), *Hitler's Mein Kampf* (trans. by Ralph Manheim, London 1969).

WEBB, MARJORIE OGILVY, *The Government Explains: A Study of the Information Services* (London, 1965).

WOODWARD, SIR LLEWELLYN, *Great Britain and the War of 1914-18* (London, 1967).

WRIGHT, QUINCY (ed.), *Public Opinion and World Politics* (Chicago, 1933).

YOUNG, HARRY F., *Prince Lichnowsky and the Great War* (Athens, Georgia, 1970).

ZEBEL, S. H., *Balfour: A Political Biography* (Cambridge, 1973).

ZEMAN, Z. A. B., *A Diplomatic History of the First World War* (London, 1971).

C   Articles

DOUGLAS, R., 'Voluntary Enlistment in the First World War and the work of the Parliamentary Recruiting Committee', *Journal of Contemporary History*, 42 (1970) 564-85.

FRASER, THOMAS, 'Germany and the Indian Revolution, 1914-18' *Journal of Contemporary History*, 12 (1977) 255-72.

FRENCH, D., 'Spy Fever in Britain, 1900-15', *Historical Journal*, 21 (1978) 355-70.

HACHEY, THOMAS E., 'British War Propaganda and American Catholics in 1918',*Catholic Historical Review*, 61 (1975) 48-66.

HOLLINS, T., 'The Conservative Party and Film Propaganda between the Wars', *English Historical Review*, 96 (1981) 359-69.

HOPKIN, D., 'Domestic Censorship in the First World War', *Journal of Contemporary History*, 5 (1970) 151-69.

KENNAN, GEORGE, 'The Sisson Documents', *Journal of Modern History*, 28 (1956) 130-54.

KENNEDY, P. M., 'Imperial Cable Communications and Strategy, 1870-1914', *English Historical Review*, 86 (1971) 725-52.

LUTZ, RALPH H., 'Studies of World War Propaganda, 1914-33', *Journal of Modern History*, 5 (1933) 496-516.

MCEWAN, J. M., 'The Press and the Fall of Asquith', *Historical Journal*, 21 (1978) 863-83.

—————, 'Northcliffe and Lloyd George at War, 1914-18', *Historical Journal*, 24 (1981) 651-72.

MORISON, STANLEY, 'Personality and Diplomacy in Anglo-American Relations', in R. Pares and A. J. P. Taylor, *Essays Presented to Sir Louis Namier* (London, 1956).

NATION, THE, 'Kadaver', *The Nation*, 38 (1925) 171-2.

NEILSON, K., '"Joy Rides?"?: British Intelligence and Propaganda in Russia, 1914-17', *Historical Journal*, 24 (1981) 885-906.

NICHOLSON, I., 'An aspect of British Official Wartime Propaganda', *Cornhill Magazine*, 70 (1931) 593-606.

PARKER, SIR GILBERT, 'The United States and the War', *Harper's Monthly Magazine*, March 1918, 521-31.

PIERCE, ROBERT N., 'Lord Northcliffe: Trans-Atlantic Influences', *Journalism Monographs* (August 1975) *Association for education in journalism.*

SANDERS, M. L., 'Wellington House and British Propaganda in the First World War', *Historical Journal*, 18 (1975) 119-46.

STEINER, Z. S., 'The Foreign Office and the War' in F. H. Hinsley, *British Foreign Policy Under Sir Edward Grey* (Cambridge, 1977).

STREET, MAJ. C. J. C., 'Propaganda Behind the Lines', *Cornhill Magazine*, 48 (1919) 490-95.

STUBBS, J. O., 'Lord Milner and Patriotic Labour, 1914-18', *English Historical Review*, 87 (1972) 717-54.

TAYLOR, PHILIP M., 'The Foreign Office and British Propaganda during the First World War', *Historical Journal*, 23 (1980) 875-98.

———, 'Publicity and Diplomacy: The Impact of the First World War upon Foreign Office Attitudes towards the Press', in D. N. Dilks (ed.), *Retreat from Power,* 2 vols (London, 1981) I, pp. 42-63.

WARMAN, ROBERTA, 'The Erosion of Foreign Office Influence in the Making of Foreign Policy, 1916-18', *Historical Journal*, 15 (1972) 113-59.

WILSON, TREVOR, 'Lord Bryce's Investigations into Alleged German Atrocities in Belgium, 1914-15', *Journal of Contemporary History*, 14 (1979) 369-81.

WRIGHT, D. G., 'The Great War, Government Propaganda and English "Men of Letters", 1914-16', *Literature and History*, 7 (1978).

D Unpublished theses

BUCHANAN, ALBERT RUSSELL, 'European Propaganda and American Public Opinion, 1914-17', Stanford University, Ph.D., 1935.

BURK, K. M., 'British War Missions to the United States, 1914-18', Oxford University, D.Phil., 1976.

JARAS, T. F., 'Promoters and Public Servants: The role of the British Government in the Expansion of Submarine Telegraphy, 1860-70', Georgetown University, Ph.D., 1975.

JONES, R. A., 'The Administration of the British Diplomatic Service and the Foreign Office, 1848-1906', University of London, Ph.D., 1968.

REEVES, N., 'Film Propaganda in the First World War', University of London, Ph.D., 1981.

SANDERS, M. L., 'Official British Propaganda in the First World War', University of London, M. Phil., 1972.

SPROTT, MARY ESTHER, 'A Survey of British Wartime Propaganda in the U.S.A. issued by Wellington House', Stanford University, Masters thesis, 1921.

Index